Sustainable
Marketing

Sustainable
Marketing
Managerial-Ecological Issues

Donald A. Fuller

SAGE Publications
International Educational and Professional Publisher
Thousand Oaks   London   New Delhi

For information:

SAGE Publications, Inc.
2455 Teller Road
Thousand Oaks, California 91320
E-mail: order@sagepub.com

SAGE Publications Ltd.
6 Bonhill Street
London EC2A 4PU
United Kingdom

SAGE Publications India Pvt. Ltd.
M-32 Market
Greater Kailash I
New Delhi 110 048 India

Printed in the United States of America

Library of Congress Cataloging-in-Publication Data

Fuller, Donald A.
    Sustainable marketing: Managerial-ecological issues/
Donald A. Fuller.
        p.   cm.
    Includes bibliographical references and index.
    ISBN 0-7619-1218-5 (acid-free paper)
    ISBN 0-7619-1219-3 (pbk.: acid-free paper)
    1. Green marketing. 2. Consumption (Economics)—
Environmental aspects. I. Title.
    HF5413   .F85   1999
    658.8—ddc21   98-40124

99   00   01   02   03   04   05   7   6   5   4   3   2   1

Acquiring Editor:	Harry Briggs
Editorial Assistant:	Mary Ann Vail
Production Editor:	Astrid Virding
Production Assistant:	Stephanie Allen
Typesetter/Designer:	Marion Warren
Indexer:	Cristina Haley

Contents

Preface

Sustainable Marketing was written to heighten awareness of environmental issues among marketing managers, marketing students, and marketing educators. I always have been puzzled by my own field's disinterest in examining how marketing decisions affect the ecosystems that sustain our lives and the lives of those to come. To me, it seems perfectly reasonable to take steps now to prevent very likely negative future environmental outcomes from occurring. To "take steps" translates into modifying the ways in which we live, consume, and make marketing decisions. It also suggests that marketing's current, and almost unquestioned, dogma of "sell, sell, sell—give 'em what they want regardless" requires adjustment as we enter the 21st century. I believe that recognizing and taking into account the impact of marketing decisions on the earth's ecosystems is a step in the right direction.

Sustainable Marketing is not a pious exercise in corporate altruism. To the contrary, it challenges marketers to cope with a relentless issue—ecosystems degradation caused by consumption. The point is that marketers can reinvent strategy and craft "win-win-win" outcomes in which customers win (obtain genuine benefits), organizations win (achieve financial and other objectives), and ecosystems win (functioning is preserved or enhanced) at the same time. Such outcomes are beginning to be labeled sustainable consump-

tion, and because marketing is the core discipline of consumption, it is uniquely empowered and positioned to influence their development. Marketers cannot conveniently turn their backs and walk away and leave this challenge to others. To do so would be negligent and would brand marketing as disrespectful of the natural world on which we utterly depend and of which we are an integral part. Education is the key to developing an environmental ethic that will promote study and action. Hopefully, this book will make a small contribution in this regard.

The odyssey leading up to this book started when I completed an environmentally oriented marketing dissertation at Georgia State University in 1972 and then began writing about "reverse channel systems" as a way in which to link marketing practice to environmental issues. As a participant in the high-level economy of America, I always had been profoundly struck by the surreal nature of landfills, those exotic places where society's excreta were continuously entombed "out of sight, out of mind" in a manner analogous to the operation of a southern outhouse (i.e., dig a hole, fill it up, dig another hole . . .). I marveled at all the "stuff" we Americans had and how we threw away many things after only one use in the name of economics and customer convenience. Disposable everything—the modern marketer's answer. But I wondered, what was our obsession with customers' convenience doing to those same customers' air, water, and land habitats?

During the mid-1980s, a defining mentality began emerging worldwide that recognized the true importance and relevance of the environment in business decisions. Yet, beyond a few (sometimes misguided) "green marketing" initiatives, the marketing profession has remained less than vocal on the subject of how marketing mix decisions—product, channels, communications, and pricing—are linked to ecosystems quality. And some voices still decry the need for environmental action; they say the issue is a nonproblem. I respectfully disagree and have structured this work around how marketing mix decisions can and do influence environmental outcomes.

Because I firmly believe that we are now damaging the earth's ecosystems but cannot prove it with absolute scientific certainty, I position myself among those who urge adoption of the precautionary principle. This proposition mandates that decision makers act now based on evidence that we are likely to incur irreversible, and unacceptable, future environmental damage if we maintain present marketing practices. Waiting for exact scientific determination puts us in the vulnerable position of not being able to make a mid-course correction if we need to do so. I believe that Parkin (1991) has it right:

Our numbness, our silence, our lack of outrage could mean we end up the only species to have minutely monitored our own extinction. What a measly epitaph that would make: "they saw it coming but hadn't the wit to stop it from happening." (p. 7)

I would like to thank the many people who helped get this work done. Those most important are members of my family, who provided the necessary day-to-day setting in which I could pursue the subject, put in a productive day's work, and come home to an excellent meal every time. Oldest son Daniel, a graduate in communications at the University of Central Florida and a writer in his own right, knew well the professional need to maintain a "feel like writing" mind-set, and he provided encouragement all along the way. Youngest son, Michael, a graduate in industrial design at Auburn University, provided a direct connection with the subject matter. His choice of major at Auburn led me to the "green design" literature and opened my mind to the ultimate conclusion that product design is the core issue in sustainable marketing. My wife Jane's continuous and loving home support (those excellent meals and many other things) made everything else work—period!

In the workplace, I thank the many graduate and undergraduate students, student assistants, and marketing department staff for their assistance in performing research, clerical, and editing tasks. In addition, colleague Bill Neace, Professor of Environmental Management at Mercer University, and longtime personal friend Pete Gillett, Professor of Marketing at the University of Central Florida, provided constructive and insightful reviews of the manuscript that greatly improved the final work. I also thank the University of Central Florida for granting a one-semester sabbatical that provided time to remain focused on the effort.

During the writing process, my father, Ernest "Bunny" Fuller, passed away. He was a member of the first graduating class in aeronautical engineering at the Georgia Institute of Technology in 1932 and was an aviation pioneer. That event heightened my resolve to stick with the project and get the job done. Pop, this work is dedicated to you.

DONALD A. FULLER
University of Central Florida

cHAPTER 1

Sustainable Marketing: An Overview

During humankind's recorded history, extensive and sophisticated consumption systems have evolved to meet the needs of the earth's human population. When the population was small, the activities involved in providing the food, clothing, housing, and other products (goods and services) demanded by people left virtually no "footprint" of pollution in the air or on the land, freshwater bodies, or oceans. But with world population now estimated at approximately 6.0 billion and expected to surge to between 7.7 billion and 11.2 billion by the year 2050 (Robinson 1998:7), the damage inflicted by consumption on the earth's ecosystems has become a world-class issue. The question is, "How do we manage consumption processes to continue to meet the needs of people while also preventing the devastation of our basic life-support systems?"

Why Sustainable Marketing—Now?

In *The Ecology of Commerce,* Hawken (1993) places the major responsibility for addressing this question squarely on business corporations. He notes, "Corporations, because they are the dominant institution on the planet, must squarely address the social and environmental problems that afflict humankind" (p. xiii) and "Business has three issues to face: what it takes, what it makes, and what it wastes" (p. 12). "What it takes" refers to the material and energy resources that are removed from the earth's ecosystems through mining, extracting, cutting, growing, hunting, and other means. "What it makes" represents the products of commerce, goods and services, that are derived from those resources through industrial conversion-transformation processes. "What it wastes" represents eco-costs, defined here as the collective costs to businesses, customers, and societies of cultural garbage/waste, pollution, and the ongoing destruction of natural systems, which are the consequences of *taking* and *making* processes. A closer examination of *taking, making,* and *wasting* leads to an inescapable conclusion: *these issues describe marketing activities and the effects of those activities on ecosystems.*

Ignoring the ramifications of *taking, making,* and *wasting* leads to unacceptable outcomes, as demonstrated by two articles from the respected *National Geographic.* In "The U.S.S.R.'s Lethal Legacy," Edwards (1994) presents a startling and damning scenario of unspeakable environmental pollution and human birth defects that has occurred in the former Soviet Union, a result of decades of industrial activity taking place in the total absence of environmental laws, policies, ethics, and common sense. Similarly, in "Exploiting the Ocean's Bounty: Diminishing Returns," Parfit (1995) chronicles the practices leading to the relentless decline of the last major resource that humans "take" by hunting in the wild—the fisheries of the world. For example, the "taking" of 1 pound of marketable seafood by high-technology commercial fleets also nets 4 pounds of "by-catch" (p. 19), that is, unwanted species and organisms that are destroyed and then returned to the sea, all in the name of efficiency. As he sadly reports,

> The unthinkable has come to pass. The wealth of oceans, once deemed inexhaustible, has proven finite, and fish, once dubbed "the poor man's protein," have become a resource coveted—and fought over—by nations. . . . "We've come to a day of reckoning," says one marine scientist. "The next ten years are going to be very painful, full of upheaval for everyone connected to the sea." (p. 2)

These examples and many others, ranging from highly publicized global tragedies (e.g., the Exxon *Valdez* oil spill, the Bhopal chemical poisonings) to local issues (e.g., the need for curbside recycling programs to stem the avalanche of consumer garbage), are symptoms of a fundamental flaw in business practice—our disregard of ecosystems. All send the same message: the time for action is now.

Sustainable Marketing Defined

The implications of all this for the future practice of marketing management are enormous. Business and marketing are inseparable concepts, for has not management guru Peter Drucker taught, "There is only one valid definition of business purpose: to create a customer" (Drucker 1973:61)? That is, the marketing function fulfills business and human purpose by providing benefits to customers through products such as the fish people eat, the cars they drive, the clothes they wear, and the computers they use. In other words, the decisions concerning *what products to make* and how to offer them to customers are the classic substance of marketing strategy. They involve interpreting target customer needs, developing product concepts in response to those needs (often described as form and function), and making them available in the marketplace through appropriate channels, communications, and pricing decisions. Traditionally, marketing success has been defined as satisfied customers and concurrent profits for the firm, a result known as the "win-win" outcome.

But decisions concerning *what products to make* also determine *what to take* (i.e., the resources required to make and market those products), and both the *making* and *taking* processes have side-effect eco-costs in the form of wastes, follow-on pollution, and damage to ecosystems. This is because *determining* the attributes of products, and the specific systems through which they are made available to markets, also *determines* resource/energy use and waste generation patterns, the antecedents of pollution and ecosystems degradation. In this regard, *The Economist* wryly notes, "The Product Is the Problem" (1990:12). But this also clearly suggests an opportunity; that is, reinventing product systems to achieve "zero-waste, zero-discharge" outcomes while providing the same or improved benefits to customers is a logical solution to pollution.

A Managerial Definition

"Sustainable marketing," a term coined by Sheth and Parvatiyar (1995), addresses the "ways and means" for reconciling economic and ecological factors through reinvented products and product systems. A number of other labels have been used to identify this subject, including "green marketing" (Ottman 1993; Peattie 1992), "environmental marketing" (Coddington 1993), "ecological marketing" (Henion 1976), and "eco-marketing" (Fuller and

Butler 1994), resulting in both confusion and misunderstanding. By convey-ing a sense of consistency with the broader construct of sustainable develop-ment (defined later in this chapter), the term *sustainable marketing* brings much-needed standardization to this important and emerging area.

In this book, *sustainable marketing* is defined as

> the process of planning, implementing, and controlling the development, pricing, promotion, and distribution of products in a manner that satisfies the following three criteria: (1) customer needs are met, (2) organizational goals are attained, and (3) the process is compatible with ecosystems.

This definition is a logical extension of contemporary marketing's managerial orientation, not a radical departure from it. It retains a focus on actively managing processes through which customers are satisfied and organizational goals are achieved. The differentiating factor is the requirement that the entire process be compatible with ecosystems to reduce eco-costs and serve the long-term well-being of society.

Pollution Prevention and Resource Recovery

Making product systems "compatible with ecosystems" requires integrat-ing the waste management strategies of pollution prevention (P2) and resource recovery (R2) into marketing decision making, and doing so attacks the root sources of eco-costs. P2 is achieved through *preventive action;* the approach is to manage wastes and wasting through marketing strategies that stop it from happening in the first place, thereby reducing present and future eco-costs. R2 is achieved through *remedial action;* the approach is to manage unavoidable waste streams through marketing strategies that recover economic values (resources) for future use and render any remaining residuals harmless if discharged into ecosystems. As will be discussed in Chapter 3, design-for-environment is the process through which sustainable marketing strategies are actualized to achieve P2 and R2 goals.

Fundamental Tenets

Sustainable marketing represents a new paradigm (Exhibit 1.1), one embracing the idea that production-consumption systems must function in ways that mimic circular natural systems. Its adoption suggests recognition of five fundamental tenets.

---

exhibit 1.1

▓▓▓▓▓▓▓▓▓▓▓▓▓▓▓

The New Paradigm of Sustainable Marketing

Marketing systems can be compared with circular natural ecosystems in which plants and organisms consume minerals, water, sunlight, and each other in interdependent processes that continually produce waste, which then becomes food or fuel for another cycle. Sustainable marketing systems operate much the same way—consuming resources and creating wastes—while providing benefits/values to customers and organizations and also maintaining or enhancing ecosystems functioning.

When marketing systems involve relatively small numbers of customers, both resources and waste sinks can be considered infinite free goods. However, because of large population increases, resources have become more limited and waste sinks have become sources of pollution that threaten long-term human survival. Accordingly, sustainable marketing adopts a circular, "zero-waste, zero-discharge" approach. Preventing waste (pollution prevention) and recovering and reusing materials (resource recovery) to reduce eco-costs are crucial strategies/goals. Using design-for-environment processes, environmental considerations are incorporated into all aspects of marketing decision making over the broad expanse of the product system life cycle.

SOURCE: Adapted from National Science and Technology Council (1994), *Technology for a Sustainable Future,* Washington, DC: Government Printing Office (386-802/00037), p. 26.

Tenet 1: Ecosystems are a physical limiting factor on marketing decisions. Ecosystems impose a non-negotiable mandate on decision makers. Therefore, screening marketing strategies for environmental impact and the full payment of eco-costs must become standard operating procedures.

Tenet 2: The product system life cycle is the appropriate decision framework. Ecosystems impact is not the function of one organization or one customer at one time and place. Rather, it is the collective result of numerous interrelated decisions by many people and organizations over time. The product system life cycle (PSLC) represents the holistic decision framework necessary for gaining an understanding of ecological impact, issues, and sustainable marketing solutions. (The PSLC concept is fully introduced in Chapter 2.)

Tenet 3: Pollution prevention and resource recovery are appropriate strategies for achieving sustainability. Implementing P2 and R2 strategies will preserve and enhance ecosystems functioning through the development of zero-waste, zero-discharge product systems.

Tenet 4: A "multiplier effect" exists in which small environmental improvements (i.e., eco-cost savings) by firms and customers at the micro level translate into large absolute improvements at the macro level. Billions of marketing decisions by organizations and customers represent sources of waste and wasting, each of which contributes in a small way to a problem of gigantic proportions; through the multiplier, small individual improvements sum into large overall gains in environmental quality. Broad acceptance of sustainable marketing practices, by organizations and customers, is a prerequisite for sustainability. The cooperation of a few will not suffice; the total elimination of "free riders" is necessary.

Tenet 5: Sustainable marketing is not an exercise in corporate altruism. Sustainable marketers must not lose sight of the fact that satisfying customers and attaining organizational goals, financial and otherwise, remain absolutely necessary conditions that must be met while achieving environmental compatibility. It also must be noted that the "best" product from a purely environmental impact standpoint is *no* product at all (i.e., no product = no *taking,* no *making,* and no *wasting*), an unacceptable state of affairs. Thus, the challenge is to reinvent the ways and means of delivering desired customer benefits and meeting organizational goals while leaving no discernible environmental footprint on the planet.

The Resource Scarcity/Depletion Issue

Although the tenets of sustainable marketing clearly place emphasis on proactively managing any damaging aspects of *waste* and *wasting* as the key to pollution abatement, the issue of resource scarcity/depletion is not overlooked. Obviously, one of the central issues underlying P2 is whether or not to use a given scarce resource in the first place. But it must be noted that the relative abundance of many natural resources is a function of best available technology (BAT). As technology advances, this often translates into increased physical access, or improved management approaches, that make available greater quantities of given resources on an economical basis (Sagoff 1997; Simon 1981). For example, new bleached chemical thermomechanical pulp technology has made it possible to increase the use of a tree's cellulose mass from 50 to 90 percent (Associated Press 1996), and improvements in fish farming management techniques have created an abundant economic resource alternative, thereby reducing reliance (and stresses) on wild fisheries (Friedland 1997). Similarly, the availability of substitute products and processes made possible by advances in technology also can affect the relevance of specific natural resources in ways that are good for the environment. For example, the substitution of glass fiber optic cables for copper in the telecommunications industry has increased data transmission efficiency more than tenfold while reducing demand for elemental copper and the attendant negative environmental impacts associated with copper mining (Young 1992).

The Master Equation

Environmentalists Ehrlich and Ehrlich (1990) have developed an equation for environmental impact as a way of visualizing and isolating the major forces causing stresses on ecosystems. The equation is $I = PAT$, where $I =$ environmental impact, $P =$ population, $A =$ affluence, and $T =$ technology.

Population (P) is a major driver of environmental impact (I) because it represents the number of human customers who have needs to be fulfilled. Affluence (A), defined as per capita gross domestic product, reflects the aspirations of people, especially those in the less developed world, to live resource-intensive Western lifestyles. The technology coefficient (T) represents the current level of efficiency through which resources are converted into products and marketed to meet the needs of customers.

The relentless upward movement of both population (P) and affluence (A) represents social phenomena that obviously are beyond the control of marketing managers. However, marketing strategy decisions are controllable and can be considered an aspect of the technology coefficient (T) as follows: technology applications, which reflect a propensity to consume resources and generate waste, influence the product forms offered; the amounts and types of materials and energy used to make products; and the relative efficiency at which production, marketing, and consumption activities are carried out. They determine the profile of environmental burdens (eco-costs) associated with given product delivery systems—the *waste* and *wasting* that go along with *taking* resources and *making* products. Thus, the sustainable marketing strategies discussed in this book—P2 and R2—can be viewed as relatively controllable technology (T) decisions that can reduce eco-costs. The short-term goal of these strategies is to gradually reduce the use of "dirty" technologies and to increase the use of "clean" technologies. Over the long term, the goal is reduce T to zero, which theoretically reduces I to zero given any quantity PA.

The Ecological Imperative

In his text, *Marketing and the Ecological Crisis,* Fisk (1974) formalized the relationship between marketing and environmental impact (I) as the "ecological imperative" that is detailed in the following scenario (Figure 1.1). Ecosystems serve as the source of all resources and also as depositories for waste. The marketing function facilitates consumption and, in so doing, sets in motion many interrelated types of industrial, commercial, and customer activities that take resources, make and distribute products, generate wastes/pollution, and degrade ecosystems. As the human population (P) grows and affluence (A) moves to higher levels, this triggers corresponding increases in the scale of activities necessary to meet consumption needs. It also triggers increases in waste generation/pollution and habitat destruction. This calls for intervention in the form of sustainable marketing practices (T) to stem the tide of eco-costs. Decades ahead of his time, Fisk (1974) summed it up:

> Increasing consumption increases pollution, which reduces habitability. Hence, the consequences of pollution on habitability create a sanction curbing levels of consumption relative to pollution. In order to consume at high levels, it is imperative to provide for waste disposal. (pp. 15-16)

In this scenario, pollution is defined as any "substance that adversely affects the physical, chemical, or biological quality of the earth's environment or that accumulates in the cells or tissues of living organisms in amounts that threaten the health or survival of those organisms" (Kaufman and Franz 1993:18). The introduction of waste/pollution can directly impair the func-

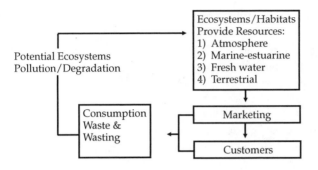

Figure 1.1. The Ecological Imperative: Marketing's Linkage to Potential Ecosystems Pollution/Degradation

tioning of ecosystems. This same dysfunctional effect also results from indiscriminate methods of *taking* resources that result in the literal *wasting* of ecosystems in the truest sense of the word (e.g., destroying, ruining, squandering, emaciating, eliminating, extincting). The previously described harvesting methods of the commercial fishing industry is a timely case in point.

The ecological imperative is an absolute mandate, not a suggestion, for as economies around the world continue to grow, ecosystems do not. Unless appropriate actions are taken to control and reduce eco-costs, consumption at high levels will not be sustainable. Stopping pollution of the earth's ecosystems is not something that *should* be done; rather, it is something that *must* be done.

The Nature of Sustainable Development/Consumption

Serious concerns about the decline of the earth's ecosystems, as well as the prospect of regressive consumption in the future, have led to the concept of sustainable development. First articulated by the Bruntland Commission, this broad term describes the need to harmonize economy and ecology in business decision making (World Commission on Environment and Development 1987). Under sustainable development, the earth's resources are viewed as assets to be responsibly managed, not as "free" goods to be ruthlessly taken. As Willums and Goluke (1992) note,

> [Sustainable development] . . . is a simple phrase with profound implications. It means, first and foremost, that we must put our way of life on a foundation that is based on generating income, not drawing down [ecological] assets. (p. 13)

From a sustainable marketing perspective, the purpose of sustainable development is to create production-consumption systems that "keep going," or regenerate themselves, without degrading ecosystems in the process. In this regard, the term *sustainable consumption* is beginning to emerge as a label for this outcome, one that emphasizes sustainability's direct linkage to the product/market decisions that underlie the marketing management process ("Of Consuming Interest" 1998).

Intergenerational Equity

Maintaining intergenerational equity in terms of the earth's resources is the recurring, forward-looking theme of sustainable development (Graedel and Allenby 1995:83). This refers to the use of resources to satisfy human needs in the present without compromising the ability of future generations to do so. Proponents of sustainable development are quick to suggest that

> the present design of the industrial ecosystem is flawed. Rather than acting according to the circular principles of natural ecosystems, the flow of goods and services is essentially linear. Products are produced, purchased, used, and dumped with little regard for environmental efficiency or impact. (Schmidheiny 1992b:109)

This linear flow to dead-end disposal is the result of inherently wasteful business practices and consumer lifestyles that lead to excessive eco-costs being incurred and passed on to future generations for payment (Cairncross 1992a; Hawken 1993; Neace 1995; Ruckelshaus 1989; Schmidheiny 1992b; Willums and Goluke 1992). Stuart L. Hart, director of the Corporate Environmental Management Program at the University of Michigan Business School, bluntly sums up the situation: "The simple fact is this: in meeting our needs today, we are destroying the ability of future generations to meet theirs" (Hart 1997:67). By contrast, the practice of sustainable development stresses circular processes that promote the preservation of ecosystem capital and quality over the long run, thereby reducing eco-costs and fostering intergenerational equity.

The Global Commons

Over 30 years ago, *Science* published Hardin's (1968) now-famous article, "The Tragedy of the Commons," a classic explanation of why ecosystems become stressed and damaged by economic activity. A professor of biology at the University of California, Berkeley, he described how each herdsman would act in his own self-interest and overgraze public pasture land (the commons), thereby destroying this "public good" in the process. The reason? No cost was charged for the herdsmen's actions. In a recent cameo appearance in *The Last Hunters* (Mare Holstrum Productions Inc. 1995), Hardin restated the "tragedy proposition" in the context of the modern commercial fishing industry:

> I view the seas as a commons because anyone who wants to can go out there and hunt for fish. And as long as there aren't too many people in the world, it works fine. But once there are too many, which is our situation now, then they overexploit the seas, and finally they may even extinguish some species. . . . The trouble is that if 95 percent of the people do exercise restraint—they have good consciences—and 5 percent do not exercise restraint, the 5 percent will prosper at the expense of the others. The second effect is, as years go by, seeing that 5 percent prosper more, the 95 percent start becoming corrupted, and they start joining the minority. . . . And once that happens, all is lost because they'll ruin the commons through overharvesting it. And what you have to get people to see is that there is no escape from this tragedy. And it is a tragedy because even though people see what's coming, they can't avoid it. There's no escape from this tragedy *unless you change the system.* (emphasis added)

Hardin continues to point out what has become painfully obvious during the past three decades: the earth is a global commons made up of interrelated political, social, economic, and ecological systems that define the quality of humans' existence as well as that of all other species. Given a finite communal resource, individuals will seek to maximize their own gains given that no costs are charged. If there is no outside force to keep them in line, then they eventually will destroy the resource for all. This predictable long-term ecological outcome, the result of allowing unfettered access to the commons without imposing eco-costs, must be avoided. The mission of sustainable marketing is to take responsible action now to avoid this fate in the future.

Fostering Corporate-Product Stewardship

Because of the dominant role of corporations in our world, the personal worldview of the decision makers within them is important. Worldview is influenced by culture and religion and generally has been defined as the way in which a people perceive reality, in this case their beliefs, values, attitudes, and behaviors in relation to the environment (Kaufman and Franz 1993:19).

An anthropocentric (or human-centered) worldview is based on the idea that humans are superior to and have dominion over nature and can take and use any resources at will. As Kaufman and Franz (1993) note,

> An anthropocentric worldview . . . may cause some people to abuse or overexploit natural resources, may encourage some people to disregard the needs of other species for habitat and food, and may cause some people to consider pollution and resource depletion as simply necessary and natural consequences of economic progress. . . . Anthropocentric decisions often produce solutions that work in the short term but are not sustainable. (pp. 552-53)

Most important, hard-core anthropocentricists see the "human system" as functioning apart from nature, not as a part of nature.

By contrast, a biocentric worldview holds that

> humans are as much a part of nature as anything else on earth. Humans are subject to all natural laws. Although human inventiveness appears to have circumvented many natural laws, it is only a matter of time before humans must confront the consequences of their activities. (Kaufman and Franz 1993:24)

This approach conveys an unreserved sense of respect and caring for the natural world; it suggests that humans, as an inextricable part of this system, must learn to live in harmony with nature. Furthermore, biocentricism essentially takes a long-term view of environmental problems, seeking solutions that achieve a "balance" within the natural world over time.

Corporate-product stewardship is the core philosophy of sustainable development. It is a largely biocentric worldview that does not diminish humans' position of intellectual superiority and dominance. Rather, it demands that we use this position of "empowered decision maker" to serve as a caretaker/nurturer in relation to ecosystem resources; doing so clearly is in our self-interest. Simply put, corporate-product stewardship is an expression of the belief "that the environment is the basis for all life and for all production. Rather than being an interest competing with other interests, it is in reality the playing field on which all interests compete" (Viederman 1992:180-81). Decision makers holding this worldview tend to see environmental issues as marketing opportunities to be proactively addressed. Those who do not hold this view tend to engage in reactive behaviors that meet minimal standards set by governments.

Environmentalism: The Next Cold War

The main thesis of this book is straightforward: business leaders must understand that the solution of environmental problems is a trade-off necessary to achieve long-term human survival. Protecting, preserving, and enhancing the environment must become legitimized as a necessary part of the value-added equation, a high-priority proposition, an issue worthy of corporate action and commitment. To bring this point home, Anthony Carnevale, chair of the National Commission for Employment Policy, suggests the following analogy (paraphrased in Laitner, Goldberg, and Skeeham 1995). During our past, and unquestioned, preoccupation with defense during the cold war years, billions of dollars were spent on stemming the threat of communism, a threat that was uncertain but not improbable. Why not adopt a similar position on the environment? Is not the threat to the world's ecosystems every bit as uncertain, but nonetheless pressing, as the threat of communism? Does not the need to confront this threat head-on translate into marketing opportunities? The chance for marketing to fill the void as internal corporate educator and environmental champion is clear.

In short, the "ecology versus economy" debate must be ended with the final conclusion that *economics and environmental quality are interrelated.* Fortunately, there are signs that *environment* is beginning to be viewed in corporate circles as something of value that should advance in priority. The necessity for establishing this point of view is echoed by the co-chairs of the President's Council on Sustainable Development—David Buzzelli, vice president of Dow Chemical, and Jonathan Lash, president of the World Resources Institute—who jointly write,

> Environmental progress will require the adoption of stewardship as an individual, institutional, and corporate value. A paradigm shift must occur,

changing a "have to do it" society to a "need and want to do it" society. Ultimately, we must have zero-discharge manufacturing. (quoted in Makower 1995b:8)

The Ecological Setting

Ecology is the study of organisms (plants and animals) in the context of the habitats in which they live (Odum 1971). A branch of biology, ecology is concerned with four basic habitats: (1) atmosphere, (2) terrestrial, (3) ocean and estuarine, and (4) fresh water. Humankind's perpetual quest for life, liberty, and the pursuit of happiness through consumption occurs within these habitats that also are components of ecosystems.

The Nature of Ecosystems

An ecosystem is the basic unit of analysis in ecology and is defined as "the physical environment and all the organisms in a given area, together with the network of interactions of these organisms with that physical environment and with each other" (Ehrlich 1986:239). The fundamental notion of "ecosystem" is one of constant interaction and dependency relationships between organisms of the same species and organisms of different species and the physical habitats within which they exist. Depending on purpose, ecosystems can be delimited quite narrowly (e.g., city block, neighborhood, county) or very broadly (e.g., country, continent, the earth as a whole).

A requisite condition that often is taken for granted is that ecosystem habitats must remain "clean and safe" for humans to survive. If the air, water, or land become polluted, then the prospect for continued survival comes into question. In this regard, humans' production-consumption activities create conflicts that must be resolved. The field of ecology offers unique insights into what must be done to avoid these conflicts and achieve the goal of sustainability.

Ecosystem Support Services and Carrying Capacity

Ecosystems perform a number of interrelated "support services" that are *absolutely essential* for humans' survival (Gladwin 1995). Three general categories are listed in Exhibit 1.2: (1) resource supply, (2) recycling-housekeeping mechanisms, and (3) preservation-control functions. If these services become inoperative (dysfunctional), then the carrying capacity of an ecosystem (i.e., the maximum population of a species that can be supported) is diminished (Buchholtz 1993). The various factors that signal the erosion of habitat quality and diminished carrying capacity include (1) the decline/ extinction of species (a failure to propagate, loss of biodiversity), (2) the depletion of physical resources, (3) the interruption of food chains, and

---

ɛxhibiт 1.2

Ecosystem Support Services: Three General Categories

1. Resource supply:
   Materials supply
   Freshwater supply
   Food supply (sea/land)
   Oxygen supply
2. Recycling-housekeeping mechanisms:
   Nutrient cycling/conversion
   Waste disposal
3. Preservation-control functions:
   Flood control
   Pest control
   Disease control
   Crop pollination
   Climate moderation
   Soil formation
   Soil preservation
   Temperature regulation

SOURCE: Gladwin, Thomas N. (1995), "Sustainable Development and Sustainable Enterprise," paper presented at the Bell Conference, a program of the Management Institute for Environment and Business, University of Texas at Austin, July 20.

(4) the general infiltration of unacceptable levels of pollution into the four basic habitats.

When natural releases of waste occur (e.g., volcanic eruptions, forest fires, decay of dead vegetation and organisms, carbon dioxide exhaled by organisms), the ecosystem's equilibrium is disturbed to varying degrees. However, multiple ecosystem support services immediately go to work to restore habitat quality and carrying capacity, and ecosystem equilibrium often is reestablished within a relatively short period of time, thereby maintaining carrying capacity. In a very basic way, all waste generated in nature serves as food or fuel for other species/organisms/systems or as an input to complementary natural processes. As a result, natural waste is continuously consumed, absorbed, or converted into natural products, carrying capacity is maintained, and the buildup of pollutants in the environment is avoided.

However, when natural events release extremely large quantities of waste, carrying capacity is exceeded and disaster follows. For example, the periodic mass extinctions of the dinosaurs are believed to have occurred when asteroids collided with the earth, causing catastrophic, worldwide atmospheric pollution caused by large quantities of dust and debris. This led to long-term global cooling, which very quickly reduced carrying capacity to very low levels (Gore 1989).

Problems of Cultural Wastes

An old adage states, "The solution to pollution is dilution." However, the large volume of the cultural (man-made) waste and its composition pose special problems for ecosystems that make the preceding proposition inoperative (Kaufman and Franz 1993). Of course, both the quantity of waste and its composition are driven by the factors of population (P), affluence/lifestyles (A), and technology (T).

Durning (1992) notes that huge disparities in waste generation exist between developed and less developed cultures. In Table 1.1, he divides the world into three consumption classes: (1) consumers (20 percent), (2) middle income (60 percent), and (3) poor (20 percent). Given that the familiar 80/20 principle holds, the majority of income (64 percent) is controlled by a few at the top (20 percent), who by proxy consume the most resources and generate the most waste per capita (p. 27). Durning concludes,

> Only population growth rivals high consumption as a cause of ecological decline, and at least population growth is now viewed as a problem by many

TABLE 1.1

World Consumption Classes, 1992

Factor	Consumers (1.1 billion)	Middle Income (3.3 billion)	Poor (1.1 billion)
Diet	Meat, packaged food, soft drinks	Grain, clean water	Insufficient grain, unsafe water
Transport	Private cars	Bicycles, buses	Walking
Materials	Throwaways	Durables	Local biomass
Percentage of world population	20	60	20
Percentage of world income	64	33	3

SOURCE: Durning, Alan (1992), *How Much Is Enough?* New York: Norton, p. 27, Table 2-1. Reprinted by permission of Worldwatch Institute.

governments and citizens of the world. Consumption, in contrast, is almost universally seen as good—indeed, increasing it is the primary goal of national economic policy. (p. 21)

Durning also analyzes what is consumed (Table 1.2). This is accomplished by defining the inhabitants of the industrial countries as the consumer class and combining those of the developing countries (i.e., the middle income and poor) into a comparison group. The contrast demonstrates two things. First, the high-income (consumer class) populations of the industrial countries outconsume the others by magnitudes ranging from 3-to-1 to 19-to-1. In addition, the combined middle and poor classes tend to have consumption patterns that leave behind less environmental damage; that is, they eat mostly grains and vegetables (not red meat), rely on long-lasting durable products (not disposables), and use mass transportation (not personal automobiles). By contrast, the consumer class is a heavy user of disposable products and personal automobiles; its high-technology products require metals, cellulose fibers (e.g., paper), plastics, glass, fossil fuels, and a host of complex chemicals, the production of which causes much greater impact on world ecosystems in terms of wasting, waste generated, energy used, and habitat destruction per capita. The consumer class also relishes fashion merchandise that often is discarded for purely aesthetic reasons long before the end of its functional life.

In addition, high-technology processes affect consumption in the consumer class economies by enhancing productivity, which increases the sheer

TABLE 1.2

Consumption of Selected Goods: Industrial versus Developing Countries, Late 1980s

Goods	Industrial Countries' Share of World Consumption (percentage)	Consumption Gap Between Industrial and Developing Countries (ratio of per capita, consumption rates)
Aluminum[a]	86	19
Chemicals	86	18
Paper	81	14
Iron and steel	80	13
Timber	76	10
Energy	75	10
Meat	61	6
Fertilizers	60	5
Cement	52	3
Fish	49	3
Grain	48	3
Fresh water	42	3

SOURCE: Durning, Alan (1992), *How Much Is Enough?* New York: Norton, p. 50, Table 4-1. Reprinted by permission of Worldwatch Institute.
a. The entry for aluminum reads, "The industrial countries use 19 times as much aluminum per capita as do the developing countries."

quantity of goods and services available for consumption per capita. High-technology applications also influence the composition of waste in the industrialized countries in terms of its "naturalness." Since the early 1900s, high-technology science has unleashed a plethora of invented materials, substances, and chemicals that are hardly "natural" by any standard, a situation that creates additional stresses on ecosystems. As Carson (1962) pointed out more than three decades ago in *Silent Spring,* the creation of man-made molecules, like the pesticide DDT and related chemicals, introduces substances into ecosystems for which there are no natural recycling mechanisms or nutrient conversion counterparts. In addition, many engineered product materials (e.g., plastic, metals, composites) and many classes of chemicals do not biodegrade or break down into natural components on their own. They are not food or inputs for any natural system; they just persist forever. High-technology production processes also often use toxic and hazardous materials in product-making activities, which further complicates pollution abatement efforts—again, be-

TABLE 1.3

Solid Waste Generation in the United States

Panel A: Estimated Total Solid Waste Generation in the United States as Defined Under
Resource Conservation and Recovery Act, Subtitles C and D, 1988

Source/Type	Percentage	Tons (millions)
Hazardous	6.0	700
Municipal solid waste	1.6	180
Mining	14.6	1,700
Agricultural	8.6	1,000
Oil/gas	12.1	1,400
Manufacturing	56.0	6,500
Other	1.1	130
Totals	100.0	11,610

Panel B: Trend in Daily per Capita Municipal Solid Waste Generation in the
United States, 1960-2010

Year	Municipal Solid Waste Generated (millions of tons)	Population (millions)	Per Capita per Day (pounds)
1960	87.8	180.7	2.7
1970	121.9	205.1	3.3
1980	149.6	227.7	3.6
1988	180.0	245.0	4.0
2000	216.0	274.6	4.3
2010	250.6	297.7	4.6

SOURCES: Panel A: Office of Technology Assessment (1992), *Green Products by Design,* Washington, DC: Government Printing Office, p. 6. Panel B: U.S. Bureau of the Census (1997), *Current Population Reports* (P25-1045, P25-1103, P25-1126), World Wide Web: http://www.census.gov/prod/3/97pubs/97statab/pop.pdf; U.S. Environmental Protection Agency (1990), *Characterization of Municipal Solid Waste in the United States, 1990 Update: Executive Summary,* Washington, DC: Government Printing Office, Figure ES-6.

cause they are "unnatural." The result often is the generation of problematic waste streams that may be characterized as complex, high volume, and difficult to handle and that become sources of lingering pollution when dissipated into ecosystems.

An estimate of the total solid waste output of the world's premier industrialized country, the United States, is given for 1988 in Table 1.3 (Panel A). Of the 11.6 billion tons total, only 1.6 percent (180 million tons) represents municipal solid waste (MSW), a component that includes post-consumer garbage (Office of Technology Assessment 1992:6). The vast majority, an overwhelming 98.4 percent, is attributable to conversion and marketing activities that take place prior to final consumption and disposal. The totals in Table 1.3 translate into an astounding waste per capita of 259 pounds/day, more than double the weight of the average 125-pound female consumer and nearly one and three quarters that of the average 150-pound male consumer.

The trend in the MSW component over a number of available years also is estimated in Table 1.3 (Panel B). Between 1960 and 1988, the U.S. per capita per day estimate rose from 2.7 pounds to 4.0 pounds, a 48.2 percent increase. From 1988 to 2010, it is projected to increase from 4.0 pounds to 4.6 pounds, a 15.0 percent increase (U.S. Bureau of the Census 1997; U.S. Environmental Protection Agency 1990). So, while consumer-related waste continues to increase in the United States, at least the rate of increase is declining. This may be attributable to increased P2 and R2 efforts that reduce waste flows to begin with and also divert them from traditional landfill disposal.

Now, imagine all 6.0 billion inhabitants of the earth living at the level of the typical U.S. consumer and the corresponding waste they would generate. Combining population increases (P) with higher living levels (A) is the point behind the "Malthusian-type trap," a proposition that basically says that population increases spell doom because more consumption and more waste must follow. But although technology (T) may be viewed as a waste-generating culprit, it also must be considered an important part of the solution; that is, the threat of the Malthusian-type trap must be eliminated by technological advances implemented through sustainable marketing practice. The new paradigm of sustainable marketing (Exhibit 1.1) makes this connection while also suggesting that changes in population (P) and affluence/average consumption (A) also are important issues—but ones to be resolved by public policymakers, not marketing practitioners.

Irreversibility and Risk

Ecosystems, and the species and resources within them, are subject to the phenomenon of "irreversibility." This means that a failure to manage waste can lead to ecological conditions that cannot be undone at any cost. For example, the queen conch fishery in the Florida Keys remains totally collapsed eight years after a harvesting ban finally was imposed after years of extreme overfishing (Associated Press 1994d). Similarly, the unrestrained plundering of the world's rain forests correlates with an alarming rate of mass extinctions of both plant and animal species (Wilson 1988). Both examples represent resources that are lost forever.

The prospects for irreversibility are even more troubling because ecology is not an exact science in terms of its ability to predict future events. For example, concerning the reality of global warming (Is it happening or not?), the scientific community has not reached a really satisfactory consensus, with many notable experts to be found arguing on opposite sides of the issue (Kahl et al. 1993; Ray 1990; Singer 1992; Walsh 1993). This sort of quandary has led to what is called the "precautionary principle," the crux of which is this: environmental issues deal with risks and irreversibility. A crucial dimension is lead time, because to wait too long to take action on an ecological issue to guarantee "certainty" (i.e., no risk of being wrong) might allow irreversibility to set in. Therefore, it sometimes might be wise to take action based on scientific evidence that supports probable, although not certain, future outcomes.

Environmentalist David Suzuki has put together an interesting scenario that further demonstrates the relationship between lead time and irreversibility. Called the "Analogy of the 29th Day" (cited in Hawken 1993), he describes how an exponentially growing algae population, one that doubles itself daily, quickly overtakes a lake, consuming all the oxygen in the water and killing off all life forms as well (Exhibit 1.3). The point, of course, has to do with timing. In short, when you finally see the freight train barreling down on you on the 29th day, a point in time when you still have 50 percent of original carrying capacity available, it already is too late to change your ways. This is because even if you were able to increase the lake's remaining capacity by 100 percent at the end of the 29th day, the exponentially growing algae still would annihilate all life in the lake 12 hours into the 31st day. The lesson? Take action now, even though information might be incomplete, to avoid likely (but not absolutely certain) ecological catastrophes in the future.

Although the loss of a single species, such as the queen conch in the Florida Keys or an insect species in a distant rain forest, might seem inconsequential to some, such an event can have a much more sinister meaning for both business interests and scientists. From the business perspective, the demise of conch fishery leads to a direct loss of jobs and markets for conch products—forever. On a much larger scale, the dramatic decline in the Georges Bank fisheries off biologically diverse New England, caused by decades of overharvesting, has resulted in a ban on fishing by the U.S. Department of Commerce, resulting in millions of dollars of lost revenues to fishermen (Noah 1994b:A20). Is this action by the Department of Commerce too much

exhibit 1.3

David Suzuki's Analogy of the 29th Day

Assumptions:

1)   There exists a rectangular lake represented by the diagrams below.

2)   Algae invade the lake; they grow exponentially, doubling in number every 24 hours.

3)   Algae growth will totally cover the lake, remove all the oxygen from the water, and kill all life forms by the end of the 30th day.

Scenario:

0% algae coverage - - beginning of 1st day:

25% algae coverage - - end of 28th day:

50% algae coverage - - end of 29th day:

100% increase in remaining lake carrying capacity - - end of 29th day:

Remaining carrying capacity

100% increase in remaining carrying capacity

100% algae coverage of orginal lake - - end of 30th day:

100% increase in remaining carrying capacity

Algae coverage - - end of 31st day: time saving due to 100% increase in carrying capacity:

Algae growth in past 24 hours

Non-existent capacity

12 hours saved

SOURCE: Created from a description in Hawken, Paul (1993), *The Ecology of Commerce: A Declaration of Sustainability,* New York: HarperCollins, pp. 206-7.

too soon, or is it too little too late? A recent study reports that of 128 types of commercial fish stocks in existence, most are in decline but could possibly rebound if careful resource management is practiced to prevent overfishing over the long term. Three species—two types of Pacific pink salmon and the spring herring—appear to have declined to the point of no return (Langreth 1995a). Lemonick (1994) reports a similar scenario of broad-base decline unfolding in 13 of 17 of the world's major fisheries. What will it be—the loss of jobs, fisheries, or both due to the failure to intervene?

From a scientific perspective, extinctions of species do occur naturally. However, the dramatic and unrestrained increase of one species, *Homo sapiens,* currently appears to be triggering large numbers of extinctions well beyond any norm. This reveals a most dangerous aspect of irreversibility that centers around the general role played by ecosystem support services (Exhibit 1.2). As Ehrlich (1988) notes, "The most important anthropocentric reason for preserving diversity is the role of microorganisms, plants, and animals in providing free ecosystem services, without which society in its present form would perish" (pp. 22-23). For example, scientists report that tropical rain forests, which are rich sources of medicines and other chemicals that currently are unknown, are particularly vulnerable to the current round of extinctions. Recently, a Danish firm, Novo-Nordisk AS, isolated a promising epilepsy drug linked to a rain forest betel nut that might offer significant hope to the world's 50 million epileptics (Moore 1995:B12D). Eliminating rain forests effectively forecloses economic discoveries of this type, which have the potential to become a major source of benefits for humankind.

Beyond extinctions, there are other troubling signs that humans' activities might be irreversibly altering the earth's ecosystems in unintended ways through the introduction of pollutants. Respected oceanographer Roger Payne reports that human populations in North America currently are carrying in their bodies organohalogens, a class of DDT-like chemicals that imitate hormones, at about the levels expected to cause serious reproductive disorders (Discovery Communications Inc. 1995). Colburn, Dumanoski, and Myers (1996) develop the case further and openly suggest that ecosystems are being subjected to a subtle poisoning by man-made chemicals that threatens fertility, intelligence, and the very survival of *Homo sapiens.* The Florida Department of Environmental Protection is investigating cases of human illness associated with outbreaks of fish mutations in nine of the state's saltwater/freshwater estuaries (i.e., fish have been discovered with mysterious holes in their heads and their entrails hanging out). At some locations, scientists have found crypto cells, a close cousin of the "cell from hell" that heavily damaged fisheries and caused human sickness in North Carolina and Maryland in the summer of 1997. Usually dormant, crypto cells feed directly on fish tissue and are believed to be transformed into fish-devouring monster organisms by pollutants such as citrus pesticides and heavy metals (Bouma 1998a). Similarly, scientists around the world are investigating a puzzling 500 percent increase in the occurrence of mutations among frog populations (i.e., they are born with extra or missing limbs, eyes, etc.); again, chemicals and their "breakdown products" are suspect ("Technology Watch" 1998:22). Although it is stressed that the exact nature of any linkage among chemicals, pollution, and mutations is unknown, one thing is clear: these occurrences signal risk and must be thoroughly investigated. As one source notes, "Frogs are a 'sentinel species'; what happens to them could happen to us" (p. 22).

The Global Dimension

Another unique aspect of the ecosystems challenge is that once waste/pollution is generated, in most cases it is impossible to physically contain within a designated area such as a specific tract of land (site) or a municipality, county, country, or nation. For example, Chernobyl's "nuclear cloud" slowly migrated across Eastern Europe at the whim of the winds. Similarly, sulfur omissions in the midwestern United States are suspected of causing forest-killing acid rain thousands of miles away in the Adirondacks (Tracey 1993), and the buildup of toxic DDT in the flesh of fish in the Great Lakes is believed to come from the continued use of this pesticide in Mexico and Central America (Reilly 1991).

The point is that a myopic, geographic view of waste/pollution issues must be avoided if the larger challenge is to be addressed. In the final analysis, global problems such as ozone depletion, acid rain, and the greenhouse effect (global warming) all begin with local waste discharges into local ecosystems that eventually migrate into the earth's commons. The need for international and interjurisdictional cooperation at all levels is obvious.

Enter Industrial Ecology

This discussion of ecology would be incomplete if the new field of industrial ecology were not introduced (Graedel and Allenby 1995). Although there are many similarities between industrial ecology and sustainable marketing, there is one subtle difference. Industrial ecology is based on the notion that the residue of one industrial process can become the anticipated input (resource) for another process, which parallels natural ecosystems in which all waste is food, fuel, or input for some other system. This means that industrial ecology focuses more on finding a home for residue, which is now considered a valuable resource destined for another industrial process, than on P2 to begin with. For the record, the similarities to sustainable marketing far outweigh this one difference, so industrial ecology remains a fertile and complementary source of ideas for sustainable marketers.

Commoner's Informal Laws of Ecology

One value of studying ecology lies in the insights it provides marketing decision makers. In this regard, Commoner's (1972) informal laws of ecology condense a lot of relevant thought into commonsense statements that people remember. These laws, and the lessons they provide sustainable marketers, are reviewed in what follows.

The First Law: Everything Is Connected to Everything Else

As Commoner (1972) notes, ecosystems consist of elaborate networks of interconnections "among different living organisms and between populations, species, and individual organisms and their physicochemical surroundings . . . which act on one another" (p. 29). For example, if one level of a food chain is damaged, then this damage affects the survival of other species that feed on the now missing link in the chain.

Natural systems provide a direct analogy with decisions and resulting actions in marketing systems. A decision to market a product "causes" other decisions and actions by extractors of raw materials, suppliers of various components and materials, manufacturers, and distribution companies as well as actions by customers who ultimately use/consume products and dispose of them at the end of service life. This means that sustainable marketers must adopt a holistic view of consumption to be able to determine what is and what is not compatible with ecosystems. The PSLC decision framework (see Chapter 2) provides this perspective.

The Second Law: Everything Must Go Somewhere

In natural ecosystems, all wastes have counterpart mechanisms to recycle or decompose them into forms that preserve system integrity. "All waste is food or fuel" and "ashes to ashes, dust to dust" is the normal routine. This means that at the end of a life cycle, wastes created by one species or natural event become inputs to another natural system or simply break down into beneficial natural products. Therefore, streams of natural wastes created by living things (e.g., excreta, carbon dioxide, biomass) continually enter natural recycling/conversion systems (e.g., nutrient cycles) from which benign and useful constituents emerge. In other words, natural wastes "go where they should." This constant circular process maintains the quality and carrying capacity of ecosystems.

Furthermore, laws of physics dictate that matter is neither created nor destroyed. Therefore, resource conversion processes that ultimately provide benefits to people through products continually leave behind various quantities of cultural (man-made) wastes, depending on the inherent efficiency of those conversion processes. Unfortunately, development of ideal zero-waste, zero-discharge processes currently is not possible given the best available technology; however, it is an entirely addressable issue. Therefore, it is the responsibility of marketers to take steps to curb the unnecessary generation of cultural wastes, to make a full accounting of any such wastes that are generated, and to ensure that they are properly managed so that they do not end up as pollution buildups in ecosystems. Because "everything must go somewhere," anticipating such problems is what P2 and R2 strategies are all about.

The Third Law: Nature Knows Best

As noted earlier, many technology-derived (man-made) products do not have natural counterparts. This implies that the production and use of "non-natural" products must be accompanied by the very careful planning of their "final fate" so that undesirable buildups in ecosystems do not occur (e.g., DDT and other pesticides). The literal explosion of man-made chemicals is of particular interest to ecologists. For example, a new technique called *combinatorial chemistry* now makes it possible for a single scientist to create and test hundreds of new (non-natural) molecules in the time it formerly took to create and test one or two (Langreth 1995b). As more and more biotechnology companies adopt this technique, the proliferation of non-natural chemicals and substances will be astronomical. Major emphasis must be placed on the health, safety, and waste management aspects of these non-natural, man-made products.

The Fourth Law: There Is No Such Thing as a Free Lunch

As Commoner (1972) explains,

> In ecology, as in economics, the [Fourth] Law is intended to warn that every gain is won at some cost. In a way, this ecological law embodies the previous three laws. Because the global ecosystem is a connected whole, in which nothing can be gained or lost and which is not subject to overall improvement, anything extracted from it by human effort must be replaced. Payment of this price cannot be avoided; it can only be delayed. (p. 42)

Eco-costs, such as the payment of social costs by governments and the expenditures by businesses and customers associated with environmental regulatory compliance and P2 and R2 activities, possess the same inevitability as do death and taxes. For example, the National Association of Manufacturers reports that an average U.S. household pays $6,000 annually in higher prices to cover the costs of environmental regulation alone (cited in Cronkite 1995). But this represents only a partial payment, and ignoring the balance of eco-costs is similar to disregarding future asset replacement costs in depreciation schedules. However, even some politicians are now suggesting that eco-costs must somehow be covered. For example, former British Prime Minister Margaret Thatcher says quite bluntly, "No generation has a freehold on earth. . . . All we have is a life tenancy—with full repairing lease" (quoted in Cairncross 1992a:6). Admittedly, political talk is cheap, and the idea of actually paying the costs of planetary repairs and maintenance "as you go" remains novel. It also is still resisted by many because such charges were not assessed in the past under the assumption that ecosystems provided "free goods" on the front end and "a free dumping ground" on the back end.

Because of this need to continually pay for and reinvest in ecological capital, some see sustainable marketing as a force that inevitably dampens competitiveness by increasing business costs, an issue that has sparked a major public policy debate. Protecting ecosystems while minimizing the costs of doing so is a clear concern of sustainable marketing. Enlisting the market mechanism as a way in which to make polluters pay (known as the *polluter pays principle* [PPP]) while rewarding and encouraging ecologically compatible behaviors is seen by many as a way in which to resolve the issue. The PPP is reintroduced later in this chapter and also is discussed in Chapter 7.

Evolving Ecological Concern

Concern about the deterioration of ecosystems and the implications this can have for lifestyles has evolved slowly over the years. Buchholz (1993) describes this evolution as a series of the following stages: (1) conservation, (2) preservation, (3) protection, and (4) survival. Conservation focuses on the prudent use of limited, nonrenewable natural resources, whereas preservation emphasizes the intrinsic value of nature apart from any services or material values it might provide humankind.

The final two stages represent today's position. Protection is a response to the perceived threat that pollution poses to human health and well-being (i.e., the notion of irreversibility and risk discussed earlier), a topic that first received widespread publicity in Carson's (1962) *Silent Spring*. By documenting the detrimental long-term health effects of DDT and other pesticides, Carson became the founder of the modern environmental movement. Raising these issues led to serious concerns about the future survival of humankind and reinforced the idea that sustainability must be achieved through thoughtful decisions by business, customers, and governments; it is simply too important a proposition to be left to chance.

The Green 1990s

The solidification of positive environmental sentiment and the desire for positive environmental action that appears to be taking hold today may well lead to the current decade being called "The Green 1990s." However, the situation might be more aptly be described as one in which "more waste intrusion breeds more concern" within the general population.

Examples of waste intruding into the daily lives of ordinary people abound. Smog in Los Angeles, Denver, Phoenix, Madrid, and Mexico City is so monumental at times that those with respiratory ailments must avoid outside activities when an inversion occurs. Sulfur dioxide concentrations in Prague have exceeded the level previously defined as a natural disaster by 400 percent, resulting in street demonstrations and the forced evacuation of pregnant women from affected areas ("Czech Republic's Air Pollution" 1993). On May 20, 1998, residents of the state of Florida, a windswept peninsula known for its pristine air quality, awoke to a first-ever statewide ozone alert. The state's Department of Environmental Protection recommended that "asthmatics, children, and elderly people stay indoors as much as possible" (quoted in Bouma 1998b:A1). In addition, 68 central Florida waterways remain under a mercury advisory, which means that eating fish from those sources is likely hazardous to human health (Regan 1993a). In what is being called the "Shetland Islands Disaster," the tanker *Braer* dumped 25 million gallons of oil into the North Sea after running aground in one of the most ecologically sensitive areas of the world (Regan 1993b). Known eco-costs already include land pollution and crop damage due to airborne oil, loss of salmon and whitefish fisheries, decimation of wildlife, and the overnight demise of the tourism industry. Mountains of MSW continue to force their way into over-burdened landfills and to pollute local water supplies, a situation local administrators try to cope with through the development of composting systems and curbside recycling programs (Steuteville 1996). Although the reality of these sometimes distant scenarios is hard to deny, consumers often still do not get the message until it hits them squarely in the pocketbook, as was the case when a local utility suggested raising the average monthly water and sewer bill from $50 to $325 (Exhibit 1.4).

The pressures of real pollution might even be pushing the U.S. automotive industry, long a bastion of conservative, "wait and see" environmental attitudes, to change its position. In January 1998, the "Big Three" auto makers announced a surprising consensus: new engine technologies are necessary to reduce air emissions and increase basic fuel economy (Blumenstein 1998). Massive expenditures on research and development projects involving fuel cell technology, hybrid electric-and-gasoline power systems, improved diesel engines, and nickel-metal-hydride electric batteries are in the works. As one General Motors executive puts it, "We need to do it. We want to do it. And we're going to do it" (p. A3).

Disagreement and Deception

There are some who sandbag the issue by simply denying the existence of what Postel (1992) labels "the global disease of environmental degradation" (p. 4). For instance, in *Earth in the Balance,* Vice President Al Gore reports that many measures of ecological health show that a decline in habitat quality is under way (Gore 1992). This position is flatly contradicted by others including Bailey (1993), author of *Eco-Scam,* and Ray (1990), author of *Trashing the Planet.* Similarly, in his book *The Ways Things Ought to Be* (Limbaugh 1992) and on the air, conservative radio talk show host Rush

ExhibiT 1.4

The Real Cost of Water: A Rude Awakening

Water customers fight planned rate increases

By Derek Catron

OF THE SENTINEL STAFF

SANFORD — Flush your toilet, or buy a sports car?

The options would seem unrelated, but the monthly payments would be about the same for some Southern States Utilities customers if a proposed rate increase is approved by the state.

About 100 of those customers from Seminole and Volusia counties were on hand Tuesday to protest the increases at a hearing before Florida's Public Service Commission in the Sanford Civic Center.

A final ruling isn't expected until August, but the customers already had made up their minds. They objected to what they perceived as an exorbitant cost for poor service and water quality from Florida's largest private water and wastewater utility, with about 150,000 connections.

Jack Shreve, the public counsel who represents customers before the PSC, called the proposed rates "atrocious" and said SSU is attempting to make its current customers foot the bill for expansions that would increase the utility's customer base.

"Rates are supposed to be fair, just and reasonable," Shreve said. "No one can convince me [the proposed rates] are fair, just and reasonable."

SSU contends the rate increases are reasonable considering the expense the company incurred in upgrading its equipment to meet higher regulatory standards for environmental protection.

The PSC approved an interim rate increase Jan. 5, but it is subject to refund if SSU fails to convince the commission the higher rates are necessary.

Three different final rate proposals are under consideration, but SSU favors a uniform rate in which nearly all customers would be billed the same for base and per-gallon charges.

The other two final rate proposals and the interim rates are different versions of a "stand-alone formula" — in which the cost is figured differently for each system.

The variables involved in the case can be mind-numbing.

Still, the bottom line in almost every instance is a rude awakening, customers said.

How rude depends on the customer's water system. Chuluota residents in Seminole County could wind up with monthly water and sewer bills that are higher than car payments or mortgages.

If the stand-alone rates are approved, the average monthly water and sewer bill in Chuluota for a customer using 8,500 gallons would top $325 — an increase of 550 percent from the former average of $50.

SOURCE: Catron, Derek (1996), "Water Customers Fight Planned Rate Increases," *Orlando Sentinel*, January 31, p. D3. Reprinted by permission.

Limbaugh regularly portrays those who suggest the existence of serious ecological issues as "environmentalist whackos" creating what he believes is a "nonproblem." The major concern appears to be a lack of an airtight case in terms of reliable, valid, and up-to-date data.

Disagreement often is couched in terms of "it's simply not an environmental problem." For example, packaging expert Judd Alexander suggests that garbage no longer is a pollution danger because "now even standard garbage is treated as hazwaste [hazardous waste] was 25 years ago" (quoted in Poore 1993:42). In other words, new handling regulations and landfill construction rules have made waste management practices much safer. Alexander (1993) further notes, "The real problem, of course, is not the growth of garbage or the quantity of garbage; it is the closing of landfills and the failure to provide replacement sites or alternative ways to handle the discards of towns and cities" (p. 21). This reveals a social dimension to the waste challenge, NIMBY (Not In My Back Yard), which simply says that finding politically and socially acceptable sites for new landfills is the issue, not ecology.

Finally, some observers believe that too often business misuses the environmental issue for the sole purpose of enhancing short-term profits. For example, in *The Green Report I* (State Attorneys General 1990), the attorneys general of 10 states conclude that "attempts to take advantage of consumer interest in the environment have led to a growing number of environmental claims that are trivial, confusing, and even misleading" (p. 1). More defiantly, the *GreenPeace Book of Greenwash* (Bruno 1992) contentiously reports that the environmental initiatives reported by many of the world's leading transnational corporations are merely deceitful public relations ploys designed to allow business-as-usual to continue.

The Competitive Setting

In Western economies, competition is not the only thing, it is everything. Marketing is all about winning the competitive game by providing benefits to customers through products at a profit. This is accomplished through the market mechanism, which allows customers to make informed choices (market transactions) after considering the various competitive offerings.

The New Competitive Game

Traditionally, customers are one party to the transactions that define the competitive game; businesses are the other party. Success is thought of in terms of "win-win" outcomes; that is, customers win when desired benefits are delivered through products, and businesses win by simultaneously attaining their objectives, usually financial in nature. As an additional factor, sustainable marketing assumes that ecosystems are parties to, or the underpinnings of, all transactions, and ecosystems also must win. This occurs when traditional win-win outcomes are achieved *and* ecosystems quality and functioning is preserved or enhanced at the same time. Thus, the revised dogma of sustainable marketing success may be described as achieving "win-win-win" outcomes.

An example of win-win-win from the health care industry demonstrates this. This particular industry currently is under intense pressure to reduce costs, and one cost-cutting approach is the purchase of remanufactured (used) medical equipment at prices as much as 50 percent lower than those for comparable new equipment (Tomsho 1996:B1). From an environmental perspective, remanufacturing is an R2 strategy that extends the life of products that have already been manufactured once (see Chapters 3 and 4). Not making new products from scratch avoids a host of materials-creating and primary manufacturing activities that would have generated large eco-costs in the form of waste and pollution. Therefore, less waste translates into a win for the ecosystems, the lower cost of equipment translates into a win for health care firms in the form of lower costs and higher profits, and customers win by having continued access to high-quality medical technology. From a business point of view, one also might describe this outcome as a case of self-interested environmentalism.

Admittedly, it is not very sensational to tout the environmental virtues of remanufactured equipment purchases, but it does demonstrate the type of consistently executed, low-key solutions that form the bedrock of environmental progress. The work of sustainable marketing must be channeled toward developing similar win-win-win outcomes for other products and industries, not toward rehashing the horrors of accidents such as the Exxon *Valdez* and Bhopal, which already speak for themselves.

The Market Mechanism

In any market transaction, the profit equation may be generalized as follows: Price – Cost = Profit. From the buyer's side, price reflects perceived value (i.e., the benefits received in relation to price), whereas the seller's cost structure is of no concern. From the seller's side, a successful outcome occurs only when profits are positive over the long run; both prices and costs are a concern. In the end, products with perceived values higher than their unit costs are winners; they produce profits.

But the market mechanism assumes that *cost* reflects a fair and equitable accounting of all relevant factors, including ecological impact (see Chapter 7). When this is the case, the market self-corrects in response to the signals it receives through the cost-price structure. But although Commoner's (1972) Fourth Law proclaims that eco-costs must be paid now or later, to date they generally have been ignored, underpaid, or improperly allocated to the products responsible for them. The point is this: not requiring products to pay their ecological way sends false signals that distort the functioning of the market mechanism, and it fails to self-correct. As one observer points out, "Today's market system operates on the fictitious premise that resources are unlimited and the dumps are free" (Breen 1990:42).

In any competitive system, individual firms cannot be expected to voluntarily add eco-costs to their internal cost structures if this creates a competitive disadvantage, a circumstance called the competitive dilemma. As Tenet 5 states, sustainable marketing is not an exercise in corporate altruism. Delivering customer benefits and profits is the driving force that makes things happen or not happen. Sustainable marketing strategies must demonstrate commercial feasibility within the context of current competition, or they will not be undertaken.

One way in which to correct the functioning of the market mechanism is through the adoption by all firms of "full-cost" accounting practices through which eco-costs are systematically internalized in cost structures and product prices (see Chapter 7). Full-costing is the first step in implementing the PPP as the ultimate solution to pollution. The PPP works as follows. Full-costing results in the inclusion of eco-costs in a product's profit equation. Because these costs are now allocated to the products responsible for them, the costs and prices of polluting products will increase relative to those of nonpolluting alternatives. Informed buyers will now likely purchase the latter over the former given parity in terms of primary benefits delivered. Schmidheiny (1992b) sums it up neatly:

> This was the point of the principle [PPP] from its very inception. Though there are various types of pollution charges and they have various primary objectives, most result in higher product prices. Higher prices for more environmentally damaging products send a market signal to the consumer to

seek a cleaner substitute. As consumers respond, so do producers. The polluter pays principle is meant to affect the choices of consumers. Open competitive markets ensure that industry reacts to changes in consumer demand swiftly and efficiently. (p. 19)

Debate over Ways and Means

But what ways and means should be used to induce all firms to uniformly engage in full-costing practices to bring markets into line? There are two major approaches: (1) voluntary private investment in technological innovation (i.e., research and development) that (hopefully) will lead to cost reductions and more efficient product solutions while achieving ecological improvements and (2) public policy initiatives that mandate or provide incentives for the adoption of nonpolluting practices. A balanced approach involving both would appear to offset the weaknesses and capitalize on the strengths of each.

Voluntary private investment in technology relies on the traditional inventiveness of firms to find lower cost ways in which to compete as competitive conditions change and then use them as a basis for establishing competitive advantage, that is, reducing the T factor. It emphasizes the need to let those most knowledgeable about given business circumstances choose the most appropriate techniques and methods for solving given environmental problems.

Public policy, on the other hand, is interventionist by definition and attempts to force action when it will not occur voluntarily. Its implementation has sparked an emotional, high-stakes political debate over how eco-costs will be paid, and by whom, to achieve a "level playing field." Public policy options include (1) directly regulating waste/pollution outputs (e.g., enforcing air, water, and solid waste disposal rules and regulations, called "command and control" policy), (2) imposing economic mandates (e.g., the direct levying of taxes and charges related to pollution outputs), and (3) providing economic incentives to induce firms to aggressively pursue and implement high-technology solutions to pollution (e.g., offering tax breaks for investing in clean technology, technology development and transfer grants, etc.). These approaches supposedly link costs with environmental behaviors in such a way as to force higher costs on polluting products and to reward lower environmental cost alternatives through the functioning of the market mechanism, again for the purpose of reducing the T factor. This costing issue is discussed in more detail in Chapter 7.

The Social-Moral Imperative

Because consumption and human well-being are background issues for all of the subjects in this book, social-moral issues cannot be ignored. Who is responsible for instigating sustainable marketing practices? Is there a social-moral imperative to be observed? How might culture and religion influence the outcome? Like it or not, character and beliefs about personal responsibility will have a tremendous bearing on the final outcome.

Zero Tolerance for Free Riders

Earlier, the startling disparity in average consumption between the industrial and less developed countries was noted. This fact reveals something few want to discuss: companies, customers, countries, and societies that are heavy consumers often do not cover the waste and wasting they cause; rather, they merely transfer this burden to the world's collective ecosystems sans payment. The notion of sustainability clearly places the issue of "covering one's own waste" squarely on the table.

Because all production-consumption activities consume resources and generate waste, all contribute to the stressing of ecosystems to some degree. In fact, some of these activities might be better described as the "production-destruction" processes. Yet there remains a tendency for companies and customers alike to believe that because their contributions are so little, no actions on their parts are necessary (i.e., they ignore Tenet 4). Worse, some companies know that they pollute (sometimes legally, sometimes illegally) and still refuse to address the issue. What they are saying is that they are not responsible for the waste and wasting their actions provoke.

Marketing decision makers have an obligation to correct this misperception. Just as marketers are morally obligated to make available products that are safe and legal to use, they also must offer consumption solutions that maintain the quality of the ecosystems within which customers live. No enterprise, no matter how small or seemingly inconsequential, is exempt from this requirement. The social-moral imperative is this: the cooperation of all individual businesses and customers (industrial buyers and consumers) is necessary to cope with the ecological challenges confronting us; there is no room for free riders.

Nor can there be free-rider countries or societies. The resources needed to feed the voracious lifestyles of the developed/industrial (consumer society) countries often are imported from undeveloped countries, leaving these countries and their peoples resource poor. For example, noted oceanographer Roger Payne reports that the United States makes up only 5 percent of world population yet consumes 25 percent of world resources (cited in Discovery Communications Inc. 1995). When combined with home country resources, converted into products, and consumed, the waste and wasting that flows from U.S. consumption is inherited by world ecosystems. The bottom line is that the U.S. consumption excrement is regularly exported to Third World countries that do not have the technical capacity to process it (Moyers 1990). On a broader level, it appears that a north-south polarization has emerged. The Northern Hemisphere creates pollution, whereas the Southern Hemisphere is depleting/destroying its natural resources base and serving as the garbage dump for the industrialized world.

To compound the problem, reducing average consumption (A) anywhere is politically "taboo"; increasing consumption levels is the major yardstick by which the success of political administrations is judged. Human attitudes in consumer societies and elsewhere are "More is better" and "You [politicians] had better provide more." In the 1994 U.S. presidential race, was not the perennial question "Are you better off now than you were four years ago?" Imagine the repercussions that would ensue if either the Republican or Democrat presidential candidate had advocated lowering the consumption level of American households rather than pledging to increase it. The cooperation of all countries, but especially the industrial countries that contribute disproportionately in terms of negative environmental impact, is necessary to cope with the ecological challenges confronting us.

Influence of Culture and Religion

The moral aspects of environmental action, or inaction, are addressed quite vocally by many cultures and religions. Obviously, this represents a legitimate ways and means for instilling pro-environmental values in the people who make boardroom and consumer decisions. For example, the American Iroquois Indian culture expresses its profound respect for and understanding of the long-term aspects of the natural world through the following saying: "In our every deliberation, we must consider the impact of our decisions on the next seven generations."

In the West, Christianity sometimes is cited as the source of anthropocentric attitudes that suggest the humans have absolute and unrestrained dominion over nature (Kaufman and Franz 1993). This may or may not have been a true interpretation in the past, but there definitely appears to be a trend toward an enlightened, stewardship-biocentric position among some religions. As Kaufman and Franz note,

> The past few decades, however, have witnessed a shift in the thinking and philosophy of some organized religions. Concern for the earth and the belief that humans are to act as stewards of God's creation are increasingly popular ideas among many religious groups. (p. 552)

This appears to be borne out by the latest edition of the *Catechism of the Catholic Church* (Libreria Editrice Vaticana 1994), which states,

> The seventh commandment enjoins respect for the integrity of creation. Animals, like plants and inanimate beings, are by nature destined for the common good of past, present, and future humanity (Gen 1:28-31). Use of the mineral, vegetable, and animal resources of the universe cannot be divorced from respect for moral imperatives. Man's dominion over inanimate and other living beings granted by the Creator is not absolute; it is limited by concern for the quality of life of his neighbor, including generations to come; it requires a religious respect for the integrity of creation. (Section 2415, p. 580)

Of course, some will find attaching a social-moral dimension to environmental business issues laughable and will counter with the "business of business is to make a profit and enhance shareholder value—period" approach. However, a small but growing number of companies and managers believe otherwise. They suggest that blindly adopting a "Wall Street" mentality, which leaves the influence of character, morals, and social responsibility at the boardroom door, is simply an inappropriate approach to business decision making. This emerging sentiment is expressed through organizations such as the Coalition for Environmentally Responsible Economies (1993) and the Global Environmental Management Initiative (1994), whose signatory companies agree to engage in responsible environmental management practices.

But actions in terms of real business decisions based on environmental values speak louder than words. One example is Unique Restaurant Concepts Inc., a firm operating 12 seafood restaurants in Florida. They have eliminated popular and profitable swordfish entrées from their menu (product line). The reason? They have taken the "Give Swordfish a Break" pledge in an attempt to reduce demand and save this seriously depleted billfish species from

exhibit 1.5

The E-Factor: Confessions of an Eco-Savvy Chief Executive Officer

The following is excerpted from remarks given by Ray C. Anderson, chairman and CEO of Atlanta-based Interface, Inc., at the "Building the Sustainable Economy II" conference last month in New York. Anderson can be reached at 770-437-6801.

IN OUR COMPANY LAST YEAR, WE made and sold $802 million worth of products. We operated factories that processed raw materials into finished, manufactured products (carpets, textiles, chemicals, raised-access floors), and our raw material suppliers operated factories. And if we think of the entire supply chain comprehensively, we find that last year the technology in our factories and our suppliers' technologies together extracted from the earth and processed 1.2 billion pounds of material from earth's stored natural capital. I asked for that calculation to be done and when the answer came back, I was staggered. I don't know how it strikes you, but it made me want to throw up.

Of those 1.2 billion pounds, I learned that about 400 million pounds were relatively abundant inorganic materials, mostly mined from the earth's lithosphere, and 800 million pounds were petro-based, either oil or natural gas.

Now, here's the thing that gagged me the most: Two-thirds of that 800 million pounds of irreplaceable, nonrenewable, exhaustible, precious natural resource was burned up to produce the energy to convert the other one-third, along with the 400 million pounds of inorganic material, into products. That fossil fuel is gone forever, except for the carbon dioxide produced in the burning of it, which was dumped into the atmosphere to

accumulate, and to contribute to global warming, to melting polar ice caps, and someday in a distant future to flooding coastal plains, including maybe even the streets of New York City.

DON'T GET ME WRONG. I APPRECIATE the business! And we're committed to producing the best possible products to meet our customers' specifications as efficiently as possible. But really, this cannot go on indefinitely, can it?

My company's technology, and that of every other company I know of anywhere, in its present form, is plundering the earth.

Am I a captain of industry . . . or merely an ecological plunderer and thief?

However, is anyone accusing me? No! No one. I stand convicted by me, myself, alone, and not by anyone else, as a plunderer of the earth.

But by our civilization's definition, I am a captain of industry, in the eyes of many a kind of modern-day hero, the entrepreneur who founded a company that provides 5,300 people with jobs, that also supports spouses and upwards of 12,000 children.

Besides, haven't we paid fair market prices for every pound of material we have bought and processed? Doesn't the market govern?

Yes, but does the market's *price* cover the *cost*? Well, let's see. Who has paid for the military power that has been projected into the Middle East to protect the oil at its source? Why, you have, in your taxes. And who will pay for the

cost of the flooded, abandoned streets of New York City someday in the distant future? Do you see how the market system of the first industrial revolution allows companies like mine to shift costs to others, to *externalize* those costs, even to future generations? My God! Am I a thief, too?

BY THE DEFINITION THAT I BELIEVE will come into use during the *second* industrial revolution, and by my own definition today, I am a plunderer of the earth and a legal thief. The tax laws are my accomplice in crime; and I am part of the endemic process that is going on at a frightening, accelerating rate worldwide to rob our children and their children, and theirs, and theirs, of their futures.

There is not an industrial company on earth and—I feel pretty safe in saying—not a company of any kind, that is sustainable, in the sense of meeting its current needs without, in some measure, depriving future generations of the means of meeting their needs. When earth runs out of finite, exhaustible resources, and ecosystems collapse, our descendants will be left holding the empty bag.

Someday, people like me may be put in jail. But, maybe, just maybe, the second industrial revolution can keep my kind out of jail. I hope so.

We have to begin where we are, to take those first steps in the long journey to sustainability—and begin to dismantle the destructive, voracious, consuming technologies of the first industrial revolution, and start to replace them with the kinder, gentler technologies of the second industrial revolution. And begin to reinvent this whole civilization.◆

SOURCE: Anderson, Ray C. (1996), "The E-Factor: Confessions of an Eco-Savvy CEO," *The Green Business Letter,* July, p. 8. Reprinted by permission.

extinction (Bell 1998). A second example is Ray Anderson, the chairman and chief executive officer of Atlanta-based Interface Inc., whose penetrating comments about sustainability are given in Exhibit 1.5 (Anderson 1996).

Establishing Ultimate Responsibility

Some ask, "Who ultimately is responsible for the waste and wasting that is occurring?" But can the blame be pinned individually on greedy business interests, mindless government bureaucrats, or insatiable consumers?

The point of view here is that all of the above are responsible. As will be noted again and again in this book, waste and wasting is a jointly induced outcome, one that breeds joint responsibility by definition. Therefore, all parties to exchanges must play a significant role in the joint efforts necessary to change the system for the "cleaner." The shell game of attempting to shift the blame to others in the system is counterproductive and will not result in progress toward sustainability.

Reasons for Studying Sustainable Marketing

Even after digesting what has been said thus far, you still might be wondering out loud, "Why is sustainable marketing so important?" Worse, you might feel that this is an "activist" subject, not a business subject. The aim of this book is to show that this is not the case, that it is important to be familiar with the subject and issues surrounding sustainable marketing for a number of reasons.

First, *sustainable* thinking is an established long-term trend, not a short-term fad. Customer sentiment and corporate practice worldwide suggest that a competitive advantage can be earned by implementing sustainable marketing practices. Conversely, a failure to do so may automatically position a firm as unresponsive, uncompetitive, and out of touch with emerging global markets.

Second, ecological factors already translate into significant costs for compliance and other mandated activities that deeply affect bottom-line profits. Furthermore, one might easily assume that as pressures on ecosystems mount as the population increases, this will spur additional government regulatory initiatives. A failure to be knowledgeable and proactive in this area invites additional government regulation—tighter emissions standards, more restrictive waste disposal, and more restrictive packaging regulations, to name a few—which in turn increases costs. During the late 1980s, state legislatures in the United States saw fit to pass hundreds of laws designed to control waste and pollution in an attempt to minimize ecosystems damage and maintain local environmental quality (National Solid Wastes Management Association 1991). As a result, the so-called "greening" of business became noticeably less voluntary. As J. Water Thompson USA (1990) notes, business was being "greened by law, not choice" (p. 4). This shows that adopting a reactive attitude can be self-destructive. As the *Florida Retailer* suggests, "Involvement or . . . more regulation? It's in your hands" (Walpert 1994:49). Therefore, implementing sustainable marketing practices may be looked at as strategy that defends business's freedom to implement voluntary (non-government-imposed) environmental solutions and also protects organizations' bottom lines.

Third, if you do personally conclude that we do have an environmental problem, then your only rational conclusion must be that a failure to act eventually will kill the planet and the market of humans and that there will be no marketing to do. Short of that, continuing environmental degradation is bound to affect your financial lifestyle in a number of ways. For example, owners of "multimillion-dollar palaces" in upscale Naples, Florida, recently have formed an environmental association to save endangered mangroves, a type of aquatic tree. The reason: the dying trees are visually blighting the landscape and reducing property values (Binkley 1995). In other words, adopting a sustainable worldview can be an act of personal, societal, and tangible property self-preservation.

Fourth, you might already possess significant ecological sensitivities that tell you that engaging in sustainable marketing is simply "doing the right thing" and that "trashing the planet" is wrong. You might even be into the semireligious world of deep ecology (Devalle and Sessions 1985) and the Gaia hypothesis (Lovelock 1979) and believe that humans are only one of many species on this planet—and not necessarily the most important one at that. Having a passionate feeling for Mother Nature as an important mystic force is easily coupled with the belief that engaging in sustainable marketing is one way in which to save her.

Philosophy of This Book

At this juncture in history, the author adopts the position that ecosystems are being heavily affected and damaged by humankind's consumption activities and that steps must be taken to preserve the planet for ourselves and also for future generations. We already are paying real eco-costs, and they have to be paid regardless because the loss of the global commons is an unacceptable outcome. So, it is not a matter of *if* we will pay; the real questions are the following: How much? For what purpose? Who will pay? How will we go about it? What are the benefits? In the face of all this, the oxymoron task of sustainable marketing remains "getting more from less resources" and "getting more from the same resources" through cleaner, cheaper, and smarter strategies.

Various groups—academics, scientists, environmental activists, religious denominations/orders, business/corporate leaders, government regulators, politicians, and customers—are direct stakeholders in the Earth's commons. In the past, these groups have chosen, more often than not, to fight each other to see to it that their respective views prevailed. Obviously, more creative solutions will be reached if adversarial relationships are avoided and all factions work together as partners. One innovative plan for bringing environmental stakeholders together is called The Natural Step (TNS). Founded in 1989 by Karl-Henrik Robert, a Swedish research oncologist, and championed in the United States by Paul Hawken, TNS's stated purpose is "to develop and share a framework comprised of easily understood, scientifically based principles that can serve as a compass to guide society toward a just and sustainable future" (Hawken 1996:1). TNS's intriguing goal is to train 1 million people in the next five years in the workings of a new model of sustainability. Central to the model are the "Four System Conditions," reproduced in Exhibit 1.6 (Robert, Daly, Hawken, and Holmberg 1996:5). Although clearly in the start-up phase in the United States, TNS principles have been used in strategic planning applications by 29 Swedish corporations and 49 Swedish municipalities (p. 5). Every indication is that TNS brings to the table an ability to unite stakeholders in common action, a factor that is so utterly important in the solution of ecological problems.

Intelligent men and women cannot believe in short-term environmental fixes that set up long-term environmental disasters. Furthermore, environmental issues must not be reduced to a simplistic sort of morality play in which "bad" business is pitted against "good" Mother Nature. Clearly, the time to act is now, and one purpose of this book is to bring all stakeholders together and promote a dialogue through which a gradual and reasoned shift to sustainable practice can occur. This has to be done if we are to leave the legacy of a respectable future for the generations that follow. The biggest danger is being lulled into complacency by the shortsighted who prefer business as usual. In *Changing Course* (Schmidheiny 1992b), Toshiaki Yamaguchi, president of Tosoh Corporation, sums up what is needed:

exHibiT 1.6

The Natural Step (TNS): The Four System Conditions

System Condition	This means:	Reason:	Question to ask:
1. Substances from the Earth's crust must not systematically increase in the ecosphere	Fossil fuels, metals and other minerals must not be extracted at a faster pace than their slow redeposit and reintegration into the Earth's crust	Otherwise the concentration of substances in the ecosphere will increase and eventually reach limits—often unknown —beyond which irreversible changes occur	Does your organization systematically decrease its economic dependence on underground metals, fuels and other minerals?
2. Substances produced by society must not systematically increase in the ecosphere	Substances must not be produced at a faster pace than they can be broken down and integrated into the cycles of nature or deposited into the Earth's crust	Otherwise the concentration of substances in the ecosphere will increase and eventually reach limits—often unknown —beyond which irreversible changes occur	Does your organization systematically decrease its economic dependence on persistent unnatural substances?
3. The physical basis for productivity and diversity of nature must not be systematically diminished	We cannot harvest or manipulate ecosystems in such a way that productive capacity and diversity systematically diminish	Our health and prosperity depend on the capacity of nature to reconcentrate and restructure wastes into new resources	Does your organization systematically decrease its economic dependence on activities which encroach on productive parts of nature, e.g., over-fishing?
4. Fair and efficient use of resources with respect to meeting human needs	Basic human needs must be met with the most resource-efficient methods possible, and their satisfaction must take precedence over provision of luxuries	Humanity must prosper with a resource metabolism meeting system conditions 1-3. This is necessary in order to get the social stability and cooperation for achieving the changes in time	Does your organization systematically decrease its economic dependence on using an unnecessarily large amount of resources in relation to added human value?

SOURCE: Robert, Karl Henrik, Herman Daly, Paul Hawken, and John Holmberg (1996). "A Compass for Sustainable Development," *The Natural Step News*, Winter, p. 5. Reprinted by permission.

The change in corporate strategy requires the establishment of an environmental management system that includes grasping the connection between business activity and its environmental impacts from a long-term perspective; reassessing corporate philosophy, activities in research and development, production, and sales; and finally evaluating progress. (p. 113)

Plan of This Book

This book continues by first introducing sustainable marketing's unique PSLC decision framework in Chapter 2, followed by a discussion of basic sustainable marketing strategies in Chapter 3. In Chapters 4 through 7, sustainable marketing management is adapted to each of the elements of the marketing mix: Chapter 4, product; Chapter 5, channels; Chapter 6, communications; Chapter 7, pricing. Chapter 8 concludes with a discussion of markets and market development issues.

Chapter Summary

Increasing world population, coupled with the desire of more individuals to adopt resource-intensive lifestyles, has placed significant stresses of the earth's ecosystems. The continuous conversion of large quantities of resources into products (goods and services) to meet these human needs consumes immense quantities of resources. It also generates large quantities of cultural wastes that threaten to pollute our basic life-support systems. We face an ecological imperative: to manage the wastes and wasting associated with all production-consumption processes.

Sustainable marketing recognizes that marketing strategy decisions have a major impact on the use of resources, on the generation of wastes, and on subsequent pollution. Sustainable marketing requires that marketing strategy be designed to be compatible with ecosystems. Achieving compatibility involves integrating the waste management strategies of P2 and R2 into the marketing decision-making process. P2 deals with preventive action; the point is to design product systems so that waste is eliminated from the start. R2 deals with remedial action; the point is to design product systems so that resources can be used over and over again. To attain these goals, sustainable marketing strategies are actualized through the design-for-environment process.

Sustainable marketing views ecosystems as a non-negotiable physical limiting factor in marketing strategy decisions. Because the preservation of clean and healthy ecosystems is a prerequisite for human survival, sustainable marketing must not be viewed as an exercise in corporate altruism. Rather, it challenges marketers to reinvent product systems so that they are zero-waste, zero-discharge in character while also delivering equivalent benefits to customers through products and meeting organizational goals (financial and other).

Sustainable marketing is a component of the broader concept of sustainable development, an approach for promoting intergenerational equity in the use of resources. Sustainable development seeks to harmonize economy and ecology; that is, we must not make economic decisions today that result in denying future generations access to and use of resources. Sustainable development treats the earth as a commons whose economic resources gradually will be destroyed if unrestricted access continues without the payment of eco-costs. This is because both businesses and customers naturally act in their own self-interest when taking resources from the commons, and neither currently pays the full eco-costs of their actions.

Understanding the ecological setting is crucial for developing and implementing sustainable marketing. Ecosystems perform support services that can be classified into three general categories: (1) resource supply, (2) recycling-housekeeping mechanisms, and (3) preservation-control functions. The proper functioning of ecosystem support services ensures the existence of the carrying capacity necessary to sustain human and other species. But support services in the various categories can be rendered dysfunctional by the intrusion of cultural (man-made) waste/pollution into ecosystems. The result is lowered carrying capacity, that is, the ability to support human and other populations.

The large quantities of cultural waste being generated by present production-consumption systems, as well as its composition, represent serious challenges. This is seen in contrasts between the developed countries (high-level economies) and the less developed world. The developed world represents the 80/20 phenomenon in action in that a small number of high-level consumer economies are disproportionately high per capita users of resources and also disproportionately high per capita generators of wastes. The high-technology processes associated with high-level economies also tend to generate large quantities of non-natural wastes, many of which are difficult to dispose of. In addition, waste/pollution is a transmigratory phenomenon in that once it is created, waste/pollution is difficult to contain within set physical boundaries or countries.

A major concern among ecologists is the prospect of irreversibility, which means that once damaged or altered, a natural system will not recover or return to its former status. Rain forest decimation and species extinction are examples. Avoiding irreversibility is difficult because the scientific prediction of future ecological events, such as global warming, lacks certainty. This creates a quandary because failing to preserve ecosystems will lead to our extinction, and long lead times are necessary to develop and implement corrective action; yet, some policymakers demand certain knowledge of future ecological events as a prerequisite for action. In response, the precautionary principle holds that in the case of environmental matters, it is absolutely necessary to err on the side of prudence because irreversible outcomes pose a fundamental threat to our continued existence. The precautionary principle suggests the need for only reasonably certain science, not absolutely certain science.

Four informal laws of ecology help to further set the context of sustainable marketing challenges and solutions: (1) everything is connected to everything else, (2) everything must go somewhere, (3) nature knows best, and (4) there is no such thing as a free lunch. In short, these laws demonstrate the interconnected nature of business decisions and relationships (i.e., channel members are interconnected in a PSLC), that the wastes created by consumption activities must be recognized and managed, that the unnatural materials/ product wastes created by humans must be carefully managed to not disrupt ecosystems, and that the payment of eco-costs cannot be avoided because they represent the price of achieving a sustainable future.

Concern over the degradation of ecosystems has evolved from past notions of basic resource conservation and preservation to today's view, which stresses the need to protect human health and well-being and to ensure long-term human survival. Waste is beginning to overtly intrude into the lives of ordinary people in the form of air pollution, water pollution, oil spills, and mounting quantities of local MSW requiring immediate disposal. However, not all agree on the seriousness of the problem. Dissenters often cite the lack of scientific certainty about future events as the reason not to take more aggressive pro-environmental actions now.

Successfully bringing ecosystems impact into marketing decision making creates win-win-win outcomes. Business firms and customers are the traditional parties to the transactions that define the competitive game. Sustainable marketing assumes that ecosystems are additional (third) parties to any transaction. The ideal outcome is where (1) customers win by receiving benefits through the products, (2) businesses win by achieving a fair profit or other goals, and (3) ecosystems win because product systems have been designed not to pollute or waste or otherwise impair ecosystems functioning.

Ecosystems impacts can be brought to bear on marketing decisions by harnessing the market mechanism. The profitability of any transaction is a function of price and cost. In general, the market mechanism allows customers to make informed choices based on price. But the market mechanism assumes that cost reflects a fair and equitable accounting of all relevant factors. The fact that the cost of ecological damage and pollution often is underpaid or ignored in product cost structures introduces a fundamental distortion into the market mechanism. This may be corrected through the PPP, which mandates the full-costing of products to include all environmental charges. The result? Polluting products will bear more and higher costs, which likely will translate into generally higher prices than those of nonpolluting products offering equivalent benefits. The market mechanism will then function appropriately, as customers generally will respond by choosing lower priced nonpolluting products over higher priced polluting products.

Determining exactly how to achieve the adoption of full-costing practices by business is a major issue. The two major approaches, public policy intervention and voluntary initiatives, both have their benefits and shortcomings. Overall, the idea is to link costs (and prices) with environmental behavior to force higher costs (and prices) on polluting products and to reward equivalent nonpolluting alternatives with lower costs (and prices).

Because production-consumption processes and human well-being are totally interconnected, the study of sustainable marketing cannot ignore social-moral issues. The ultimate answer to the question "Who is responsible for waste management?" will largely reflect the character and moral beliefs of the managers and customers who have to address it. The need for all parties to "cover their wastes" mandates that free riders cannot be tolerated; this includes customers, firms, and countries. In addition, the cultural and religious orientation of individuals represents an important force for bringing pro-environmental beliefs to bear on business and customer decisions.

CHAPTER **2**

New Decision Boundaries:
The Product System Life Cycle

One of the major lessons of ecology is that we live in a very interconnected world in which, to quote Commoner (1972), "Everything is connected to everything else" (p. 29). This means that environmental impact (I) is an eclectic phenomenon that results from the collective actions of many people and organizations, each of which has a role to play in maintaining ecosystems quality. It follows that to develop an understanding of ecosystems impact and the associated eco-costs of product systems, as well as to craft appropriate sustainable responses, marketing decision makers must revise traditional decision boundaries to include a much broader range of organizations and activities than usually is associated with the problem-solving process.

The Product System Life-Cycle Concept

The product system life cycle (PSLC) defines the new, extended decision boundaries that marketers must address when responding to the ecological challenges posed by consumption. It represents the merger of two concepts: (1) the resource life cycle and (2) the marketing channel network.

The Resource Life Cycle

The term *life cycle* is commonly used to describe any birth-to-death, cradle-to-grave sequence of events through time. For example, human biological age is used to segment medical practice into age-based specialties (e.g., pediatrics, adolescent medicine, gerontology) that reflect changing physiological needs over time. A fundamental assumption of all life-cycle representations is that the phenomenon under examination can be depicted (i.e., modeled) as a series of interdependent stages, events, or activities that occur over time and that a holistic, total systems orientation is useful for meaningful interpretation.

In environmental engineering, resource life cycles are described as cradle-to-grave materials flows often depicted by five nominal stages (Figure 2.1): (1) raw materials extraction, (2) materials-components manufacturing, (3) finished products manufacturing, (4) product use/consumption, and (5) waste disposal (Hunt, Seller, and Franklin 1992; Tchobanoglous, Theisen, and Vigil 1993). Stages 1 to 4 occur in a first-to-last progression; Stage 5, waste disposal, is a concurrent activity associated with all stages of the life cycle.

Each stage in Figure 2.1 is viewed as an input-output process. In Stages 1 through 4, input flows consist of resources and manufactured products (R/P→) that are either (1) consumed in internal processing, (2) incorporated into manufactured products passed on as outputs to the next stage (P→), or (3) discharged as waste outputs (W→) (Keoleian and Menerey 1993; Society of Environmental Toxicology and Chemistry 1991). Stage 5 activities are unique; they take place at all levels/stages to convert waste outputs into (1) marketable resources-commodities-products and (2) benign substances-materials that are safe for terminal disposal. Overall, the life-cycle representation of inbound and outbound flows and interrelated stages provides a basis for understanding the use of resources, the generation of waste, and the eco-costs associated with the total product system under study.

The Marketing Channel Network

The marketing channel network is a systems concept that charts the set of manufacturer-producer and distribution organizations that work together over time to complete transactions with given target markets. Also known as the vertical marketing system, it defines the specific companies and managements (by type, name, and location) that conceive of and carry out marketing

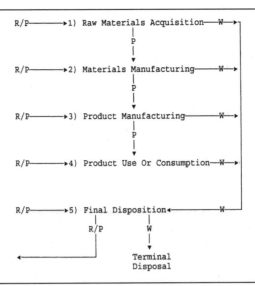

Figure 2.1. Five Stages of the Resource Life Cycle

NOTE: R→ = resource inputs = energy and raw materials; P→ = manufactured products; W→ = waste outputs = emissions into the air and water, solid waste, noise, and heat.

strategy with mutual economic self-interest and customer satisfaction as objectives.

The decision boundaries associated with marketing channel networks generally are defined as *beginning* with a production process (i.e., a manufacturing operation in which resources are converted into form and function) and *ending* with the target market transaction. Occurrences before or after these beginning and ending points are considered beyond the channel network's decision-making, administrative, and functional domain. For example, a manufacturer of lead acid automobile batteries for consumer markets would not be concerned with the waste or pollution generated by the lead mining, smelting, and fabrication processes that precede its manufacturing operations, nor would this manufacturer be concerned about how consumers accomplish the final disposal of spent batteries at the end of the products' useful lives.

Product System Life Cycle Defined

The resource life cycle and channel network concepts have a basic commonality: both depict organizations and customers engaged in purposive, resource-based activities that are performed sequentially and concurrently over time. But there are two distinct differences. First, the resource life cycle emphasizes materials and waste flows but essentially ignores business purpose, that is, the fact that the organizations involved are joined through the prospect of economic gain. Second, the resource life cycle is a cradle-to-grave proposition, whereas the typical channel network applies to only one segment of the cradle-to-grave span.

The PSLC (Figure 2.2) represents a merger of the two concepts that captures the comprehensive, cradle-to-grave coverage necessary to assess ecological problems while factoring in the element of business purpose. Simply put, the PSLC is premised on the idea that resource flows are determined by sets of organizations and customers that come together for the ultimate purpose of making profitable market transactions. The normative PSLC model depicts the five cradle-to-grave stages of the resource cycle as a set of channel networks, each consisting of combinations of manufacturers, distributors-wholesalers, retailers, and target markets. The first four stages—raw materials channel networks, materials-components channel networks, finished products channel networks, and consumer target markets—are aligned in series; Stage 5, reverse waste management networks, concurrently functions to manage wastes generated at all levels of the PSLC. Organizations and markets making up the PSLC are linked by marketing strategy (MS in Figure 2.2). In essence, the PSLC defines the totality of stakeholders relevant to the business issues of *taking, making,* and *wasting* set forth by Hawken (1993). Tracing the PSLC reveals the diversity of the organizations that must unite under the common banner of corporate-product stewardship.

New Decision Boundaries

The first recognition in marketing literature that a given product's eco-systems impact must be linked to an extended view of marketing channels is attributed to Cracco and Rostenne (1971) in their prophetic article, "The Socio-ecological Product." In this regard, what may be described as a PSLC's mutual use of resources to target an end customer also brings with it mutual eco-costs in the form of joint waste generation. Clearly, the development of meaningful sustainable marketing strategies can occur only within the context of the new, extended decision boundaries defined by the limits of the PSLC. This represents an important departure from the myopic boundaries usually associated with the notion of channel networks.

The precise point is *not* to view PSLC stages (channel networks) separately; rather, it is critical to view waste management and environmental

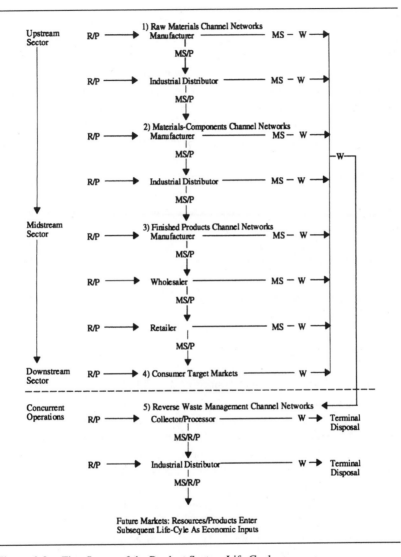

Figure 2.2. Five Stages of the Product System Life Cycle

NOTE: R→ = resource inputs = energy and raw materials; P→ = manufactured products; W→ = waste outputs = emissions into the air and water, solid waste, noise, and heat; MS→ = marketing strategy linkage.

impact as fundamentally holistic, interconnected phenomena. A marketing strategy's eco-costs are a function of a large number of wide-ranging decisions made by the many organizations and individuals making up the PSLC that occur *before, during,* and *after* the act of final consumption; therefore, all

PSLC members are part of the problem, and all are part of the solution. Limiting waste management analysis to a single stage or organization within the PSLC can result in suboptimization, the situation in which decisions based on conditions at one point in a system may minimize "local" impact but tend to increase total system impact (El-Ansary and Stern 1988). For example, when a manufacturer shifts from refillable to disposable bottles, it reduces the manufacturer's internalized packaging costs by shifting the bulk of the ultimate container disposal function to public sector reverse channels, where costs might be higher.

Adopting the broadened decision boundaries of the PSLC forces a longer run orientation necessary to understand and cope with ecological problems. PSLC members usually are diverse in character and function as well as geographically dispersed; the system itself represents a definite, but often stretched-out, chronological sequence of events that must regularly occur if consumption of finished products is to take place. Within this setting, all PSLC members must constantly think in terms of how the decisions they make at their respective levels are linked to waste outcomes over the entire production-consumption sequence.

Product System Life-Cycle Sectors

For discussion and analysis purposes, the PSLC can be generalized into three sectors (left margin of Figure 2.2): (1) upstream (Stages 1 and 2 plus concurrent Stage 5 activities), (2) midstream (Stage 3 plus concurrent Stage 5 activities), and (3) downstream (Stage 4 plus concurrent Stage 5 activities). These three sectors correspond to supply, finished products manufacturing, and final consumption levels. Working down Figure 2.2 and assuming a consumer product scenario, upstream Stage 1 and 2 manufacturers act as suppliers for the finished products manufactured and marketed by midstream firms in Stage 3. Stage 4 serves as the downstream target market in which products ultimately are consumed. By definition, Stage 5 organizations operate concurrently in all sectors to manage any waste flows (W) generated. If an industrial product scenario is assumed, then the model simply terminates at an earlier stage.

Midstream Sector

A closer examination of the hierarchy of PSLC stages reveals that midstream manufacturing and marketing organizations are in a unique position to influence waste outcome (and eco-costs) in all sectors. Organizations in Stage 3 are the locus of product design decisions; they continually go through the process of interpreting target market needs (Stage 4) and responding with substantive product and distribution solutions that deliver the necessary benefits. Product decisions at this level translate directly into materials specifications and manufacturing/processing requirements; they also determine which upstream suppliers (Stages 1 and 2) will be participants in the PSLC and which downstream target markets (Stage 4 customers) will be sought. Likewise, Stage 3 distribution decisions define the type of product handling, movement, and storage activities that must be provided by wholesaler and/or retailer intermediaries to make products accessible to target market customers. All of these determinations preordain the character of waste streams that will be generated throughout the PSLC.

For example, suppose that a Stage 3 beverage manufacturer believes that switching from disposable aluminum cans to returnable/refillable glass containers is a better environmental solution and that consumers will see this change as "public-minded" and flock to the product because of it. This decision will force the alteration of the PSLC in that new supplier networks made up of glass container manufacturers will emerge upstream. The manufacturer's midstream bottling operations also will take on different characteristics. Furthermore, switching packaging materials redefines the character of waste processing needs at all levels. The public sector curbside collection programs that handled the disposable aluminum containers after Stage 4 consumption no longer will be used, but the refillable system will require the development of alternative Stage 5 recapture and processing networks that may be internalized by the manufacturer and also require wholesaler-retailer participation.

Clearly, then, midstream marketing decision makers occupy a position that enables them to strongly influence ecological outcomes should they choose to do so. It follows that to thoroughly understand waste management issues, midstream decision makers must engage in extensive inter- and intraorganizational analysis involving nontraditional subjects and areas of expertise.

Upstream Sector

Midstream decision makers are beginning to flex their ecological empowerment. One practice that is emerging is known as "Greening the Supply Chain" (1993:2). In this case, *greening* refers to the need for upstream manufacturer-suppliers (Stages 1 and 2) to be able to show their midstream manufacturer customers that they have viable environmental management systems in place that address the issue of environmental performance. In short, midstream organizations are invoking the "clean birds of a feather flock together" approach. Being proactive in this area can be a critical prerequisite for making a manufacturer's "to consider" list. For example, Principle 11 of the International Chamber of Commerce Business Charter for Sustainable Development promotes and encourages the adoption of the charter's full set of principles for environmental management by suppliers and contractors working on behalf of any signatory organization (Willums and Goluke 1992). Further pressure is being exerted by the International Organization for Standardization, which has adopted ISO 14000, a series of standards promoting the establishment of environmental management systems within organizations (Rothery 1995). When fully implemented, ISO 14000 will become a market-driven buyer requirement that supplier organizations will have to meet through formal certification procedures. (See Chapter 5 for additional comments about ISO 14000.)

Other proactive stances can be taken by Stage 1 and 2 organizations when the environmental characteristics of the products/components they supply become an issue at midstream and/or downstream points in the PSLC. An interesting example is the intensive corporate-integrated container recycling network put in place by the Reynolds Aluminum Recycling Company, which included more than 900 redemption locations at one point, to defend the use of disposable aluminum containers and also to cultivate a low-cost source of secondary raw materials (Fuller 1977, 1991). This downstream effort by Reynolds Aluminum certainly has contributed to the aluminum container industry's record 66.5 percent recycle rate (Ridgley 1998a:1).

Downstream Sector

It also is clear that the traditional approach of "determining what the customer wants and then providing it" without regard for ecosystem consequences (i.e., eco-costs) no longer is acceptable on its face. This suggests that a major mission of marketing must be to educate downstream customers about how product choice and subsequent product disposal affect ecosystems, both positively and negatively, and influence long-term quality of life. It is argued throughout this book that maintaining ecosystems quality is really a fundamental customer need, something to which people have a right. But it is admittedly perceived as an indirect benefit and not recognized as a "felt" need by most consumers (see Chapters 7 and 8). In commenting on the need to address this state of affairs, Sheth and Parvatiyar (1995) note, "It is marketing's task to redirect needs and wants towards consumption that is ecologically least harmful" (p. 11).

Concurrent Reverse Waste Management Networks

Stage 5 operations are concurrent at all stages and, therefore, should not be considered a separate sector of the PSLC. The general nature of Stage 5 activities is common regardless of the sector in which they occur. For example, the label *reverse* is used because the function of Stage 5 processes is to turn around linear flows of waste to terminal disposal (i.e., landfills or discharges into ecosystems) and make them circular. This is accomplished by diverting by-product wastes through systems designed to recover products, materials, and energy values that subsequently are redeployed as economic resources (inputs) in new life cycles (Fuller and Allen 1995; Zikmund and Stanton 1971). In fact, ideal "zero-waste, zero-discharge" PSLCs are not really cradle-to-grave systems; rather, they are cradle-to-cradle systems in that no terminal disposal would be required because outbound residual waste streams would be reduced to zero by processing through Stage 5 operations.

Legislative mandates, increasing environmental compliance costs, and changes in consumer ecological consciousness have led to the formalization of eco-costs on accounting statements. Consequently, the management of existing waste streams (i.e., Stage 5 activities) has assumed the status of a functional area that significantly affects the bottom line. Therefore, it is necessary to treat both internal waste management activities and subcontracted Stage 5 services as important cost-profit centers to be professionally managed, not as "out of sight, out of mind" waste dumping operations. Furthermore, the careful management of these activities results in the tracking of costs that eventually can be allocated to the products responsible for them, thus making sure that the true costs of doing business end up in the right product cost structures. Known as "full costing," this aspect is the major concern of the field of environmental accounting and also an emerging influence on pricing decisions (see Chapter 7).

In the public sector, the business of managing Stage 5 reverse municipal solid waste systems is a function that is only indirectly linked to the upstream and midstream managements of PSLC firms. Producers find themselves selling to large numbers of end users from whom they are physically estranged in terms of time, place, and product ownership; they have little control over actual disposal behavior and processes once title passes to the customers.

Nevertheless, it is vitally important for producers to design marketing strategies that are as compatible as possible with the needs of downstream public waste management networks to enhance the efficiency of these operations. For example, in the area of packaging, this has meant making packages easier to recycle, which involves using fewer types of materials in product composition and standardizing around a limited number of specific types of materials (see Chapter 4).

A few manufacturers find it in their immediate self-interest to become managerially involved in Stage 5 reverse channel networks to varying degrees. The earlier example of the Reynolds Aluminum integrated recycling network demonstrates how the firm protected itself from the ecological criticism surrounding its manufacture of disposable, nonbiodegradable packaging while creating a strategic, long-term source of valuable raw materials in the process (Fuller 1991). Another firm, Canon Canada, has found it important to recover its laser copier cartridges because they contain toxic materials that cause pollution when dumped in landfills. Because Canon Canada is not in a "functional" position to actually perform downstream Stage 5 retrieval/ collection activities on a large-scale (nationwide/worldwide) basis, the company manages this process through a strategic alliance with Canada Post, which routinely collects used cartridges from thousands of widely dispersed office locations and returns them to manufacturer-designated facilities. A major designed-in factor that expedites recovery is the innovative outbound packaging that doubles as the return packaging system complete with instructions, mailing labels, and prepaid postage ("Canon Canada Taps Canada Post" 1993).

From these examples, one can conclude that a first step in implementing sustainable marketing is delineating a product's PSLC from which will come an understanding of the waste burdens generated by the interrelated decisions of upstream, midstream, and downstream sector participants. Although no individual organization or customer in a PSLC can be said to be legally responsible for the waste of other system participants, it is clear that the totality of the system's waste must be understood if it is to be moderated through coordinated sustainable marketing efforts.

Quantitative Life-Cycle Assessment

As noted in *The Economist* ("Life Ever After" 1993), "To discover how "green" a product is, companies increasingly look at its environmental effects before, during, and after its existence" (p. 77). This "look" takes the form of life-cycle assessment (LCA), an emerging discipline that quantitatively studies the cradle-to-grave impact of industrial processes and consumption activities on ecosystems.

Definition of Life-Cycle Assessment

LCA logically follows from the PSLC framework. It is formally defined by the Society of Environmental Toxicology and Chemistry (1991) as

> an objective process to evaluate the environmental burdens associated with a product, process, or activity by identifying and quantifying energy and material use and environmental releases, to assess the impact of those material uses and releases on the environment, and to evaluate and implement opportunities to effect environmental improvements. (p. 1)

Practiced by environmental engineers, environmental scientists, and consultants worldwide, LCA is becoming a source of relevant insights and information for sustainable marketing decisions. The major objectives of LCA as a field of study and practice are as follows:

1. to provide as complete a picture as possible of the interactions of process, product, or an activity with the environment;
2. to contribute to the understanding of the overall and interdependent nature of the environmental consequences of human activities; and
3. to provide decision makers with information that defines the environmental effects of these activities and identifies opportunities for environmental improvements. (Society of Environmental Toxicology and Chemistry 1993b:5-6)

In a nutshell, LCA attempts to add flesh, muscle, and sinew to the bare bones of the PSLC framework. It does this by assessing resource use and waste generation over the system designated appropriate for the analysis; that is, it focuses on (1) determining the sources and composition of waste (actual or potential) in qualitative and quantitative terms and (2) using the findings as a basis for moderating or eliminating unacceptable ecological burdens.

In linking LCA to ecology and marketing, it is easy to see that this style of analysis gives full recognition to Commoner's (1972) informal laws of ecology. This can be shown through a respectful restatement of the four laws as follows:

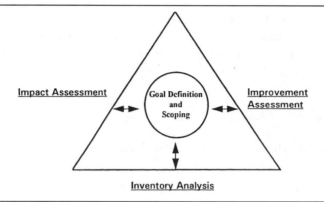

Figure 2.3. Technical Framework of the Life-Cycle Assessment Process
SOURCE: Society of Environmental Toxicology and Chemistry (1993b), *Guidelines for Life-Cycle Assessment: A "Code of Practice"* (1st ed.), Pensacola, FL: SETAC, p. 11. Reprinted by permission. Copyright 1993 by Society of Environmental Toxicology and Chemistry.

- ▧ First Law (restated): Everything is connected to everything else; so, let us determine various organizations and markets involved and then determine the interrelationships that are relevant.
- ▧ Second Law (restated): Everything must go somewhere; now, let us find out what waste there is, where it comes from, where it goes, and what it does when it gets there.
- ▧ Third Law (restated): Nature knows best; also, let us look at our use of unnatural products, chemicals, and materials, eliminate those that might cause problems, and develop a managed approach for controlling those remaining.
- ▧ Fourth Law (restated): There is no such thing as a free lunch; overall, let us eliminate waste when we can, make any remaining waste go where it should, and develop an approach for assessing the full costs of doing so.

The Life-Cycle Assessment Process

The technical framework of the LCA process consists of four interrelated phases (Figure 2.3): (1) goal definition and scoping, (2) inventory analysis, (3) impact assessment, and (4) improvement assessment (Society of Environmental Toxicology and Chemistry 1993b). They logically fit together in an investigative sequence that begins with problem definition and data collection and ends with environmental solutions.

Goal Definition and Scoping

This first phase deals with identifying study goals (objectives), defining the functional unit of analysis, and setting up peer review control procedures

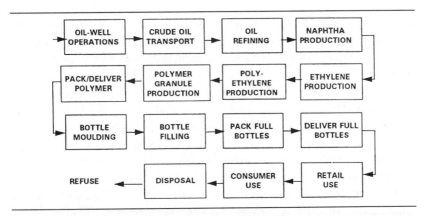

Figure 2.4.   The Product System Life Cycle for Polyethylene Terephtahalate
Containers
SOURCE: Society of Environmental Toxicology and Chemistry (1993b), *Guidelines for Life-Cycle Assessment: A "Code of Practice"* (1st ed.), Pensacola, FL: SETAC. Reprinted by permission. Copyright 1993 by Society of Environmental Toxicology and Chemistry.

to review data quality. These determinations lead to study scoping, that is, the specification of the PSLC organizations/activities that will be subject to investigation including the geographic extent of coverage. For example, objectives may confine the analysis to selected or limited segments of the PSLC to investigate the unique waste burdens imposed by specific suppliers, manufacturers, or retailers. In any case, scoping can become quite complex and extensive because every organization, process, component, raw material, manufactured product, service, or customer that has any association whatsoever with the product under study could be included. The complexity factor is amply demonstrated in Figure 2.4, which shows the full PSLC for a single product component, the polyethylene terephtahalate container used for beverages and other food products. In addition, whether the analysis is to be used internally to improve functional performance or externally in support of promotion or other communications programs is another key factor in determining what PSLC coverage is relevant.

Establishing the relevant functional unit of analysis for the study is another early decision linked to objectives and scoping. This step defines an unambiguous measure of system performance that is relevant in the analysis at hand. For example, the functional unit for a study of volatile organic carbons leaching from paint applied in the home might be defined as "unit surface area covered by paint for a defined period of time," a packaging analysis might be defined in terms of "the packaging required to deliver a given volume, say, 1,000 liters of beverage," or a study of laundry products might focus on "the amount of detergent necessary for a standard household wash" (Society of Environmental Toxicology and Chemistry 1993b:14). In addition, it is important that comparative studies employ the same functional unit of analysis.

Data quality assurance is another important aspect of any LCA that must be addressed during the first phase. This refers to "the degree of confidence in the individual input and output data, in the data set as a whole, and ultimately in the decisions based upon using the data" (Society of Environmental Toxicology and Chemistry 1993b:14). One approach to maintaining data quality is the use of peer review procedures to verify the validity of the data themselves, the collection procedures, and any other analytic techniques employed. Peer review is especially critical for achieving a consensus on "what the results mean" in LCAs designed for external applications.

Additional examples of the decisions involved in goal definition and scoping are given through the example LCA described in Part A of Exhibit 2.1. This work, prepared by the respected consulting firm of Franklin Associates Ltd. (1992), compares reusable cloth and disposable diaper systems (see also Sauer et al. 1994). It is presented to demonstrate what a field LCA looks like, not to answer the question as to whether disposable or reusable diapers are better for ecosystems.

Inventory Analysis

The inventory phase is the most advanced and developed aspect of current LCA field technology and methodology. It is a data-based approach that quantifies resource use and waste generation over a PSLC (Fava, Consoli, and Denison 1991; Hunt et al. 1992; Keoleian and Menerey 1993; Society of Environmental Toxicology and Chemistry 1991; Vigon et al. 1992). The goal is to provide measures in physical terms. After specific variables have been identified and measured, an additive model generally is employed to sum relevant data sets over defined PSLC stages.

The LCA inventory approach models each PSLC unit/activity (e.g., manufacturer, industrial distributor-wholesaler, retailer, collector/processor, consumer target market) as a detailed input-output process (Figure 2.5). In simplified terms, inputs consist of resources (R→) and manufactured products (P→), whereas outputs consist of both manufactured products (P→) and waste (W→). These processes are limited by two principles of physics. First, the principle of conservation of mass applies; that is, the total quantity of input resource materials must equal the output, where output is the sum of usable products, waste, emissions, and other releases. Second, the principle of

exhibit 2.1

Energy and Environmental Profile Analysis of
Children's Single-Use and Reusable Cloth Diapers

PART A: GOAL DEFINITION AND SCOPING

Study objective: To thoroughly assess energy use, water requirements, and environmental emissions through a cradle-to-grave analysis of children's single-use and cloth diaper systems.

Scope: The product diaper systems examined in this study were (1) single-use diapers, (2) commercially laundered cloth diapers, and (3) home-laundered cloth diapers.

System boundaries: Diaper systems analyzed in this study included (1) the acquisition of raw materials including crude oil production, wood harvesting, and cotton growing; (2) production and distribution of the diapers; (3) reuse involving the laundering and transporting of cloth diapers; (4) waste management options such as recycling, composting, combustion, and landfilling; and (5) production and disposal of packaging for the diapers and diaper components.

Functional unit of analysis: The systems are compared on an average use over a six-month diapering period. Examination of diaper systems revealed a daily usage rate of 9.7 cloth diapers compared to 5.4 single-use diapers per day; this resulted in a diaper usage ratio of = 9.7/5.4 = 1.8.

Peer review: In accordance with practices recommended by the Society of Environmental Toxicology and Chemistry, Procter & Gamble contracted Roy F. Weston to coordinate and participate in the peer review process.

PART B: INVENTORY ANALYSIS

Note: Selected figures from the report demonstrate comparisons in five areas: (1) energy requirements, (2) water use, (3) solid waste generated, (4) atmospheric emissions generated, and (5) and waterborne waste generated.

(text continues on page 64)

conservation of energy applies; that is, energy input to each organizational unit/activity will equal the output, where output is the sum of heat losses,

exhibit 2.1   (Continued)

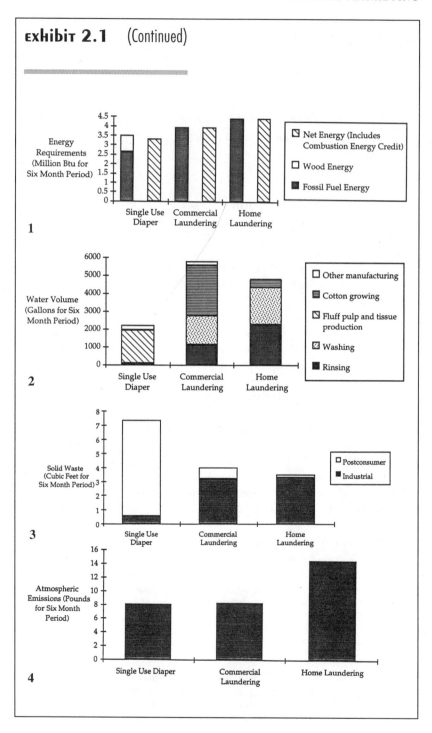

Exhibit 2.1 (Continued)

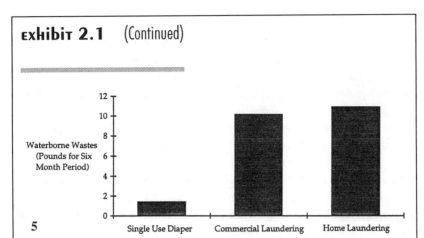

PART C: STUDY CONCLUSIONS

Individual diaper systems:

■ Home cloth diapers consume 33 percent more energy than single-use diapers and 12 percent more energy than commercial cloth diapers.

■ Single-use diapers produce about twice the total solid waste by volume of home or commercial cloth diapers.

■ Home cloth diapers produce nearly twice the total atmospheric emissions of single-use diapers or commercial cloth diapers.

■ Home or commercial cloth diapers produce about seven times the total water-borne waste of single-use diapers.

■ Home or commercial cloth diapers consume more than twice the water volume of single-use diapers.

SOURCE: Franklin Associates Ltd. (1992), *Energy and Environmental Profile Analysis of Children's Single-Use and Cloth Diapers,* Prairie Village, KS: Franklin Associates. Reprinted by joint permission of the American Forest and Paper Association Inc. and Franklin Associates.

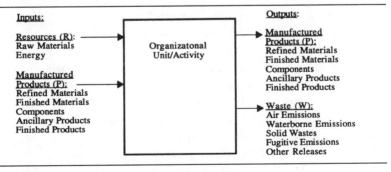

Figure 2.5. The Product System Life-Cycle Organizational Unit/Activity as an Input-Output Process

SOURCE: Adapted from Society of Environmental Toxicology and Chemistry (1991), *A Technical Framework for Life-Cycle Assessment,* Washington, DC: SETAC, p. 13, Figure 2-4.

waste, and energy that is effectively "banked" or "embedded" within finished products. Stated another way, neither materials nor energy is created or destroyed during processing/conversion; what goes in comes out as either a product or a waste component. It is noted in passing that environmental engineers generally refer to these calculations as mass balances, whereas LCA practitioners often refer to them as eco-balances.

LCA inventory measurement involves highly detailed and complex techniques, which clearly fall in the domain of science and engineering. Although coverage of these techniques is beyond the scope of this book, the marketer's "need to know" revolves around screening the information for marketing strategy implications. Selected examples of the types of variables measured and the data developed through those measurements are given for the continuing diaper LCA in Part B of Exhibit 2.1.

Impact and Improvement Assessment

Both the impact assessment and improvement assessment phases of complete LCA are in the embryonic stages of development. Impact assessment refers to the determination of the interrelationships among waste and resource depletion, human health, and ecosystem health. Specifically, it attempts to quantitatively assess damage to ecosystems and human health through analysis of the various waste burdens identified through the LCA inventory analysis. Although protocols for impact analysis are not yet agreed on, some consensus exists that the following general steps define the impact assessment process (Society of Environmental Toxicology and Chemistry 1993a): (1) classification, (2) characterization, and (3) valuation. Classification is an initial step in which data from the inventory are grouped into a number of general and specific impact categories (e.g., items that relate to meeting compliance standards) or by type of emission (e.g., air, water, solid waste). Characterization is a step that further categorizes impact categories in an attempt to facilitate analysis (e.g., grouping compliance items into categories made up of those meeting standards vs. those not meeting standards). Valuation involves assigning weights to the various variables rather than assuming that all factors have equal weight in the model. For example, if two PSLCs are inventoried and the first makes a lesser contribution to global warming and the second makes a lesser contribution to ozone depletion, then one cannot tell which system has the lesser overall impact unless the categories of global warming and ozone depletion are implicitly weighted 1:1 or arbitrarily weighted in some other manner.

Whereas impact assessment attempts to develop a better picture of the meaning of inventory findings, improvement assessment is the logical conclusion of the LCA process, one that suggests solutions to the challenges uncovered. It deals with the systematic identification, evaluation, and selection of alternatives that will lead to environmental improvements. However, it must be pointed out that "improvement assessment has not yet undergone the consensus examination of the methodology, as has the inventory analysis and, to some extent, the impact assessment component" (Society of Environmental Toxicology and Chemistry 1993b:28). Given the high level of research activity underway in this area, substantial progress toward consensus can be expected during the next few years.

Criticisms and Cautions

PSLC-LCA is a relatively new approach that has its fair share of critics. From a technical, quantitative perspective, a comprehensive (or full-blown) PSLC-LCA application has yet to be achieved at any time or place by any person or organization. Criticisms and cautions have been organized into the following areas: (1) simple products analyzed, (2) project scoping, (3) measurement and evaluation errors, and (4) timeliness of information.

Simple Products Analyzed

Even applications of inventory analysis, the most advanced aspect of LCA, generally focus only on relatively simple, nondurable products such as single-use diapers and selected packaging containers/materials (Chem Systems Inc. 1992; Franklin Associates Ltd. 1990a, 1990b, 1992). Detractors assail these limited applications for costing too much and delivering very little in terms of substantive quantitative data and technical analysis.

Project Scoping

In addition, some charge that study parameters are deliberately gerrymandered to support the sponsoring firm/industry's position, a practice called "cooking the books" (Stipp 1991:B1). For example, in three single-use versus reusable cloth diaper LCA studies (Franklin Associates Ltd. 1992; Lehrburger, Mullen, and Jones 1991; Lentz and Franke 1989), each produced substantially different results based on different scope decisions, thereby clouding any conclusions as to which product is best for the environment. This type of outcome naturally has raised questions about the ethics and efficacy of the science behind the numbers (Holmes 1991).

The problem of identifying the excruciatingly complex web of organizations and customers that make up a full-blown PSLC has been noted as particularly problematic by Portney (1994a). This is especially true in the case of complex products made of many different materials, parts, and components (e.g., high-design durable goods). Theoretically, a full-blown PSLC application accounts for all waste trails, which means identifying every raw material, component part, processing activity, support service, transportation movement, wholesale-retail distribution function, consumption activity, and the like that has any connection with the product. When full coverage is not the case, critics argue that the selectivity imposed invites suboptimized answers that reflect biases.

Measurement and Evaluation Errors

Major criticisms also center around the related factors of measurement and evaluation. Although the scientific and technical aspects of measuring waste streams and emissions are beyond the scope of this book (but see Graedel and Allenby 1995; Society of Environmental Toxicology and Chemistry 1991, 1993a, 1993b), let it be sufficient to say that several measurement errors may be present. For example, LCA applications almost always involve multiple product/material situations that require "allocation" decisions (e.g., what percentages of solid waste output stream X are to be allocated to products Y and Z, respectively?). Inappropriate assumptions obviously can lead to overallocation, which can undermine the environmental credibility of any product. Furthermore, measurement biases may be induced through improperly executed field procedures and by the existence of missing values (no data are available). The use of surrogate measures, such as replacing actual company data with industry averages, may induce additional bias. Finally, the wrong variables may be measured, or relevant variables may be excluded from the analysis.

Portney (1994a) notes other measurement and evaluation difficulties found in LCA applications. First is the matter of weighting the variables in the analysis, which would occur in the valuation step of impact assessment. When treated as implicit, the assumption is that a 1:1 ratio holds. But in a given situation, is air pollution more important than water pollution? Second, all waste discharges of a given type and magnitude are not of equal consequence in terms of time and place. Given discharges in densely populated urban centers are one thing, but in rural settings they represent quite another. Third, the actual products contrasted in LCAs are assumed to be apples-to-apples equals in terms of benefits delivered, but do disposable diapers deliver the same level of preventive care (i.e., absence of diaper rashes and skin infections) as do cloth diapers, or is this an apples-to-oranges comparison? Fourth, doing an in-depth LCA might require access to trade secrets and other proprietary information, and suppliers might see requests for such data as simply too compromising to comply.

Timeliness of Information

Finally, not unlike survey research results, the value of LCA data is a function of timeliness. This suggests that the rapidly changing technologies associated with production, distribution, and waste recovery systems can cause LCA interpretations to become obsolete overnight. For example, Diatec Recovery Technologies USA Inc. introduced at Waste Expo '97 the Diapactor, a machine that recycles used disposable diapers into reusable paper and plastic pellets (NaQuin 1997). Given that this technology proves to be commercially viable, this new alternative to landfill disposal will moderate the (former) major negative disposable diaper factor identified by the Franklin Associates Ltd. (1992) LCA, that is, the generation of large quantities of solid waste by disposable diaper systems.

Progress toward Applications

LCA technologists are slowly moving the discipline forward on a number of fronts. Two trends are particularly apparent: (1) standardization of methodology and (2) refinement and implementation of partial LCAs.

Standardization of Methodology

An important trend is the international movement toward standardization of LCA methodologies, procedures, and protocols. A worldwide coalition of government agencies, professional/trade organizations, and consultants (e.g., American Society of Testing and Materials, Battelle Institute, Business in the Environment, Ecobalance, Franklin Associates Ltd., Green Cross, International Organization for Standardization, Roy F. Weston, Scientific Certification Systems, Society for the Promotion of LCA Development, Society of Environmental Toxicology and Chemistry, SustainAbility Ltd., U.S. Environmental Protection Agency) continues to make credible progress in this regard. Separately and jointly, this coalition also is responsible for an impressive set of design and guidance manuals, specialty publications, and data sources that serve to educate users and practitioners and to foster LCA quality assurance. The Society for Environmental Toxicology and Chemistry's (1993b) *Guidelines for Life-Cycle Assessment: A "Code of Practice"* and SustainAbility Ltd.'s (1993) *The LCA Sourcebook: A European Guide to Life-Cycle Assessment* are particularly noteworthy accomplishments because of their international orientation.

Refinement of Partial Life-Cycle Assessments

As LCA technology advances, partial LCA inventory analyses currently are being used to quantitatively support what are called report card, or Type III, environmental labeling approaches (see Chapter 6). These limited-scope assessments also involve a restricted set of inventory variables. The assumption is that the 80/20 principle is operative; that is, a large portion of the actual/potential waste problem is accounted for by a relatively small number of variables, sources, products, processes, suppliers, organizations, activities, or customers within the PSLC. This suggests that a selective focus will produce meaningful information about product environmental advantages and disadvantages or areas in need of change or action. Exactly what to address in a given study (i.e., scope coverage and variables) is approached by rigorous consensus building among knowledgeable practitioners and other interested parties. Small contributor waste sources, defined as materials that account for less than 5 percent of end-product mass by weight, may be eliminated from study (Berube and Bisson 1991). The Scientific Certification Systems' Certified Eco-Profile program demonstrates this type of methodology. It consists of selected measurements in two areas: (1) resources and energy use and (2) emissions and wastes (L. Brown 1995). Exhibit 2.2 shows the Certified Eco-Profile label that directly compares 100 percent recycled-source polyester fiber to its virgin-source counterpart.

Qualitative Life-Cycle Assessment

Whereas developing credible quantitative waste management analyses has intrinsic appeal, the qualitative *decision-domain-stretching* aspect of

exhibit 2.2

Scientific Certification Systems' Certified Eco-Profile:
100 Percent Recycled Polyester versus Virgin Polyester Fiber

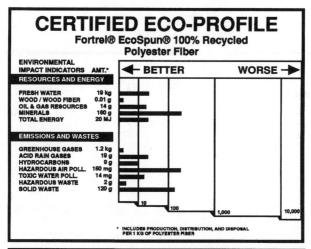

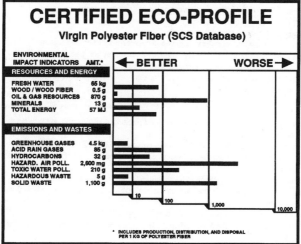

exhibiт 2.3

The Robert Mondavi Environmental Fact Sheet

Contact:
Margaret Kearns
(707) 226-1395 x3299
(707) 224-3995 Facsimile
NASDAQ:MOND

ROBERT MONDAVI WINERY AND THE ENVIRONMENT

Robert Mondavi Winery is the recognized industry leader in environmental responsibility. Dedicated to growing its wines naturally, the Robert Mondavi family introduced its natural farming and conservation program more than 20 years ago with worker health, environmental protection and enhanced grape quality as its goals.

IN THE VINEYARD

Natural Farming Techniques
- Adopted natural winegrowing philosophy in the early 1970s and is a leader in on-going research and experimentation.
- Currently owns and manages more than 1,000 naturally-farmed acres in Napa Valley.
- Uses alternatives to chemicals whenever possible:
  - Replaces herbicides with hoe plowing or other means of mechanical cultivation.
  - Fruit trees and raptor roosts used to encourage the proliferation of natural predators to control vine pests.
  - Reduces insect pests, powdery mildew and bunch rot by removing leaves.
  - Uses composted pomace, a natural grape byproduct, for soil building.
  - Cover crops and added organic matter used to naturally replenish the soil with nitrogen. Cover crops also reduce need for fumigation and provide diverse sources of food for pests.

Ecological Accomplishments
- Participates in a number of conservation projects, including hillside and soil erosion control, and water-use reduction.
- Has teamed with researchers at U.C. Davis to conduct a $100,000 seven-year irrigation study to determine the minimum amount of water needed to produce fruit of high quality and appropriate yields.
- Participates in a national pilot land stewardship program to preserve the habitat.
- Retains, enhances and actively encourages the proliferation of natural wetlands and woodlands on vineyard properties.
- Controls noise pollution to prevent disturbing nesting birds.
- 1991 "Conservationist of the Year" – Mitchell Klug, Director of Robert Mondavi Napa Valley Winegrowing Operations.

---

exhibit 2.3 Continued

▨▨▨▨▨▨▨▨▨▨▨▨▨▨▨▨▨▨▨▨▨▨▨

Endangered Species Preservation
- Hillside erosion controls have been adopted at Robert Mondavi's Carneros Vineyard in an effort to protect the Huichica Creek watershed, home to the endangered California freshwater shrimp.
- Implemented a stream bank stabilization program to preserve Huichica Creek's banks and natural flow.

AT THE WINERY

Environmental Packaging
- Created the revolutionary Robert Mondavi capsule-free design, eliminating use of lead, tin or plastic.
- A small disk of recycled paper affixed to the top of the cork provides the seal.
- Wine bottles are labeled and packaged with 100% post-consumer recycled and recyclable paper products, using soy-based inks and food-grade glues.

On-Site Environmental Efforts
- An in-house task force studies and implements new environmental projects.
- Maintains an aggressive recycling program for glass bottles, paper products, corks and cans.
- Recycles more than 1 million gallons of winery waste water annually for use in the vineyards.
- Conducts seminars on natural farming and conservation techniques for grape growers.
- Uses only biodegradable soaps and food-grade paints.

SOURCE: Reprinted courtesy of Robert Mondavi Winery, Oakville, CA.

PSLC-LCA currently represents its greatest contribution to marketing decision making. As Fava notes, LCA "is applied conceptually . . . to weave awareness of environmental liabilities throughout clients' operations" (quoted in "Life Cycle Analysis" 1993:11).

Encouraging Long-Term Thinking

As a qualitative tool, it cannot be understated how positively the PSLC-LCA viewpoint encourages comprehensive, long-term thinking, which is a vast improvement over the single factor, short-term (and shortsighted) decision framework of the past. By definition, the approach heightens top management's consciousness of environmental issues at all stages of the PSLC and encourages routine environmental screening upfront rather than after the fact. A commitment to this way of thinking provides the foundation on which corporate-product stewardship programs are built. Such thinking is demonstrated by the management of Robert Mondavi Winery in Exhibit 2.3.

Identification of "Hot Spots"

Similarly, the qualitative aspects of the conclusions attached to an LCA inventory analysis may reveal "hot spots" of customer dissatisfaction, points of competitive weakness and superiority, and the like that lead to better marketing mix decisions. For example, Part C of Exhibit 2.1 lists the conclusions of the Franklin diaper LCA. Certainly, the pluses and minuses that show up under each diaper system provide food for thought for the marketing decision makers behind these alternative products.

Debate over External Marketing Applications

Curiously, discussions of the marketing use of LCA findings often provoke a heated debate in which some suggest that applications external to the organization are out of bounds. This view is expressed by noted Battelle Institute LCA practitioner Bruce Vigon, who comments: "It's unfortunate that life-cycle analysis has been picked up by ad and marketing people" (quoted in Stipp 1991:B1). This seems to suggest that LCA findings should be used only in internal applications by the "technical types." However, on deeper inspection, it appears that the "red flags" might stem from a misunderstanding about the fundamental role of marketing in the organization. Specifically, the prohibition in regard to LCA data use appears to be mainly concerned with one aspect of marketing strategy: applications of LCA data to back up green product claims in external promotion and environmental labeling programs. This type of external use certainly is controversial at this time (see Chapter 6). However, moving toward LCA-based consumer information and eco-labeling systems as the "ways and means" of providing meaningful information to customers who desire to purchase ecologically compatible products is a logical and inevitable application. The continuing refinement and standardization of LCA protocols will provide a much-needed basis for establishing the validity and credibility of such applications in the future.

The debate underscores the need for interaction among sustainable marketers, LCA practitioners, and the technical types who use LCA to make internal assessments (e.g., cutting the costs of manufacturing waste, improving product performance) without recognizing the inevitable linkage to marketing strategy, particularly in the area of product development. Understanding this linkage would come about more easily if all would simply accept the premise that the only legitimate purpose of a business is "providing benefits to customers through products" and that all functional areas of enterprise play a role in achieving this outcome. Therefore, any information, whether LCA derived or otherwise, may well serve a legitimate marketing purpose—internal or external. To fail to use LCA information in the quest to establish ecological competitive advantage represents the misuse of a valuable marketing resource.

An example of the productive use of LCA-style analysis in an external application is provided by Baxter International Inc., a leading supplier of health care products and services to major hospitals and medical institutions. First, the firm positioned itself through its 1995 *Environmental Performance Report* as follows: "We will work with our customers to help them address their environmental needs" (Baxter International Inc. 1995:4). In moving beyond internal boundaries, Baxter International managers essentially decided that their "customers' waste problems are our waste problems." To implement this thinking, a waste auditing service was developed to assess the waste management needs of downstream customers, followed by an extensive redesign of products and packaging to minimize adverse waste handling impacts of Baxter International products and services (Sandborg 1995).

Path to the Future?

Overall, the PSLC-LCA approach offers a usable qualitative decision framework for identifying and gaining insights about environmental issues. Although quantitative results might be limited, the power of the approach is that it forces scrutiny of all PSLC stages and the specific firms and customers within each stage, thereby revealing points where marketing reinvention opportunities might exist to cut waste, emissions, releases, or resources and energy use.

Sustainable marketing must balance three factors: (1) customer satisfaction, (2) organizational goals, and (3) ecosystems compatibility. While cleaning up the consumption process, marketers must not lose sight of customer satisfaction or of the organization's financial prospects. The PSLC-LCA approach defines a path for striking a reasonable balance. Given the belief that it is necessary to move toward the goal of sustainable development, why not take this path to the future—now?

In their discussion of industrial ecology, Richards, Allenby, and Frosch (1994) construct a continuum of three progressively more efficient resource use systems—labeled Types I, II, and III—to depict how societies provide benefits to customers through products. In Type I systems, material flows remain linear; resources are used once and then experience terminal disposal. Type II systems feature some reintegration of resources, but the systems remain dependent on virgin inputs and on terminal disposal. Type III systems exhibit very high levels of material conservation and reuse and spin off very little true waste to terminal disposal; they approach the ideal zero-waste, zero-discharge prototype.

Currently, we occupy the territory between Type I and Type II systems. Achieving more movement toward Type II systems is the short-term objective, and achieving full transition into true zero-waste, zero-discharge Type III systems is the long-term goal. In this endeavor, the approach of PSLC-LCA is compelling because it builds the holistic perspective required to understand and act on ecological challenges that face us. Current qualitative levels of LCA technology and practice already provide a starting point for inching down the path toward Type II and III systems.

Chapter Summary

The PSLC represents the total network of organizations and activities that collectively account for the cradle-to-grave ecological impact of a product. The normative PSLC consists of a set of five interrelated channel networks beginning with raw materials extraction (Stage 1) and continuing on with materials-components manufacturing (Stage 2), finished products manufacturing and marketing (Stage 3), and consumer target markets (Stage 4). The fifth channel network, reverse waste management (Stage 5), consists of concurrent activities that handle waste outputs at all stages of the PSLC.

The PSLC is an extension of the marketing channel network concept in which the organizations involved are bound together by business purpose and marketing strategy over the cradle-to-grave resource use cycle. The decision boundaries associated with traditional channels usually are defined as beginning with a production process that substantially alters resources into form and function and ending with the next market transaction; what occurs before or after these defined beginning and ending points is considered beyond the decision domain. By contrast, the PSLC extends the decision domain to include these *before* and *after* stages because they are extremely relevant for gaining insights into the waste management challenges posed by consumption. Just as all PSLC members play a mutual role in serving the ultimate customer, they also contribute mutually to the joint wastes that are generated by doing so. In short, waste management is a holistic and interconnected phenomenon that must take into account the wide-ranging waste-generating activities of PSLC organizations and customers that occur before, during, and after the act of final consumption. The restricted range of the marketing channel ignores these ramifications, whereas the PSLC represents a broadened decision domain that includes them.

The PSLC can be generalized into three sectors: (1) upstream, (2) midstream, and (3) downstream. The midstream sector, consisting of Stage 3 finished product manufacturers and marketing organizations, basically determines product form and function and the delivery systems (wholesaling-retailing) necessary to reach Stage 4 target markets. These decisions set the character of the total PSLC and determine its subsequent waste impact. The upstream sector, made up of raw materials and materials-components producers-suppliers and marketing organizations (Stages 1 and 2), exists to meet the needs of the Stage 3 manufacturers that are their customers. Some Stage 3 manufacturers are beginning to engage in the practice of greening the supply chain, which means that supplier organizations (Stages 1 and 2) must formally address environmental management issues to make the "to consider" list. The downstream sector, consumer target markets (Stage 4), is the logical focus of all PSLC activities. Many consumers do not recognize how product choice and consequent product disposal affect the environment and overall quality of life. This creates an opportunity for marketers to redirect customer choices and disposal behaviors toward alternatives that are more compatible with ecosystems.

Stage 5 networks complement all sectors of the PSLC by concurrently managing the unavoidable wastes generated by production-consumption activities. Because of legislative mandates, increasing compliance costs, and changing consumer ecological consciousness, these activities must be considered important profit centers that require professional management. Stage 5 waste management activities also may serve as a source of environmental cost information (tracking) that can be used to develop product pricing approaches that reflect the full costs of doing business.

LCA is an emerging discipline that studies the cradle-to-grave impact of industrial and consumption activities on ecosystems. Its goal is to objectively evaluate resource use (i.e., energy and materials) and environmental releases (i.e., waste generation) over the PSLC and to evaluate and implement changes that will result in environmental improvements. The LCA process consists of the following phases: (1) goal setting and scoping, (2) inventory assessment, (3) impact assessment, and (4) improvement assessment. At this time, inventory assessment (i.e., the measurement and quantification of energy-resources use and releases to the environment) is the most developed aspect of quantitative LCA. However, skeptics hold that potential measurement errors, the lack of agreement about what to measure in the first place, and wide-ranging scope of analysis required to conduct a full-blown LCA make the process impossible to fulfill in quantitative terms. In response, partial LCAs, covering only selected sectors/aspects of PSLCs, have been shown to offer important insights into improving environmental performance.

Although the quantitative dimension of waste management analysis has intrinsic appeal, it is the qualitative decision-domain-stretching aspect of PSLC-LCA that contributes most to progress toward sustainability at this time. The approach offers a usable decision framework and suggests basic thought processes for identifying and gaining insights about environmental issues. Its power lies in the systematic scrutiny of all PSLC stages and the specific firms-customers-activities within each, which reveals points where marketing reinvention opportunities might exist for developing strategies that are truly compatible with ecosystems.

cHapter 3

Sustainable Marketing Strategies

Sustainable marketing is an extension of, not a radical departure from, traditional marketing management practice. Overall, the basic strategies presented here, pollution prevention (P2) and resource recovery (R2), should be viewed as logical responses to the need to develop production-consumption practices that preserve and enhance the ecosystems within which we live.

Framework for Sustainable Marketing Management

Developing a framework provides a convenient way in which to define and organize the various elements that make up and influence a process. In this case, it also reinforces the idea that the essence of marketing management is decision making, the outcome of which provides benefits to customers through products. Both traditional and sustainable marketers approach the decision-making task in the same way as a planning→implementing→controlling sequence that is subject to various influences. But although the approach is the same, the decision outcomes may be quite different.

Business as Usual Marketing Management Model

The "business as usual" model of marketing management, as described in various introductory texts, consists of the following elements: (1) target market, (2) marketing mix, (3) company resources and objectives, and (4) external factors (Figure 3.1) (Boone and Kurtz 1992; McCarthy and Perreault 1993; Stanton, Etzel, and Walker 1994). Within this setting, managers make decisions that involve (1) deciding what to do and why (planning); (2) deciding on the how, who, where, and when of carrying out the plan (implementing); and (3) measuring progress of the plan toward objectives (controlling). A typical strategy development and deployment scenario would be the following:

1. Using the decision criteria of *customer satisfaction* and *organizational goals* as basic points of reference, managers set objectives and make concurrent decisions about target market selection and each of the elements of the marketing mix as follows:

   Target market selection: Suppose that a major bank decides to pursue the rapidly expanding "Wealthy Seniors" segment, defined as age 60 years or over with deposit accounts of $100,000 or more.

   Marketing mix decisions:

   A. *Product:* determining individual product attributes (i.e., form and function) and the product mix (Wealthy Seniors are offered a "packaged account" featuring free services including credit card, checking, travelers checks, a 1 percent interest rate incentive on consumer loans, and an assigned personal banker)

   B. *Channel networks (place/distribution):* determining the membership of channel networks (i.e., independent intermediaries such as wholesalers-retailers and/or corporate facilities) and other "ways and means" of achieving customer access to the product (Wealthy Seniors will interact with the bank through a direct "in-home house call banking" program)

   C. *Communications (promotion):* determining the promotion mix (i.e., components of personal selling, advertising, sales promotion, publicity/public relations) appropriate for communicating with channel members, target markets, and other stakeholders and the messages to be delivered by each (Wealthy Seniors are reached through the publications of the American Association of Retired Persons, and messages stress "safety of principal")

   D. *Pricing:* determining price level, discounts, allowances, and other terms of sale to be used when presenting the "price offer" to channel members (the trade) and target market customers (Wealthy Seniors are offered "no-fee value banking" in exchange for maintaining $100,000 or more in total deposit balances)

2. These decisions are adjusted by considering the following:

   A. the internal resources of the firm (i.e., marketing, production, research and development, financial, and personnel) (the bank already has a

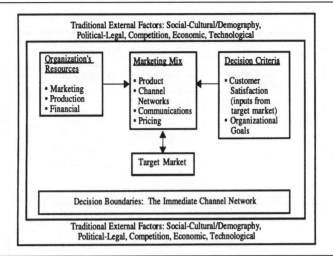

Figure 3.1. "Business as Usual" Marketing Management Setting

significant "seniors" franchise and a well-developed personal banker
program)

B. traditional external factors (called business environments) that influence
how the firm operates (i.e., social-cultural/demography, political-legal,
competition, economic, and technological) (a recent merger of major
competitors under an out-of-state name has left many "seniors" interested in establishing a new "local" affiliation)

The marketing strategy/plan that emerges is implemented, and periodic
evaluations (the control function) are made to assess progress toward objectives and to make changes as necessary. Once the strategy is under way, it is
subject to only one rule: the only thing constant is change.

Sustainable Marketing Management Model

Figure 3.2 presents the sustainable marketing management model. On
examination, three major differences are apparent. First, whereas a few
authors do routinely include "the natural or physical environment" in the
business as usual model as one of the external factors bearing on marketing
decisions (Kotler and Armstrong 1991; Zikmund and d'Amico 1993), the
placement of "ecosystems" in Figure 3.2 is deliberate and meaningful. Spe-

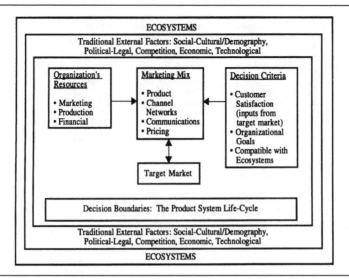

Figure 3.2. Sustainable Marketing Management Setting

cifically, it is shown as encompassing the entire decision-making process. This signifies the mandated, non-negotiable role ecosystems play as a physical limiting factor, one that transcends all other decision influences. (This corresponds to Tenet 1 in Chapter 1.) In short, the screening of marketing strategies for environmental impact and the payment of eco-costs must become standard operating procedures.

The second difference is that the position of dominance given "ecosystems" in Figure 3.2 is complemented by the addition of a third marketing mix decision criteria: the need for marketing strategy to be compatible with ecosystems. This makes a simple but powerful point: *The marketing mix is the vehicle through which sustainable marketing strategy is implemented in pursuit of P2 and R2 strategies/goals.* (This corresponds to Tenet 3 in Chapter 1.) This follows because marketing mix decisions set in motion inevitable cycles of resource use and waste generation and thereby dictate the nature of any environmental impact (positive or negative) attributable to consumption. As noted in Chapter 1, the master equation for environmental impact, $I = PAT$, is a function of population (P), affluence (A), and technology (T). In this context, marketing mix decisions represent factors within the technology coefficient (T) that directly influence its level. Therefore, reinvented/

redesigned marketing mixes represent major ways and means of achieving compatibility with ecosystems.

Third, in the business as usual marketing management process, decisions are focused on the immediate channel network, with occurrences *before* and *after* these traditional boundaries given little, if any, consideration. As discussed in Chapter 2, sustainable marketing extends decision boundaries to include the total set of organizations, functions, and activities that make up the product system life cycle (PSLC). (This corresponds to Tenet 2 in Chapter 1.)

Dematerialization: An Outcome

Dematerialization is an outcome that occurs when fewer resources (e.g., materials, energy) are used to create the same or equivalent benefits for customers, thereby reducing burdens on ecosystems (Herman, Ardekani, and Ausubel 1989). The basic sustainable marketing strategies, P2 and R2, contribute directly to this outcome because both have the general effect of reducing the quantities of materials and energy that must be mined, grown, harvested, or generated from ecosystems over time to support given levels of consumption.

Rethinking Products as Services

A key dimension of dematerialization is the idea that customers seek benefits, not products per se. For example, social activist Alan Durning (1992) notes,

> The crucial distinction is between physical commodities and the services [benefits] people use those commodities to get. For example, nobody wants telephone books, newspapers, or magazines for their own sake; rather, we want access to the information they contain. In an economy of permanence, that information might be available to us for much the same price on durable electronic readers. That would enable us to consult the same texts but eliminate most paper manufacturing and associated pollution. (p. 108)

Durning, however, is simply restating what already is obvious to marketing practitioners; that is, to develop the right product solutions, decision makers first must fully understand the benefits customers seek. The design of appropriate form and function and the other elements of the marketing mix then follow.

Implementing Dematerialization

Dematerialization can come about in at least three ways. One approach is to deintensify all products (and packaging) in terms of the quantities of materials used in their construction. For example, since 1972 the weight of a 16-ounce, glass, one-way bottle has been reduced from 12.1 to 6.6 ounces, thus dematerializing these packaging systems by more than 45 percent based on weight (Saphire 1995:9). This represents a major application of P2 strategy (see Chapter 4).

A second approach is to influence customers' buying and product use behaviors, which includes the act of product disposal. For example, in *Prosperity without Pollution,* Hirschhorn and Oldenburg (1991) point out that a shift from disposable products to durable alternatives (e.g., replacing disposable razors with a single electric razor) will result in a major decrease in waste generated given benefits received. Even within the realm of disposable products, they suggest the following three principles that dematerialize purchases of packaged convenience goods: (1) buy products in large, economy-sized packages, (2) buy products in concentrated forms, and (3) buy products with the fewest layers of packaging (i.e., depackaging) (p. 229). Obviously, evolving product design technology also is a contributing factor. In addition, participation in recycling and product take-back programs, which are R2 approaches, is another major way in which consumers can reduce the amount of materials a society uses up to obtain a given level of benefits.

Third, dematerialization occurs when durable product transaction formats are shifted from traditional ownership (i.e., a title transfer transaction) to product as service (i.e., a rent/lease transaction). Consider the following example:

> A chainsaw manufacturer produces 50 units that are sold to individual home owners in a given neighborhood. Each homeowner uses the chainsaw approximately 30 minutes a year. In terms of available capacity, one chainsaw could easily provide the annual sawing capacity (total benefits) required by all 50 home owners in the neighborhood.

In a nutshell, the environmental burdens (or eco-costs) associated with manufacturing and marketing 50 chainsaws could be reduced by changing the style of transaction. By renting to meet occasional needs rather than owning, just a few chainsaws (and their attendant eco-costs) might easily accommodate the total demands of all homeowners. Obviously, environmentally enlightened distribution, promotion, and pricing decisions could contribute toward shifting exchanges for certain products away from traditional ownership to the rent/lease format.

Dimensions of Waste Management

A constant theme of this book is that production-consumption processes generate waste, the antecedent of pollution. Therefore, the prevention and remediation of waste is the constant concern of sustainable marketing managers.

Definition of Waste

Waste has been defined as "any material released to the environment through the air, water, and/or land that has no beneficial use" (Society of Environmental Toxicology and Chemistry 1993b:67); it is something that is valueless by definition. Like the old adage "The poor will always be with us," it is clear that some waste will always accompany production-consumption processes. With tongue in cheek, Joel Makower notes in *The Green Business Letter,*

> Waste, as one pundit put it, is a terrible thing to mind. With good reason: Whether in the form of omissions, excess packaging, or outdated equipment, the definition of "waste" inevitably boils down to the same thing for most companies: something they bought but couldn't use and had to pay to dispose of. ("Waste Not" 1995:1)

Traditional Waste Management: A Process

One way in which to gain an initial understanding of the issues and challenges of waste management is to view it as an ongoing, remedial process involving the following functional stages (Figure 3.3): (1) waste generation, (2) waste processing at the source, (3) collection and transportation, (4) non-source waste processing, and (5) terminal disposal (TD) (Tchobanoglous,

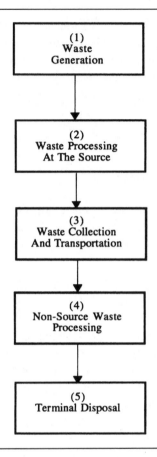

Figure 3.3.   The Waste Management Process

Theisen, and Vigil 1993). The focus is on managing known waste streams that spin off from resource conversion activities including personal consumption.

Waste Generation

Resource inputs become waste under two circumstances. First, materials are identified as having no immediate further economic value by their owner and are either thrown away or set aside for disposal (e.g., a consumer tosses a soft drink container into the household trash can, industrial workers set metal clippings aside in a stamping plant). Second, other by-products of production, such as air- and waterborne emissions, become waste as they are deliberately discharged into ecosystems or accidently discharged in the case of fugitive emissions. An unfortunate example of the latter is the infamous Bhopal incident in which the accidental release of menthyl isocyanate gas from a Union Carbide chemical facility killed or maimed thousands of people in India in 1984 (Cairncross 1992a).

Processing at the Source

Waste processing at the source involves the internal operations of collecting, moving, separating, packaging, and storing waste in anticipation of further on-site and off-site waste handling and disposal activities (e.g., consumer households participate in curbside collection programs by sorting out newspapers, paper, plastics, glass, and metal containers for separate collection; supermarkets bale [package] and set aside corrugated materials for pickup by commercial paper dealer-processors). Industrial firms may conduct on-site activities such as prompt industrial recycling (materials are immediately returned to the production process), composting, landfilling, or the processing of liquid wastes through settling ponds to eliminate contaminants. The point is that these activities occur on the site where the waste is generated.

Collection and Transportation

Collection and transportation involve the pickup and movement of materials to off-site facilities for further processing. The characteristics of waste sources again play a major role in determining the types of efforts necessary. For example, postconsumer waste is generated in small quantities at millions of household locations. This circumstance has led to weekly or twice-weekly curbside pickup systems using specialized vehicles. By contrast, industrial waste collection involves a much smaller number of generating sources that typically generate much larger individual quantities of homogeneous waste at each location (e.g., a manufacturing plant is a high-volume source of aluminum stamping clippings of a given alloy, a supermarket continuously generates large quantities of clean, corrugated box material).

Non-Source Processing

Non-source waste processing (off-site processing) involves the transfer of materials to second- or third-party specialists for final handling. Activities involve extracting useful materials and energy values for future use and rendering any residuals, which are now devoid of any functional or monetary value, safe for TD. For example, a curbside collection company will operate a municipal recovery facility in conjunction with the local landfill, where postconsumer materials are accumulated and sorted into general quality classes. They are then sold to dealer-processors who accumulate large quantities from multiple sources, further refine/sort the materials into specific quality classes, and sell them in large lot sizes to industrial users.

Terminal Disposal

The TD of solid waste typically is accomplished either through landfilling (i.e., materials are buried in a controlled landspace) or landspreading (i.e., materials are dispersed over the surface of the land). Gaseous and liquid wastes are released directly into the air, freshwater habitats, or marine-estuarine habitats after contaminants (hopefully) have been removed.

Integrated Waste Management

Traditional waste management tends to focus on after-the-fact waste streams and the associated goal of R2. But as noted earlier, waste management must be heavily concerned with P2. The relationship between P2 and R2 is clarified by integrated waste management (IWM), which establishes the well-accepted hierarchy of priorities shown on the left side of Figure 3.4 (Freeman et al. 1992). The *first* priority is P2, that is, the elimination or reduction of waste at the source. The *second* priority is R2, which involves the recapture of energy, materials, and products from waste streams for future use. The *third* priority is TD, which involves the ultimate release of residuals into ecosystems. The clear intent as one moves down the priorities (i.e., P2→R2→TD) is to progressively downsize waste streams. In ideal "zero-waste, zero-discharge" systems, all by-products (wastes/residuals) at the prior level are either avoided through P2 applications or systematically recovered and converted into resources for future economic use through R2 initiatives; waste output to TD is nonexistent. The IWM hierarchy has been adopted by the U.S. Environmental Protection Agency as its official environmental policy for the 1990s and also has been adopted by many state and local governments.

While recognizing the priorities and sequential nature of the IWM hierarchy, one also must note the complementary nature of the relationships among the components. For example, when P2 acts to "reduce waste at the source," this affects the quantity and character of by-products available for

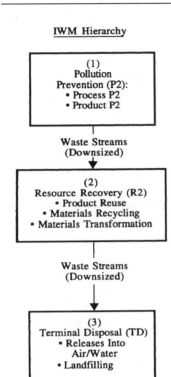

IWM Hierarchy

(1)
Pollution
Prevention (P2):
• Process P2
• Product P2

Waste Streams
(Downsized)

(2)
Resource Recovery (R2)
• Product Reuse
• Materials Recycling
• Materials Transformation

Waste Streams
(Downsized)

(3)
Terminal Disposal (TD)
• Releases Into
  Air/Water
• Landfilling

**Sustainable Marketing Strategies Actualized
Through Design-For-Environment**

(1) Proactive Strategy: Pollution
Prevention (P2)

Conserve resources and eliminate
waste through up-front process and
product design changes/decisions;
eliminate after-the-fact waste
processing costs.

(2) Proactive Strategy: Resource
Recovery (R2)

Manage unavoidable waste streams
by recapturing materials, energy
values, and products for future
use; enhance efficiency-
effectiveness of recovery functions
through reverse channel and product
design changes/decisions; build
markets for recovered materials,
energy, and reusable products.

(3) Default Option: Terminal Disposal

Wastes are released into
ecosystems; this is not a strategy
- - it is an occurence/event often
beyond the marketer's control;
prior implementation of P2 and R2
strategies will reduce TD volume
and also render benign products/
wastes that undergo TD due to
uncontrollable and varying
local circumstances

Figure 3.4. The Integrated Waste Management Hierarchy and Analogous
Sustainable Marketing Strategies
NOTE: P2 = pollution prevention; R2 = resource recovery; TD = terminal disposal.

input into subsequent R2 and TD. Thus the IWM hierarchy represents a system
of interconnected, interacting strategies/goals.

Strategy Options

Sustainable marketing strategies are derived and actualized through two
interrelated concepts: (1) IWM and (2) design-for-environment (DFE). As
noted in the previous section, the IWM hierarchy serves as the source of the

basic types of strategies to be employed; DFE is the process through which sustainable marketing strategies are developed and implemented.

Basic Sustainable Marketing Strategies

The first two levels of the IWM hierarchy provide the analog for designating the proactive sustainable marketing strategies discussed in this book: (1) P2 and (2) R2 (see the right side of Figure 3.4). Each is described in the following sections as subsets of proactive, sustainable approaches that are actualized through the DFE process. However, the third level of the IMW hierarchy, TD, is not regarded as a strategy per se. Rather, it is treated here as a default option/event, one that must be minimized in the sustainable economies of the future. In the interim, the idea is to gradually phase out reliance on TD while phasing in P2 and R2 as standard operating procedure for business and customers alike.

Design-for-Environment

The term *design-for-environment* originated in industrial design/product engineering, where it describes focusing the design process on building sets of positive ecological attributes into products (Graedel and Allenby 1995). But marketing strategy consists of much more than product decisions; it involves interrelated marketing mix decisions that define specific actions that collectively influence resource use and waste outcomes as consumption needs are met. Therefore, the key to reducing the technology factor (T) in the equation for environmental impact (I) is to ensure that all marketing mix elements have passed DFE scrutiny.

A firm's marketing mix represents decisions that reflect how a given situation has been interpreted by managers and translated into specific marketing actions. Making marketing mix decisions is the raison d'être of the firm. As shown in Exhibit 3.1, each marketing mix element represents sets of specialized decisions that reflect either a direct role in waste generation or a facilitating role in the exchange process. Because they involve the physical processes of making and moving-storing products, product and channel decisions have the distinction of being directly associated with waste generation. On the other hand, communications decisions provide market information, and pricing reflects transaction value in regard to type (e.g., own vs. lease) and terms of sale (e.g., discounts, allowances, payment timing). Therefore,

exhibiт 3.1

Marketing Mix Elements: Decision-Making Areas and Strategic Role in Waste Generation

Marketing Mix Element	Decision-Making Areas	Strategic Role in Waste Generation
Product	Determine individual product attributes (i.e., form and function) and the product mixes appropriate for meeting the needs of target markets	Product design determines the types of resources and manufacturing processes to be used to create form and function; these factors are the primary determinates of the volume and characteristics of all product system life-cycle waste streams
Channel networks (place)	Determine the composition, intensity of market coverage, and functional capabilities of the organizational networks that are necessary to link products with target markets	Channel organizations continuously generate process and product/packaging waste as they perform logistics (move-store) functions
Communications (promotion)	Determine the promotion mix (i.e., components of personal selling, public relations, sales promotion, and advertising) appropriate for reaching channel members, target markets, and other stakeholders as well as the messages to be delivered by each component	Although channel members and suppliers generate some process waste when undertaking promotion activities, this source is a very limited waste generator
Pricing	Determine price level, discounts, allowances, and other terms of sale to be used when presenting the "price offer" to channel members and target markets; evaluate cost data and other indicators of perceived value when setting price	Pricing is the managerial function of valuing the marketing mix; it is not a functional activity that generates waste

both communications and pricing decisions serve as facilitators of the exchange process.

Under the DFE approach, sustainable marketers first must develop a comprehensive understanding of how waste is generated and prevented in PSLCs to make product and distribution decisions that moderate ecosystems impact. Collateral communications and pricing decisions can then be made that build on the environmental actions taken and information generated in the areas of product design and channel networks (distribution). The point of subjecting all marketing mix elements to the DFE process is to increase the likelihood that environmentally compatible products, which also are satisfactory to customers and business, will be made available in the marketplace.

Proactive Strategy: Pollution Prevention

P2 is described by the U.S. Environmental Protection Agency as follows:

> Pollution prevention is the use of materials, processes, or practices that reduce or eliminate the creation of pollutants or wastes at the source. It includes practices that reduce the use of hazardous materials, energy, water, or other resources and practices that protect natural resources through conservation or more efficient use. (quoted in Freeman et al. 1992:619)

The approach of P2 is to eliminate wastes and wasting at the point of origin; their presence is an indicator of inefficiency in conversion processes or activities. They also represent a product quality defect under total quality management (TQM), one that negatively affects overall customer satisfaction and/or profits. Therefore, the value of P2 is found in its front-end attack on pollution at all levels of the PSLC, as opposed to the mere treatment of end-of-pipe symptoms. Hawken (1993) concurs, "The logical response to our current predicament would be to design or redesign manufacturing systems so that they do not create hazardous and biologically useless waste in the first place" (p. 49).

Goal: Getting More from Less

Overall, P2 applications are long-run solutions that must be designed in as production-consumption systems evolve over time. Initiating P2 early in the PSLC results in two benefits that have been dubbed the "double whammy." One benefit is associated with inputs, and the other is associated with outputs. Concerning inputs, initial upstream conversion processes are necessary to produce energy and material inputs for midstream product manufacturing and downstream consumption, and all such conversions incur eco-costs in the form of waste generated. Using fewer such inputs to make products that deliver the same benefits (value added) to customers reduces the investment in front-end eco-costs per unit of customer benefit. On the output side, P2 accrues savings by directly reducing the quantity of after-the-fact waste that must be managed locally, or downstream, at some future cost (Freeman et al. 1992; Porter and Cannon 1992; Reilly 1991; "Waste Reduction Works" 1993).

The novel marketing strategies of two Washington, D.C. hotels demonstrate the double whammy in action. The Embassy Inn and the Windsor Inn have offered a discounted "green rate" of $50 per night; the regular rate is $79. In exchange for the $29 difference, the customer agrees to use the same sheets and towels over a three-day period, as opposed to having a daily change out (J. Schroeder, The Embassy Inn/The Windsor Inn, personal communication, July 1995). One wash cycle per three days is now required instead of three, which requires one-third the amount of resource inputs measured in terms of electricity, water, and detergent. This reduces immediate hotel expense but also reduces the eco-costs of producing electricity, water, and detergent elsewhere. On the output side, requiring one wash cycle generates X gallons of wastewater, whereas maintaining the former approach would have generated $3 \times X$ gallons; it simply costs more to clean up three cycles of wastewater than one. An additional benefit is that the sheets themselves last longer because they experience less wash cycle wear and tear.

In essence, the economics of P2 are summarized by the old axiom, "An ounce of prevention is worth a pound of cure." Because the goal of P2 is to use fewer resources on the front end and require less cleanup on the back end, it has been labeled the "getting more from less" strategy. Some experts take it a step further by suggesting that P2 always is the lowest cost waste management strategy, a position supported by Freeman et al. (1992): "It makes far more sense for a generator [of waste] not to produce waste than to develop extensive treatment schemes to [e]nsure that the waste poses no threat to the quality of the environment" (p. 619). However, this unquestioned belief that "cure always costs more than prevention" is openly challenged by some who suggest that individual circumstances play such an important role in outcomes that a case-by-case analysis often is more appropriate (Oates, Palmer, and Portney 1993).

Pollution Prevention as a Generalized Marketing Strategy

P2 has major applications in the upstream and midstream industrial stages of PSLCs, where the vast majority of waste is generated. It is implemented through two types of substrategies: (1) process P2 and (2) product P2 (Figure 3.4 and Exhibit 4.2) (Fuller 1993).

Process Pollution Prevention

The activities involved in product and materials making, and in their movement through channel networks, are actually a series of resource conversion processes linked by marketing purpose that create form, time, place, and possession utilities. The PSLC unit/activity input-output process model developed in Chapter 2 fully applies (see Figure 2.5). Therefore, process P2 involves systems redesign with the objective of reducing resource inputs and waste outputs directly associated with manufacturing activities and inventory handling/storage and transportation functions that occur during distribution. In short, all products are held accountable for the wastes and wasting left behind by the set of manufacturers, suppliers, and channel members that create form, time, place, and possession utilities for end customers.

The extended decision boundaries introduced by the PSLC suggest that when a firm investigates the environmental implications of its processes, scrutiny of the processes of its PSLC partners is an escapable part of the analysis. Each PSLC member must be concerned about the ecological impacts of the processes of those firms preceding it in the channel and also about the impacts of those that follow. In the field of distribution, the waste minimization aspects of process P2 has become the basis of the practice of what is called green/reverse logistics, the new label for the study of how physical distribution systems can be designed to lessen overall impacts on ecosystems (Stock 1992). Further details concerning process P2 strategies are given in Chapters 4 and 5.

Product Pollution Prevention

In contrast to the processes that make and move products/materials, the "product proper" that leaves a manufacturing facility is a de facto future source of waste. Therefore, product P2 involves designing products to minimize waste generated downstream both during and after personal consumption or industrial use. The focus of product P2 is on (1) the choice of materials that go into product construction, (2) the quantities of materials used in product construction and packaging, (3) the implications of durability versus disposability (i.e., the duration of use cycle or useful life), (4) the minimization of product operating wastes, and (5) the potential for making fundamental changes in the ways in which products deliver benefits to customers. This last factor, changing the product's core benefit delivery system, is a particularly challenging and exciting aspect of sustainable marketing (see Chapter 4).

As with process P2, product P2 translates into "getting more from less," which makes one thing crystal clear: *Planned obsolescence, the strategy under which products are deliberately designed to wear out/fail early in the physical or fashion sense (thereby generating a self-perpetuating replacement market), is truly the antithesis of P2/sustainability and must be abandoned.* For example, if a radial automobile tire could be designed to achieve an average of 100,000 miles of service, then the massive waste stream generated by tire replacement would be reduced by an estimated 60 to 75 percent (Westerman 1978). However, long service life products generally require a high initial entry price because a large quantity of future product benefits are bought at one time on the front end, a situation that is analogous to discounting a future stream of cash benefits to the present time period. This sort of challenging sustainable pricing issue (e.g., compact fluorescent vs. incadescent light bulbs) is discussed in Chapter 7.

Pollution Prevention over the Product System Life Cycle

In Figure 3.5, the P2 symbols show points of application at all levels of the PSLC, although the manufacturing and distribution stages have the most potential for environmental improvement from P2 strategies. Note that the symbol P2 is present on both the inbound and outbound flows at all stages. On the inbound side, P2 indicates the upfront choices of resources/materials/products that affect the generation of process/activity waste or potentially decimate/waste a resource. For example, a manufacturer may decide to eliminate a toxic solvent in a paint stripper; this decision eliminates the eco-costs associated with original solvent production. On the outbound side, P2 signifies decisions that reduce the volume of waste generated internally by a given activity. For example, a manufacturer may choose to continue using hazardous materials but take steps to minimize the quantity, thereby reducing the physical hazards and regulatory costs associated with these materials as well as the volume of outbound hazardous waste that must be disposed.

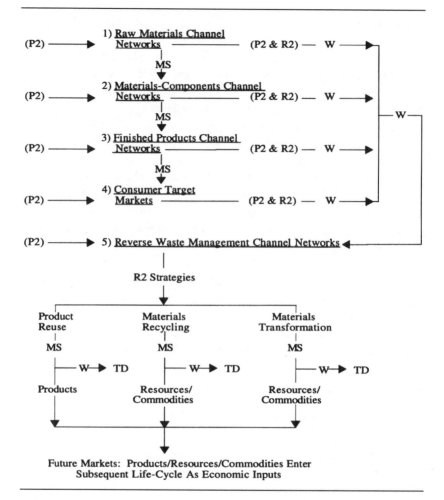

Figure 3.5. Sustainable Marketing Strategies over the Product System Life Cycle
NOTE: W→ = waste outputs = emissions into the air and water, solid waste, noise, and heat; P2→ = pollution prevention strategy; R2→ = resource recovery strategy; TD→ = terminal disposal default option; MS→ = marketing strategy linkage.

Proactive Strategy: Resource Recovery

R2, the second priority of IWM, assumes that wastes are an inevitable residue of production-consumption activities at all levels of the PSLC. This currently is true for three reasons. First, all products eventually wear out or become obsolete, requiring replacement. Second, at least some minimal levels of packaging are necessary to ensure the timely availability of safe, sanitary, economical, reasonably convenient products. Third, the laws of conservation of mass and energy dictate that the transformation of resources into products through industrial processes will generate waste streams. The development of zero-waste, zero-discharge systems is simply beyond the capability of current best available technology. Therefore, although waste may be minimized and its character altered, it cannot be eliminated entirely at this time.

R2 may be described as the processes through which products, materials, and energy values are routinely recaptured from waste (residual) streams and returned to economic use (redeployed) in future production-consumption cycles. As shown in Figure 3.5, this is accomplished by diverting waste streams (designated by W) through Stage 5 reverse channel networks. Therefore, R2 may be described as an ecosystem housekeeping function that moderates the negative impacts of waste streams that have been *first* down-sized through P2 efforts. It is important to reemphasize this *first-second priority* relationship between P2 and R2. Specifically, R2 strategically and tactically serves as the second line of defense for minimizing ecosystem impacts. After P2 strategies are employed to minimize waste streams, R2 "kicks in" to "close the loop" by extracting any remaining resource values. Under ideal conditions (i.e., the zero-waste, zero-discharge model holds), there would be no residuals remaining requiring TD. The result would be a state of continuous recirculation of all matter and energy (i.e., a cradle-to-cradle system) that mimics the natural world.

Goal: Getting More from the Same

A major argument for R2 is that it further writes off the initial investment in eco-costs (described earlier) that always is present after the "first time" conversion of resources has occurred. All "already made" products leaving manufacturing facilities possess this investment because energy and materials have been expended during the transformations of resources into form and function and remain embedded in any product discards (e.g., energy equivalents, purified metals). So, at the end of the product's useful life, the (former) product assumes the transient status of waste (i.e., it is temporarily a valueless residual) until appropriate processes liberate this initial investment, thereby creating value.

For example, an aluminum container begins as bauxite ore that is transformed through applications of labor, energy, and other resources into virgin aluminum ingot, sheet stock, and (finally) aluminum containers. As this process unfolds, an investment in eco-costs (waste) accrues as an unavoidable side effect. R2 further writes off this investment as follows: used beverage containers are accumulated in large quantities and sorted into strict homogeneous categories (i.e., occasional steel cans and other "out-throws" are removed), converted into ingots, rolled into sheet stock, and fabricated into new containers—all at a 95 percent savings in energy consumption compared to virgin production. This suggests that once eco-costs accrue through resource transformations, it often makes sense to initiate additional materials use cycles. Failure to do so represents a forgone opportunity. In fact, the continuous future redeployment of resources is really an act of conservation. Because R2 extends the life of manufactured (already-made) resources, it can be called the "getting more from the same" strategy.

It is important to note that R2 is the only sustainable marketing strategy that creates marketable materials/products/energy as outputs. These outputs must be competitive in terms of cost of recovery, price, quality, and availability when compared to direct and indirect competitive counterparts in the marketplace; otherwise, the economic transactions necessary to "close the resource loop" will not occur. Therefore, R2 must be viewed as a normative marketing process linking resource sellers and buyers on an ongoing basis.

Resource Recovery as a Generalized Marketing Strategy

R2 strategies focus on the disposition path a product (or material) is expected to take at some point in the future. The point is to anticipate expected disposition and then design product systems that enhance future resource redeployment opportunities. Three R2 substrategies define alternative disposition paths: (1) product reuse, (2) materials recycling, and (3) materials transformation (Figure 3.4 and Exhibit 4.5) (Fuller 1993).

Product Reuse

All product reuse strategies share a common basis: they involve the continuing use of an already-made product that is recaptured and then remarketed to create an ongoing series of back-to-back use cycles. In other words, the original form and function is largely retained, thereby eliminating the basic materials extraction and conversion processes that underlie first-time products. The different approaches within the reuse category are based on the type of product involved and the degree to which the original physical good is modified prior to remarketing. Reuse differs from the P2 strategy of product useful life extension as follows: reuse involves programming a series of back-to-back use cycles, whereas P2 life extension involves lengthening the individual use cycle. The three major product reuse substrategies are (1) adopting reusable packaging systems, (2) remanufacturing/reconditioning/repairing (R/R/R), and (3) reusing in an alternative application.

Reusable packaging systems can be implemented at both industrial and consumer levels. These systems avoid generation of disposable packaging waste; however, they require significant product design changes and development of efficient reverse channel systems (recapture networks) to build trippage rate (i.e., the number of times reuse is achieved by the system). In consumer applications in particular, overcoming consumer resistance to participating in take-back (i.e., the redemption/return process) is a major marketing challenge. Various aspects of both industrial and consumer container/package design and the dynamics of high-efficiency recapture systems (Stage 5 reverse channels) are discussed in Chapters 4 and 5.

R/R/R applications are durable goods strategies distinguished from each other by the degree or extent of product upgrading prior to remarketing as follows:

> Remanufacturing: [This is] a process in which "improvable products" (worn-out or technically deficient products) are remade to a condition at least as good as new. The process is extensive; the product is disassembled, and every part, material, or structure is examined.
> Reconditioning: [This] involves upgrading through the cleaning or replacement of critical parts. However, the item is examined and reworked to a lesser extent, and disassembly and reassembly are not as comprehensive as in remanufacturing.
> Repairing: [This] refers to the process of "fixing" something that is broken. Repair is focused on replacing a specific broken part or component and does not generally include total disassembly and reassembly. (McConocha and Speh 1991:25)

R/R/R has been a substantial form of business activity since the late 1920s, when Arrow Automotive Industries began rebuilding auto parts (McConocha and Speh 1991). It has been standard operating procedure in the aircraft industry, where engines and other assemblies are routinely replaced with remanufactured components after functioning for a predetermined (standard) number of hours. But this behavior has been driven by traditional economic advantage (cost-effectiveness), not savings in terms of environmental impact.

Recognition that R/R/R also spawns ecological benefits (i.e., it eliminates the eco-costs associated with building products from scratch), as well as traditional economic benefits, has revitalized interest by the electronics and other manufacturing industries. For example, the "win-win-win" case of the U.S. health care industry's purchase of remanufactured equipment for 50 percent less was cited in Chapter 1. As another example, the author recently replaced a dishwasher timer, which involved trading in (exchanging) the old unit at a local parts distributor for a remanufactured unit at a price savings of about 45 percent compared to a newly manufactured item with the same warranty. Savings in the range of 40 to 60 percent on remanufactured capital equipment have been reported (McConocha and Speh 1991:27). This new-found linkage to ecology and economics is now discussed in the management literature under the topic "product recovery management," which is defined by Thierry et al. (1995) as follows:

> Product recovery management . . . encompasses the management of all used and discarded products, components, and materials that fall under the responsibility of a manufacturing company. The objective of product recovery management is to recover as much of the economic (and ecological) value as reasonably possible, thereby reducing the ultimate quantities of waste. (p. 114)

The final reuse strategy involves using an already-made product "as is" in an alternative application. For example, old radial tires can be left intact and used as playground devices, or jelly jars can be retained as bathroom or kitchen drinking glasses. Admittedly, this approach is not viable for most products, but it is mentioned here and in Chapter 4 to ensure completeness.

Materials Recycling

Materials recycling involves the processes of recapturing large quantities of targeted products and materials from waste streams, sorting them into homogeneous categories, upgrading them to the quality specification levels required by industrial buyers, and then making them available to those buyers. In contrast to product reuse and materials transformation strategies, materials recycling involves a total physical reduction of recovered products and materials back to the level of raw materials/commodities; original product form and function is discarded. After processing, the materials compete against their virgin-source counterparts in meeting the specifications demanded by buyers (e.g., quality, purity, quantity, exact chemical composition). To compete head-to-head with virgin materials, high volumes must be achieved, strict quality control must be exercised, and prices must be competitive. In short, materials recycling creates alternative competitive sources of supply for industrial markets. When recaptured materials cannot be returned to the level of quality required in primary (original product) applications, they may be used in lower quality applications. For example, mixed plastics may be made into low-grade plastic (composite) lumber. This application of recycling, referred to as "downcycling," is a clear signal that the highest and best use of materials was not achieved.

The economic success of materials recycling is dependent on three enabling conditions: (1) establishment of supply continuity, (2) development of Stage 5 reverse channel networks (infrastructure), and (3) development-maintenance of markets for recycled-source materials (Fuller 1993). Supply continuity means that large quantities of specific quality feedstocks must be made available to industrial customers on a continuous basis. After materials sources are located, Stage 5 reverse channel networks are necessary to achieve functional materials recapture and processing and to maintain exchange continuity (see Chapter 5). The development of reliable and continuous markets for recycled-source outputs is the linchpin of materials recycling. Key issues include building demand by specifying recycled-source materials in new finished products construction and maintaining the generally high-quality specifications demanded by industrial buyers (see Chapter 8). Quality maintenance is important because of the positive correlation between market prices and quality level. Maintaining high quality also translates into less downcycling of materials into lower quality (low-value) applications.

A critical factor influencing the economic feasibility of materials recycling is the avoidance of entropy. An engineering term, *entropy* refers to the condition in which materials become so randomly mixed or otherwise combined/contaminated that it is not economically feasible to physically sort them into homogeneous categories (Purcell 1980). In general, high levels of entropy are a barrier to efficient R2. One strategy for avoiding entropy is to sort materials (waste) at the immediate point of generation. For example, it is much more efficient to sort basic consumer wastes (e.g., paper, glass, plastics, metals, organics) within households as they are created than to attempt to recover the same materials from a commingled (mixed-garbage) source. This explains the widespread adoption of curbside collection systems for handling postconsumer recyclables. It also points out the major role that Stage 5 reverse channel networks play in the materials recycling process (see Chapter 5).

Entropy avoidance also is an important element of product design. This is because all products start out as sets of homogeneous materials that are assembled (i.e., combined, joined, welded, screwed, bonded, bolted, laminated, or otherwise brought together) to create the desired form and function. In general, as one moves down the PSLC, products become more complex— and entropy builds. Materials recycling must efficiently reverse this process; therefore, designing future "recyclability" into products is an important strategy that prevents and reverses entropy (see Chapter 4).

Materials Transformation

Materials transformation involves thermal (incineration-combustion), chemical, or biological processes that convert original materials into alternative forms or directly extract energy values. Alternative product outputs include soil enhancers derived through aerobic composting and energy/fuel sources developed through incineration/waste-to-energy (WTE) systems and pyrolysis/gasification technologies. The last two approaches also are referred to as thermal recycling/energy harvesting.

Municipal and industrial solid waste (MSW) often becomes unavoidably commingled and contaminated as it is generated and handled (i.e., entropy is maximized). In this case, materials transformation strategies are the only approach through which any remaining resource values can be recaptured while also reducing the flow of materials to TD. Simply put, materials transformation accommodates the dredges of society's waste streams and provides one last chance to extract any resource values for future use. TD then follows as a finale.

One specific form of transformation, incineration, has a shabby public image built around the fear that contaminants (e.g., dioxins, furans, heavy metals) are released directly into the air or become concentrated in the residual ash as a result of the waste burning process. In this regard, the Supreme Court has ruled that incinerator ash is legally defined as a hazardous waste and must be tested prior to its TD in landfills. This action has reinforced incineration's unsafe image and has added a significant cost factor that now clouds the economic feasibility of this alternative (Integrated Waste Services Association 1994).

In the case of those materials that are both combustible and recyclable, the strategies of incineration/WTE and materials recycling are direct competitors. One of the most obvious conflicts involves plastics. Because they are made from petrochemicals, plastics are particularly sought for incineration because their high BTU content enhances burn efficiency. This had led to local turf battles over "who gets the garbage" when large WTE facilities already are in place. This is because such facilities have a voracious appetite for combustibles. If other local interests successfully promote materials recycling as a cleaner alternative, then this diverts prime incinerator feedstocks and undermines the economics of WTE operations. Although such battles are beyond the control of marketing decision makers, the lesson is that products might need to be designed with both strategies in mind.

As a distinct strategy, materials transformation can be strategically supported through product design decisions such as including natural, combustible, degradable, and nonhazardous/nontoxic materials in product and package construction and by the development of Stage 5 reverse channel networks that consistently deliver large quantities of appropriate waste materials to facilities for energy recycling/harvesting or the production of compost. In what must be classified as a "sleeper," the composting of MSW currently is undergoing a major resurgence in the United States, as evidenced by the fact that 3,484 composting projects that handle yard trimmings were reported in 1997 (Glenn 1998:33). The banning of yard trimmings from landfills in 27 states has been a major contributing factor (Garland, Grist, and Green 1995:53), and this trend will continue. In addition, the use of compost no longer is limited solely to its role as a soil amendment. New market applications include using compost for erosion control, cleaning up contaminants in storm water runoff, and remediating soils contaminated with heavy metals or toxic compounds. Yet another benefit is that the diversion of organic materials to composting processes eliminates the natural formation of methane, a major greenhouse gas, in landfills. The positive trade-off is that composting activity alternatively generates carbon dioxide, a gas that has a greenhouse effect that is 22 times less than that of methane (Garland et al. 1995:53).

Resource Recovery over the Product System Life Cycle

It is important to emphasize that R2 is a concurrent strategy that supplements P2 at all levels of the PSLC and to avoid the misconception that R2 is only a downstream, end-of-pipe solution. As Figure 3.5 clearly shows, output waste streams (designated by W) emerging from all levels must go somewhere. A solution is for them to enter Stage 5 reverse channel networks at their respective levels, where various R2 substrategies are implemented, or to use TD as the default option of last resort.

Default Option: Terminal Disposal

TD is at the bottom of the IWM hierarchy. It involves the final release, or discharge, of valueless wastes (residuals) into ecosystems through both legal means (e.g., landfilling, emission of treated waste into air/water) and illegal dumping. In this book, TD is not treated as a strategy per se; rather, it is a default option/event that must be respected and tolerated while P2 and R2 strategies gain ground and eventually eliminate the need for it.

Weaning Society's Dependence

This is not to say that TD is to be ignored. In 1997, an estimated 61 percent of the MSW generated annually in the United States was routinely disposed of through the TD approach of landfilling, compared to 62 percent in 1996 and 70 percent in 1993 (Glenn 1998:34; Goldstein 1997:62; Steuteville 1994:48). TD is truly a deeply ingrained business/consumer practice that will not go away quickly or quietly. This should not be surprising given that America has been the global leader in "disposable everything" for decades. As a result, the American industrial complex is enmeshed in processes and systems that cater to disposable lifestyles. This contributes to the relative inelasticity of waste streams in the short run that will cause TD to remain the dominant disposal approach for society's discards into the foreseeable future.

Weaning society from dependence on TD will be accomplished only gradually as P2 and R2 strategies make inroads, thereby causing a reduction in TD volume. Ironically, one nonecological pressure that will shift more emphasis to P2 and R2 approaches is the "NIMBY" (Not In My Back Yard) syndrome (mentioned in Chapter 1), which makes it difficult to develop additional landfill capacity in urban areas, which in turn tips the scales in favor of P2 and R2 options. But landfilling will remain the most likely disposal scenario for many products for years to come.

Disposal under Uncertainty

When developing sustainable P2 and R2 approaches, marketers simply do not know, nor do they control, the time, place, or type of disposal that will occur at downstream points in the future. In the United States and elsewhere, the character and availability of local R2 system infrastructure, markets, and other waste disposal alternatives vary widely. In addition, waste management laws and ordinances are not consistent or standardized across jurisdictions. This introduces uncertainty into the waste management equation.

Not unlike the stock market, this uncertainty manifests itself daily. As products move forward through marketing channels, absolute control over disposal also passes along with title/ownership. In most cases, manufacturers of finished products lose all control over the disposal of their products (including packaging) when ownership changes. The reality of this situation in relation to packaging is well stated by Alexander (1993):

> When marketers pack their goods, they do not know in which state or city any particular package will be discarded. . . . Will it be used and disposed of in northern New Jersey, with disposal costs of $140 per ton, or in a small town where the landfilling charges are $6 per ton? Will the city have a recycling program, and [if so] for which materials? If the disposal location uses WTE plants, [then] ash quantity, energy content, and air pollution are more important considerations. (p. 81)

An exception to the loss of control scenario is the lease transaction in which title does not pass. As applied to durable goods, such as automobiles and industrial equipment, the final fate of the product is specified in the lease agreement and might involve return to the manufacturer. For a more detailed discussion, see the "Rent/Lease Pricing" subsection in Chapter 7.

Benign by Design

Because of this, sustainable marketers must develop "benign by design" approaches that serve as fail-safe mechanisms if the TD option were exercised. This again suggests an emphasis on the design of clean burning products that use natural, combustible, degradable, and nonhazardous/nontoxic materials in product and package construction as a way in which to guard against unintended detrimental ecosystem impacts.

In the case of landfilling, a particularly widespread practice at the municipal level, Reinhart (1994) notes, "Ideally, land should be a repository exclusively for inert 'earthlike' materials that can be assimilated without adverse environmental impact, a conviction held by landfill regulators, designers, and operators throughout the world" (p. 1). But with more than 6 out of 10 pounds of municipal waste going into the ground, the inappropriate inclusion of massive quantities of "non-earthlike" materials in landfills is a daily fact of life. Advances in landfill design technology will reduce some of the risks associated with landfill operations. The modern engineered landfill is a far cry from the "open sink" of the early 1900s and can be loosely classified into four types (Reinhart 1994): (1) the *secure landfill* (entombs waste and postpones environmental consequences to a future time period), (2) the *monofill* (used for inert materials), (3) the *reusable landfill* (allows later excavation to recover materials previously entombed), and (4) the *reactor landfill* (operates to minimize ecological impact while waste degradation is activated within it). These design alternatives make it possible to accommodate the variations in climatological, geological, and hydrological factors that represent unique local conditions.

The fact remains that entombing society's discards in landfills is a temporary "out of sight, out of mind" solution at best—and one to be avoided in the future. In fact, the phrase "environmentally sound landfill" is a classic oxymoron because the liners that contain toxic lechate in today's secure landfills have a service life of only about 20 years (D. R. Reinhart, University of Central Florida, personal communication, April 1995). So, building a safety net through benign-by-design approaches certainly is a prudent step but still is only a stopgap measure.

Organizational Strategies

At a broad level, the general organizational strategies that firms may employ to move toward sustainable practices are identified in Figure 3.6. The "products" dimension of the exhibit (Columns 1 and 2), which reflects internal company decisions to alter form and function and delivery systems to achieve ecosystems compatibility, is used to create two general categories of strategies: (1) environmentally improved products and (2) environmentally reinvented products.

Environmentally Improved Products Strategies

The strategies in Column 1, market penetration and market development, suggest making minor alterations or adjustments to products and manufacturing processes and delivery systems (i.e., minor ecological attribute changes) as the ways and means of achieving traditional marketing objectives (i.e., growth, profits, customer satisfaction) while also pursuing sustainability objectives. Some of the basic questions addressed would be as follows:

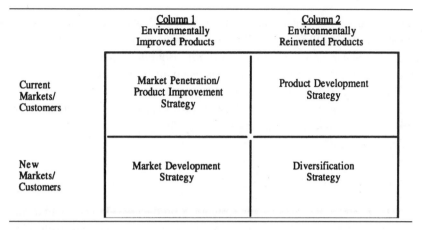

	Column 1 Environmentally Improved Products	Column 2 Environmentally Reinvented Products
Current Markets/ Customers	Market Penetration/ Product Improvement Strategy	Product Development Strategy
New Markets/ Customers	Market Development Strategy	Diversification Strategy

Figure 3.6. Environmentally Improved and Reinvented Products
Strategy Matrix
SOURCE: Adapted from Ansoff, H. I. (1957), "Strategies for Diversification," *Harvard Business Review,*
Vol. 35, September-October, pp. 113-24.
NOTE: Column 1 strategies imply making minor environmental product improvements within the confines
of the present product system life cycle; they largely represent applications of resource recovery strategy.
Column 2 strategies imply a "clean sheet of paper" approach, or a product reinvention approach, which may
radically change the product benefits delivery system and product system life-cycle configuration; they
largely represent applications of pollution prevention strategy.

- What are the waste streams associated with our product (1) during the manufacturing and (2) during movement through channels?
- What waste is generated by our product during customer use and on retirement
  at the end of useful life?
- What is our product's typical final disposition pattern?
- Are there environmentally friendly processes, materials, and other product
  improvements that can be used or made within the context of our present
  production systems and technologies?
- How "green/sustainable" are our suppliers? How can we help our suppliers
  eliminate the use of hazardous or toxic materials?
- Do our customers perceive our product as environmentally friendly or damaging?

Thus, Column 1 strategies would involve modest product-process
changes and add-on fixes that attempt to clean up the present PSLC. The likely
emphasis would be on present technology; overall, the present product's core

benefit delivery systems (i.e., form and function) would essentially remain intact, as would PSLC participants. So, the initiatives would be largely R2 in character and would focus on the short run. Both the amount of change and the commitment to product stewardship would be minimal and might be classified as reactive in nature if the changes are largely driven by the need to comply with federal, state, and local regulations. But these strategies also might be viewed as the voluntary start of building a bridge to future sustainable practice.

Environmentally Reinvented Products Strategies

By contrast, the strategies in Column 2, product development and diversification, stem from fundamental product concept reinventions made with ecosystems impact as a criterion. In product development terms, the core benefit delivery system is substantially altered to accommodate ecological attributes (see Chapter 4). Such major environmentally driven changes in product form and function may well lead to important shifts in PSLC composition. This also implies the need for a high level of managerial commitment to the stewardship ethic if these strategies are to become operational over the long run. In particular, diversification is a movement into the "high-risk zone" because both product and market are new. In the sustainable setting, this might involve relying on strategic alliances as a way in which to move into functional areas of ecosystems strategies that are beyond the firm's expertise. The changes in the grand design implied by Column 2 strategies suggest a focus on P2 approaches.

Sustainability as Competitive Advantage

Unique waste management initiatives, particularly those in the environmentally reinvented products category, may provide the basis for a firm to separate itself from competitors in ways that are very hard to imitate and duplicate, thus establishing what is called competitive/differential advantage (Alderson 1957; Porter 1986). Porter (1991) points out that developing a true competitive advantage based on environmental considerations will likely involve strategies that "stress pollution prevention rather than merely abatement or cleanup" (p. 168). Furthermore, Porter suggests that environmental innovations can result in "a process that not only pollutes less but [also] lowers costs or improves quality" (p. 168). This enhancement of so-called "eco-efficiency" (Schmidheiny 1992b:10) is a characteristic of dynamic competition and translates directly into competitive advantage for innovator firms. Thus, Porter essentially supports the existence of win-win-win scenarios that simultaneously achieve lower costs (business objectives), meet customer needs, and reduce impacts on ecosystems. In particular, the T factor in the equation for environmental impact (see Chapter 1) is reduced because certain cost-reducing "innovation offsets" kick in (Porter and van der Linde 1995). This is the essence of the Porter hypothesis: organizations that are proactive and act early to phase in advanced/innovative P2 technologies may experience lower long-run costs than those that simply wait for the regulators to come up with more rules and are then caught up in the "rush to comply."

The Porter hypothesis is supported by limited case histories, as well as other anecdotal evidence, that suggest its potential cost-effectiveness over the long run. A long-standing example is the aggressive development and implementation of innovative P2 technologies by the 3M Corporation, which claims to have saved $500 million during 1975 to 1989 by implementing P2 initiatives (Ottman 1993:60). More recently, the Aspen Bay Pulp & Fibre of Menominee, Michigan has constructed an innovative mill that uses bleached chemical thermo-mechanical pulp (BCTMP) technology. This process allows the use of more than 90 percent of a tree's cellulose mass, whereas standard chemical pulping processes use only 50 percent. In addition to this whopping increase in resources productivity, BCTMP uses hydrogen peroxide as the bleaching agent, which breaks down harmlessly in the environment. This avoids potential dioxin contamination, as well as the costs associated with protecting against it, that is associated with the chlorine bleaching systems used in standard chemical pulping. Already known as an innovator, Aspen Bay Pulp & Fibre is a good example of how "outsider" firms can gain market entry on the basis of an environmental competitive advantage (Associated Press 1996). Other examples of innovation offsets are provided by Porter and van der Linde (1995).

However, the Porter hypothesis does not go unchallenged. Critics see Porter's results as a manifestation of the "low-hanging fruit" phenomenon. In particular, Oates et al. (1993) claim to generally disprove the Porter hypothesis using "a simple economic model of the sort used in analyses of innovation in pollution control" that shows that "the addition (or tightening) of constraints on a firm's set of choices cannot be expected to result in a higher level of profits" (p. 2). Furthermore, they note that the positive case for the Porter hypothesis "seems to us to rest largely on the existence of some 'slack' [in the system], that is, some preexisting opportunities for cost savings or profitable product enhancement that have, for some reason, gone unrealized" (p. 3). In other words, for the Porter hypothesis to hold, low-hanging fruit has to be on the tree to begin with; the imposition of more stringent regulations simply forces firms to go looking for it as a way in which to cut costs. Conversely, firms already operating at high levels of industrial efficiency have no low-hanging fruit to pick, so additional regulations just add to their costs. Such firms are in a "lose-win-win" situation; that is, any environmental advances come at costs that are not offset elsewhere in production systems, customer needs are met, and ecosystems are protected. In short, after picking the fruit that is easy to reach, the harvester faces a very steep learning curve.

From another perspective, Clark (1993) suggests that when governments impose regulations, this creates the "potential for significant changes in the distribution of competitive advantage" (p. 57). Two classes of firms may emerge: (1) winners, for whom market opportunities are created by the imposition of regulations, and (2) losers, or those who must pay additional costs or otherwise face diminished market opportunities. For example, Oates et al. (1993) point out that government-inspired "cleanups of hazardous materials at sites under programs like Superfund . . . have already (or soon will) become big business that involves research and development and a variety of sophisticated technologies including bioremediation" (pp. 4-5). Providers of such services are market winners and face an opportunity of global proportions. The firms paying for such services are losers because they will incur additional costs as a result.

Similarly, packaging regulations mandating the use of refillable, reusable containers would create instant winners among firms already supplying such products and losers among those dependent on the continuing replacement market created by the use of disposal packages. In particular, because refillables can be made only from glass or plastic (both of which feature two-way closures), suppliers of paperboard and metal sheet stock packaging materials would suffer negative consequences, whereas suppliers of plastic and glass would likely advance in market share.

In summary, it is only natural to suspect that covering ecological costs, after they have been treated as "free" for decades, will add to costs and put some upward pressures on prices—and might result in some basic reshuffling in competitive position among firms. At the same time, Porter is right to suggest that man's ingenuity in the realm of science and technology constantly introduces the dynamic element of change into the competitive equation, thus opening up the potential to dramatically reinvent lower cost ways and means of providing benefits to customers through environmentally compatible products. A good example is the fiber-optic telecommunications cable, which is simply a "better" solution because it provides higher transmission capacities and more customer value at less ecological cost than does copper or aluminum wire (Gilder 1990; Young 1992).

Marketing's New Mission

Viable micro-level sustainable marketing strategies can be developed only within organizations that are truly committed to ecological concerns and are willing to translate those concerns into action through marketing mix decisions. Consequently, sustainable marketing must embark on a new mission summarized by the following "three R's" (Sheth and Parvatiyar 1995): (1) *redirecting* customer choices, (2) *reorienting* the marketing mix, and (3) *reorganizing* delivery systems.

Redirecting Customer Choices

Traditional marketing management practice has been to give customers, both industrial buyers and consumers, what they want within the constraints of economics and the business as usual context shown in Figure 3.1. Sustainable marketing faces the additional challenge of harmonizing economy and ecology (Figure 3.2). It has been noted previously that healthy ecosystems represent an absolute precondition necessary for human survival. But at the same time, the threat to this factor is not appreciated by consumers. As Sheth and Parvatiyar (1995) point out, this suggests that *redirecting* customers is necessary, which means "to intervene to appropriately change the criteria for consumer decision making in favor of ecologically benign consumption" (p. 10). The reality is that customers will need convincing that changing product delivery systems and consumption practices to modes that might offer less short-term convenience is in their self-interest. Likewise, organizations within the PSLC must buy in and understand why joint ecological action is necessary to support P2 and R2 strategies. This boils down to a slow and steady transition through which both companies and markets will move in the appropriate direction. To facilitate this process, sustainable marketing must assume a major role in educating customers and channel members about the nature of environmental needs and how consumption decisions influence both ecosystems and the quality of life.

To bring about gains in dematerialization, redirecting customer choices also suggests changing the basic format of some durable goods transactions. As noted earlier in this chapter in the chainsaw example, the norm of traditional ownership of consumer durable goods may give way to the notion of renting/leasing "units of service" as the need arises in the short run. This could evolve into the leasing of nontraditional durables (e.g., appliances, carpets, electronics) for extended time periods, at the end of which the worn-out assets revert to the dealer/manufacturer as inputs into reuse, recycling, materials transformation, or TD. Implementing such fundamental changes in transaction strategy format undoubtedly will raise many reinvention challenges for marketers, one of which is the area of pricing decisions.

Reorienting the Marketing Mix

Obviously, the process of *redirecting* customers must be simultaneously matched by *reorienting* the marketing mix in deference to ecological considerations. This means actually making the decisions that develop and implement zero-waste, zero-discharge systems that support sustainability objectives while also providing necessary benefits to both customers and organizations.

Marketing Mix Changes

Exhibit 3.2 summarizes some of the changes in marketing mix orientation that are associated with a sustainable paradigm. First and foremost, product decisions require a focus on building in appropriate ecological benefits (product attributes) by employing the process of product DFE as the major ways and means of influencing process and product waste streams. The attack on process waste is carried into distribution channels and beyond by developing appropriate reverse/green logistics functions and by selecting channel partners on the basis of demonstrated environmental commitment and practice. Communications (promotion) is reoriented to include coverage of environmental information and values, and pricing is refined by activity-based accounting procedures that allocate ecological costs to the products responsible for them. Pricing also is revised to reflect appropriate shifts from title transfer to rent/lease transactions. A subsequent chapter discusses each marketing mix element in detail.

ᴇxʜɪʙɪᴛ 3.2

Marketing Mix Changes: Traditional Marketing versus Sustainable Marketing

Traditional Marketing ⟶	*Sustainable Marketing*
Product	
1. Focus on traditional customer benefits	1. Focus on traditional customer benefits *and* ecological benefits
2. DFX, where "X" designates traditional product attributes	2. Product DFE *in addition to* DFX, where "E" designates ecological attributes
Channel networks (place/distribution)	
1. Traditional functional, product support, and customer access issues within the immediate channel network	1. Addition of "reverse/green" logistics functional support for P2 and R2; use of strategic alliances to cover the extended product system life cycle
2. Traditional channel member selection criteria	2. Addition of "green factor" as channel member/ supplier selection criterion
Communications (promotion)	
1. Appeals based on direct consumer functional and emotional benefits	1. Appeals based on direct consumer functional and emotional benefits *and* on indirect, long-term ecological benefits
2. Educate customer about product benefits	2. Educate customer about long-term ecological benefits and values; provide information to aid the purchaser in determining ecologically sound product choices; stimulate participation in R2 programs
Pricing	
1. Short-term focus on costs/ prices and value added	1. Focus on long-term life-cycle costs/prices and life-cycle value added
2. No separate costing to identify or allocate eco-costs	2. Use of activity-based costing to identify eco-costs and allocate them to the products responsible for them
3. Pricing to reflect traditional product ownership (title transfer)	3. Pricing to reflect "products as services" (potential for rent/lease vs. title transfer)

NOTE: DFX = design-for-X; DFE = design-for-environment; P2 = pollution prevention; R2 = resource recovery.

Sustainable Marketing Objectives

The requirement that sustainable marketing be compatible with ecosystems introduces an *additional dimension* in the area of objectives. The word *additional* is carefully chosen to indicate that the main mission of the firm still is (1) to make available products that deliver real benefits to customers and (2) to meet the financial and other objectives of the firm. Therefore, the need for traditional marketing and financial objectives that (1) are measurable specific, (2) have defined time lines for achievement, (3) are realistic/attainable, and (4) are consistent/congruent with other objectives of the firm is no less pressing. (See Guiltinan and Paul 1991 and Kotler 1997 for excellent discussions of traditional marketing objectives.)

The nature of the *additional dimension* brought to the table by sustainable marketing is made clear when sustainable objectives and marketing mix elements are linked as shown in Exhibit 3.3. Sustainable objectives have this additional distinction: both product and channel are waste-influencing activities, so objectives for these elements are variants of the common P2 and R2 themes of eliminating, reducing, and remediating waste streams across the PSLC. On the other hand, communications and pricing are information-providing and transaction-valuing functions, respectively; they are not classic waste-generating activities. Instead, they use the P2 and R2 (environmental) decisions made in the product and channel areas as inputs when designing communications programs and for establishing product costs, value, and price. The objectives for these elements of the marketing mix follow a more traditional pattern.

Reorganizing Delivery Systems

Reorganizing firms into boundary-spanning delivery systems capable of meeting environmental challenges is necessary if *reoriented* marketing mixes are to be delivered to *redirected* customers. The shift in paradigm requires changing the way in which environmental issues are approached both within organizations (the intraorganizational dimension) and between organizations (the interorganizational dimension). These changes in managerial perspective show up in many of the contrasts made in Exhibit 3.4 that reflect the generally broadened and longer-term PSLC orientation associated with the sustainable paradigm.

exhibiт 3.3

Sustainable Marketing Objectives

Marketing Mix Element ⟶	*Objectives*
Product	To minimize the waste and pollution generated by a product over the product system life cycle as a result of decisions about product attributes and manufacturing processes.
Channel networks (place/distribution)	Outbound/forward channels: To minimize the waste and pollution generated by the transportation, storage, and handling functions associated with any product.
	Reverse/backward channels: 1. To minimize the waste and pollution generated by the transportation, storage, and handling functions associated with recaptured products and materials. 2. To provide appropriate coverage of waste sources to maximize collection convenience and to recapture efficiency-effectiveness.
Communications (promotion)	To educate stakeholders about environmental issues; to foster an image of environmental responsibility (in terms of products and corporate practice) that will directly or indirectly have a positive impact on sales now or in the future.
Pricing	To set product prices that reflect the inclusion of full eco-costs in the unit cost structure.

Implementing Sustainable Marketing Strategies

Implementing the sustainable paradigm requires a major change in managerial and marketing thinking. Therefore, the incorporation of sustainability into everyday decision making likely will require an extended transition process.

exhibit 3.4

Changes in Managerial Perspective: Traditional Marketing versus Sustainable Marketing

Traditional Marketing ————————————→ *Sustainable Marketing*

Criteria/goals

Traditional Marketing	Sustainable Marketing
1. Customer satisfaction	1. Customer satisfaction
2. Organizational goals	2. Organizational goals
	3. Ecosystem compatibility

Decision-making frame of reference

Traditional Marketing	Sustainable Marketing
1. Immediate channel network	1. PSLC: cradle-to-grave
2. Fragmented thinking	2. Integrated thinking
3. Non-boundary spanning	3. Boundary spanning
4. Short-term orientation	4. Long-term orientation

Philosophical basis

Traditional Marketing	Sustainable Marketing
1. Anthropocentric	1. Biocentric
2. Ecosystem an open "sink"	2. Ecosystem a physical limiting factor; eco-costs must be paid

Ecological accountability/responsibility

Traditional Marketing	Sustainable Marketing
1. Limited product risk	1. Product risk over the PSLC
2. Local/regional/national	2. Global/international
3. No/underpaid ecological costs	3. Full accounting of ecological costs
4. Individual organization alone is accountable	4. PSLC members are mutually accountable
5. A public sector responsibility	5. Joint public-private sector responsibility

General tools/approaches

Traditional Marketing	Sustainable Marketing
1. Use planning to minimize the costs of local waste disposal	1. Use life-cycle assessment and environmental audits to minimize and redirect PSLC waste streams
2. Reactive approach to waste management	2. Proactive approach to waste management
3. Isolated department functions	3. Use of cross-functional teams
4. Focus on industrial functions	4. Focus on industrial processes
5. Total quality management	5. Total quality environmental management
6. Use of strategic alliances to accomplish traditional goals	6. Use of strategic alliances to accomplish sustainable goals
7. Focus on tangible goods	7. Focus on "products as services"

NOTE: PSLC = product system life cycle.

Transition Process

In this regard, McDaniel and Rylander (1993) provide the following 10-step plan:

> Step 1—Develop an environmental corporate policy. This policy should state the company's mission and objectives with regard to the environment and should allow for environmental considerations to be integrated into all company decisions.
>
> Step 2—Build environmental leadership at the top level of the organization. Doing this should communicate a long-term commitment to environmental action.
>
> Step 3—Hire or develop environmental advocates on the inside. These people can concentrate on environmental concerns and provide a consistent environmental voice for the organization. Some companies may even create an entirely new department dedicated to environmental planning.
>
> Step 4—Educate and train all employees on environmental awareness. From the boardroom to the mailroom, an environmental consciousness must pervade the organization.
>
> Step 5—Maintain active dialogue with outside environmental groups and government agencies. It is essential to stay abreast of outside needs and concerns.
>
> Step 6—Develop an assertive environmental action program. This program should be integrated into all parts of the strategic planning process.
>
> Step 7—Integrate all departments to facilitate flexibility in responding to environmental needs. Doing this may require building bridges between competing interests in the organization.
>
> Step 8—Allocate adequate resources to show commitment. This environmental commitment must be demonstrated by provision of money and personnel to implement the environmental action program effectively.
>
> Step 9—Through effective advertising and publicity, communicate to customers what you are doing. This communication will not only build customer loyalty toward your organization, but also encourage customers' cooperation in environmental efforts.
>
> Step 10—Monitor consumer response with an active marketing research program. The dynamic nature of environmental needs and demands requires constant monitoring with flexibility to adapt. (pp. 7-8)

The marketing function's roles in this 10-step plan can be described variously as those of champion, educator, and integrator/implementer. As champion, the marketing department can take the initiative of bringing the environmental issue to the table while also serving as an inside advocate. As educator, it can endeavor to heighten environmental awareness among the firm's personnel while maintaining a focus on those issues most germane to the firm's product lines or industry. It also is important to "teach" the fundamental notion that *environmental issues know no functional boundaries and are both intrafirm and interfirm in nature.* As integrator/implementer, marketing can bring various functional and organizational units together in cross-functional teams and strategic alliances to tackle PSLC-related environmental challenges. Marketing also can instigate changes in business practice, such as inserting formal DFE procedures in the product development process, regularly including environmental issues when conducting customer research, and incorporating environmental information in promotional communications to customers and other stakeholders.

Stewardship Ethic: Core Corporate Value

As the 10-step plan indicates, top management must first genuinely "buy into" the stewardship ethic (see Chapter 1) and then take appropriate steps to instill this philosophy as a *core corporate value* throughout the organization. As Neace (personal communication, July 26, 1995) comments, "From a business (marketing) perspective, product stewardship is the policy component of the implementation of sustainable development within the enterprise." In particular, corporate leaders must end the economy versus ecology debate with the conclusion that ecological and economic systems are interdependent. Then they must make an overt commitment in the form of a written environmental policy outlining principles and goals. The format can be short and sweet or long and detailed. For example, AT&T's Environmental Policy succinctly reads as follows:

> AT&T is committed to protection of human health and the environment in all operations, services, and products. AT&T will integrate life-cycle environmental quality into design, development, manufacturing, marketing, and sales activities worldwide. Implementation of this policy is a primary management objective and the responsibility of every AT&T employee. (K. Brown 1995:17)

Additional examples of environmental policy statements by The Home Depot and the The Clorox Company are reproduced in Exhibits 3.5 and 3.6.

Fortunately, there are signals that "environment" is being viewed in corporate circles as something of value that should advance in priority. The importance for establishing this point of view is echoed by the co-chairs of the President's Council on Sustainable Development, David Buzzelli, vice

exhibit 3.5

The Home Depot's Statement of Environmental Principles

THE HOME DEPOT ENVIRONMENTAL PRINCIPLES

We are committed to improving the environment by selling products that are manufactured, packaged and labeled in a responsible manner, that take the environment into consideration, and that provide greater value to our customers.

We will support efforts to provide accurate, informative product labeling of environmental marketing claims and impacts.

We will strive to eliminate unnecessary packaging.

We will recycle and will encourage the use of materials and products with recycled content.

We will conserve natural resources by using energy and water wisely and seek further opportunities to improve the resource efficiency of our stores.

We comply with all environmental laws and will maintain programs and procedures to ensure compliance.

We are committed to minimizing environmental health and safety risks for our employees and our customers.

We will train employees to enhance understanding of environmental issues and policies and to promote excellence in job performance in all environmental matters.

We will encourage our customers to become environmentally conscious shoppers.

13

SOURCE: Brown, Kendra (1995-96), "First Step to Corporate Environmental Stewardship: Put It in Writing," *Keep Florida Beautiful Magazine*, Fall-Winter, p. 13. Reprinted by permission. *Keep Florida Beautiful Magazine* is published by Keep Florida Beautiful Inc., Tallahassee, FL.

exHibit 3.6

The Clorox Company's Policy on Public
Health, Safety, and the Environment

THE CLOROX COMPANY POLICY ON PUBLIC HEALTH, SAFETY, AND THE ENVIRONMENT

Clorox designs, manufactures and markets only those products which satisfy consumer needs, meet our quality standards, and are safe for their intended use. Building on existing company policies, Clorox will continue to promote public health, safety and environmental quality in all aspects of our operations, products, and packaging. Clorox also will meet or exceed all applicable industry standards and laws governing public health, safety and the environment; and will disseminate appropriate and accurate information on these issues. The following activities will be carried out to meet this commitment.

Product and Packaging

Design products and packaging which achieve the optimum balance of safety, product performance and environmental quality within the limits of commercially available technology.

Reduce or prevent environmental effects of products and packaging whenever feasible.

Manufacturing

Insist on safety for our employees and for the communities in which we operate.

Design and maintain process controls which ensure that our quality standards and product safety requirements are met.

Minimize waste in the manufacture and distribution of our products and packaging.

Develop and use manufacturing processes which advance what is commercially feasible in safeguarding the environment from pollutants which cause damage to air, water and earth.

Information and Interaction

Develop and maintain programs which enhance awareness and provide prompt, accurate information to our employees, customers and consumers on Clorox public health, environment and safety measures.

Inform and motivate employees about their responsibilities associated with public health, safety and the environment and seek their suggestions to continually improve in these areas.

Work with regulatory and public interest groups to define controls and programs related to our industry which both protect the environment and provide safety and value to the consumer.

Implementation:

We will maintain appropriate organizational structures and dedicate sufficient management and financial resources to implement this policy.

SOURCE: Brown, Kendra (1995-96), "First Step to Corporate Environmental Stewardship: Put It in Writing," *Keep Florida Beautiful Magazine*, Fall-Winter, p. 16. Reprinted by permission. *Keep Florida Beautiful Magazine* is published by Keep Florida Beautiful Inc., Tallahassee, FL.

president of Dow Chemical, and Jonathan Lash, president of World Resources Institute, who jointly state,

> Environmental progress will require the adoption of stewardship as an individual, institutional, and corporate value. A paradigm shift must occur, changing a "have to do it" society to a "need and want to do it" society. Ultimately, we must have zero-discharge manufacturing. (quoted in Makower 1995b:8)

Total Quality Environmental Management

TQM is premised on customer satisfaction that is achieved through the continuous improvement in quality over time. TQM is seen as a pervasive function/activity in an organization; likewise, an organization's ecological "footprint," or perceived environmental performance, is a function of the collective actions/efforts of all of its constituent parts and represents a major element of customer satisfaction. Therefore, achieving improvement in terms of sustainability represents another way of achieving the TQM objective of enhancing customer satisfaction. In fact, the congruence between sustainability and TQM is now being discussed in management circles under the label *total quality environmental management* (TQEM), where making environmental gains is seen as an element of the continuous (incremental) quality improvement process (Global Environmental Management Initiative 1992).

Cross-Functional Teams and Strategic Alliances

The boundary-spanning nature of sustainable marketing decisions, functions, and activities, as well as the diversity of disciplines and interests that must provide input on ecological problems, suggests the employment of cross-functional teams and strategic alliances as problem-solving and administrative mechanisms. This applies to both intra- and interorganizational dimensions. On the intraorganizational level, the use of concurrent product development teams makes it possible to achieve a multidiscipline focus on ecological impact from Day 1 during the product development process, thus avoiding the costly redesigns and time delays associated with linear design efforts. Similarly, the need for high levels of cooperation between the organizations in the PSLC calls for the use of strategic alliances (i.e., liaisons, environmental partnerships) that represent de facto interorganizational teams (Fuller 1994a; Long and Arnold 1995). The lesson is clear: no one organization, function, or discipline can solve ecological problems individually; a team/alliance approach must be employed to bring to bear the necessary skills and to achieve consensus among the varied disciplines, interests, and stakeholders who are part of the problem as well as the solution.

Product-Specific Sustainable Marketing Audit

The first step in marketing planning is to gather appropriate information concerning "where we are now." This requires conducting a traditional marketing audit, a process that has a fundamental purpose—to provide guidance for building the marketing plan. Marketing audits vary tremendously in exact coverage and complexity depending on products, markets, company size, organizational specialization, and management goals. Kotler (1997) defines the audit process as follows:

> A marketing audit is a comprehensive, systematic, independent, and periodic examination of a company's—or business unit's—marketing environment, objectives, strategies, and activities with a view to determining problem areas and opportunities and recommending a plan of action to improve the company's marketing performance. (p. 777)

The framework of a traditional marketing audit is outlined in Kotler (1997:780-81).

Sustainability Dimension: An Added Component

In this book, the term *marketing audit* means a product-specific analysis as opposed to a focus on either facilities, functions, or processes. Therefore, a sustainable marketing audit concentrates on understanding the ecological burdens and implications of the firm's current and proposed marketing strategies for a product. But because environmental subject matter is specialized, it should be viewed as a component (module) to be added to Kotler's traditional outline. Because the major issues involve resource use and waste generation, and these factors are a function of the firm's marketing mix decisions, the approach adopted here is to structure the audit primarily around the "four P's" (i.e., product, place/channel networks, promotion/communications, and pricing), the target market(s), and the current environmental culture of the firm. A suggested component outline is shown in Exhibit 3.7.

exhibit 3.7

Components of a Product-Specific Sustainable Marketing Audit: General Questions and Issues

1. Audit coverage:

   Set scoping and objectives.

2. Corporate environmental culture:

   Identify: environmental policy/mission statement; environmental reporting beyond compliance; present environmental programs/involvements; awareness/attitude of top management, middle management, and rank-and-file employees.

3. Product assessment:

   What specific waste generation patterns/insights/issues emerge in relation to product manufacturing processes and inventories?

   What specific waste generation patterns/insights/issues emerge in relation to product design, function, use, materials composition, and final disposal?

   What are the respective roles of product reuse, materials recycling, and materials transformation?

   Is changing/modifying the core benefits delivery system an option?

   Is changing manufacturing processes or process control systems an option?

   Have processes been designed to minimize the generation of solid, liquid, and gaseous manufacturing residues?

   Do product packaging materials generate large amounts of wastes/residuals (solid, liquid, gaseous) at production or user levels?

   Can disposable product packaging be downsized or shifted to reusable systems?

4. Channels (distribution) assessment:

   What specific waste generation patterns/insights/issues are posed by the channels/logistics requirements associated with product manufacturing and sale?

   Can channel inventories be further minimized and simplified?

   Do upstream materials used in product construction or manufacturing processes require energy-intensive transportation?

(continued)

exhibit 3.7   (Continued)

Do current transportation modes create significant operating residuals (solid, gaseous, liquid) as they operate?

Has materials/product movement been minimized to reduce air emissions from transportation?

Have transportation modes been selected to minimize air emissions?

Have personnel been trained in ecologically sound driving techniques?

Have industrial packaging sizes and types been standardized?

Have reusable packaging systems been analyzed as replacements for disposable systems?

If disposable packaging is unavoidable, are the materials recycled or designated as a supplier take-back item?

Have "sustainable criteria" been established for the selection of channel partners?

Are our reverse channel operations considered a profit center (enterprise approach) or merely a cost center?

5. Communications (promotion) assessment:

Can the specific environmental characteristics of our products be used to project a positive aura through marketing communications?

Can the overall environmental track record of our company be used to project a positive aura through marketing communications?

Are strategic alliances with environmental advocacy groups a possibility?

Does funding an environmental certification/labeling approach make sense?

Are our sustainable communications efforts coordinated across promotion mix elements?

Do we regularly feature our top management team in sustainable communications?

Has our sales force been trained about the environmental implications/ attributes of our product line(s) and overall company operations?

Have environmental product brochures been developed and distributed to relevant target groups?

Is "the environment" a constant "subject" within our current advertising program?

Do we publish a separate corporate environmental report (CER) or have a major environmental section within the usual annual report?

Is there an industry/product-related trade association actively promoting environmental issues on our behalf? Can we tie in more effectively?

---

exhibit 3.7   (Continued)

---

6. Pricing assessment:

   What environmental challenges are reflected in the pricing of this product?

   Has the accounting function developed environmental cost allocations that result in the full-cost approach to pricing?

   What is the relevance of the following pricing strategies to our situation: meet-the-competition/level pricing, premium green pricing, larger quantity pricing, complementary product pricing, service life pricing, take-back pricing, rent/lease pricing?

   Do our quantity discount schedules reasonably reflect the packaging reductions/efficiencies associated with larger individual-size purchases?

   Are any reduced environmental burdens experienced by our customers (designed in by us) adequately communicated as an element of "value added" in the pricing equation?

7. Target market(s) assessment:

   Has research examined the environmental issues associated with our product(s) as they relate to current and potential market segments?

   Has research examined the disposal behaviors of our customers?

   Is product final disposal by the customer an untapped opportunity to tie the customer to our brand or product on a relationship basis?

   What is the current environmental perception of our products by customers?

   What is the current environmental perception of our company by customers?

   Are specialized "green" segments relevant to our product lines?

NOTE: The reader is reminded that the questions and issues germane to the audit will largely be a function of the "position(s)" occupied by the firm in the product system life cycle.

In contrast to quantitative life-cycle assessment (LCA), the sustainable marketing audit is a decidedly qualitative, interpretative exercise. An important aspect is the ability to identify important issues and to discard information that is not important (i.e., engaging in the process of triage). In this regard, the opportunity to enhance sustainability through revised marketing plans will be realized only if the analyst understands the nature of P2 and R2 strategies from the start. This means that findings about resource use and waste generation become classified as "strengths/weaknesses" or "opportunities/threats" (SWOT analysis), depending on the firm's ability to implement realistic P2 and/or R2 solutions as a marketing response. For example, a small firm might find it a "weakness" to market its product in a disposable container. However, given limited financial resources, its only "opportunity" might be to attempt to neutralize this weakness by actively supporting local municipal recycling programs through marketing communications and package labeling approaches. By contrast, a large firm might be able to address the same concern (weakness) and convert it into a significant source of competitive advantage (strength) by seizing the opportunity to engage in a multimillion-dollar total package redesign effort that yields an innovative refillable consumer container system.

Product System Life-Cycle "Position(s)" of the Firm

When making environmental interpretations, the firm's "position(s)" in the PSLC is a major determinant of the types of ecological impacts relevant to the product under study. A firm can occupy one or more positions in the upstream, midstream, and downstream sectors of the PSLC. Depending on position(s) occupied, firms face different immediate sets of ecosystems concerns/challenges that are under their immediate control as well as different sets of upstream and downstream partners to whom they are linked in the waste generation sense. An auditor's job is to systematically review the firm's position(s) and linkages to other firms for their ecological relevance and significance in terms of the product's resource inputs (R/P→) and waste outputs (W→). For example, issues facing midstream manufacturers of finished products include industrial process waste, product design attributes/specifications, and any "green" requirements-standards imposed by ultimate buyers. By contrast, intermediaries (e.g., industrial distributors-wholesalers, retailers) face issues relating to product-related move-store process wastes, industrial/shipping packaging systems, and the need to conform to a variety of local waste management ordinances.

Audit Coverage and the 80/20 Rule

The extent of coverage of a given sustainable marketing audit will be governed by the objectives and scoping appropriate for the investigation. Many initial audits will be guided by the firm's given position(s) in the PSLC or will bounded by the channel network partners immediately adjacent in the channel, resulting in a partial LCA approach. In addition, audits may be limited to a product's impacts in designated facilities or to specific waste management areas/issues of immediate concern to management (e.g., the recycling of disposable packaging, product take-back, buyer disposition behavior).

As noted in Chapter 2, the justification of partial LCAs is the 80/20 principle. When conducting a sustainable marketing audit, 80/20 can be extended to include all aspects of the investigation; that is, the analyst must be alert to the likelihood that the process of triage will uncover a limited number of "hot spots" (e.g., products, processes, variables, customer factors) that represent the areas in which significant gains in environmental performance can be achieved.

Sustainable Marketing Audit Checklists

It must be emphasized that each sustainable marketing audit is an "original" in its own right; no two situations are identical. With this in mind, highly detailed checklists are available to assist the analyst in developing the correct set of questions to ask under the prevailing circumstances (Callenbach et al. 1993; Graedel and Allenby 1995; Winter 1988). As an interim step, Exhibit 3.7 identifies general-level questions and issues within each component (section) of the audit from which a more refined analysis can be developed.

Chapter Summary

Sustainable marketing is an extension of current marketing management practice but differs in three important ways. First, sustainable marketing adds *ecosystems* to the list of external factors that influence marketing decision making, where it serves as a physical limiting factor (mandate) that transcends all others. Second, in addition to the traditional decision criteria of (1) customer satisfaction and (2) meeting organizational goals (financial and other), sustainable marketing adds the requirement that marketing strategies be designed to (3) be compatible with ecosystems. Third, the decision domain of sustainable marketing is extended to include the PSLC as opposed to the much more limited range of the immediate channel network.

Sustainable marketing strategies ultimately derive from two interrelated concepts: (1) the IWM hierarchy and (2) the DFE process. The IWM hierarchy identifies the basic types of strategies to be employed, whereas DFE is the process through which sustainable marketing strategies are developed and implemented.

The first two levels of the IWM hierarchy designate the proactive sustainable marketing strategies discussed in this book: (1) P2 and (2) R2. P2 strategies focus on eliminating waste upfront through the more efficient conversion and use of resources. Besides using fewer resources to create equivalent customer benefits, P2 also generates less after-the-fact waste requiring costly cleanup (remedial actions). It is a long-term solution that must be designed in as production-consumption systems evolve over time. Therefore, P2 is equivalent to "getting more from less." Two substrategies are involved: (1) process P2 and (2) product P2. Process P2 focuses on eliminating product making and distribution of process wastes. Product P2 concentrates on product design factors that eliminate wastes inherent in the product proper.

By contrast, R2 strategies involve the routine recapture of products, materials, and energy values from waste (residual) streams after use and their eventual redeployment in a future life cycle. The idea is to create a circular system of continuing resource use, recapture, and reuse. Therefore, R2 is equivalent to "getting more from the same." R2 assumes that waste streams always will exist and attempts to make the recapture of resource values as efficient as possible. Theoretically, R2 kicks in after P2 applications have first been employed to downsize any waste outputs requiring handling. Three R2 substrategies are involved: (1) product reuse, (2) materials recycling, and (3) materials transformation. Product reuse involves remarketing already-made products to achieve additional use cycles. Materials recycling involves recapturing materials from waste streams, reducing them to generic raw materials (commodity) status, processing them to required quality specifications, and selling them to industrial buyers. Materials transformation involves incineration or chemical/biological alteration to recapture energy values or to create inert materials.

The IWM hierarchy also identifies a third approach: TD. This involves the direct release of emissions into ecosystems (e.g., landfilling, air and water releases, illegal dumping). For our purposes, it is regarded as a default option that must be deliberately minimized in the future, not as a proactive sustainable marketing strategy. But because maintaining absolute control over products, their use, and disposal is generally not possible once they are sold to customers, making products benign-by-design (which is largely accomplished by P2 efforts) is suggested as a fail-safe measure to accommodate unanticipated and inappropriate disposal scenarios. In addition, whereas P2 and R2 strategies contribute to dematerialization, TD does not because it represents a major form of linear disposal.

DFE originated in industrial design/product engineering and describes how the design process may be focused on building sets of positive ecological attributes into products. However, its application is generalizable to the other elements of the marketing mix, so it serves to actualize sustainable marketing strategy. Under the DFE approach, sustainable marketers first develop a comprehensive understanding of how waste is generated and prevented and then apply the DFE process to each element of the marketing mix. The idea is to enhance the probability that environmentally compatible products will be made available that also are satisfactory to customers and business.

The "products by markets" matrix approach to categorizing organizational strategies can be used to further delineate sustainable marketing efforts. Environmentally improved product strategies (i.e., essentially the same products with minor changes in ecological attributes) can be categorized as market penetration and market development approaches that also feature modest changes in the supporting PSLC. Environmentally reinvented product strategies (i.e., products featuring major changes in ecological attributes) can be categorized as product development and diversification approaches that likely will involve significant changes in the structure of the supporting PSLC. In particular, product reinvention strategies may represent major sources of environmental improvement that also translate into competitive/differential advantage for the firm.

Sustainable marketing requires the commitment of the organization to translate ecological concerns into action through marketing mix decisions. This suggests a new mission based on redirecting customer choices toward ecologically compatible consumption choices, reorienting the marketing mix to include such choices, and reorganizing firms into boundary-spanning delivery systems capable of meeting environmental challenges. Implementation will require a transition process that must occur over an extended period of time. A key ingredient is the total acceptance by top management of the stewardship ethic. An indicator that this has occurred is the presence of a written corporate environmental policy that articulates the issues and the desire of the firm to meet the ecological challenge. In addition, TQEM, cross-functional teams, and strategic alliances are tools/approaches that are relevant for implementing sustainable marketing strategies.

The first step in marketing planning is conducting a sustainable marketing audit, a product-focused analysis to determine "where we are now." Sustainability issues are an added component that supplement traditional marketing audit coverage. The position(s) of the firm in the PSLC (i.e., upstream, midstream, downstream) will determine the general issues and questions relevant to the inquiry. The extent of audit coverage (scoping) is governed by immediate objectives as defined by management. It also is likely that application of the 80/20 rule will be relevant to the investigation; that is, a small number of hot spots likely will emerge as areas in which significant environmental gains can be achieved.

chapter 4

Sustainable Products

Consumption is defined by the *American College Dictionary* as "the using up of goods and services (products) that have an exchangeable value" (Random House 1958:260). Because resource use and waste generation are the inescapable consequences of making and consuming products, product design is the core issue of sustainable marketing strategy. As the congressional Office of Technology Assessment (1992) has noted,

> Product design is a unique point of leverage from which to address environmental problems. Design is the stage where decisions are made regarding the types of resources and manufacturing processes to be used, and these ultimately determine the characteristics of waste streams. (p. 3)

Role of Product

As an element of the marketing mix, product is the true embodiment of the customer benefit delivery system. It has been defined as "a set of tangible and intangible attributes including packaging, color, price, quality, and brand, plus the seller's services and reputation" (Stanton, Etzel, and Walker 1994:211). The term *product,* also referred to as *form and function,* includes both physical goods and services as well as any combination of the two.

Product attributes (also called features, characteristics, or dimensions) may be described as core or auxiliary (Zikmund and d'Amico 1993). A product's core attributes deliver the basic benefits sought by customers and tend to be somewhat common within a product category (e.g., the ground beef patty in a hamburger). Auxiliary attributes provide supplementary benefits that differentiate one product version from another (e.g., the condiments on a hamburger) or serve to point out the distinctions among the offerings of different sellers (e.g., speed of service associated with a fast-food restaurant hamburger versus a gourmet restaurant hamburger). It is very important to note that product attributes, both core and auxiliary, are only a means to an end, not an end in themselves. Therefore, from a marketing perspective, it is important to remain simultaneously focused on what a product *is* (the bundle of attributes) as well as on what it *does* for the customer (the benefits derived through those attributes).

Sustainable Products: Solution to Pollution

Obviously, the introduction of genuinely sustainable products into economic systems on a massive scale would be a major solution to pollution. In the United States, the so-called "green products" category continues to show strong growth, as evidenced by the introduction of items ranging from Scotch Brite Never Rust Wool Soap Pads by 3M Corporation (made from 100 percent recycled high-density polyethylene [HDPE] plastic), to Rayovac's Renewal rechargeable battery, to Xerox's Verdefilm (a dry processing film system for commercial applications). As a percentage of all new product introductions in the United States, the "green products" category has increased its share from only 2.8 percent in 1988 to 9.5 percent in 1997. Within the 1997 totals, the "household products" subcategory had the largest percentage of introductions at 29.5 percent ("Green Product Introductions" 1998:3).

Sustainable Product Defined

But what defines sustainable (green) products? They possess positive ecological attributes that are nothing more than enhanced waste management factors that have been purposely designed in (embedded) through decisions concerning how products are made/manufactured, what they are made of, how they function, how long they last, how they are distributed, how they are used, and how they are disposed of at the end of useful service life. These decisions essentially operationalize pollution prevention (P2) and resource recovery (R2) strategies, and in so doing, they reduce eco-costs.

Nature of Ecological Attributes

Product ecological attributes may be classified as either (1) process specific or (2) product specific; both contribute to dematerialization. Process-specific ecological attributes reflect waste management characteristics that stem directly from the raw materials and processes used to manufacture products and make them available to customers through channel systems. Waste streams generated by manufacturing, wholesaling, or retailing facilities are examples.

Product-specific ecological attributes are inherent in the product form and function of the "product proper" that leaves the production facility and moves downstream through channel networks. They are part and parcel of "what the product is" and "what it does" in the future. The types and quantities of materials used in final product construction, including packaging, are examples. Others include factors such as product useful service life (e.g., disposable vs. durable), the waste streams that "spin off" as a product is used/operated by a customer (e.g., automobiles generate tailpipe emissions as they are driven), and how easy it is to disassemble a product for recycling.

Secondary/Auxiliary Role of Ecological Attributes

In most cases, ecological attributes are intangible, invisible, and of secondary importance to customers. They do not reflect the immediate core benefits that are the primary reason(s) why a product is purchased in the first place. Rather, they reflect long-term ecosystem needs that eventually revisit customers in terms of improved quality of life. For example, the use of recycled-source aluminum in new container manufacture can result in lower eco-costs due to the potential 95 percent energy savings. However, consumers simply do not know (nor do they care) about this ecological attribute because its presence affects neither product form (e.g., appearance, container strength) nor function (e.g., making available an effervescent and fresh-tasting drink).

In a few cases, ecological attributes have represented major, high-profile, core product features. For example, Deja Shoe, a product of Deja Inc., used recycled rubber components to differentiate its consumer products in an ill-fated attempt to stimulate environmentally driven purchases (White 1995);

however, any immediate customer benefits from purchasing shoes made from recycled rubber components were likely emotional at best (e.g., "I've helped the environment by buying this product; fewer tires will end up in landfills"). Any eventual impacts on consumers would be subtle, indirect, future improvements in quality of life—a factor that is very difficult for customers to comprehend and appreciate at the time of purchase (J. Walter Thompson USA 1991). This is one of the more challenging aspects of sustainable marketing—the need to educate short-term-oriented customers about the real long-term benefits to be derived through ecological attributes. (See Chapter 6 for a discussion of the educational objectives of sustainable communications.)

The Industrial Design Process

The term *design,* according to the *American Heritage Dictionary of the English Language,* means "to create or contrive for a particular purpose or effect" (Houghton Mifflin 1992:506). For better or worse, all products are designed. In the past, the power of design as a strategic weapon has been underestimated by marketers (Kotler and Rath 1984). But an understanding that superior design can be a basis for establishing competitive advantage is emerging in the marketing discipline (Berkowitz 1987; Blaich 1988; Lorenz 1986).

Likewise, the industrial design community is beginning to embrace the concept of total design management, an approach that recognizes that designing for customer satisfaction is an important element of total quality management (TQM), one capitalized on only by understanding customer needs. The result has been more marketable products "incorporating quality features which engage and delight the user" (Zaccai 1994:5).

Creating Form and Function

The purpose of industrial design is to literally bring to life product form and function. In undertaking this task, industrial designers have been described as "technology interpreters providing the humanizing link between technology and the user" (B. Bullock, Georgia Institute of Technology, personal communication, January 4, 1994). The goal of industrial design is "to improve the function, manufacture, and appropriateness of industrial products while raising them to the level of art" (Burnette 1990:4).

This goal typically is approached by developing a set of product attributes that reflect the needs of a diverse set of internal and external customers including manufacturing, marketing, regulators, and (most important) the customer (i.e., industrial user or consumer). The types of attributes considered include quality, performance, ergonomic-anthropometric-gerontological needs, style-image-appearance, manufacturing economy, ease of assembly/disassembly, user economy-costs, ease of repair-maintenance-service, durability/useful life, reliability, user convenience, ease/simplicity of operation, statutory-regulatory-legal requirements, and safety (Kotler and Rath 1984; Parsons 1989).

Attributes → Specifications

Attributes describe products at a general level. During the design process, attributes are translated into specifications that define in detail what the product is and "what the product has to do" (Ulrich and Eppinger 1995:55). Specifications can be stated as subdimensions that have operational definitions that include a metric value (i.e., how the specification will be measured) and a target value (i.e., the objective/criterion level sought). For example, one attribute of an automobile is "operating economy," one subdimension (specification) of which is "gasoline consumption rate." Final translation into a metric and target value could be as follows:

▓ Attribute: Operating economy
Specification: Gasoline consumption rate
Operational definition:
Metric: Miles per gallon at sea level
Target value: 40 miles per gallon

As a product is developed, designers, taking a holistic view, make trade-offs among attributes and specifications in an attempt to achieve optimal form and function. For example, given the product attribute "disposable aluminum container," complementary specifications and their corresponding metrics and target values could be as follows:

▓ Attribute: Disposable aluminum container
Specification 1: Container weight
Operational definition:
Metric: Grams
Target value: 16 grams per 12-ounce container

Specification 2: Distribution durability

Operational definition:

Metric: Breakage per 1,000 containers under normal distribution conditions

Target value: $\leq$ 20 per 1,000 (i.e., 2 percent)

Suppose that it is proposed that this container be downsized 15 percent to a new target value of 13.6 grams in an attempt to reduce packaging costs and the resultant waste stream volume attributable to its disposable design. However, the attribute "distribution durability" also must be considered, that is, the ability of the container to simultaneously withstand normal handling within the distribution system and deliver the product intact (see Specification 2). Furthermore, a test run of downsized containers is produced and shipped (i.e., the 13.6-gram version) and experiences a breakage in transit rate of 300 per 1,000 (i.e., 30 percent) in trials. Container weight is then reconfigured to 14.4 grams (this represents a 10 percent downsizing from the original configuration), and testing of this version achieves the breakage target value of $\leq$ 20/1,000, which represents and overall improvement. Bullock summarizes, "Effective industrial design results in customer satisfaction, reduced costs, and increased sales through striking a balance between the human and technical requirements of industry" (B. Bullock, Georgia Institute of Technology, personal communication, March 8, 1994).

Product Design-for-Environment

Like any other managed activity, the efficiency and effectiveness of the product design process can be enhanced by limiting the field of alternatives and developing a focus (purpose) for the effort. This is accomplished through a general narrowing strategy called design-for-X (DFX), where "X" is any specific set of product attributes (e.g., manufacturability, assembly, safety, serviceability, quality, ease of use) that goes beyond basic performance and functionality (Gatenby and Foo 1990).

Product Design-for-Environment Defined

Design-for-environment (DFE) is a subset of DFX, where "E" stands for the set of ecological attributes that makes a product compatible with ecosystems (Allenby 1991). Therefore, DFE may be defined as "a practice by which environmental considerations are integrated into product and process engineering design procedures" (Keoleian, Koch, and Menerey 1995:124). Because all products consume energy and material resources and thereby leave an environmental footprint, DFE is a design constant; that is, it is a design consideration associated with all products. Indeed, the Industrial Designers Society of America, a major professional association, expresses its support of this position through its publication of the "Design Principles of Environmental Stewardship" (Exhibit 4.1).

But DFE is not an end in itself. If it were, then the only acceptable product would likely be no product at all because this would create an absolute zero-waste, zero-discharge condition. Rather, products still must be designed with a focus on core and ancillary "X" attributes that deliver benefits to customers and reward companies with profits for efficiently doing so. The role of DFE is to concurrently add those attributes that moderate ecosystem impact along the way.

When "thinking" DFE, designers must take care to extend their vision to include both P2 and R2 goals. Within the extended product system life-cycle (PSLC) setting, they must be careful to include ecosystems as parties to transactions whose needs must be met along with those of traditional customers, manufacturing, distribution, and regulatory interests under TQM's definition of customer satisfaction. The logic is this: any wastes/pollution attributable to a product/process system represents a quality defect, one that erodes potential customer satisfaction. Consequently, removing such defects through DFE decisions directly enhances ultimate customer satisfaction (Keoleian and Menerey 1993:28).

Product Design-for-Environment Strategies

The sustainable marketing strategies developed in Chapter 3, P2 and R2, serve as the basis for categorizing product DFE applications. Although maintaining this separation is necessary to facilitate discussion and allow subtle distinctions to be made, several undercurrents should be kept in mind. First, DFE applications generally follow the "serial" priority of P2 *first* and R2 *second*. Second, DFE applications tend to be complementary and interactive rather than mutually exclusive; that is, final product solutions frequently involve blends of P2 and R2 that are supportive of each other. Finally, exercising the "null option" (i.e., deciding not to market a product or to

exhibit 4.1

Industrial Designers Society of America's
Design Principles of Environmental Stewardship

The concept and philosophy of DFE has been embraced by the Industrial Designers Society of America, a key professional association. This group recommends adoption of the following Design Principles of Environmental Stewardship:

1. *Advocacy of safe products and services.* Designers will advocate with their clients and employers the development of buildings, landscapes, products, communications, and spaces that minimize environmental harm and are safe for use by people.

2. *Protection of the biosphere.* Designers will seek to minimize the release of any pollutant that might endanger air, water, or the earth.

3. *Sustainable use of natural resources.* Designers will strive to make sustainable use of renewable natural resources including the protection of vegetation, wildlife habitats, open spaces, and wilderness.

4. *Reduction of waste and increasing recycling.* Designers will try to minimize waste. To this end, they will design for durability, adaptability, repair, and recycling and will include these criteria in their purchasing and specifying.

5. *Wise use of energy.* Designers will choose environmentally safe energy sources and adopt energy-conserving means of production and operation whenever possible.

6. *Reduction of risk.* Designers will seek to minimize environmental risk to the health of their employees and the users of their designs.

7. *Sharing of information.* Designers will share information that will help their peers make the best choices in specifying materials and processes.

SOURCE: Reprinted with permission from *Innovation* (1992), "The Design Principles of Environmental Stewardship," Vol. 11, No. 3, p. 3. *Innovation* is the journal of the Industrial Designers Society of America, Great Falls, VA.

eliminate a product feature because adverse ecological impacts are simply not correctable) remains a constant possibility.

Sustainable Product Objectives

At the general level, sustainable product objectives deal directly with waste management concerns and are reflected by DFE P2 and R2 decisions that (1) reduce the amounts of resources used (energy and materials) and waste generated as a consequence and (2) increase the amounts of waste by-products that are recovered and returned for future economic use (see Exhibit 3.3). The focus is on improving what might be described as the ecological utility of the product itself and the processes through which it is created. Several hypothetical examples of DFE P2 and R2 objectives are given in the following:

> Pollution prevention:
> 1. To eliminate the use of toxic substances in Product X and its production processes by January 1, 20___
> 2. To increase the service life of Product X from two years to five years by January 1, 20___
>
> Resource recovery:
> 1. To increase the recyclability of Product X by decreasing the number of materials in product construction from 12 to 4 by January 1, 20___
> 2. To make Product X 100 percent compatible with present recycling technology by using only standardized materials in construction by January 1, 20___

Of course, the firm must continue to emphasize traditional product objectives, which include (1) modifying product attributes to accommodate market change; (2) developing totally new products; (3) dropping obsolete, outdated, and unprofitable products; and (4) strengthening line coverage and relationships within the product mix. The intention in the short term is to make sure that the primary benefits sought by customers and profitability issues continue to be addressed while adding necessary ecological attributes. However, if present trends continue, then ecological product attributes likely will increase in importance relative to other product attributes as drivers of purchase behavior.

Product Design-for-Pollution Prevention

As noted in Chapter 3, the thrust of P2 strategies is to eliminate waste before it is generated. This means addressing the following question: how can net investment in resources per unit of ultimate benefit received by the customer be minimized? Given that zero-waste, zero-discharge technology currently is not available, P2's short-term objective is to make significant reductions in existing PSLC waste streams. Two P2 strategies for moving toward these goals are (1) manufacturing process specific and (2) manufacturing product specific (Exhibit 4.2).

Manufacturing Process-Specific Strategies

This subset of strategies focuses on the waste streams that spin off from product manufacturing and inventory processes. It builds on the idea that "product and process design are integrated end to end" (Gatenby and Foo 1990:4).

Changing Manufacturing Processes

Many industrial processes have relatively "dirty" or "wasteful" components. One way in which to correct this in the short run is to improve the present process by making relatively minor adjustments. Longer-term solutions are (1) to change out major process components and (2) to adopt totally new technologies. The degree of change opted for (i.e., minor change vs. major change) will be a function of the firm's present technological position and corporate philosophy. The discussion that follows focuses on how changes of various types/degrees can affect waste reduction in general.

One effect of process changes designed to enhance ecological performance can be immediate cost savings in terms of process materials, reduced waste stream processing, and reduced energy use. The following are some examples of process change applications that have such effects:

- Lockheed has replaced a paint stripping system that used solvents with a process that now uses high-speed plastic pellets to remove the paint, thereby avoiding costly hazardous waste disposal ("Paint Busters" 1993).
- In the steel industry, researchers have devised a breakthrough direct steel-making process that eliminates coking and sintering, two major sources of waste and pollution ("Science Newsfront" 1991).
- In the paper industry, unbleached paperboard can be substituted for its bleached equivalent, which eliminates a process (chlorine bleaching) that is directly linked to dioxin contamination (Boulton et al. 1991). Similarly, a hydrogen peroxide process can be substituted for traditional chlorine bleaching to achieve a bleached paper equivalent ("Hydrogen Peroxide Supplies" 1995).

---

exHibiT 4.2

▓▓▓▓▓▓▓▓▓▓▓▓▓▓▓▓▓▓

Product Design-for-Environment Strategies: Design-for-Pollution Prevention

Basic question addressed: How can net investment in resources per unit of ultimate benefit received by the customer be minimized?

Manufacturing process-specific strategies:
- Changing product manufacturing processes
- Changing manufacturing inventory processes

Product-specific strategies:
- Reducing materials intensity
- Modifying materials mix[a]
- Extending useful life
- Minimizing operating waste/energy consumption
- Reinventing the core benefit delivery system

---

a. Includes simplifying, eliminating, standardizing, substituting, reformulating, detoxifying, and avoiding dissipative materials as well as avoiding energy-intensive materials.

▓ In the fashion industry, Wrangler introduced Earth Wash jeans, which are made using low-impact dyes requiring 35 percent less water and 65 percent less sulfides than regular processes ("An Ecostyle Listing" 1993:29).

▓ In the printing industry, digital prepress technologies, such as "computer-to-printing-plate" systems, totally eliminate the need for traditional photographic plate making and the toxic chemicals and solid wastes associated with those processes ("Good Impressions" 1995).

It should be noted that many of the these examples demonstrate process detoxification, an approach useful for achieving environmental improvement. Because toxic materials are involved, this has implications for inventory management that are discussed later in this chapter.

Specific improvements also can be achieved by changing the ways in which given materials are routinely handled in the production setting. For example, acids are used extensively in production operations. The WADR (waste acid detoxification and reclamation) Process Spent Acid Recovery System is a P2 application that rejuvenates used acid, reduces the amount of hazardous waste (spent acid) that must be disposed by 90 percent, and reduces demand for virgin acid (E. Jones, Viatec Recovery Systems Inc., personal communication and sales literature, 1996). Similarly, Safety-Kleen Corporation has developed an equipment cleaner system that internally reprocesses toxic solvents, which reduces total solvent use as well as costly toxic waste disposal by a factor of 5 to 10 times (Kusz 1990).

Several other types of process changes are worthy of note. The first is the avoidance of processes that are inherently dissipative. A dissipative process is one that creates a waste stream at the time the process is undertaken that is not amenable to later resource recovery efforts (Ayres 1994); that is, there is no possibility of recapturing these materials at a later point in time because they have become contaminated or have been dispersed (dissipated) into the product itself or directly into ecosystems (i.e., entropy has been maximized; see discussion in Chapter 3). For example, processes that insert chlorofluorocarbons (CFCs) as refrigerants in air-conditioning systems would be classified as nondissipative because recycling systems are available to recover CFCs from old units/appliances at a later date. But the use of CFCs as a foam-blowing agent in polystyrene manufacture is a dissipative process because the spent CFCs are not recoverable during polystyrene recycling. Similar circumstances surround processes involving many types of heavy metals, sulfur, ammonia, and phosphoric acid (Ayres 1994).

Changing one manufacturing process sometimes can cause the dissipative factor to emerge because a complementary process also changes, resulting in a negative, although often unintended, impact on future recycling economics. For example, as its latest salvo in the cola wars, Pepsi is test marketing a two-liter "grip" bottle made from polyethylene terephthalate (PET). The advanced blow-molding technology that creates this "shaped" (i.e., non-straight-sided) container mandates the use of a heat-transfer process to embed labels in the plastic of the container body. This introduces pigment discoloration, a serious physical contaminant that reduces the value of subsequent recycled materials from this source because they do not meet the stringent "clear" color sort standard demanded by buyers (Ridgley 1998b). The lesson clearly is to avoid dissipative processes because they inhibit the efficiency and effectiveness of follow-on applications of R2 strategy.

In addition, opting for less energy-intensive technologies and process materials produces an automatic dividend of reduced demand for electric power and fossil fuels. For example, switching away from traditional painting or plating processes to powder coating technology to apply finishes reduces energy consumption as well as volatile organic compound (VOC) emissions. Also, because the overspray is a dry powder, up to 98 percent of it is retrievable, resulting in significant reductions in materials costs (Powder Coating Institute, personal communication, 1996).

How well manufacturing operations are controlled also influences waste generation. Improved process controls can lead to a reduction in the number of "out-of-spec" production runs that otherwise become waste. For example, when making coated papers, 3M Corporation experienced variations in oven temperatures during the initial phases of a drying cycle that led to a considerable amount of waste product. Development of a computerized climate control system reduced this variation and dramatically cut the amount of out-of-spec (waste) product experienced on each run (3M Corporation 1990). In a comprehensive plant redesign, Owens-Corning Fiberglass Corporation recently reopened its Jackson, Tennessee, fiberglass facility, which uses a new blend of materials and technologies as well as extensive computer-based process controls to virtually eliminate all air pollution and waste disposal costs associated with production (Bleakley 1994).

Simplification of products and the industrial processes that produce them also can reduce waste generation as follows. The avoidance of unnecessarily complex process and product designs automatically reduces the number of conversion, assembly, and fabrication steps in manufacturing and simplifies support services such as inventory handling and storage. This, in turn, translates into less opportunity for waste-generating errors to occur in the form of (1) out-of-spec production runs and (2) inventory-related accidents, including spills and the occurrence of damaged/deteriorated goods. In the Owens-Corning Fiberglass plant redesign example, part of the P2 gains are attributable to simplifying the plant's processes and reducing the number of products produced from three to only one—fiberglass (Bleakley 1994).

Changing Manufacturing Inventory Processes

Maintaining inventories of hazardous/toxic materials in support of production processes is problematic because such materials pose inherent risks to human health and safety as well as to the environment. They also represent definable eco-cost centers. In particular, inventory management requires compliance with a variety of statutes (i.e., local, state, federal) governing handling, cradle-to-grave record keeping, transportation, and disposal procedures, all of which translate into traceable administrative costs (Government Institutes Inc. 1995). Detoxifying processes and products eliminates this burden as well as the upstream demand for these materials and their attendant eco-costs.

Similarly, tighter inventory and material handling controls in general, including the way in which materials are stored, can moderate the risks of accidents/spills due to unnecessary handling and can reduce waste from deterioration or evaporative losses (i.e., fugitive emissions). Simplification of products and manufacturing processes has an additional inventory effect: it allows a given level of production to be supported by smaller and less diverse inventories. Standardizing materials has a similar effect. This is important because waste generation is positively correlated with inventory size for two reasons. First, wastes (eco-costs) are generated by the conversion processes necessary to bring inventoried items into existence. When less inventory is necessary in the first place, upstream eco-costs are reduced at various points in the PSLC. Second, smaller inventories translate into less potential to generate waste through accidents and the occurrence of damaged/deteriorated goods.

Finally, creative materials handling and storage solutions often pay un-expected dividends in terms of environmental improvement, risk reduction, and lower costs. For example, a major U.S. electronics firm has developed an on-site system for producing highly toxic arsine, a chemical with no known substitutes that is used in semiconductor manufacturing. The system produces arsine from less toxic chemicals only in the small quantities needed just prior to its use in production. This eliminates the need for three large-scale arsine storage facilities, each of which costs more than $1 million to build and maintain (Ember 1991). It also eliminates significant upstream eco-costs associated with off-site production and distribution of arsine.

Product-Specific Strategies

Product-specific P2 strategies focus on embedding waste-reducing attri-butes in the product proper; they include the aspects of primary, secondary, and industrial packaging. The need to adopt a front-end perspective is pointed out by Hawken (1993): "Designers must factor in the future utility of a product, and the avoidance of waste, from its inception" (p. 71). Product P2 substrategies affect five aspects of product design (Exhibit 4.2): (1) reducing materials intensity, (2) modifying materials mix, (3) extending product useful life, (4) minimizing product operating waste and/or energy use, and (5) reinventing the core benefit delivery system.

Reducing Materials Intensity

All materials incorporated into a product already have created a trail of past waste streams (eco-costs) associated with their initial resource conversions. Obviously, the absolute quantities of materials embodied in a final product directly influence the volume of past waste streams and also preordain those that must be managed in the future on disposal. Therefore, materials minimizing/downsizing strategies have the objective of reducing the quantities of resources in each unit of final product necessary to meet the needs and applications for which the product is intended.

First and foremost, the quantities of materials used in the end product can be analyzed and then minimized to a point consistent with expected use requirements, a practice called lightweighting, downsizing, or rightsizing. This is not to suggest that designers/engineers are not already sensitive to the costs of materials; it simply suggests going further and including an environmental rationale/perspective in the decision. This could involve the reconsideration of style factors that consume significant quantities of materials but do not enhance functional performance. However, materials should not be arbitrarily reduced to the point where performance reliability is eroded, causing premature product failure that generates unintended waste. For example, the automotive steel industry is fighting aluminum's "light weight" advantage through the development of steel body components that are 35 percent lighter. The well-known design firm, Porsche Engineering Services, designed this weight reduction while also cutting costs by 18 percent—and while maintaining the same crash resistance/impact standard as regular steel (Norton 1995:A4).

Materials lightweighting-downsizing-rightsizing is a particularly relevant strategy when considering product packaging. In this application, packages/containers are redesigned to use less materials or different materials while maintaining the ability to meet the needs of physical handling conditions within distribution channels (i.e., the distribution durability specification mentioned earlier in this chapter). For example, reducing the weight of Clorox bottles by switching from 3.5-pound (56-ounce) glass units to 3.5-ounce HDPE units reduced transportation fleet requirements by 25 percent (M. Riley, Clorox Company, personal communication, September 3, 1992). Substitution of plastic for glass also resulted in a dramatic 94 percent reduction in waste stream weight (i.e., reduction = 56.0 – 3.5 ounces / 56.0 ounces = .9375 = 94 percent). Less breakage during transit and improved consumer product safety were additional positive features.

When looking at other highly visible types of consumer packaging, important advances in materials downsizing can be documented as follows (Saphire 1995:9):

- Between 1972 and 1992, the weight of a 2-liter PET bottle dropped from 3.0 to 1.9 ounces, a 37 percent reduction.
- Between 1972 and 1995, the weight of a 12-fluid-ounce aluminum can dropped from 0.72 to 0.54 ounce, a 25 percent reduction.

The variety of package sizes offered also represents an important factor that influences materials costs and the quantity of packaging waste generated when delivering a given volume of product to the marketplace (Table 4.1). For example, it takes 24 percent less steel sheet stock to "can" one 6-ounce portion of cat food than to can two 3-ounce portions. This simply demonstrates a commonsense law of packaging: the ratio of packaging to product tends to go down as the size of the individual package increases. Eliminating small package sizes and offering products in larger packages is a waste reduction strategy that usually delivers significant decreases in packaging materials per unit of delivered product.

Conversely, proprietary packaging decisions that focus exclusively on enhancing sales may have the opposite effect. For example, in 1997, The Coca-Cola Company began extensive test marketing of a shaped 12-ounce aluminum container that emulates the famous Coke bottle profile. But the container's curvilinear sides require 10 to 15 percent more metal than its straight-sided counterpart to maintain equivalent tensile strength (LeMaire 1997:1). Obviously, the introduction of this container would represent a clear conflict with the objective of materials downsizing and the broader goal of dematerialization. Fortunately, perhaps, the company abandoned the experiment because "consumers weren't willing to pay more for the same product and contents they could buy at a cheaper price" ("Coke Crushes Experiment" 1998:B10).

Modifying Materials Mix

The quantities of materials used in product construction are one thing; the mix of materials is quite another. For example, standardizing materials is

TABLE 4.1

Package Volume and Materials Intensity/Efficiency

Package Material, Weight, and Volume	Package Weight per Ounce (grams)	Package Weight Saving[a] (percentage)
High-density polyethylene, 44.34 grams, 64.0 ounces	0.6928	—
High-density polyethylene, 69.39 grams, 128.0 ounces	0.5421	22
Polyethylene terephthalate, 28.92 grams, 20.0 ounces	1.4460	—
Polyethylene terephthalate, 59.61 grams, 67.6 ounces	0.8818	43
Aluminum, 14.37 grams, 12.0 ounces	1.1975	—
Aluminum, 38.53 grams, 32.0 ounces	1.2041	-1[b]
Steel, 27.55 grams, 3.0 ounces	9.1833	—
Steel, 41.89 grams, 6.0 ounces	6.9817	24

a. Package weight saving demonstrates the generally *higher efficiency* (i.e., lower materials intensity) of larger packages. The example calculation for high-density polyethylene is as follows:

$$1 - \frac{0.5421}{0.6928} = 0.2175 = 22\%$$

b. In the case of aluminum,, the larger package is actually slightly less efficient.

supportive of future R2 efforts because it simplifies the accumulation function that is crucial for efficient materials recycling (see additional comments under "Materials Recycling Strategies" subsection later in this chapter). Avoiding dissipative materials (i.e., those for which there are no resource recovery remedies) and hazardous/toxic materials also simplifies future accumulation and reduces costs by keeping contaminants out of future waste streams. The result is less downcycling or less need to dispose of unusable mixed wastes by landfilling or incineration. Specifying benign materials for product construction and packaging also ensures that the fail-safe "benign by design" default option will become operative if an item were unintentionally landfilled or incinerated. Using less energy-intensive materials has the background effect of reducing the eco-costs associated with forgone energy generation using fossil fuels.

Using hazardous/toxic materials as product components also might pose an eminent health threat under certain conditions. For example, vinyl mini-blinds manufactured in Mexico and Asian countries recently were found to contain lead to make the blind slats rigid and colorfast. However, it is known that prolonged exposure to heat and sunlight (i.e., normal conditions of use) causes decomposition that leaves behind a leaden dust that can be inhaled, thereby raising the possibility of lead poisoning, a severe health threat especially among children. The *Wall Street Journal* reports that 25 million sets of such blinds are imported into the United States each year by stores such as The Home Depot, which currently is removing all lead-contaminated mini-blinds from its stores and replacing them with lead-free models ("Vinyl Miniblinds" 1996). This costly action could have been avoided entirely if the products had undergone an environmental assessment/screening prior to marketing.

Some states have banned the inclusion of certain toxic materials in products, assuming that such items eventually will be landfilled or incinerated. For example, when L.A. Gear introduced running shoes containing a 1-gram, mercury-activated light switch in the heel, the company immediately ran afoul of Minnesota's ban on mercury (a toxic heavy metal) in product construction. After the company paid a $70,000 fine, the shoe was redesigned using steel ball bearings to activate the switch ("L.A. Gear to Pay" 1994; "Shoe Company" 1994). Other cases tell similar stories. For example, the packaging card for Duracell 9-volt batteries is now prominently labeled "Environmentally Improved—No Mercury Added," and lead-leaching brass impellers in submersible water well pumps have been replaced by impellers of benign composition ("Pump Makers" 1994).

The presence of dissipative or toxic/hazardous materials may represent a marketing opportunity to eliminate offensive materials, substitute benign materials, or reformulate the product. For example, paints commonly contain VOCs in the form of solvents that leach out of surfaces (evaporate) as the product dries—substances that are both dissipative and hazardous. As a marketing response, Glidden Company developed reformulated SPRED 2000 paints that are VOC/solvent-free (Exhibit 4.3). Similarly, the Clean Air Act triggered the reformulation of gasoline to eliminate lead anti-knock compounds as a way in which to reduce lead air pollution (Keoleian and Menerey 1993). Note that in both cases, the clear choice was to eliminate the offending material up front. However, after reformulation to accommodate environmental concerns, both products retain the ability to deliver the original product's benefits.

Extending Useful Life

Product useful life has been defined as "how long a system (product) will operate safely and meet performance standards when maintained properly and not subjected to stresses beyond stated limits" (Keoleian and Menerey 1993:63). As a P2 strategy, *extension* specifically refers to lengthening the

exhibit 4.3

Glidden SPRED 2000 Zero-VOC Paint

Concern For The Environment Is Changing The Way We Live. It Could Also Change The Way You Paint.

From the simple, personal act of recycling, to the complex international efforts to understand global warming, there is no denying the impact that concern for our environment will have on the way we, as caretakers of the planet, live in years to come.

Just as there is also no denying the responsibility that business and industry have to take positive steps today to ensure a cleaner and healthier tomorrow.

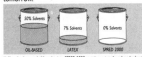

50% Solvents   7% Solvents   0% Solvents

OIL-BASED   LATEX   SPRED 2000

Unlike other latex and oil-based paints, SPRED 2000 contains no petroleum-based solvents.

One company taking just such an important first step is Glidden.

As a corporate goal, Glidden has committed itself to eliminating petroleum-based solvents from its entire line of decorative paints by the end of this decade.

Toward this end, the company recently introduced SPRED® 2000, the first high-quality latex paint made in America that is totally solvent-free.

The result is a paint that contains no volatile organic compounds,* or VOCs, that can react with nitro-
*According to EPA Test Method 24.

gen oxides in the presence of sunlight to form ground-level ozone, a component of smog.

Plus, unlike conventional latex paints, SPRED 2000 gives off none of the solvent odor that can spoil the air you and your family breathe.

CERTIFIED
No Smog-Producing Ingredients (VOCs)

Scientific Certification Systems has awarded SPRED 2000 its Certification Seal to verify Glidden's "No Smog-Producing Ingredients" technology breakthrough.

Yet, in both lab and field testing, SPRED 2000 wall paint has been shown to sacrifice nothing in terms of coverage or durability. In fact, it meets the same high standards established with Glidden's best-selling SPRED Satin® wall paints.

Reaffirming the fact that environmental responsibility does not have to come at the expense of quality.

For the name of the Glidden retailer nearest you, call **1-800-367-0862**. And make the clean air choice." With SPRED 2000.

To learn more about what Glidden is doing to address the concerns of the future, write to:

Glidden and The Environment
925 Euclid Avenue
Cleveland, Ohio 44115.

SPRED 2000 is available in flat and semi-gloss finishes.

Glidden

A Better Way To Paint.™
©1993, The Glidden Company

ICI *Paints World Leader*

SOURCE: Glidden Company (1993), "Concern for the Environment Is Changing the Way We Live . . .," advertisement in *National Geographic*, Vol. 183, No. 4, p. 141. Reprinted with permission of the Glidden Company.
NOTE: VOC = volatile organic compound.

duration of the use cycle that begins with product purchase and ends with product retirement, an event triggered by any number of factors including technological or fashion obsolescence, planned obsolescence, premature failure, need for cleaning, environmental or chemical corrosion, damage caused by accident or inappropriate use, or simple wear-out. The P2 strategy of extending a product's use cycle length clearly differs from the R2 strategy of product reuse, which involves achieving an extended series of back-to-back use cycles over time (see "Product Reuse Strategies" subsection later in this chapter). As pointed out in Chapter 3, extending product useful life is the antithesis of planned obsolescence, a practice that attempts to deliberately, and unethically, shorten a product's use cycle.

The length of a product's use cycle and the terms used to measure it are product specific. Some representative measures include (1) number of uses or operating cycles expected before average product failure; (2) length of operation in terms of minutes, hours, or years; and (3) shelf life. These measures give clues as to how DFE decisions can influence use cycle length. For example, a clothes dryer may be designed to withstand 10,000 duty cycles (cycle = a standard drying process), a 100-watt lightbulb is designed to deliver 1,710 average lumens for an average of 750 hours, and a radial tire is constructed to withstand an average of 45,000 miles of noncommercial use. Other products, such as chemicals, adhesives, and bonded materials, are subject to gradual deterioration, so they are designed and packaged to achieve a given shelf life in terms of years.

A basic approach for extending product life is to enhance physical durability. This usually requires an up-front investment in more materials per unit as a trade-off for extending product life. For example, products such as Tupperware storage containers are designed to withstand continual consumer refilling in the home. The benefit is an almost infinite number of use cycles achieved at the cost of using more materials on the front end (M. Cousins, Tupperware International, personal communication, April 23, 1992). Similarly, Procter & Gamble's concentrated Downey fabric softener is now supplied in a more durable container designed to be refilled in the home and to last for several years in this extended application ("Source Reduction" 1990).

Another life extension approach that applies to complex durable products is to make them adaptable and upgradeable to meet changing future user needs and to take full advantage of advances in technology. A classic example is the addition of disk storage and RAM capacity to personal computers to accommodate sophisticated software programs, whereas the basic machine remains intact. Adaptation/upgrading is accomplished through the use of replaceable modules, which represent a continuing after-market for manufacturers. Attention also must be given to providing customer education for do-it-yourselfers who may choose to perform the product changes themselves. A similar approach applies to mechanical products, where realized useful life is a direct function of proper maintenance, service, and repair. For example, the Saturn automobile, notable for user-friendly access to regularly serviced components, has door panels designed for easy removal and replacement by consumers using simple hand tools and without the need for extensive collateral body work.

It should be noted that successful life extension, while having a positive impact on the environment, likely will have a major negative impact on the demand for some products. For example, the automobile as we now know it might be a "loser" product in the making. As the *Wall Street Journal* comments, "Because automobiles are more expensive and durable, consumers won't purchase them as frequently" (Simison 1995:A2). This basic change in vehicle-buying habits reflects increased product service life, causing some to predict continuing flatness in auto sales in the short run and a permanent long-term decline (Suris and Stern 1995).

In the "rush to judgment" that suggests that extending product useful life always is the best solution, a caveat must be observed. When rapidly changing technology is a major competitive factor in a product market, continuing the use of older, inefficient technologies might be environmentally counterproductive. This is arguably the case for aging automobiles as follows. In 1991, it was reported that 22 percent of the vehicles in the collective U.S. fleet were pre-1980 vintage. These vehicles accounted for only 8 percent of the miles driven but emitted 40 percent of the hydrocarbons, 40 percent of the carbon monoxide, and 25 percent of the nitrogen oxide accounted for by all automobiles in the United States (Alberini et al. 1994:vii). Retiring these vehicles, rather than continuing their high-emissions operating lives, is a superior strategy from an air quality point of view.

Minimizing Operating Waste/Energy Consumption

Some products, durable goods in particular, possess the characteristic of consuming energy resources (e.g., electricity, fuel) and/or generating a continuing waste stream as they function; emissions from automobiles are a classic example. But the presence of this "continuous waste stream" characteristic is not always obvious. For example, as automobile tires wear, zinc oxide (a heavy metal) in the rubber compound is left behind on roadway surfaces, from which it migrates into local water systems through storm runoff, where it constitutes a subtle form of non-point source pollution (Silver and Rothman 1995).

Product reformulations and technological advances are useful approaches for combating the particular problem of waste derived from or associated with product use/operation. Taking the lead out of gasoline, and the corresponding major decline in lead pollution, is one of America's major environmental success stories. The gains made in basic gasoline engine technology are another example. A recently announced two-stroke gasoline engine technology promises dual benefits: (1) increased miles per gallon/reduced energy consumption and (2) reduced emissions (Smithers 1993). In yet another instance, the incorporation of "power down" technology in computers and related hardware is saving significant amounts of electricity, which in turn eliminates pollutants associated with power generation elsewhere. Known as the U.S. Environmental Protection Agency's (EPA) Energy Star Computer Program, President Clinton has mandated that the world's largest purchaser of computers, the U.S. government, purchase only Energy Star certified equipment (Betts 1994).

A recent case demonstrates the need to constantly monitor the functioning of mechanical products that generate pollutants because failing to do so can lead to costly penalties for violating environmental regulations. In this instance, General Motors recently agreed to pay a record fine of $45 million to settle federal charges that it installed devices on certain Cadillac engines that resulted in carbon monoxide emissions of as much as three times the legal EPA standard to go unchecked since 1991 (Gruley and Davidson 1995).

Relatively low-tech, commonsense approaches also may have a very positive impact on wastes generated by some products during their operation. For example, the typical residential flush toilet built before 1990 creates a waste stream of approximately 3.5 gallons of water per flush. However, the addition of a simple, retrofitted plastic part to a supply line functions to balance unequal tank and lower bowl filling rates, thereby reducing the waste stream by 1.5 gallons per flush (J. Levin, aquaSaver, personal communication and sales literature, 1994). This savings potential was recognized and developed as a product adaptation (brand name aquaSaver, installation time 1 minute) after a careful and insightful review by a master plumber. Looking forward, the Energy Policy Act of 1992 requires that all new residential flush toilets use no more than 1.6 gallons per flush, thus prompting Kohler and other manufacturers to design commodes that meet this specific waste management standard ("Details" 1996; U.S. Congress 1992).

Other approaches that demonstrate reducing/eliminating waste during use or associated with product operation are as follows:

- A camera features a built-in flash, thereby eliminating the process of buying, using, and disposing of used flashbulbs/cubes.
- A copying machine is programmed to copy on two sides as the standard option to minimize the use of paper.
- A lawn mower is redesigned as a mulcher to eliminate the need to bag and dispose of yard waste.
- Fashion merchandisers make garments "machine washable," which eliminates the need for perchloroethylene (PCE), a hazardous solvent used when fabrics are "dry clean only."

Reinventing the Core Benefit Delivery System

The format through which a product delivers its benefits, the core benefits delivery system, always has been a major focus of marketers operating under the dictum that "It is not what the product is, but what it does, that people buy." A product's core benefit delivery system is a major determinant of waste streams to be generated over the PSLC because it defines the materials and processes required to fulfill form and function. Changing the core system to achieve a cleaner delivery of equivalent or superior benefits probably is the most radical application of sustainable marketing P2 strategy. In this undertaking, the ideal scenario would be to lower costs, increase environmental benefits, maintain or increase customer satisfaction, and increase profits.

High-technology breakthroughs can represent an important source of core benefits delivery system change that translates into environmental improvement. For example, the *Encyclopedia Britannica* provides access to information. The traditional hard copy (bound set) version costs $1,500, but interacting with the new, paperless CD-ROM version provides not only equivalent information but also enhanced educational benefits—for a price of only $995. Whereas both options provide customer benefits, each is the result of a decidedly different form of delivery system that initiates a unique set of PSLC-associated ecosystem impacts to consider. The greeting card industry and catalog marketers, such as Spiegel Inc., also are embracing such paperless product delivery approaches (Bounds 1996; Coleman 1996).

Similarly, the new Helios digital imaging technology by the Polaroid Corporation makes it possible to meet the highest quality medical imaging

exhibit 4.4

▓▓▓▓▓▓▓▓▓▓▓▓▓▓

Greener Imaging: Polaroid's Helios System

Traditional radiographic film recording systems, used by radiologists, use silver halide technology. Although silver halide was an enormous imaging breakthrough, its viable image quality and mandatory "wet" processing contribute to inconsistent results and serious toxic chemical disposal issues.

Polaroid's new "dry" laser system is a breakthrough technology that is cost-effective and environmentally friendly. The Helios laser system for ultrasound and nuclear medicine diagnostic studies eliminates wet chemical processing, cassettes, darkrooms, and toxic waste disposal. It produces high-quality images with consistency and adds additional cost savings due to higher patient throughput. It also eliminates the environmental and Office of Safety and Health Administration problems associated with chemical processing. With dry imaging, no chemical waste is discharged, and this in turn eliminates the legal responsibilities of cradle-to-grave responsibilities.

The benefits of the Helios system are numerous. Environmental hazards are eliminated, the annual cost savings are considerable, the imaging is superior to that of silver halide, and more patients can be examined each day because the images can be viewed while they are being taken.

SOURCES: Helios System Data Sheet 1 and personal communication dated June 16, 1996.

standards using a "dry" technology, thereby avoiding the hazardous waste streams associated with the use of "wet" photographic development processes (Exhibit 4.4). Finally, the technological superiority of glass fiber-optic materials over copper in telecommunications lines has eliminated demand for large quantities of copper, which eliminates the damaging environmental impacts associated with basic copper mining at the extraction level. In addition, this new technology offers vastly increased information-carrying capacity and enhanced system longevity as well as immunity from lightning strikes and corrosion damage, which dramatically reduces future replacement, maintenance, and waste management costs (Gilder 1990; Young 1992).

TABLE 4.2

Product Concentration, Package Volume, and Materials Intensity/Efficiency

Package Material	Package Weight (grams)	(ounces)	Package Weight per Use (grams)	Package Weight Saving[a] (percentage)
High-density polyethylene (1)	69.39	128	2.1684	—
High-density polyethylene (2)	44.34	64	1.3884	36

NOTE: Assumptions:
  High-density polyethylene (1) = unconcentrated liquid product = 4 ounces per use.
  High-density polyethylene (2) = concentrated liquid product = 2 ounces per use.
Both packages deliver 32 uses.

a. Relative decrease $= 1 - \dfrac{1.3884}{2.1684} = .3597$, or 36%

Low-technology adaptations also are a source of core system change. For example, product concentration alters the form of a product but not its function. When Procter & Gamble concentrates a detergent by reducing the water content, the reduced weight and volume translates into reduced shipping costs. Consumers add water at the time of use or simply use the product in concentrated form to obtain equivalent results. This alternative also triggers a collateral packaging benefit: less intensive use of packaging materials because more units of use (i.e., wash loads) are now delivered to customers in smaller packages (Table 4.2). Concentrated products also are key elements of the in-home refillable systems that use durable containers to capitalize on the benefits of extended product useful life.

Product Design-for-Resource Recovery

R2 accepts the proposition that even after the rigorous application of P2 approaches, generation of at least some waste/residuals is an unavoidable by-product of production-consumption activities at all levels. Because materials/residuals bearing the label "waste" are valueless by definition, design-for-R2 decisions have the underlying purpose of making "waste" a transient phenomenon. Therefore, product design-for-R2 addresses the following question: how can investment in resources in "already-made" products be efficiently recaptured for future redeployment?

---

exhibit 4.5

▦▦▦▦▦▦▦▦

Product Design-for-Environment Strategies: Design-for-Resource Recovery

Basic question addressed: How can investment in resources in "already made" products be efficiently recaptured for future redeployment?

Product reuse strategies:
- Adopting reusable packaging systems
- Remanufacturing/reconditioning/repairing
- Reusing in an alternative application

Materials recycling strategies:
- Modifying materials mix[a]
- Designing for disassembly (demanufacturing)
- Designing for recycling process compatibility
- Adopting materials coding systems
- Specifying recycled-source materials

Materials transformation strategies:
- Designing for waste-to-energy conversion
- Designing for composting

---

a. Includes simplifying, eliminating, standardizing, substituting, reformulating, detoxifying, and avoiding dissipative materials.

Waste streams are generated by both manufacturing-distribution processes and the product proper. As noted earlier, process P2 can have the collateral effect of simplifying the waste streams generated by facilities, thus reducing entropy and enhancing potential materials recovery efficiency. The actual recovery of materials is a channels strategy decision (see Chapter 5). The product R2 design strategies discussed in this chapter relate to the future downstream recapture of resources from already-made products. In this regard, three R2 strategies serve to focus design decisions on the recapture challenge: (1) product reuse, (2) materials recycling, and (3) materials transformation (Exhibit 4.5). Whereas the life of the materials in products is extended in all cases (i.e., getting more from the same), these strategies are differentiated by the degree to which the original product's form and function is retained for future use.

Product Reuse Strategies

Product reuse strategies involve continuing the use of an already-manufactured durable or nondurable good in essentially its original form. Whereas the process P2 strategy of extending product useful life refers to the length of a single use cycle, R2 product reuse applications involve programming a set of back-to-back use cycles over time. In short, at the end of Use Cycle 1, the product is recaptured (recovered) and returned to service (Use Cycles 2, 3, . . . *n*) after undergoing some degree of cleanup, repair, upgrading, or other modification. Within the product reuse category (Exhibit 4.5), substrategies are distinguished by the degree of cleanup, modification, or change that takes place before the product is returned to service in a subsequent use cycle and include (1) adopting reusable packaging systems, (2) remanufacturing/reconditioning/repairing (R/R/R), and (3) reusing in an alternative application.

Adopting Reusable Packaging Systems

Reusable packaging systems involve virtually no modification of the packages in question once they have been produced but do subject them to a cycle of recapture, cleaning and inspection, and additional handling within reverse channels/logistics networks prior to their return to service. The point is to keep the packages "going and going and going" (circulating) like the well-known Energizer rabbit. Reusable industrial packaging systems and reusable consumer packaging systems are the two major forms of this strategy in which product DFE decisions play an aggressive role.

Reusable industrial packaging systems are used for handling a wide variety of consumer food products, beverages, and retail and industrial merchandise. They consist of crates, containers, boxes, pallets, banding, sheeting, and void-fill materials (e.g., polystyrene peanuts). Traditional packaging objectives remain in force: (1) product protection, (2) preservation, and (3) unitization (i.e., holding units of products together for efficient/economic distribution). In contrast to traditional one-way (disposable) shipping systems, reusables require the general design attribute of being structurally durable to withstand the rigors of repeat handling in reverse channel systems. This enhanced durability factor is achieved through an up-front investment in additional materials in product construction. But as the trippage rate (i.e., the number times the package goes through the reuse cycle) increases, this investment is rapidly paid back. The magnitude of savings is documented by Saphire (1994) as follows:

> Over the course of its lifetime, a 2-cubic-foot plastic reusable shipping container weighing 5.5 pounds and making 250 trips will replace 250 1.5-pound single-use corrugated boxes weighing a total of 375 pounds. The single-use container will generate 98.5 percent more waste measured in weight than [will] the reusable container (5.5 vs. 375 pounds). (p. 5)

Reusable industrial packages also may exhibit a number of other design features that facilitate large-volume shipping, handling, and storage functions within channel networks. Under various conditions, these may include the following (Saphire 1994:8):

- Collapsibility: Container walls fold down to minimize the space (capacity) required to transport and store empty containers.
- Nestability: One container nests inside another, thereby facilitating the transportation and storage of empties.
- Stackability: Container tops and bottoms lock together to allow greater stacking height in storage facilities.
- Lids: To protect contents, separate lids facilitate access to the container's contents; attached lids may save handling time.
- Side access: This involves mounting side doors that allow entry to stacked containers without disturbing the stack.
- Solid versus lattice-work walls and bottoms: Solid walls facilitate the handling of bulk materials (e.g., liquids, chemicals) and protect against contamination; lattice construction downsizes materials, allows ventilation, and facilitates drainage when containers must be sanitized.
- Size: This will tend to be a function of whether the container will be manually or mechanically handled; container size also is tied to preset standards within given distribution systems.

As already noted, the value of these attributes depends entirely on the conditions associated with the industrial packaging problem at hand. For example, it is reported that Toyota ruled out collapsibility in a parts shipping system because the containers were used to return dunnage (i.e., cushioning and padding materials) to suppliers; nestability also was ruled out because nested containers require slanted walls that reduce cubic volume (Saphire 1994:8). Similarly, conditions facing Xerox, a multinational producer of copiers, printers, computer software, and other electronic products, led the company to adopt a middle-ground variant of pure reusability—a system that uses only nine standard extended-life (i.e., limited reusable) corrugated packages (Saphire 1994:10).

Reusable consumer packaging systems often involve refillable beverage containers, made of either glass or plastic, that incorporate a resealable closure system in the design. By contrast, metal containers often feature one-way tab pulls that generally preclude their use in refill systems. Consumer refillables also require the design attribute of being structurally stronger than one-way packages because they have to withstand 8 to 25 trips through distribution channels before they are retired. Again, this dictates an up-front investment in additional product construction materials to meet the distribution durability objective and a well-developed reverse channel network (concurrent Stage 5 of the PSLC) to perform the recapture function (see Chapter 5). But the investment in materials can be paid back quickly as trippage increases, as is demonstrated by the exponential decreases in the weight of glass and plastics packaging materials required to deliver the given quantities of consumer products shown in Exhibit 4.6. However, other factors, including collection, transportation, and sanitization costs, have to be considered when comparing refillable and single-use (disposable) alternatives. It also should be noted in passing that the plastic and paper bags used by grocery stores and other retailers also have "reuse as is" potential that is largely a function of customer awareness and training.

Remanufacturing/Reconditioning/Repairing

R/R/R strategies have particular application to durable consumer goods, industrial capital equipment, and components. They represent a hierarchy of applications based on how much the original product is modified before a new use cycle is initiated (see detailed definitions in Chapter 3). The DFE objective is straightforward: design in attributes that make it economical to routinely remanufacture, recondition, and repair products as appropriate. Relevant attributes include ease of disassembly and reassembly, which often involves incorporation of easy-to-replace components and/or modules, and the avoidance of one-way press fit, spot-weld, and adhesive bonding technologies that impede disassembly-reassembly operations (McConocha and Speh 1991:31).

Overall, R/R/R considerations largely parallel those discussed under the P2 strategy of extending product useful life. The difference is the planned recapture of the product at the end of its use cycle, its return to acceptable

exhibit 4.6

Comparison of Weight (in pounds) of Glass and
Plastic Refillable Bottles versus One-Way Bottles[a]

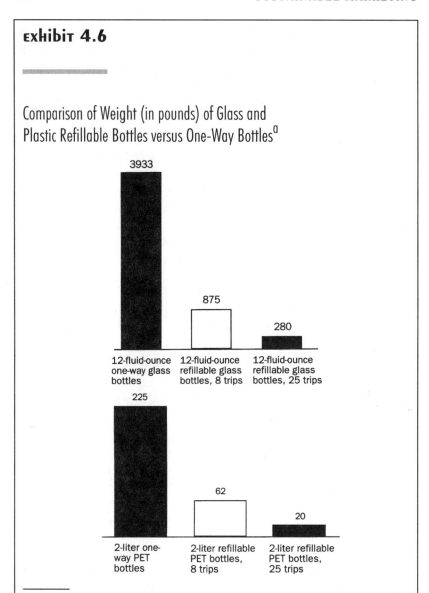

SOURCE: Saphire, David (1995), *Case Reopened: Reassessing Refillable Bottles,* New York: INFORM Inc. Reprinted with permission of INFORM Inc., 120 Wall Street, New York, NY 10011; phone: (212) 361-2400.
a. To deliver 1,000 gallons of beverage.

specifications, followed by its launch on a new use cycle. Of course, a key
marketing consideration associated with R/R/R strategies is designing the

Stage 5 channel networks necessary to perform the recapture function (see Chapter 5).

Reusing in an Alternative Application

The final product reuse strategy involves using the product "as is" in an application that differs in some basic way from its primary use. Some design changes may be warranted if this strategy is deliberately sought by the seller. For example, Welch's packages some of its jellies in drink-glass-size containers, known affectionately as "jelly glasses," which are specifically intended for long-term use in the home once the primary product (jelly) is consumed (Bechtel 1990). Product design enhancements include added durability and stylistic/functional touches to accommodate the secondary application. In this case, the jelly glass is emblazoned with permanent renderings of endangered species and feature a smooth-lipped, snap-on closure system.

A second and perhaps more mundane example is the reuse of the standard 5,000-sheet, 8.5 × 11-inch paper shipping carton as a record storage carton, as opposed to recycling the corrugated materials or terminal disposal. In this case, physical product modifications are superficial; the end of the carton is simply printed, so its contents can be easily marked for future identification (e.g., spaces are available for writing in the box's contents and date). Admittedly, this sort of reuse has very limited applications and is not viable for most products, but it does contribute to dematerialization, the conservation of resources, and the diversion of waste from landfills.

Materials Recycling Strategies

Materials recycling reduces products to the sets of basic materials out of which they are made; therefore, DFE decisions focus on enhancing the efficiency and effectiveness of future collection (recapture) and processing activities so that large quantities of specific quality, cost-competitive materials continuously flow from Stage 5 reverse waste management systems to user markets. The physical composition of products in terms of materials and the ability to break down products into their constituent material components are critical issues. Product decisions in this area often are referred under the broad label "design-for-recyclability" and relate to five aspects of product design (Exhibit 4.5): (1) modifying materials mix, (2) designing for disassembly (demanufacturing), (3) designing for recycling process compatibility, (4) adopting materials coding systems, and (5) specifying recycled-source materials. Each is discussed in turn in the following subsections.

Modifying Materials Mix

The mix of materials used in product construction, as well as the selection of specific materials, preordains future waste handling characteristics, both favorable and unfavorable, in the later stages of the PSLC. This is because materials decisions influence entropy, an engineering concept that states that as materials become more and more randomly mixed, it becomes more difficult or impossible to economically separate them for any further use (see discussion in Chapter 3). Therefore, increasing the complexity of the materials mix making up a product exacerbates entropy, making it harder to get to the desired result—the separation of large quantities of "on-spec" homogeneous materials from the mix of materials making up former products.

One approach for making any product more recyclable is to reduce the number of different materials used in its construction, that is, to simplify the mix of materials. A good example is the typical soft drink bottle. A 1-liter bottle constructed of the single polymer PET featuring no base cap, a PET plastic bottle top (not metal), water-soluble label glues, and paper labels is much more recyclable than the same bottle made from multiple plastics (PET bottle, HDPE base cap, low-density polyethylene label), a metal bottle cap with attached ring, and nonsoluble label glues (Flemming 1992). More recently, the Plastic Redesign Project, an initiative co-funded by the EPA and the University of Wisconsin, has sought to develop a consensus on 13 bottle redesign recommendations that industry could enact to simplify containers and thereby improve the overall efficiency of community recycling programs (Ridgley 1997).

The use of standardized materials is another approach that enhances recyclability. Standardization has the effect of reducing entropy; it facilitates the accumulation of the large quantities of recycled-source feedstocks by reducing the number of sorts required to achieve homogeneity. The increase in quantities allows the realization of economies of scale in processing, handling, and transportation activities. By contrast, the following two cases demonstrate the power of nonstandardized materials to retard recycling efforts. In September 1993, T. G. Lee Foods Inc. introduced the yellow milk jug (a 1-gallon HDPE container) in Central Florida markets as a way in which to differentiate its product (Stutzman 1993). This immediately unleashed a recycler backlash due to the fact that the nonstandard yellow containers had to be sorted out because colored HDPE commands a low price in comparison to clear HDPE products. In the second case, the brewing industry is considering the introduction of a new plastic resin called polyethylene naphthalate (PEN), which provides the barrier characteristics necessary to contain beer. Because PEN and soda bottle PET are chemically incompatible "look-alikes," the potential for nonstandard PEN to become a contaminant in present recycling sorting processes is enormous (Egan 1996b).

Finally, as noted earlier in the "Manufacturing Process-Specific Strategies" subsection, the incorporation of hazardous/toxic or dissipative processes in product manufacturing can abruptly surface later as a serious source of contamination when materials recycling is attempted (recall Pepsi's use of a heat-transfer labeling process). Obviously, then, controlling the materials mix is a major strategy for ensuring that recycling systems can economically achieve homogeneous sorts of materials.

Designing for Disassembly (Demanufacturing)

A related factor is the relative ease of separating (sorting) complex products into sets of homogeneous materials (components) for further handling. If materials recycling is the intended recovery alternative for durable products (e.g., appliances, automobiles, machinery, electronics), then the products should be designed for easy disassembly, a process also called demanufacturing. This involves designing in self-contained components and two-way (reversible) fastener systems that make possible the rapid mechanical separation and sorting of constituent parts. (Note: Many of the same attributes associated with R/R/R strategies also apply.) For example, as an outgrowth of German take-back legislation (i.e., the manufacturer is held responsible for product disposal), European automakers including BMW, Mercedes-Benz, Peugot, Renault, and Volkswagen currently are developing vehicles intentionally designed for easy disassembly (demanufacturing) at the ends of their useful lives (Corcoran 1992; Young 1992). Progress in this regard may be reflected in a recent Chrysler advertisement that states that 75 percent of the current Chrysler automobile is recyclable ("If We're Going to Save the Planet" 1995).

Designing for Recycling Process Compatibility

The recycling processes from which recovered materials eventually emerge as marketable commodities represent an interface that needs to be considered when designing future recyclability into a product. The presence of incompatibilities at this juncture can create unintended barriers to recycling efforts down the road. Likewise, the opportunity presents itself to build in enhancements that leverage recycling efficiency.

One aspect of recycling processing deals with the interaction of combinations of materials as they pass through sorting and upgrading systems at the end of product life. For example, take the case of a product that is to be made from two polymers (plastics), where one option is to use Polymers X and Y and a second option that achieves the same product functional result is to use Polymers X and Z. However, a recycling process compatibility analysis shows that Polymers X and Z are easily separated using a wet reclamation process after grinding (i.e., X sinks, Z floats), whereas Polymers X and Y both float and cannot be effectively separated. A decision to use the X-Z combination will enhance recycling processing efficiency (Abler 1990).

Another aspect of recycling process compatibility is transporting and handling large volumes of materials. Subtle changes in product design can lead to cost savings in these functional areas. For example, plastic containers feature the peculiarity of being difficult to densify for transporting; in short, light, uncompact shipments are uneconomical. Recognizing this, Evian has developed a PET bottled water container that easily compacts when empty. With future recyclability in mind, crumple creases were molded into the container's surface, which allow customers to easily crush (compact) them to 25 percent of their former volume before depositing them in recycling bins.

Adopting Materials Coding Systems

Downstream recycling also is enhanced when materials can be easily identified for physical sorting into homogeneous categories. This is particularly important when either physical properties (e.g., magnetic characteristic, weight) or visual appearance (e.g., many plastics look alike) make positive identification difficult. It follows that the use of materials coding systems may be an appropriate strategy on items such as metals and plastics. A standard coding system for plastic containers has been voluntarily implemented in the United States to facilitate the separation of incompatible look-alikes, such as PET (Code 1) and polyvinyl chloride (Code 3), the mixing of which drastically alters end-product quality and market value. This situation will be further exacerbated if the new look-alike plastic PEN is introduced as consumer packaging; obviously, it will have to be assigned a new code number to separate it from Codes 1 and 3. Taking this idea into the arena of complex products, Apple Computer now codes the plastic parts in its Macintosh Color Classic to facilitate later recycling (Betts 1994). Automakers in Europe and the United States also are moving to code materials to make it easier to recycle a higher percentage of the typical automobile.

Specifying Recycled-Source Materials

Specifying that a product be made from recycled contents materials has the basic effect of building demand for recycled-source materials in general. This general approach, called "buy recycled" in both the public and private sectors, is discussed in detail in Chapter 8.

Materials Transformation Strategies

Because materials transformation involves processes that cause the physical, chemical, or biological alteration of materials from one form to another or from one form to energy, only certain materials qualify for this alternative; therefore, materials selection is the key product design issue. The two major transformation substrategies are (1) waste-to-energy (WTE) conversion and (2) composting.

Designing for Waste-to-Energy Conversion

Obviously, materials destined for WTE conversion must be combustible in nature. This strategy features the co-objectives of (1) waste volume reduction and (2) the harvesting of energy values. Because the major drawback is the possibility that the combustion process will release air pollutants in the form of dioxins, furans, and heavy metals and also might leave behind heavy metal contaminants in the residual ash that remains after combustion, materials selection is the critical product/package design issue. Specifically, the selection of clean-burning materials that do not contain toxic/hazardous elements is required. This includes the avoidance of heavy metal-based printing inks in package labels. The use of soy-based organic inks is a solution to this problem and also eliminates the eco-costs (waste streams) associated with the former manufacture of heavy metal-based inks (Bechtel 1990; Kaldjian 1990).

Designing for Composting

Similarly, composting involves chemical-biological transformations; therefore, inputs must consist of degradable materials. The types of materials amenable to composting include paper/cellulose fibers, various forms of yard waste, food scraps/grease/oil, and treated sewage sludge. However, overt product design decisions revolve largely around packaging considerations. If composting is to be a package's recovery option, then specification of biodegradable materials is a requirement along with the avoidance of toxic/hazardous elements including heavy metal-based inks. In addition, some traditional consumer products, such as single-use diapers made from manufactured (unnatural) and natural materials (i.e., plastics and cellulose fibers), can be designed to facilitate the chemistry and effectiveness of composting processes. For example, Procter & Gamble has redesigned disposable diapers so that 80 percent of the materials contained in its present product lines do effectively biodegrade when subjected to proper composting conditions (Freeman 1991).

Product Classification Systems: Design-for-Environment Insights

Traditional product classification systems provide an opportunity for gaining useful insights about the development of sustainable products. As noted in the classic article by Murphy and Enis (1986), product typing systems can be based on any number of classification schemes. Exhibit 4.7 offers some proposed product classifications that are linked specifically to the sustainability/waste management dimension. However, it is clear that overlaps between classifications still occur and that using a multiclassification approach provides a richer understanding of the complexities and challenges involved.

Durability: Durable/Nondurable Products

This classification is based on the anticipated useful life of products in their initial use cycle. Durable product strategies that maximize useful life must emphasize designs that can withstand the rigors of customer use. Likewise, reusable container systems must be able to withstand repeated handling through multiple refilling/handling cycles, which means heavier construction

exнiвiт **4.7**

Product Classification Systems: Relationship to Sustainable Design

Classification System	*Sustainability/Waste Management Dimension*	*Sustainable Product Design Insights/Issues/Implications*
Durability: durable/ nondurable	Length of service life of resources in first or reuse applications.	1. Durables have long-term waste impacts and product life extension ramifications; opportunity to design for eventual demanufacturing. 2. Nondurables tend to be disposable and have immediate recycling implications; packaging is a major issue.
Design intensity: high design/low design	Product complexity factor in regard to construction and production processes.	1. High-design products tend to involve complex benefit delivery mechanisms; opportunity exists to reinvent form and function using breakthrough technologies. 2. Low-design products tend to be standardized and process intensive (constrained); immediate recycling implications; packaging is a major issue.
Degree of conversion: raw materials/components/ finished products	Stage in product system life cycle.	1. Different stages of the product system life cycle create vastly different waste streams. 2. Finished products manufacturers must consider their "ecologically empowered" position in the product system life cycle.
Naturalness: natural/ unnatural	Impact of resource use on survival of natural populations/stockpiles; potential incompatibility of unnatural products with natural systems.	1. The potential to deplete natural resources must be considered. 2. The careful management of unnatural materials flows is important.

and the development of retrieval systems. Durable products that are electrical and/or mechanical in nature can be designed to be maintainable, repairable, and upgradeable—factors that suggest applications of modular construction as well as "drop-in" components that make user-friendly the systematic changing out of assemblies. Consideration also must be given to waste generation and energy consumption during product use.

By contrast, nondurable products often reflect single-use/disposable strategies; therefore, the intensiveness of packaging materials is a major issue. Materials mix simplification and materials standardization, to facilitate recycling collection and processing on a large-volume basis, are additional factors of major importance. For example, Johnson Controls Inc. recently changed the construction of its 1- and 2-liter soda containers from two-piece construction (PET body and HDPE base cup) to the one-piece "big foot" configuration (i.e., PET body with no base cup required) to accommodate and complement PET recycling efforts (White 1994a).

Design Intensity: High-Design/Low-Design Products

The high-design/low-design distinction reflects the degree of complexity of the form and function required to deliver customer benefits; it places products on a continuum, with high design and low design occupying the bipolar extremes. On this continuum, high-design products may be characterized as being made up of large numbers of different materials and components; functional output often is achieved through an intricate set of interrelated components (e.g., visualize the complex electrical-mechanical systems that deliver "holes" via a Black & Decker $\frac{3}{8}$-inch, variable-speed hand drill).

It follows that high-design products often are technology driven, such as the Polaroid Helios digital imaging systems mentioned previously (Exhibit 4.4), which suggests an opportunity for achieving ecological advances through breakthrough technologies, functional approaches, and industrial process improvements. The inherent complexity and long service life of many high-design products also suggest that future recyclability must receive special attention. In this regard, the development of extensive expertise in the field of design-for-disassembly by German automakers in response to public and government concern for the environment has been cited previously. In addition, the high-design distinction often implies the potential for extending product life, so DFE must consider modular construction, maintainability, serviceability, and the strategy of product upgrading over time. This also underscores the need for marketing systems that deliver parts, service, and training (consumer and professional) in support of these design attributes.

By contrast, low-design products are relatively simple in materials mix and construction and are produced in relatively large quantities (e.g., packaging for high-turnover consumer goods). Sometimes, a minor product change can significantly reduce ecological impact, such as when plastic ties replace metal ties in boxes of trash bags. However, the manufacturing economics of many low-design products are process driven in the sense that product design and process design are inseparable. Examples include food, packaging, chemicals, and paper products that are mass produced. Adding sustainable attributes to such products might seem easy, but the unavoidable process design linkage might require significant changes in total production systems (e.g., retooling, major factory changes) because economies of scale are easily affected. In the case of the Johnson Controls "big foot" container cited previously, the move to the single-material PET design was accomplished only after developing and patenting a sophisticated, totally new production process involving significant expense (White 1994a). In addition, because many low-design products are high-turnover nondurables, packaging materials intensity is a very important design attribute.

Degree of Conversion: Raw Materials/ Components/Finished Products

This classification is linked to the stages in the PSLC. In a basic sense, the design challenge intensifies as products move toward ultimate consumption as finished products in either industrial or consumer markets as product complexity follows this same path. The most overt environmental insight provided by this classification is the constant reminder that the raw materials extraction and various other materials and components fabrication processes precede finished products manufacture and must be reviewed for ecosystems impact. Therefore, finished products manufacturers and distributors, who make up Stage 3 of the PSLC, have the opportunity to take advantage of their ecologically empowered position by selecting upstream partners who engage in appropriate waste management practices, perhaps as evidenced in the future by ISO 14000 certification (see Chapter 5).

Naturalness: Natural/Unnatural Products

This classification system emphasizes two ecological linkages. First, it points out the need to examine the expected ecological consequences of overusing given natural resources, a circumstance that can lead to depletion/ extinction. The general decline of the world fisheries due to overharvesting was cited in detail in Chapter 1. Although one might argue that the product "fish" is not subject to design decisions in the usual sense, certainly the design of sustainable aquaculture systems to make protein available for human consumption is a very overt production-consumption application.

This suggests that the conditions under which natural products are harvested is an important distinction that reflects a marketable ecological attribute. For example, farmed salmon from Chile and northwestern U.S. salmon harvested in the wild might taste the same to the average consumer and meet the same need, but they represent totally different ecological consequences and benefits. Similarly, manufacturers of housing and fine furniture are beginning to recognize the value of using "good wood" as opposed to wood of unspecified origin. Specifically, good wood refers to forest products that are harvested under managed/sustainable guidelines and are so certified by organizations such as Scientific Certification Systems (Schatz 1996).

Second, the distinction between natural and unnatural materials used in product manufacturing can be useful in screening for potential undesirable waste consequences. For example, the use of so-called "naturally colored cotton" eliminates the need for unnatural chemical dyes (and their attendant eco-costs) in later manufacturing processes (Schoonover 1993), an advantage that Australian cotton farmers hope to fully exploit (Witcher 1995). Similarly, making fashion garments out of "dry clean only" fabrics creates derived demand for PCE, a hazardous, unnatural solvent used in dry-cleaning processes. The uncontrolled dumping of PCE already has created a $1.4 billion cleanup problem in the state of Florida (Associated Press 1997:C3). The ecosystem hazard posed by this chlorine derivative is seen as so significant a threat that the state imposed a tax of $5 per gallon on its purchase several years ago (Associated Press 1994c:C3). Obviously, a major product option is to redesign the garment using natural, washable fabrics, thereby eliminating the market for this unnatural chemical along with its unacceptable eco-costs.

Implementing Product Design-for-Environment

In terms of issues, expertise, functions, and breadth and depth of intra- and interorganizational involvements, the daunting task facing managers charged with implementing DFE generally may be described as incredibly diverse and complex. In this section, the roles of cross-functional teams, strategic alliances, and the sustainable marketing audit are discussed in relation to this challenge.

Cross-Functional Teams

In both product and process development, the expertise of industrial design/engineering obviously is a key component. However, both marketing and manufacturing traditionally also have claimed the product development process as a unique area of functional concern. Because decisions and actions by these three organizational areas (called the basic triad) are inextricably intertwined, the need for a strong internal working partnership is axiomatic, especially when ecosystem impact is under scrutiny. This sets the stage for organizing internal work into cross-functional teams that bring together the necessary functionaries and participants. An expanded list of the disciplines/ functions playing a direct role on these teams includes (1) marketing, (2) industrial design, (3) environmental engineering, (4) process design engineering, (5) materials engineering, (6) production management, (7) ecology-chemistry-biological science, (8) industrial ecology, and (9) environmental law.

The cross-functional team approach, also called concurrent design, operates on the assumption that it is desirable for all of the relevant functional disciplines to be represented at the table from Day 1 of the developmental cycle (Katzenbach and Smith 1993; Wheelwright and Clark 1992). This achieves the objective of "conscious prevention," a condition in which the most important design challenges and trade-offs (ecological attributes and others) are identified early, thereby helping prevent costly and time-consuming redesign cycles at a later time. A simplified review of selected relationships and milestone events linking the major triad functions (i.e., marketing, industrial design, manufacturing) is presented in Exhibit 4.8. In this exhibit, concurrent activities within various phases of the developmental process are shown. The bottom row simply emphasizes the ongoing emphasis on ecosystems impact that must now be identified and formally addressed by team members during the total cycle.

Strategic Alliances

Strategic alliances have been described as "interorganizational liaisons where the participants (partners) make substantial investments in time, money,

exhibit 4.8

The Cross-Functional Team: Triad Interactions over the Product Development Process

Activities within the Phases of the Product Development Process/Milestone Decisions

Functional Area	Idea Generation/ Initial Screening→	Concept Development→	Business Analysis→	Product Development→	Test Marketing→	Commercialization
Marketing	Identify customer needs; eliminate loser concepts; conduct marketing research	Concept testing; conduct marketing research	Define target markets; estimate sales; conduct marketing research	Conduct product tests; conduct marketing research	Develop and implement marketing strategy; conduct marketing research	Execute rollout; achieve initial distribution and sales; measure customer satisfaction; conduct marketing research
Industrial design	Investigate feasibility of rough concepts	Refine product concepts; create prototypes; define product architecture			Resolve problems; finalize design	Evaluate product field performance
Manufacturing	Investigate process technology requirements and costs	Refine process technology requirements and costs			Finalize process systems; build test products	Ramp up production volume; meet product quotas; maintain quality
All functional areas	Assess ecosystem impact/implications as an integral aspect of each activity in each phase					

and expertise for the purpose of obtaining mutual benefits or seeking mutual objectives" (Fuller 1994a:315). In the context of DFE, these liaisons represent the natural teaming of organizations for the purpose of addressing the environmental impacts of products and the processes. This is a logical response because no one firm in the PSLC commands the expertise necessary to meet the functional, temporal, and geographic challenges ecological design problems pose. The array of potential alliance partners includes traditional competitors; industrial distributor, wholesale, and retail channel members; reverse/waste management specialists; local, state, and federal government agencies; trade associations; and environmental advocacy organizations.

The Vehicle Recycling Development Center is an example that might be described as a product-technology-process alliance. Formed by arch-competitors General Motors, Ford, and Chrysler, it has been established to move forward product technologies and processes that will make tomorrow's automobiles more recyclable ("Big Three Automakers" 1993). The growing belief among original equipment manufacturers that they bear some responsibility for improving downstream waste management efficiency and the threat of future take-back mandates are the likely instigators of this association. Solutions that emerge will represent DFE applications that focus on the specific objective of making future take-back efficient and effective in economic terms.

The strategic alliance between McDonald's Corporation and the Environmental Defense Fund (EDF) provides a second example demonstrating how traditional businesses and environmental advocacy groups can work together in partnership to conduct a meaningful analysis of the overall processes through which a product is manufactured and delivered to the market. First established in 1989, the McDonald's-EDF alliance combined the dual expertise of food system operations and environmental performance assessment into a top-to-bottom analysis of McDonald's network operations. This resulted in several initiatives including the testing of reusable shipping container systems and pallets, downsizing single-use packages, switching to alternative packaging materials (e.g., polystyrene to paper), and increasing purchases of recycled-contents products (McDonald's Corporation 1991; "A Perspective on the EDF-McDonald's Partnership" 1992).

It should be noted that the McDonald's-EDF alliance also served to defuse what might have been a bitter and dysfunctional confrontation between a high-profile business and an equally high-profile environmental advocacy group. By creating positive publicity, both McDonald's and the EDF have enhanced their credibility as organizations that are able to implement constructive, substantive, sustainable marketing solutions.

Sustainable Marketing Audit: Product Assessment

Obtaining information through a marketing audit is a prerequisite of implementation. To assist in the product assessment process, a number of generalized questions and issues are provided in Exhibit 3.7. It is very important to recognize that the "position(s)" of a firm in the PSLC will determine the significance of various product- and process-related factors in the analysis.

Chapter Summary

The product element of the marketing mix is the primary mechanism through which benefits are delivered to customers. Product design decisions determine the types of resources and manufacturing processes to be used to provide customer benefits. These decisions also determine the character of subsequent waste streams. Therefore, product design and reinvention is the core issue of sustainable marketing strategy.

Sustainable products possess positive ecological attributes that have been embedded via design decisions. These attributes represent operationalized P2 and R2 strategies that affect how products are manufactured, what they are made of, how they function, how long they last, how they are distributed, and how they eventually are disposed. But ecological attributes generally are secondary/auxiliary in character; they do not reflect the core benefits desired by the customer.

Product DFE is a special case of DFX, where "X" stands for the set of attributes focused on making the product attractive to the customer; "E" stands for the set of ecological attributes that makes the product compatible with ecosystems. Product DFE is a constant design consideration because all products create ecosystems burdens (eco-costs) to some extent. However, product DFE is not an end in itself. Products still must be designed with a focus on the set of core and ancillary attributes ("X") that deliver customer benefits and make it possible for companies to meet organizational goals. DFE's role is to concurrently add those attributes that moderate ecosystems impact.

Product DFE strategies involve P2 and R2 applications at the product level. It follows that sustainable product objectives are couched in terms of waste reduction/elimination and in enhancing the efficiency of future resource recapture. Product design-for-P2 includes two basic substrategies: (1) manufacturing process specific and (2) manufacturing product specific. The first focuses on eliminating/reducing waste streams that spin off from production activities. The second focuses on embedding ecological attributes directly in the product proper. Product design-for-R2 includes three basic substrategies: (1) product reuse, (2) materials recycling, and (3) materials transformation. Product reuse involves subjecting an already-made product to an additional use cycle (e.g., refillable containers). Materials recycling involves recapturing resources from waste streams, converting them to raw materials status, and using them in another production-consumption cycle (e.g., recapture of aluminum containers). Materials transformation involves converting materials to another form such as energy or compost (e.g., WTE systems).

Traditional product classification systems provide an opportunity for gaining useful insights about the development of sustainable products. The durability (durable/nondurable) distinction focuses on the issues of how to achieve the desired length of service life, whether it be deliberately extended (e.g., maintainable, durable items) or of short duration (e.g., disposable containers). The design intensity (high-design/low-design) distinction focuses on the issues of product complexity (e.g., the relative complexity of recycling an auto vs. a plastic bottle). The degree of conversion (raw materials/components/finished products) distinction focuses on position in the PSLC (e.g., upstream vs. midstream). The naturalness (natural/unnatural) distinction reinforces the ideas of natural resources conservation and the need to carefully manage the introduction of unnatural products/substances into ecosystems.

Implementing product DFE is a diverse and complex task that requires bringing together a plethora of skills and functional capabilities as well as achieving high levels of intra- and interorganizational involvement. Both cross-functional teams and strategic alliances are appropriate ways and means for addressing the challenge. In addition, the sustainable marketing audit product assessment is a major source of decision support information.

![decorative separator bar]

Sustainable Channel Networks

In marketing strategy, channel decisions create systems of organizations, called channel networks, that link producers of products with customers/end users. As demonstrated in Chapter 2, channel networks are the building blocks of the much broader product system life cycle (PSLC), and the organizations and markets within them are interrelated through marketing strategy. The various channel networks making up the stages of the PSLC include raw materials suppliers and manufacturers as well as intermediary organizations/ facilities (e.g., industrial distributors, wholesalers, distribution centers, transporters, retailers) that engage in pass-through trade.

Role of Channel Networks

The primary role of channel networks is to make products accessible to customers. Toward this end, channel organizations perform basic marketing functions (e.g., buying, selling, transportation, storage, financing, risk taking, standardization, developing marketing information) that add value to products by making them available at the right time, location, and price and by facilitating title transfer. These functions generally are nonmanufacturing in character and serve to enhance time, place, and possession utilities. Therefore, channel networks can be described as "value chains" in which each organization performs certain functions and is paid an appropriate markup for doing so.

Rosenbloom (1991) points out that channel decision making involves two distinct components: (1) logistics and (2) channel management. Logistics decisions (also called physical distribution) deal primarily with the movement and storage of finished and semifinished products and raw materials between points of acquisition/origination and points of consumption (Ballou 1985). Move-store functions occur at all levels of the PSLC and include detailed activities such as transportation, order processing, materials handling, inventory control, storage/warehousing facilities management, design and implementation of industrial packaging systems, management of parts and service support systems, and industrial site selection.

Channel management decisions determine the overall number and identity of organizations/facilities making up a channel network. Marketers tend to view logistics as subordinate to channel management. That is, it is first necessary to establish channel network boundaries; only then can decisions be made with the objective of maximizing the effectiveness and efficiency of moving and storing products within this framework of given organizations/facilities. Channel management decisions include (1) specifying the appropriate intensity of distribution (i.e., the number of retailers or wholesalers carrying the product); (2) identifying the different types of functional support that must be obtained from channel organizations/facilities; (3) selecting specific channel partners based on product mix fit, functional specialization, availability, costs, and other criteria; and (4) evaluating channel partner relationships over time.

Logistics and channel management components provide a basis for organizing this chapter. The logistics distinction is used to discuss channel design-for-environment (DFE) as it relates to the processing and packaging wastes generated by forward systems as well as the need for reverse channels to support resource recovery efforts. The channel management distinction is used to focus discussion on the role of retailing, channel partner selection, and various implementation issues associated with sustainable channel decisions.

Channel Design-for-Environment

It was noted in Chapter 3 that of the four elements of the marketing mix, product and channel network decisions have an important direct impact on waste generation, whereas communications and pricing decisions tend to reflect the environmental decisions and information generated in the first two areas. Because intermediary organizations making up channel networks perform move-store functions, channel DFE focuses on two factors: (1) moderating various forms of distribution process and product-packaging wastes that are generated as a consequence of forward (outbound) distribution and (2) designing effective Stage 5 reverse channel networks that concurrently manage the waste flows generated at all stages of the PSLC. (Note: Wastes associated with product manufacturing facilities were considered in Chapter 4.)

Channel Networks as Waste Generators

In the specific case of channels, the need to "make products accessible to customers" translates into a set of functional processes that require the conversion of resources at many levels. Under life-cycle assessment input-output assumptions (see Chapter 2), this means that all organizations/facilities/activities/customers in the channel network generate distribution process and packaging waste as they handle products on a pass-through basis; they also consume products/energy as they engage in functional activities. Reducing the volume of waste streams flowing from these sources represents an opportunity to apply process pollution prevention (P2) solutions; managing the waste streams that remain requires the implementation of R2 strategies.

Forward versus Reverse Channels

The usual notion of channel networks is one of forward, outbound flows of products from a manufacturer at Point A (the point of origin) to customers at Point B (the point of transaction). The idea is to efficiently and effectively accomplish Alderson's (1957) four aspects of sorting—sorting out, accumulation, allocation, and assorting—to match specialized manufacturing capabilities with specialized customer needs. The forward movement of products through channel networks is analogous to the flow of water through a pipe from the wellhead (manufacturer source) to a customer's kitchen sink for consumption by the glass.

By contrast, the term *reverse channel* is used to designate those cases in which a channel, or some portion of it, has been designed to accommodate flows of products or materials that occur in a direction opposite (backward) of that found in the usual forward setting (e.g., concurrent Stage 5 activities in the PSLC). During the past decade, the term *reverse/green logistics* has evolved to describe the various backward move-store functions that occur in such systems. The Council of Logistics Management (1993) defines reverse logistics as the logistics management skills and activities involved in reducing, managing, and disposing of hazardous and nonhazardous waste from packaging and products. It includes reverse distribution . . . , which causes goods and information to flow in the opposite direction of normal distribution activities. (p. 3)

According to Ross (1996), the goal of reverse logistics is "the effective coordination of both the forward and reverse processes necessary to fully utilize products and materials throughout their life cycles" (p. 8). This points out that managing reverse logistics is at least a secondary activity in many forward channels; however, in specialized reverse channels, it is the primary activity. In either case, reverse channels represent the implementation of R2 strategies that provide the recapture function for product reuse, materials recycling, and materials transformation systems. More recently, the term *take-back* has come into use to describe reverse channel programs/systems under which manufacturers recapture and assume responsibility for the disposal of products (or their residuals) at the end of the use cycle (Davis 1996).

Sustainable Channel Objectives

Improving the environmental performance of channel organizations still boils down to implementing P2 initiatives that reduce waste and R2 applications that remediate unavoidable waste streams. Therefore, sustainable channel objectives deal directly with both waste reduction concerns in forward channels and the efficiency of recapture operations in reverse channels (see Exhibit 3.3). Several hypothetical examples of objectives are given in the following:

Pollution prevention:
1. To reduce inventories by 25 percent by January 1, 20__
2. To reduce the number of accidental spills to zero by January 1, 20__

Resource recovery:
1. To replace 50 percent of all forward disposable industrial packaging with reusable systems by January 1, 20__
2. To increase the number of office wastepaper-generating locations served by reverse channels by 200 percent by January 1, 20__

In addition, it is important to recognize the role traditional channel objectives can play in providing customer access to products including sustainable products. This involves the usual forward issues of (1) degree of market coverage (i.e., intensive, selective, exclusive), (2) functional support requirements, and (3) creating appropriate retail image/ambiance. Just like other products, sustainable products must be functionally supported and made available on a competitive basis. Their sales success in the marketplace will move us closer to sustainability, and appropriate channels strategy can be a major contributing factor in making sales of sustainable products happen.

Channel Design-for-Pollution Prevention

Forward move-store activities generate a number of process wastes that result from (1) transportation activities, (2) the volume and handling of physical inventories, and (3) transportation/materials handling accidents. In general, a tightening up of present practices using R2 approaches is the first response. Changing the character of the delivery system occurs as longer-term P2 approaches evolve.

Transportation Wastes Minimization Strategies

Because transportation vehicles continuously consume energy (fuel) and discharge air emissions as they operate, the adoption of vehicle policies that stress fuel economy and the use of reduced emissions technology is an important consideration in achieving sustainability. Also, moving products fewer times and in large quantities (i.e., single products in bulk or consolidated shipments of different products) and avoiding distribution movement mistakes (i.e., product is shipped to the wrong location and must be reshipped) tend to lower environmental emissions per unit of delivered product.

The selection of transportation mode also is an important factor. For example, a study funded by Patagonia, a maker of outdoor clothing products and gear, suggests that using air freight increases environmental burdens (eco-costs) in the form of air emissions, whereas using intermodal ground transportation reduces them significantly (Hopkins and Allen 1994). However, as noted in the next section, transportation is only one element of the total cost of distribution, against which savings in inventory size and handling costs must be traded off.

Inventory Wastes Minimization Strategies

Minimizing inventory levels and associated storage facilities/space requirements and preventing damage/breakage within channels are areas that have hardly escaped scrutiny by logistics experts. Achieving a more precise match between supply (inventories) and demand (sales) leads to leaner (lower) inventories, a need for less storage space, and more efficient use of smaller-scale facilities, all of which suggest lower costs. Some experts even credit advances in inventory minimization with reducing volatility in the economy (Peske 1997). From the channel DFE perspective, inventory reductions are a form of P2 strategy because they result in reduced upstream conversions of materials, which spawns collateral savings in eco-costs (see Chapters 3 and 4).

Approaches for achieving a more precise match between supply and demand include electronic data interchange (EDI) and just-in-time (JIT) inventory systems. These techniques attempt to create steady flows of inventories that meet needs but avoid inventory peaks and valleys. In short, a trade-off occurs between transportation costs (TC) and inventory holding costs (IC) that minimizes the total costs of distribution (TCD): $TCD = TC + IC$ (Bowersox and Closs 1996; Stern, El-Ansary, and Coughlin 1996). Given a reasonably high correlation between eco-costs and TCD, the normal objective of TCD minimization already supports sustainability goals to a great extent. However, care must be taken to ensure that the drive to lower inventory holding costs does not occur solely for the benefit of one channel member, thereby resulting in a case of "ecological" suboptimization elsewhere in the system. For example, suboptimization may occur if the shipping of numerous small quantity orders was required as a condition of doing business by a powerful channel member and this practice increased overall transportation emissions in comparison to bulk shipments.

Fugitive Emissions Minimization Strategies

Another distribution process waste source is fugitive emissions resulting from transportation/materials handling accidents. Oil tanker spills, such as the Exxon *Valdez* debacle, are a classic example of exactly what needs to be avoided in the future. This concern is particularly relevant to organizations that routinely handle large quantities of hazardous or toxic materials. Given that such materials are absolutely essential to operations, one obvious minimization strategy is to reduce the quantities of products/materials being moved and stored in the first place to limit risk exposure. Another strategy is to redesign transportation equipment, facilities, and materials handling systems so that (1) the probability of on- or off-site spills is reduced and (2) those that do occur are immediately contained. For example, a recent *Wall Street Journal* advertisement by Mobil Corporation (1998) touts the firm's development and use of double-hulled tankers to reduce risks in oil transport. Similarly, German chemical maker Hoechst AG recently announced a $100.7 million program to clean up its operations after a series of accidents sparked public outrage. A short list of the firm's fugitive emissions problems includes (1) releasing a metric ton of herbicide (2,204.64 pounds) into the environment and failing to promptly notify authorities and (2) allowing 1.5 metric tons of acid to leak into the Main River. The firm's chairman, Juergen Dormann, has acknowledged Hoechst's difficulties and indicated that much of the money would be spent on modernizing industrial control systems. He also indicated that the practicality of producing dangerous chemicals in densely populated areas such as Frankfurt was being reexamined ("Hoechst Announces Cleanup Plan" 1996).

The Emergency Planning and Community Right-to-Know Act (EPCRA), passed by the U.S. Congress in 1986, mandates that channel members be adequately prepared to handle fugitive releases of U.S. Environmental Protection Agency-designated hazardous substances (Harrison 1992). Under EPCRA's emergency planning provisions, firms are required to cooperate with local emergency planning committees to develop evacuation plans, descriptions of available emergency equipment, and emergency notification and response procedures.

Channel Design-for-Resource Recovery

A major component of all R2 strategies is the logistics support provided by reverse channel networks that essentially divert flows of products/materials/wastes from terminal disposal (TD) in landfills. The following subsections examine reverse channels for product reuse, materials recycling, and materials transformation strategies.

Reverse Channels: Reusable Packaging System Strategies

Managing flows of product-related packaging moving both forward (outbound) and backward (reverse/inbound) in channel networks is an important logistics task. The routine and repetitive nature of within-channel shipping cycles and the bulk-breaking activities that take place within forward channels lead to situations in which large volumes of shipping/tertiary packaging routinely accumulate at, or flow through, given distribution locations called gateways. Consumer households also represent gateways where discarded product packaging accumulates.

There are two fundamental approaches to packaging: (1) disposable (single use) and (2) reusable. When discarded, disposable packaging can serve as an input into reverse materials recycling systems (see discussion later in this chapter). Reusable packaging is a form of product take-back and involves two substrategies: (1) reusable industrial packaging systems and (2) reusable consumer packaging systems.

Reusable Industrial Packaging Systems

Industrial packaging has been defined by Saphire (1994) as

> packaging used to ship goods from their point of origin, such as a production facility or farm, to their destination (e.g., to a manufacturer, wholesaler, retailer, or consumer). For distribution packaging, which includes boxes, crates, pallets, banding, and void-fill packaging (e.g., polystyrene "peanuts"), the greatest emphasis is placed on protective, functional (handling, opening, closing), and shipping considerations. The box or crate that physically contains the product is often referred to as the shipping container. (p. 3)

Under a reusable strategy, the R2 objective is to develop logistics networks that efficiently recapture containers/packages and routinely return them to service in a new shipping cycle. The fundamental benefits of reuse strategies are realized only if trippage rates are maximized; that is, the idea is to write off the extra up-front investment in materials in reusable containers/packages required to enhance durability, and any other fixed or variable handling costs, over a large number of back-to-back trips to dramatically minimize packaging resources used and costs per trip.

The ideal conditions for maximizing trippage appear to exist in closed-loop distribution systems in which industrial packages/containers routinely go back to the same point of origin while passing through the same standardized gateways. These ideal conditions include the following (Saphire 1994:7):

1. Short distribution distances: This expedites the return of containers to the point of origin.
2. Frequent deliveries: High frequency means high inventory turnover, which creates a continual availability of containers for collection at the time of delivery, which also translates into a small "float" of containers because few remain tied up in storage or the transportation pipeline.

3. Small number of parties (channel members): Controlling the return function is simplified when the number of parties handling the containers is small.

4. Company-owned vehicles: This usually implies the availability of "free" back-hauling capacity. This also applies to subcontractor fleets that are "dedicated" to a single customer.

JIT delivery is an approach for minimizing inventories that reflects conditions like those just outlined. JIT is based on making frequent deliveries of smaller quantities of materials to customers on an as-needed basis, as opposed to making infrequent deliveries of larger quantities that are then inventoried. One major JIT tactic is to bypass central receiving and deliver materials directly to the shop/plant floor location of use. This speeds up turnover and reduces inventory requirements, thereby freeing up storage space for use in production activities. JIT works best when vendors are in close proximity to customers, when the number of parties involved in transactions is small, and when participants are "dedicated" to working together (i.e., an exclusive or near exclusive relationship is maintained in regard to transportation equipment and shipping container use), a set of circumstances that are naturally compatible with reusable industrial packaging systems. As Saphire (1994) notes, "Working with fewer dedicated companies facilitates control and administration of empty containers, especially if companies use proprietary containers" (p. 10).

But reusable industrial packaging systems also can work in open-loop settings in which procedures are standardized and the packages or containers are relatively generic, meaning that a number of different firms can use them. In the open-loop case, a third-party logistics service contractor tracks and maintains a float/pool of containers and then rents them to multiple users as a generic commodity thorough regional depots (Coyle, Bardi, and Langley 1996). For example, the common use of wooden pallets in industrial shipping translates into a marketing opportunity. More than 1.5 billion pallets currently are on hand in the United States, and 400,000 more are produced each year, accounting for 27 percent of U.S. lumber production (Machalaba 1998:A1). By offering a nationwide pallet rental service to subscribers, Chep USA shifts waste management practice away from TD of old pallets in landfills to a pattern of cyclical reuse, which means that fewer pallets are needed to accomplish given product movements (Council of Logistics Management 1993).

In summary, the main environmental benefits of industrial packaging reuse are waste prevention and resource conservation, including both energy and raw materials. Potential cost benefits associated with reusable industrial packaging include (1) reduced packaging costs, (2) reduced damage in transit,

(3) avoided disposal costs, (4) reduced labor/handling costs, (5) reduced storage costs, and (6) reduced freight costs. These benefits, however, are earned only at the cost of developing and operating efficient recapture networks (reverse channels) that achieve high trippage rates (Saphire 1994:10).

Reusable Consumer Packaging Systems

Countries, states, or other jurisdictions with consumer packaging/container deposit laws often require retail and/or wholesale channel members to serve as points of take-back; that is, they are required to accept materials for entry into various R2 systems. This creates two types of reverse/backward flows of consumer containers. The first consists of single-use containers that usually are destined to be processed through reverse materials recycling channels, an application discussed later in this chapter. The second involves reusable/refillable beverage containers that are routed back to manufacturers' processing/bottling facilities.

Many of the specifics relevant to reusable industrial packaging systems also apply to consumer systems. But because the fickle consumer is now part of the take-back equation, along with scattered retail locations, some nuances exist. For instance, the admittedly small market share held by consumer beer and soft drink refillables, less than 10 percent in the United States (Saphire 1994:10), seems to be clustered in the following settings (p. 154):

1. The jurisdiction/state has a container deposit law: This tends to mandate and maintain an infrastructure that collects and refills bottles.
2. On-premises retail consumption occurs: The bottles do not leave the retail location, thereby easing the accumulation function.
3. A simplified distribution system exists: This often involves direct distribution to a limited number of local retail outlets (store door delivery systems). The number of parties handling the bottles is minimal.

Two other factors distinguish consumer refillables from reusable industrial packaging systems in terms of logistics functions. First, the widespread practice of using proprietary packages in the United States (i.e., packages that uniquely differentiate a given brand) makes it difficult to accomplish efficient quantity accumulation for refilling, especially when broad national markets and distribution is involved (i.e., packages are not interchangeable between sellers). Second, because refillables are used in human food contact applications, reverse channel networks for refillables must pay particular attention to accomplishing the functions of inspecting and sanitizing the inbound containers.

The advantages and successes of refillable consumer container systems appear to be largely dependent on local circumstances. It must be remembered that single-use (disposable) containers originally gained widespread acceptance in the United States because they played to consumers' universal desire for convenience; therefore, take-back may be seen as a "step back" by U.S. consumers. Just the opposite is true in Germany, where the share of refillable consumer containers is nearly 75 percent, clearly demonstrating that take-back (or not) is a culture-bound phenomenon (Fishbein 1994:86).

Interestingly, it has been suggested that even in the midst of the United States' "disposable everything" society, refillable systems might in fact represent a marketing promotion opportunity for some sellers to uniquely differentiate or position their products in a way that translates into brand loyalty (Saphire 1994); that is, once a beverage has been purchased in a proprietary refillable container, the implied obligation to return the container for refilling can lead to a bonding with customers that generates repeat purchases over time. An attempt to use refillable containers as a differentiating approach is demonstrated by the experience of the Schroeder Milk Company. This American firm operates a refillable milk jug system that uses one-half-gallon, high-density polyethylene (HDPE) containers. The reverse distribution problem was solved within the confines of the existing forward system by implementing a low-cost back-hauling approach that collects containers from retailers in company-owned delivery vehicles as they make their retail rounds. To guarantee product integrity, Schroeder Milk installed U.S. Food and Drug Administration-approved testing, sterilization, and refilling equipment. The refillable containers are expected to achieve a trippage rate of 50 round trips before disposal. When calculated over 50 trips, the 0.35-pound HDPE refillable jug displaces more than 5 pounds of waste when compared to its single-use counterpart (Kaldjian 1990). Obviously, a key aspect of this approach will be communications strategy designed to gain initial consumer participation and maintain it at high levels over time. Home delivery of bulk bottled water in reusable plastic containers is another example of tying the customer to the seller through an environmentally beneficial packaging system.

Reverse Channels: Remanufacturing/ Reconditioning/Repairing Strategies

Remanufacturing/reconditioning/repairing (R/R/R) represents a spectrum of reuse strategies that recapture products at the end of a base use cycle, return them to production/processing facilities for renewal to standard or upgraded specifications, and then make them available for resale through traditional forward channels. Also referred to as product recovery management, asset recovery, and take-back systems (Davis 1996; Thierry et al. 1995), the success of these strategies is dependent on the development of economic reverse channel networks that "close the loop" through which products are removed from service (recaptured) and returned to processors, including original equipment manufacturers. Although R/R/R may involve a variety of product types, the discussion in this chapter focuses on relatively high-value products such as computers, copiers, and related equipment and components. For these types of products, trade-in and exchange discounts/allowances (i.e., take-back pricing strategies) are becoming fairly common elements of marketing transactions (see Chapter 7).

Managing the Recapture Function

In contrast to the high volume and continuity that characterize materials recycling and reusable packaging channel networks, R/R/R recapture operations tend to be much more selective, sporadic, and low volume in nature. In the case of equipment, the challenge is to accomplish take-back from a wide array of user locations on an occasional, as-needed basis, frequently in conjunction with the sale of new equipment (i.e., an exchange/trade-in is part of the transaction). In such cases, recapture involves used equipment deinstallation (removal), packaging, and transportation on short notice. In this context, manufacturers have three choices: (1) using existing forward channel partners, (2) contracting with third-party specialists, or (3) having customers deinstall and directly ship used products to designated locations. The intermittent nature of the functional activities involved seems to explain the apparent lack of manufacturer-instigated corporate integrated networks to handle recapture.

Existing forward network partners might be able to provide a number of parallel functions, including collection and back-hauling, at relatively low costs. But it must be remembered that when taking back high-value products, the functional needs might be very intermittent, the locations needing service might be varied and irregular, and the work might involve a number of other requirements such as complex deinstallation and providing nonstandardized packaging and transportation services. In addition, if the forward system employs third-party carriers, then the advantages of "free" back-hauling generally are lost.

In addition, organizations in the forward channel network are specialized in carrying out forward functions. For example, most wholesalers and retailers lack the specialized equipment, facilities, and experience to deal effectively with high-value product take-back programs. If such programs are proposed, then the details of implementation must be thoroughly communicated to channel members to ensure a clear understanding of the program's objectives, the manufacturer's performance expectations, and the payback to be received by the participants. Manufacturers must be very careful to design take-back programs that do not interfere with, or dilute, the focus of outbound marketing efforts, which remain an intermediary's primary business interest.

For high-value products that require significant functional efforts to accomplish take-back, a favored option is to employ third-party specialists to handle the entire process. By consolidating the needs of several manufacturers into a unified business, such firms are able to achieve economies of scale in deinstallation, collection, packaging, and transportation activities. Serving as individual subcontractors, they represent a highly flexible alternative that can be employed as needed in different geographic markets. The manufacturer incurs costs only on a pay-as-you-go basis; overhead costs are avoided because this is a classic form of outsourcing. Another advantage is that the manufacturer is able to retain a focus on its core business. The customized third-party product take-back services available through North American High Value Products, an independent subcontractor, are described in Exhibit 5.1.

For items of lesser value, such as copier toner cartridges, it might be feasible to involve customers in a direct shipment system through which the items are returned to designated locations. Such situations are characterized by the relatively simple nature of the actions required by the end user (e.g., no complex deinstallation, outbound product packaging doubles as prelabeled and preposted return packaging). Canon Canada's international Clean Earth Campaign for the return of toner cartridges is an example that combines deinstallation by the customer with logistics provided by third-party specialist Canada Post (Exhibit 5.2). It must be noted, however, that although this program provides a good example of how to retrieve remanufacturable components, in this particular case they are not refilled; instead, they become a source of potentially recyclable materials.

Voluntary Action versus Mandated Take-Back

As noted in Chapter 3, R/R/R has been practiced for decades for purely economic reasons. Recognizing and emphasizing the parallel ecological benefits of these strategies is a natural adaptation to the changing business climate of the 1990s in which economy and ecology are beginning to merge; it also suggests a new source of competitive advantage, especially for firms already engaged in voluntary take-back. For example, the Xerox Corporation has

Exhibit 5.1

North American High Value
Products Third-Party Services

Specialized equipment deinstallation. HVP manages product returns for the Diagnostic Division of Miles Inc. When Miles sells new blood analyzer equipment to hospitals, laboratories, and clinics, it assumes reponsibility for disposing of the used units. In certain jurisdictions, only the original manufacturer can dispose of this equipment. HVP removes or "deinstalls" blood analyzers and related hardware from hospitals and clinics for analyzers and related hardware from hospitals and clinics for Miles. First, a Miles technician cleans and disinfects the equipment. Next, an HVP driver removes the certifiably disinfected property from the user facility and transports it to a Miles disassembly center, where it is reclaimed, refurbished, or destroyed.

Just-in-time leased equipment take-back. The physical condition of a product often deteriorates quickly after its lease or service contract ends. Thus, just-in-time deinstallation is essential to maintain the value of reusable products. HVP generally receives advance notification from its customer and schedules a deinstallation to be performed soon after the termination of the equipment lease contract. Risk of equipment damage is thereby reduced, and opportunities for equipment reuse or further leasing are increased.

Contract reverse distribution. One type of service that HVP anticipates will grow substantially is helping companies consolidate the return product stream within its terminal service network and redirecting such used products to other destinations and uses. Many companies in the office equipment, computer, and computer peripheral businesses have set up product take-back and lease termination programs.

HVP services for Wang Laboratories are a case in point. Wang takes back a substantial volume of used computer peripheral devices and automated office equipment from its dealer network. HVP worked with Wang to manage return product flows from dealer locations throughout the United States and to track these flows using HVP's Asset Management Product Tracking System. This system allowed Wang to better control assets in the field and to meter their flow to the Wang disassembly point, located in HVP's Boston logistics center and jointly staffed by both companies. At that center, Wang technicians disassemble used equipment, salvage parts, and dispose of the remaining material. Some equipment is refurbished for resale.

---

exhibit 5.1   Continued

~~~~~~

The program has helped increase Wang's product returns for resale by 55 percent while reducing resource requirements; Wang reduced its number of Return Product Centers from 28 to 4. In addition, the program linked all transactions and inventory controls through HVP's Asset Management Product Tracking System and, consequently, eliminated five Wang staff positions. HVP was able to efficiently consolidate reverse product flows through its existing cargo-tracking network and to redirect product flow to alternative destinations at the customer's direction.

Other returned product services. For some of its customers, HVP does more than package and transport equipment that is being taken back. For example, the company disassembles equipment in its logistics centers, separates scrap from reclaimed components, manages the return of usable parts to a customer-designated reclamation center, and consigns nonreusable parts to recycling centers. HVP also leases space in its logistics centers to allow customers to perform disassembly and reconsignment within the reverse supply chain. Although HVP has principally focused on take-backs from commercial and business sites, the company now has several projects under way that take back and deinstall equipment from individual residences.

SOURCE: Council of Logistics Management (1993), *Reuse and Recycling: Reverse Logistics Opportunities,* Oak Brook, IL: CLM. Reprinted by permission.
NOTE: HVP = North American High Value Products.

---

operated a sophisticated reverse distribution and remanufacturing system since the 1960s. It initially involved the take-back of leased Xerox units that were then refurbished and remarketed. As the purchase pattern shifted to customer ownership of machines, the company continued to offer the take-back service because significant cost savings were being realized through remanufacturing used equipment, and these savings could be passed on to customers in the form of trade-in incentives. Xerox presently accomplishes reverse distribution through a network of independent delivery recovery carriers (third-party specialists) who install new equipment and accomplish deinstallation, packaging, and transportation functions. The used equipment is returned to designated hub locations/terminals, where decisions are made to either (1) remanufacture it to new product standards or (2) disassemble it into components for future reuse or for sale as scrap to recyclers. Xerox's

exhibit 5.2

Canon's Clean Earth Campaign

THE CANON CARTRIDGE RECYCLING PROGRAM

The Canon Cartridge Recycling Program fulfills the first initiative of Canon's Clean Earth Campaign, which supports four critical environmental areas:

• Recycling in the Workplace

• Conserving Environmental Resources

• Scientific Research and Education

• Encouraging Outdoors Appreciation

The remaining "Clean Earth" initiatives are supported in the U.S. through sponsorships of the National Park Foundation, the National Wildlife Federation, and The Nature Conservancy and in Canada through donations to the World Wildlife Fund Canada and The Nature Conservancy of Canada.

Since its inception, The Canon Cartridge Recycling Program has collected millions of cartridges that otherwise would have been discarded into landfills or similar facilities. Instead, this rapidly growing program returns used cartridges to the manufacturing process, thus conserving an array of resources.

Becoming a part of this worthwhile program is easy. When your cartridge is of no further use, simply follow the instructions detailed for U.S. or Canadian residents.

We appreciate your support of The Canon Cartridge Recycling Program.

Working together we can make a significant contribution to a cleaner planet.

• Cartridges collected through this program are not refilled.

• You are not entitled to a tax deduction or rebate for the return of empty toner cartridges.

• This program may be modified or discontinued without notice.

LE PROGRAMME DE RECYCLAGE DES CARTOUCHES DE CANON

Le Programme de recyclage des cartouches de Canon répond aux exigences de la première initiative de la Campagne pour une planète propre de Canon, qui axe ses efforts sur quatre aspects essentiels de la protection de l'environnement:

• Recyclage sur le lieu de travail

• Conservation des ressources environnementales

• Recherche scientifique et éducation

• Encouragement aux activités de plein air

Les autres initiatives de la Campagne pour une planète propre sont soutenues aux États-Unis au moyen de parrainages par la National Park Foundation, la National Wildlife Federation et la Nature Conservancy, et au Canada, par le biais de dons au Fonds mondial pour la nature Canada et à la Société canadienne pour la conservation de la nature.

Depuis sa création, le Programme de recyclage des cartouches de Canon a permis de recueillir des millions de cartouches qui auraient pu être jetées dans des décharges ou des installations similaires. Ce programme en plein essor favorise le retour des cartouches usées au processus de fabrication, ce qui permet de conserver une variété de ressources.

Il est facile de participer à ce programme utile. Lorsque votre cartouche n'a plus d'utilité, vous n'avez qu'à suivre les directives relatives aux personnes domiciliés au Canada ou aux États-Unis.

Nous vous sommes reconnaissants de votre soutien au Programme de recyclage des cartouches de Canon. En travaillant ensemble, nous pourrons faire notre part pour une planète plus propre.

• Les cartouches recueillies dans le cadre de ce programme ne sont pas rechargées.

• Vous n'avez pas droit à une déduction d'impôt ni à un rabais puor le retour de cartouches de toner vides.

• Ce programme peut être modifié ou annule sans préavis.

SOURCE: Reprinted by permission of Canon U.S.A. Inc.

exhibit 5.2 Continued

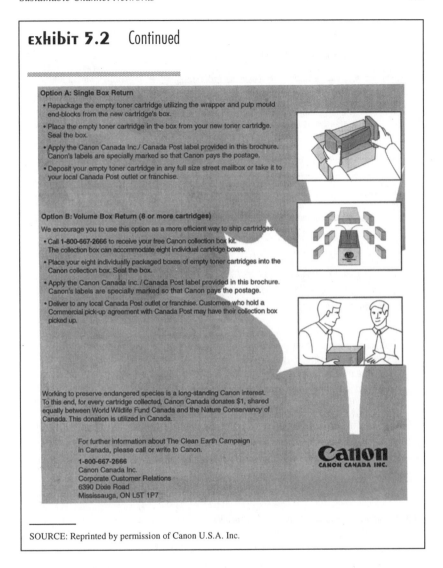

Option A: Single Box Return

• Repackage the empty toner cartridge utilizing the wrapper and pulp mould end-blocks from the new cartridge's box.

• Place the empty toner cartridge in the box from your new toner cartridge. Seal the box.

• Apply the Canon Canada Inc./ Canada Post label provided in this brochure. Canon's labels are specially marked so that Canon pays the postage.

• Deposit your empty toner cartridge in any full size street mailbox or take it to your local Canada Post outlet or franchise.

Option B: Volume Box Return (8 or more cartridges)

We encourage you to use this option as a more efficient way to ship cartridges.

• Call **1-800-667-2666** to receive your free Canon collection box kit. The collection box can accommodate eight individual cartridge boxes.

• Place your eight individually packaged boxes of empty toner cartridges into the Canon collection box. Seal the box.

• Apply the Canon Canada Inc. / Canada Post label provided in this brochure. Canon's labels are specially marked so that Canon pays the postage.

• Deliver to any local Canada Post outlet or franchise. Customers who hold a Commercial pick-up agreement with Canada Post may have their collection box picked up.

Working to preserve endangered species is a long-standing Canon interest. To this end, for every cartridge collected, Canon Canada donates $1, shared equally between World Wildlife Fund Canada and the Nature Conservancy of Canada. This donation is utilized in Canada.

For further information about The Clean Earth Campaign in Canada, please call or write to Canon.

1-800-667-2666
Canon Canada Inc.
Corporate Customer Relations
6390 Dixie Road
Mississauga, ON L5T 1P7

Canon
CANON CANADA INC.

SOURCE: Reprinted by permission of Canon U.S.A. Inc.

highly developed approach may well provide a model for future take-back applications in broader markets for appliances, electronics, and similar technology-driven products (Council of Logistics Management 1993).

As we near the end of the 1990s, it is clear that the specter of legislated take-back is turning into reality for durable goods manufacturers. For example, an outgrowth of Germany's 1991 landmark Ordinance on the Avoidance of Packaging Waste, popularly called Green Dot (see Chapter 8), is a proposal

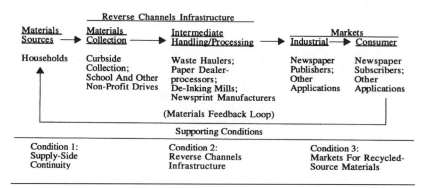

Figure 5.1. Marketing-Recycling Process for Old Newspaper

to require automobile manufacturers to take back the cars they sell at the end of the cars' service lives (Fishbein 1994). But as a recent report by Davis (1996) notes,

> The bright spot is that efforts to develop legislative programs are generally at a stage where industry has the opportunity to work ahead of the curve. A common refrain among manufacturers developing take-back programs is, "We need to find a way to do it before government tries to tell us how." (p. 8)

Of course, one key to effective take-back is the design of reverse recapture networks. Another is designing products to enhance the efficiency of the processes that will occur in relation to take-back including demanufacturing/disassembly, remanufacturing operations, and materials recycling (see Chapter 4).

Reverse Channels: Materials Recycling Strategies

When disposable (single-use) industrial packaging is used, the bulk-breaking activities that occur in forward channels result in the buildup of large quantities of standardized packaging materials at facilities performing distribution functions. Likewise, when consumers perform final bulk breaking at the household level, similar buildups of single-use packaging materials occur. In addition, household, industrial, and commercial concerns also are sources of nonpackaging waste such as discarded consumer goods, production wastes, traded-in products (e.g., automobiles, appliances), and other mandated take-back items (e.g., automobile tires, lead-acid batteries, used oil). The availability of large quantities of these items, which represent an alternative source of raw materials, sets the stage for the strategy of materials recycling.

Materials Recycling Is a Marketing Process

As defined in Chapter 3, materials recycling is a normative marketing process that involves collecting and accumulating large quantities of materials/products from waste streams, sorting them into homogeneous materials categories, upgrading them to the quality level required by industrial buyers, and making them available for sale. Recycled-source materials generally compete head-to-head against their virgin (primary) counterparts or as substitutes for other primary materials. In those cases when acceptable quality cannot be achieved, the downcycling of recycled-source materials in lower quality applications may be an option.

This notion of "marketing-recycling process" is important because it reveals the following three enabling conditions that must be fulfilled before successful exchanges will occur: (1) supply continuity must be established; (2) reverse channel networks (infrastructure) must be in place to perform various logistics, processing, and marketing functions; and (3) markets for recycled-source materials must be available (Fuller, Allen, and Glaser 1996:56). These enabling conditions are demonstrated in Figure 5.1, which shows the marketing/recycling process for old newspaper. As will be discussed in what follows, reverse channels have a major role to play in fulfilling and maintaining these conditions over time.

Condition 1: Supply-Side Continuity

For materials recycling to succeed, reverse channel networks must place an emphasis on the accumulation and sorting functions necessary to efficiently or effectively accomplish the large-scale recapture of desired materials. This is because the industrial target markets that serve as end users typically demand large quantities of high-quality feedstocks on a continuous basis. Any interruptions in supply to these customers can result in costly production facility shutdowns. In addition, from the recycled material supplier's viewpoint, volume operations are necessary to reap the economies of scale that are necessary when handling commodity-type, low-unit-value products because this allows a given operation to remain price/cost competitive in markets characterized by razor-thin margins. As an indication of the volumes required, every standard shipment of 40,000 pounds of "balled" aluminum container materials requires the collection and magnetic/visual screening of 1,185,185 containers (at 0.54 ounce each). This is equivalent to the retrieval of 197,531 six-packs of consumer beverages.

To facilitate supply continuity, channel design must address the issue of developing adequate coverage of waste sources. Type of source is a key factor. Reverse channel networks that interface with households, a postconsumer waste source, face a daunting challenge when it comes to efficiently performing accumulating and sorting functions. The scenario is as follows. There exists a very large number of extremely small-quantity waste generators (households), and each has the opportunity to commingle (mix) desired recoverables in with the other trash (Fuller 1979). Any mixing exacerbates entropy, thereby creating conditions unfavorable for economic recycling (Purcell 1980). However, the current operation of 8,937 curbside collection programs (reverse channel systems) that reach an estimated 136 million people in the United States has largely resolved this unique sorting and accumulating problem (Glenn 1998:41). These programs mandate that house-holders make an initial "free" sort of materials at the head of the channel, which is followed by routine pickup that is part of the municipal waste collection process. However, even with free initial sorting, the economic result often is a loss; that is, costs (e.g., collection, further sorting, baling-packaging for resale, marketing) are not covered by revenues over the short run. This usually is attributable to low revenues, which are a function of low commodities prices. But because eco-costs usually are not considered in the cost structures of competitive virgin materials and production systems are not yet universally designed to accept recycled-source raw materials as norm inputs, it is difficult, if not impossible, to assess the real economic benefits of this activity.

By contrast, the collection of recyclables from commercial-industrial sources faces the following scenario. A limited number of sources-locations exists, and each generates relatively large quantities of fairly homogeneous, known-quality materials. For example, retail supermarkets are bulk-breaking points for thousands of cases of products, which routinely spin off large quantities of uncontaminated corrugated packaging materials. These materials often are compacted and baled on the store's premises and then regularly picked up by a paper dealer-processor for further upgrading and eventual sale to a boxboard manufacturer. Because sorting and collection regularly occurs as the wastes (corrugated materials) are generated, there is less chance that irreversible entropy (contamination) will occur.

Condition 2: Reverse Channels Infrastructure

Given that source coverage has been achieved, Stage 5 reverse channel networks must continuously function to (1) recapture and process large quantities of materials, (2) process these materials to required quality specifications, and (3) maintain exchange continuity. Meeting the often quite demanding quality specifications of buyers is particularly important because price and quality are positively correlated in recycled materials markets. In general, high-quality, recycled-source commodities have more end uses and higher levels of application; that is, the highest quality recycled-source materials can be used in more types of applications and as 100 percent of an application, whereas lower quality materials must be downcycled to lower quality applications or heavily blended with virgin materials. In addition, many industrial processes are extremely sensitive to variations in the quality of raw materials inputs. For example, the inclusion of a single piece of ceramic material in a "lot" of container glass destined for recycling can contaminate an entire production run, lead to system shutdown, and require dumping the output as waste. Paper making and plastics production are similarly affected by the inclusion of noncompatible materials (contaminants/out-throws). Obviously, reverse channels must be designed with a combined emphasis on efficiently performing the accumulation and sorting functions to build volume while also maintaining strict quality control standards.

At any given time, the available infrastructure of reverse channel networks reflects economic conditions, legal arrangements, the functional requirements associated with specific commodities, the strategies of specific players in an industry, and public policy mandates (Guiltinan and Nwokoye 1974; Zikmund and Stanton 1971). For example, the Federal Republic of Germany literally created overnight a mandated recycling infrastructure through its Green Dot legislation (Fishbein 1994) (see Chapter 8). By contrast, Figure 5.2 presents alternative reverse channel networks that reflect strategic options that have evolved over time in the United States (Fuller et al. 1996). Some of the more important characteristics of each type are generalized in the following.

Corporate integrated networks. Corporate integrated networks use a legitimate/ownership power base to control the accumulation and sorting processes. Because it is necessary to cover a wide variety of waste sources when dealing with postconsumer materials, corporate networks require an

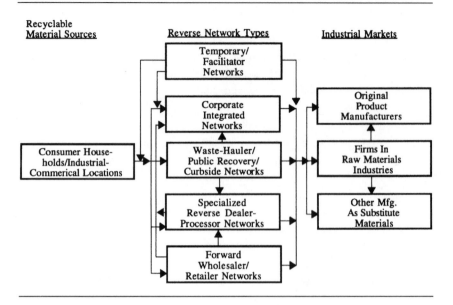

Figure 5.2. Alternative Reverse Channel Networks for Recyclable Materials
SOURCE: Fuller, Donald A., Jeff Allen, and Mark Glaser (1996), "Materials Recycling and Reverse Channel Networks: The Public Policy Challenge," *Journal of Macromarketing,* Vol. 16, No. 1, p. 58.

extensive investment in processing equipment/facilities, transportation equipment, and promotional programs to stimulate and service collection activity (Fuller 1991). The payoff is control of a large-volume, high-quality source of raw materials. For example, the Reynolds Aluminum Company, a major primary ingot producer, operated an extensive corporate integrated consumer recycling network in the United States from the early 1970s until late 1997, when it divested the subsidiary operation (the Reynolds Aluminum Recycling Company) in a major corporate restructuring (Egan 1997). Other examples of corporate integration include Tropicana's glass container manufacturing facilities (Fuller and Gillett 1990) and Adolph Coors Company's (1992) aluminum sheet stock division, the Golden Aluminum Company, which is partially supplied through its internal Recycle Division.

Waste-hauler/public recovery/curbside networks. In the United States, waste collection and disposal generally has been a public sector function, one necessary to preserve the health, welfare, and safety of citizens. As waste volume has increased, the effects of traditional "burn and bury" landfill disposal have come under increasing scrutiny, leading many states to pass legislation mandating that certain materials be diverted from landfills through curbside collection programs (National Solid Wastes Management Association 1991). Because the functions involved in curbside collection parallel those of routine garbage collection, firms already in the public sector waste-hauling business have tended to enter this new business as a natural product line extension.

Waste Management Inc. has responded to this opportunity by forming an independent subsidiary, Recycle America Inc., that collects presorted recyclables at the curbside (Fuller 1990). In Central Florida, it also manages a centralized materials recovery facility at the Orange County Landfill that receives and further sorts materials into generic categories and packages them (e.g., baling, containerization) for outbound shipment to dealer processors and/or industrial users. When relatively large geographic areas and population concentrations are covered by a waste collection franchise, it becomes possible for such networks to deliver large volumes of postconsumer recyclables on a continuous basis.

Specialized reverse dealer-processor networks. Dealer-processors are independent wholesaling specialists that often are referred to as junkyards or scrap dealers. Some are multimillion-dollar, full-function operations providing a wide variety of collection, processing, and management and marketing services backed up by extensive investments in specialized waste processing/handling/collection equipment, facilities, and vehicles. Others might be described as limited-function, "mom and pop" operations that specialize in the collection of a single material (Fuller and Gillett 1990).

Traditionally, full-function dealer-processors have engaged in the heavy-duty functional activities needed to handle industrial source waste streams such as dismantling, shredding, cutting, breaking, baling, and transporting. Their material inputs have included industrial equipment and consumer durables (e.g., automobiles, appliances) as well as large volumes of standardized materials in the form of metal and paper. More recently, the prospect of profiting from handling large quantities of postconsumer recyclables from municipal sources, which requires only lightweight processing (e.g., collection, sorting, baling), has led many full-function dealer-processors to include this area as a line extension. Such firms have continuous market contacts and can act as centralized buying/brokerage operations fed by waste-hauler networks and smaller dealer-processors.

Traditional forward retailer-wholesaler networks. Because the efficient handling of recyclables requires specialized facilities and functional capabilities, participation by traditional forward wholesalers and retailers has been limited. Such forward channels do occur as the result of mandates incorporated into state bottle bill/container deposit legislation. Where postconsumer redemption is mandatory, retailers have found that emphasizing convenience is important for achieving acceptance of the return system and in facilitating the required tasks (Crosby, Gill, and Taylor 1981; Crosby and Taylor 1982; Ginter and Starling 1978). However, the simultaneous implementation of curbside programs (waste-hauler/public recovery networks) in these same states creates channels that conflict directly with the volume goals of forward retailer-wholesaler channel systems.

Some retailers have offered voluntary postconsumer collection programs in an attempt to forestall restrictive legislation and to cultivate community goodwill. For example, the installation of reverse vending machines can provide consumers immediate rewards such as cash, receipts, tokens, stamps, or coupons for in-store discounts. One study reports locating recycling stations in the rear of the store as a means of building traffic (Westerman 1983). In other cases, the primary motive appears to be reinforcement of an image of good corporate citizenship and to reflect consumer values. An example is Publix Super Markets, based in Lakeland, Florida, which places bins for the collection of plastic and paper bags in all stores to make recycling convenient for customers ("Every Day Is Earth Day" 1992).

The role of retail locations as a source of recyclable commodities is moving beyond the retrieval of postconsumer packaging. Take-back mandates have resulted in the routine collection of used oil, oil filters, and antifreeze for recycling by quick-change oil service centers, gasoline service stations, auto parts stores, and even discount stores. Lead-acid batteries and scrap tires are similarly handled as take-back items. In a particularly innovative program, Saturn dealerships are now engaged in the recovery and recycling of polymer body panels that become available through their dealers' auto body repair shop operations (Exhibit 5.3).

At the wholesale level, some suppliers have developed reverse channels for single-use packaging to minimize their customers' waste disposal and handling problems and to differentiate their services from those of competitive suppliers. In some cases, however, this is not exactly a voluntary response on the part of suppliers. Large buyers facing high local disposal costs have the channel power to add the requirement of packaging take-back to standard terms of sale. For example, The Home Depot instituted a take-back requirement with sheetrock suppliers covering the space allocators that separate the

exhibit 5.3

Saturn Dealership Polymer Recycling Program

Saturn Reuses Polymer Panels in New Automobile Parts

US carmaker **Saturn Corporation** is taking back its polymer autobody panels and fascias for reuse. In partnership with its retailers, Saturn has established a national corporate program to recover scrapped post-consumer polymer for recycling. In spring 1993, Saturn began a pilot program to evaluate the feasibility of recycling post-consumer painted polymers. A group of Saturn retailers returned damaged painted bumper fascias for recycling. The pilot was a success and became a national program in December 1994. As of mid-April, Saturn had recovered over 18,000 square feet of scrapped polymer material.

The program runs at a minimal cost to both Saturn and its retailers. Using existing parts delivery systems, Saturn's transportation partner, **Ryder**, picks up the recovered polymer at the retailer during normal parts stops. The material is inspected and sorted at the Saturn manufacturing site in Spring Hill, Tennessee, then shipped to **American Commodities**, which reprocesses the material into pellets. The reprocessed pellets are tested for compliance and required specifications, then shipped back to Saturn for use in making new fascias, wheel liners, and rocker supports.

"With the program up and running, we're now looking at how to extend it to the non-Saturn-controlled body shops on the periphery," said **John J. Resslar**, Saturn's "design for environment (DFE) champion," and program manager, vehicle engineering and assembly, product engineering. "If a customer goes to a non-Saturn repair facility, how do we make sure the damaged fascia comes back to Saturn for recycling? Some people in the business would say there has to be an incentive, in the form of a core cost (extra charge) to make sure the part comes back. We're trying to educate these people about the environmental impact, taking a more philosophical approach."

Saturn's philosophy is to manage environmental issues through the product lifecycle, from design through post-consumer disposal. "Saturn views this program as a tool in the toolbox — we want to take a more comprehensive approach to product lifecycle management," Resslar told *BATE*. For the short-term, the company is concentrating on waste reduction and reuse, and extending the life of its product. "But to make an impact long-term, the stylists, engineers, and designers must be a heartbeat away from knowing the total environmental impact of the materials we use, including adhesives and sealants. We have total buy-in from product engineering and Saturn top management on this."

SOURCE: "Saturn Reuses Polymer Panels in New Automobile Parts," (1995), *Business and the Environment*, July, p. 9. Published by Cutter Information Corporation, Arlington, MA; telephone: (617) 641-5125; fax: (617) 648-8707; World Wide Web: http://www.cutter.com.

individual sheets during shipment after it was discovered that this item accounted for 10 percent of a store's waste stream. This arrangement reportedly has saved The Home Depot more than $700,000 in local collection and disposal fees (Council of Logistics Management 1993:166).

Temporary/facilitator networks. Schools, social clubs, and other nonprofit groups often have used recycling drives as fund-raisers. In so doing, they would enter the infrastructure as temporary or occasional intermediaries and then exit once the immediate task is accomplished (e.g., the group's fund-raising drive was completed). Much of this activity is low volume and seasonal in nature and in many cases is actually directed by permanent channel members as a means of stimulating additional volume (Fuller 1991). Despite their intermittent nature, these groups serve as temporary middlemen and, therefore, are counted as facilitating members of reverse channel networks.

Condition 3: Markets for Recycled-Source Materials

Channel infrastructures are dependent on the end markets they serve. In this regard, the volatility of recycled materials markets stacks the deck against smaller independent operators who tend to remain in the market when prices are favorable but exit rapidly when prices decline. On the other hand, the waste-hauler/public recovery, manufacturer-integrated, large-scale specialized dealer-processor, and the traditional forward retailer-wholesaler networks will likely survive. Because the waste-hauler and forward networks for postconsumer materials are mandated by legislation, they continue to function regardless of end-market conditions, even when prices are zero or even negative (i.e., the source of waste pays the buyer to take it away). Any operating losses are simply shifted to consumers as public sector eco-costs in the form of increased local waste collection fees and taxes or as higher retail prices. (Note: A discussion of factors influencing recycled materials markets is included in Chapter 8.)

Given that recycled-source materials use becomes more standardized, one might expect markets to stabilize somewhat. Revenues from public sector operations might even provide consumers (taxpayers) with some relief in the form of reduced collection fees or fewer increases in fees and other local taxes in the future. One also might expect the large manufacturer-integrated and dealer-processor systems to prosper given their advantages including (1) economies of scale (high-volume, low-cost advantage), (2) market coverage, and (3) financial staying power. They are well equipped to weather the "feast or famine" cycles that have been typical of these commodities-type markets.

Postconsumer recycling, in particular, has reached an unprecedented level of general acceptance, one totally unanticipated even five years ago. This is evidenced by the development and rapid growth of reverse curbside recycling systems. The number of programs increased from approximately 1,000 in 1988 to 8,817 in 1996 and to 8,937 in 1997 (Glenn 1998:41; Goldstein 1997:60-61). Although program growth definitely is slowing, approximately 136 million Americans continue to be reached on a daily basis. In *BioCycle,* one of the recycling industry's major trade journals, Steuteville (1996) comments on how enabling conditions for successful consumer-source recycling—source continuity, infrastructure, and markets—have come together to form an ongoing solution to pollution:

In less than a decade, curbside recycling went from a marginal activity mostly provided by nonprofit groups and a few progressive municipalities to a truly mainstream activity. The shift is due to the U.S. public, which willingly embraced recycling, and municipal officials, who have provided the convenience necessary to make it work. Haulers, who have developed tremendous expertise in providing recycling, also deserve a lot of credit, in addition to end users, particularly the paper industry, who have added billions of dollars in manufacturing capacity. (p. 59)

Reverse Channels: Materials Transformation Strategies

Industrial and commercial concerns and households also are sources of wastes that are organic and/or combustible in character. These materials include food-related and agricultural by-products, wood, plastics, rubber, and contaminated paper products/packaging. The availability of these materials creates an opportunity to engage in the R2 waste transformation strategies of (1) waste-to-energy (WTE) conversion and (2) composting.

Waste-to-Energy Conversion

WTE conversion, another name for systems that incinerate (burn) materials to harvest energy values and reduce waste volume, requires a steady stream of combustible municipal and industrial solid waste to fuel the "burn." Although energy harvesting may be the major objective, reducing the waste volume by 90 percent (a 10 percent ash component remains) leads to the important benefit of extending landfill life, often in the face of limited local capacity.

To put WTE in perspective in terms of the integrated waste management hierarchy, an ideal community R2 waste management approach would be to first engage in recycling and composting, to be followed by WTE and the landfilling of the ash residuals. The waste-hauler/public recovery networks described earlier also serve as the reverse channels for supplying the large quantities of mixed wastes necessary to implement this strategy.

Specific materials/products often contribute to the creation of unique WTE reverse channels. For example, automobile tires can be converted into tire-derived fuel, a high-energy input for WTE systems. Traditionally, tire retailers (traditional forward channels) have doubled as used tire collection centers because the typical customer requires installation at point-of-purchase (i.e., used tire carcasses are simply left behind at retail). Consequently, this has led to high levels of recovery in the United States (69 percent in 1995), of which 73 percent of the tire carcasses were used as tire-derived fuel (Scrap Tire Management Council 1997). However, special furnaces are required if tires make up a major percentage of fuel because they burn at much higher temperatures than other components of mixed garbage such as wood and paper.

The controversy over incineration as a method of waste management, which revolves around the issues of adverse air pollution and the landfilling of contaminated residual ash, was discussed earlier in Chapters 3 and 4. This has put the future of WTE in the United States in doubt because no closure has been reached on the safety issue; consequently, public distrust of WTE systems remains the norm.

Composting Organic Materials

The diversion of organic materials for composting is classified by some as a form of materials recycling. It is treated separately here because what goes in as one material input comes out as something else, that is, a material form that is totally different in terms of chemical and/or physical use properties. End results include animal feed, fertilizer, soil amendments, and erosion control media. More recently, composting processes have been used as a cost-effective pollution prevention/control and bioremediation technology (Goldstein 1995).

When organics are destined for composting, it is important to obtain early, clean sorts of materials to avoid entropy buildup. Reverse channel systems must be designed to achieve this objective because failure to do so results in an inconsistent end product. As with recyclable materials, the channels challenge differs for postconsumer and postindustrial/postcommercial locations. The collection of organics from postconsumer (household) sources parallels the curbside recycling channels for other materials operated by municipalities (i.e., the waste-hauler/public recovery network often is the choice). Consumers are asked to source separate designated items to prevent commingling with noncompostable materials. For example, the 4,700 households in Caledon, Ontario, sort vegetable and fruit matter, egg shells, coffee and tea grounds, bakery items, microwave popcorn bags, and food-contaminated paper packaging (e.g., pizza boxes, food cartons) into 64-gallon aerated carts, which are collected every two weeks on a separate collection cycle. Household yard wastes are handled similarly but are segregated from the other organics. The collected items subsequently are delivered to Caledon's municipal landfill, where a separate composting plant has been set up (Gies 1996:80).

In comparison to postconsumer sources, industrially-commercially generated organics exist at fewer prime locations—food service businesses, supermarkets, food wholesalers, and food processors—that generate relatively large quantities, an opportunity that parallels industrial materials recycling sources. Again, prompt separation at the source is the key to avoiding entropy. However, channels for composting organics from such sources are in the embryonic stage of development. Some of the factors that will influence future channel efficiency include (1) refining routing to efficiently reach prime generators; (2) developing specialized collection vehicles (standard solid waste packer trucks appear to be inefficient in this role); (3) developing specialized collection containers to accommodate semiliquid, putrefying materials; and (4) accounting for the seasonal variations in the composition of organic waste streams ("Hauling Food Residuals" 1995).

Some industrial-commercial generators are experimenting with direct channels through which they take the initiative of delivering organics to designated facilities for further processing. For example, to move vegetable and fruit trimmings and spoiled produce from its chain of 325 supermarkets located over a 60,000-square-mile area, The Vons Companies uses its own corporate integrated system to back-haul these items to the firm's centrally located distribution center. At that point, the various shipments are consolidated into Vons-owned, custom-designed composting trailers for transport to a private composting company for final processing ("The Hauler Perspective" 1995).

Composting, which used to be the domain of farmers and deep ecologists, clearly has emerged as a fundamental, technology-based strategy through which the public sector pursues landfill diversion goals. For example, the state of Iowa has targeted organics as a major factor in achieving a 50 percent reduction in its solid waste stream by the year 2000 (Wiekierak 1996:33). This suggests that rapid advances in composting channel implementation and design for both postconsumer and postindustrial organics can be expected during the next few years.

Channel Management: Sustainable/Green Retailing

Determining the appropriate types of retailers, or retailing formats, to employ in consumer channel networks is a traditional outbound channel management decision, one that is equally important for sustainable products. This involves the selection of specific retail organizations located in desired geographic markets as well as alternatives such as direct mail/catalog retailing, the Home Shopping Network's television approach, and the emerging use of on-line retail transactions over the Internet ("Wal-Mart to Operate" 1996).

Closest to the Consumer

Because retail stores occupy the position in channel networks "closest to the consumer," the retailing community serves as an interpreter of market preferences. The constant day-to-day challenge facing retailers is "What product mix should be offered?" given the basic dictum that whatever is offered must be profitable. Being in a position of intimate contact with customers also suggests that the retailing community can serve as an environmental go-between and educator. As the well-known proponent of sustainable development Stephan Schmidheiny notes, "As gatekeepers between manufacturers and consumers, retailers have many opportunities to exert pressure in favor of sustainable development" (Schmidheiny 1992b:112).

Being "closest to the consumer" also makes the retailer the major recipient of consumer scorn when things do not go right. Customers take unsatisfactory products back to the retailers that sold them when results are not up to expectations. So, if a so-called "environmentally correct" product fails to function as well as its mainstream counterpart, then retailers feel the heat first. Similarly, retailers are immediately vulnerable and held accountable by consumers when a product flaw is brought to light. An environmental example is the recent revelation that certain plastic miniblinds imported from Asian suppliers and retailed in the United States contain lead as an additive that turns into lead dust when the plastic is exposed to heat and sunlight. This toxic discovery, a particular threat to small children, led The Home Depot and other U.S. retailers to remove these products from their shelves ("Vinyl Miniblinds" 1996). The press also reports that a class-action suit has been filed in California asking that Wal-Mart recall the tainted miniblinds, replace them at no cost with "noncontaminated, child-safe" versions, and also fund and administer a program for the safe disposal of the products already sold (Reuters 1996). Obviously, what might appear at first to be a trivial environmental oversight in product design has the potential to become an expensive legal and public relations battle at the retail level.

Retailing's unique role as interpreter of market preferences adds yet another dimension to sustainable marketing decisions. Specifically, the retailing community's selection of products for pass-through sales to consumers reflects the market's current acceptance or rejection of environmentally compatible consumption alternatives. Quite important, the collective product mix decisions of individual retailers determines the general public's level of exposure to sustainable product offerings.

Character of Retailing Waste

Retailing activities spin off the same general types of distribution process and product (packaging) wastes as do other channel network organizations, so the P2 and R2 strategies discussed earlier are applicable. In individual situations, the nature of the products handled, the size of the establishment, and the operating format influence waste stream volume and contents. For example, Jiffy Lube retail locations generate large quantities of waste oil and used oil filters, Kmart discount stores produce large quantities of single-use corrugated box materials, and Publix supermarket locations are sources of significant quantities of compostable organic foodstuffs as well as recyclable corrugated boxes and other packaging materials. As noted earlier, mandated take-back laws also make individual retailers unwitting participants in reverse channel networks for products such as lead-acid batteries, automobile tires, and consumer containers.

Specialty Green Retailers

Because mainstream retailers have been cautious about adding green product lines, specialty green retailers have evolved to fill the niche. Many of the market entrants are cause-driven marketers, their major purpose being the promotion of environmental social responsibility (Gupta 1994). Specialty green retailing essentially takes two forms: (1) specialty store operations known as eco-retailers and (2) specialty green catalog retailers.

Eco-Retailers

The *1993 In Business Directory of Green Retailers* listed 123 operating locations in the United States and Canada specializing in green products, up from an estimated 11 locations in early 1991 ("The Status of Eco-Retailing" 1993:32). The stores, identified by a market survey, were relatively small, ranging in size from 250 to 4,000 square feet, with a median size of 1,000 square feet. The most popular lines sold were recycled paper products, T-shirts, cleaning products, personal care products, and organic-natural clothing. The tenuous status of many of these mom-and-pop operations is shown by the fact that 68 percent of those responding to the survey reported that they did not make a profit during the preceding year (p. 33).

Some larger operations also fall into this specialty category. Among them is The Body Shop, which formalizes its commitment to sustainability through the 10-point environmental policy statement shown in Exhibit 5.4. In the first half of 1995, The Body Shop had 1,300 retail stores in 45 countries and reported revenue of £105.4 million. However, the firm has not experienced unqualified success; it suffered a 26 percent loss in pretax profit for the six months ended August 26, 1995 (Parker-Pope 1995:B11). In addition, the firm recently was taken to task in a social evaluation conducted by Kirk O. Hanson of Stanford University, who chided the company for giving more attention to its social initiatives than to improving the social/environmental impact of its day-to-day business operations (cited in Rose 1996). The firm has indicated it is making changes in response to the problems uncovered by this evaluation and its own independently verified social/environmental audit.

Green Catalog Retailers

Green catalog retailers are direct marketers that appeal to a narrow but loyal segment of consumers driven by environmental concerns. Two major competitors in this market are Seventh Generation and Real Goods. Seventh Generation is the "green" Lands' End of direct marketing, with nearly $7 million in annual sales (Smith 1993:5). In the past, its strategy has been to offer a wide array of "deep green" consumer products exclusively through its catalog. However, the firm has been plagued by profitability problems in recent times, which has led to restructuring. Among the changes have been a reconfiguration of product lines to include so-called "light green" products that do not meet the stringent ecological guidelines that once placed all Seventh Generation offerings. In addition, in a monumental breach of tradi-tion, Seventh Generation has decided to bring its 20 strongest core products to mass markets through traditional supermarket distribution channels and natural foods stores ("Seventh Generation Repositions" 1994).

Real Goods is a catalog retailer specializing in products that deliver energy conservation benefits such as solar- and wind-driven energy systems. Its ultimate goal is to allow consumers to live "off the grid," a term signifying independence from traditional utility-provided electrical power (Smith 1993). With 1992 annual sales of approximately $12 million, the firm's management seems to prefer a marketing approach that uses controversial themes. For example, during the Persian Gulf War, Real Goods featured a catalog cover showing huge transport planes unloading Marines in the desert war zone, and underneath it was a picture of a solar-paneled house. The implicit message

exhibit 5.4

The Body Shop Environmental Policy

Thinking Globally

The Body Shop International's business is the manufacture and retailing of skin and hair care products. We have developed this policy as a constant reminder of our responsibilities to act in order to protect the environment both globally and locally. We want to do things better than they have been done before, and we want to include our staff, franchisees, subsidiaries and suppliers in making that happen.

Achieving Excellence

Sound environmental management is both good house-keeping and good sense. Through regular reviews and assessments of our operations around the world, we will set ourselves clear targets and time-scales within which to meet those targets.

Searching for Sustainability

Sustainable development is about achieving a fairer and safer world for future generations. At all levels of operation – in our head office, in our manufacturing facilities, in our subsidiaries and franchises, and in our retail outlets around the world – we will try to use renewable resources wherever feasible, and we will conserve natural resources where renewable options are not available. This will apply in particular to our purchasing which will be supported by a system of product stewardship including ecological assessments of our products and packaging.

Managing Growth

The quest for economic growth is the cause of much environmental and human exploitation. Our future planning will be balanced between the environmental implications of our business and economics. We will devote increasing efforts to establishing non-exploitative trading arrangements with communities in less developed countries as a means to protecting their cultures and their environments.

Managing Energy

Global warming, acid rain, nuclear waste – problems caused by the misuse and abuse of energy resources provide urgent reasons to achieve the highest possible energy efficiency in our operations. We will work towards replacing what we must use with renewable resources.

Managing Waste

We believe that wealthy societies have an urgent and overwhelming moral obligation to avoid waste. As a responsible business we adopt a four-tier approach: first, reduce; next, reuse; then, recycle; and finally, as a last resort we will dispose of waste using the safest and most responsible means available.

Controlling Pollution

Pollution is a special form of environmental abuse – it is more than exploitation, it involves degradation and despoilation. Environmental damage is an inevitability of most industry practice, but we are committed to protecting the quality of the land, air and water on which we depend.

Operating Safely

The reputation of any business rests on safety – for staff, for customers and for the community in which the business operates. We will minimise risk in every one of our operations – from ensuring the safety and quality of our products, to good neighbour policies in the communities where we work. We will maintain emergency plans to safeguard the environment within our workplace in the event of fires, floods or other natural disasters.

Obeying the Law

The minimum requirement for any responsible business is to observe legal requirements and regulations wherever the Company operates. We will ensure that environmental laws are complied with at all times and in the event of difficulties these will be reported to the appropriate regulatory authorities.

Raising Awareness

Our mission is to forge a new and more sustainable ethic for business. We want our efforts to set a precedent for others. We are committed to continuous education for our staff on environmental issues. We are committed to freedom of information and full public disclosure of the results of our environmental assessments.

SOURCE: The Body Shop International PLC, *The Body Shop Environmental Statement 95,* a company publication. Copyright 1996 by The Body Shop International PLC. Used by permission.

about the consequences and social costs of using fossil fuel versus solar energy is obvious (Orloske and Davis 1994).

Sustainable Initiatives by Mainstream Retailers

This is not say that traditional mainstream retailers, such as supermarket chains and mass merchandisers, are devoid of sustainable initiatives. Loblaws, a Canadian supermarket chain, uses environmental product offerings, called the President's Choice line, to uniquely position itself within the industry (Walley 1991). Other supermarket chains address the challenges of "greening" the logistics and retail store operations aspects of their businesses while also giving some attention to green product lines. For example, Publix Super Markets aggressively pursues an internal combined P2 and R2 program that follows the traditional "reduce, reuse, and recycle" approach; it focuses on store-generated packaging materials, foodstuffs/organics, and refrigerant and energy conservation programs in an attempt to moderate the day-to-day environmental impact of local store operations. Publix Super Markets also has introduced a line of recycled contents paper towels under the store brand "Publix Green" ("Every Day Is Earth Day" 1992). In recognition of its proactive environmental efforts, the supermarket chain's division in Jacksonville, Florida was awarded the prestigious Lee and Mimi Adams Environmental Award in early 1996 for recycling more than 1,700 tons of paper, 200 tons of plastics, 190 tons of waxed cardboard, and more than 1,000 pounds of aluminum (Keep Florida Beautiful 1996:6).

Mass merchandisers, including Wal-Mart and Kmart, also have made some forays into the green arena. Wal-Mart's "eco-store" prototype in Lawrence, Kansas, opened in June 1993 and represents a major attempt to incorporate ecologically friendly facilities design and operating features as a major component of new store development strategy. Innovations include the use of recycled-contents materials in building construction and in-store fixtures, CFC-free air conditioning systems, and built-in integrated solid waste management/recycling systems for both consumer- and store-generated waste (Fitzgerald 1993; "Wal-Mart Explores" 1992). Competitor Kmart also is pursuing environmental objectives through store development decisions (e.g., selection of construction materials, in-store energy conservation systems) and through take-back programs for environmentally sensitive consumer products such as batteries (auto, marine, and button types) and the recycling of industrial packaging that accumulates at both stores and distribution centers ("Quietly, Kmart Makes Environmental Push" 1993).

In addition, it would be an oversight not to point out that both Wal-Mart and Kmart have made overtures to their manufacturing partners and suppliers to provide more products that have positive ecological attributes (Kmart Corporation 1993; "Tending Wal-Mart's Green Policy" 1991). Likewise, The Home Depot has instituted the Environmental Greenprint Campaign program, which includes an opportunity for its suppliers to formally certify the environmental claims they make about their products. Claim testing and verification is carried out by Scientific Certification Systems, an independent laboratory that offers third-party environmental certification programs (S. T. Whitaker, The Home Depot, personal communication, April 20, 1993) (see Chapters 2 and 6). The basic purpose of this program is to demonstrate the firm's commitment to improving the environment by selling products that take environmental compatibility into account (M. Eisner, The Home Depot, personal communication, December 1996).

Greening the Shopping Mall

"Greening the shopping mall" refers to the strategies employed to make these concentrated hubs of retailing activity more compatible with local ecosystems. The conglomerations of stores making up mall developments are natural bulk-breaking points (gateways) in retail distribution channels that represent an R2 opportunity in urban areas. Specifically, a major component of mall/shopping center waste streams is industrial packaging (e.g., corrugated cardboard, plastic sheeting, pallets) that accompanies inbound merchandise (Fuller 1994b). The major role that both mall management (which oversees the smaller stores) and anchor tenants are now playing involves setting up systematic programs for collecting and accumulating large quantities of materials for input into materials recycling channels. Making this happen in the most economical manner possible is a proposition that might involve the cooperation of several hundred stores at one location. Because participation often was mandated by local ordinance, "economical" must be interpreted as either being able to make a profit from the sale of these materials or minimizing the cost of the added functional burden imposed by local mandates.

For many existing mall locations, setting up materials recycling systems is a challenge involving retrofitting this specific functional activity into facilities that originally were designed as one-way TD systems. This sometimes translates into the management of rather awkward collection systems. But new facilities development is beginning to take the environmental consequences of waste management into consideration from the start. A case in point is the Mall of America in Bloomington, Minnesota. The entire facility was conceived and built around the theme of environmental responsibility. Its unique feature is a self-contained, integrated, internal recycling processing system that ties together 400 retail shops on four levels. This operation, managed by Browning-Ferris Industries, can process up to 900 tons of recyclable materials each month ("Mall Will Boost" 1992).

Individual retail tenants can have an impact on the environmental management and marketing practices of mall developers and owners. For example, Gap, the $3.7 billion-a-year San Francisco-based clothing retailer, has placed itself "at the forefront of efforts to design and operate stores with minimal environmental impact" ("Minding the Store" 1996:1). The firm currently operates 1,700 Gap, GapKids, BabyGap, Banana Republic, and Old Navy Clothing Company stores. Store design and operating improvements are first tested in a series of prototype locations and then phased in to ongoing new construction and store renovation programs over time. Gap management also firmly believes in leveraging the chain's considerable buying power to "prod suppliers and vendors not just to meet increasingly greener product specifications but also to present Gap with eco-innovations that the company hadn't even considered" (p. 1). But recognizing that employee buy-in also is an important ingredient, this leadership position is driven by a management philosophy that states, "What's good for our employees' health and happiness is also good for the environment, customer satisfaction, and the bottom line" (pp. 1-2).

Other greening impacts that retailers such as Gap can have on mall operating policies include trimming the costs of mall operations and common area maintenance fees through energy and water conservation programs, zero-scaping exterior areas (i.e., the use of no-water landscaping), and purchasing nontoxic maintenance materials ("The Greening of the Mall" 1996; "Malls and Energy Management" 1990). The emphasis is on achieving results through incentive programs that reward reduced energy use and provide tenant support and discounts tied to lower trash output and recycling program participation. Although the motivation is generally cost driven, the general effect is to portray eco-efficiency as a serious form of competitive advantage that can be capitalized on by developers.

Mall managers, through their "in the mall activities" and external promotion programs, also have the opportunity to serve as educators in relation to environmental issues. In addition, they play a product gatekeeper role in the sense that they can encourage or discourage the inclusion of specialty green retailers in tenant mixes. Because malls are socially prominent gathering places in most communities, some suggest that local malls have an obligation to serve as environmentally responsible corporate role models. But although some mall managers might embrace this altruistic position, most remain logically focused on the bottom line and will continue to emphasize minimizing the short-term functional costs associated with waste management operations (Fuller 1994b).

Is Green Going Mainstream?

Some suggest that we are entering a period in which green products are beginning to significantly infiltrate mainstream retailing (Quintana 1995). This suggests that although ecological product attributes are not a top-of-mind decision criterion, they might be beginning to fully assume the role of "tie-breaker" because the ordinary person simply wants to do right by the environment when all other product attributes appear equal. This attitude apparently is influencing the retail buyers of mainstream merchants to bring more green lines into the mix. Interestingly, as true green lines begin to infiltrate the mass merchandisers, such as the Publix and Winn-Dixie supermarket chains, this fact may well spell the demise of the smaller eco-retailers that have survived by exploiting (although marginally) the green niche.

Channel Management: Selecting Sustainable Partners

One characteristic of the PSLC is that the channel network organizations making up the five general stages (see Figure 2.2) jointly contribute to the waste impact assignable to given products. In this setting, a manufacturer in Stage 3 (i.e., the finished products channel network) faces a channel member selection process that involves three levels of organizations: (1) Stage 5 reverse channel organizations, which serve to manage the firm's outbound waste streams; (2) Stage 1 and 2 upstream suppliers, which provide product-making inputs; and (3) Stage 3 wholesale and retail distributors, which represent the final link with Stage 4 consumer target markets. It follows that one approach to enhancing sustainable practice is to use environmental performance as a channel member selection criterion to construct relatively clean networks from the start. The ensuing discussion focuses on this aspect of sustainable channel management by examining the following issues: (1) legal liability, (2) current ad hoc green screening approaches, and (3) the formalizing screening role that ISO 14000 will likely play in the near future.

The Specter of Legal Liability

One reason for the concern about Stage 5 partners' environmental pro-clivities is the issue of ultimate liability for the disposal and possible mishan-dling of hazardous wastes. For example, in the United States, Section 107 of the Comprehensive Environmental Response, Compensation, and Liability Act of 1990 (Government Institutes Inc. 1994) makes any firm in the chain of disposal (manufacturer-generator, waste hauler, disposal facility operator) jointly and severally liable for the proper handling of any hazardous waste by each of the other parties. Simply put, a manufacturer could contract in good faith for the hauling and disposal of waste, but any mishandling or otherwise illegal disposal by any of these reverse channel members remains the potential responsibility of the manufacturer. The removal of this costly unlimited liability provision has been a major issue before recent past sessions of the U.S. Congress (Noah and Kuntz 1995). But because it remains law at this time, the lesson is to select as reverse channel network partners only those firms that can demonstrate a track record of total compliance with applicable environmental regulations.

Ad Hoc Screening for Green

Because it was initially applied "backward" by manufacturers to up-stream participants in the PSLC, the process of firms aligning themselves with environmentally sound suppliers/sources has been dubbed "Greening the Supply Chain" (1993). But because the idea is that "clean birds of a feather flock together" over the entire PSLC, the use of a green screening process to evaluate partners obviously is applicable to all levels.

For example, The Body Shop has begun a supplier accreditation program that uses a questionnaire to assess the ecological virtues of suppliers and finished goods manufacturers and to weed out those that are unwilling to begin modifying their actions to meet the company's standards. Similarly, The Home Depot's practice of including packaging take-back as an element of supplier trade terms (cited earlier in this chapter) also can be interpreted as a form of greening the supply chain. At the finished products manufacturing level, Apple Computer and Northern Telecom have developed programs that let their components/parts suppliers know what environmental standards are expected and to even help them develop practices and procedures that will bring them in line with those standards ("Greening the Supply Chain" 1993).

The applications of green criteria so far have been largely tailored to individual circumstances and are mainly qualitative in character. Most approaches have consisted of finding partnership solutions; that is, the emphasis clearly is on cooperative efforts and positive reinforcement, as opposed employing immediate sanctions and draconian mandates. Sun Microsystems might be typical in this regard. The firm has surveyed its suppliers and has developed a comprehensive concept for a supplier-management program. But the emphasis remains qualitative, and the firm has not set up specific standards that have to be met to qualify as a bidder ("Greening the Supply Chain" 1995). Similarly, Steelcase Inc., a major manufacturer of office furniture and fixtures, brings costs into the picture by noting that developing comprehensive procedures involving audits and surveys would be prohibitively expensive at this time. The firm's director of corporate environmental quality comments, "That's why we have chosen to stay with the partnership approach. We work with people we know and trust, explain to them what we need, and work together to make it happen" (p. 2).

But it also is clear that the present reliance on qualitative standards is due largely to the simple fact that the science of environmental evaluation is in its infancy, and consensus guidelines and measurement approaches have yet to emerge. Still, as one authority notes, "environmental purchasing standards would need to tighten up over time if companies want to make real progress in improving environmental quality and internal cost structures" ("Greening the Supply Chain" 1995:2). In addition, as more and more companies find themselves immersed in the challenge of sorting out environmental issues, some generalized review formats appear to be taking shape. For example, the noted consultant firm KPMG Peat Marwick (1993) suggests that a standardized vendor environmental review examine these areas: (1) the nature of products and services purchased by a business, (2) potential environmental impacts of those products and services, (3) the environmental track record of vendors, and (4) existing vendor programs for avoiding environmental risk (p. 7). Within this emerging framework, it is becoming standard practice to ask suppliers for immediate improvements in packaging through downsizing, implementing reusable-returnable shipping-pallet systems, and using packaging materials with high postconsumer recycled materials contents. Surveys, workshops, and award programs also are turning up as common approaches for initiating an environmental dialogue between PSLC organizations and to reward progress toward goals.

ISO 14000: Formalizing the Process

One thing is certain: sweeping changes in the future role of environmental evaluation are looming on the horizon in the form of ISO 14000, the environmental management standard (EMS) recently put in place by the Geneva-based International Organization for Standardization. The ISO 14000 series complements and parallels the well-known ISO 9000, the worldwide quality management standard that has been adopted by nearly 100,000 firms (Rothery 1995:6). As *The Green Business Letter* points out,

> ISO 14000 aims to create uniform environmental standards among products, companies, industries, and nations. Its purpose is to avoid trade barriers from conflicting national or regional environmental standards as well as provide an alternative to command-and-control regulation. And, of course, lead to improved eco-performance. ("The EMS Mess" 1996:1)

Firms seeking ISO 14000 certification must first conduct an initial environmental review, which is essentially a situation analysis (i.e., an audit or gap analysis). Although there is no required formal structure for this data-gathering exercise, Rothery (1995) suggests a general outline with 12 sections (pp. 46-55). As the British express it, the initial environmental review is a "once off" exercise that establishes a starting point or baseline. For example, Section 9.0 of Rothery's general outline bears the label "Supplier Considerations," which translates directly into the matter of channel network partner selection and greening the supply chain. Although Rothery suggests that the gathering of information for this section may be initiated through informal letters and/or detailed questionnaires, it is very likely that such methods will provide insufficient levels of detailed information; therefore, on-site follow-up vendor audits might be necessary. The difficulty of securing supplier cooperation in what may be considered the forced revelation of proprietary information can hardly be understated. Obviously, the partners involved must share a sense of mutual trust and confidence (known as a referent relationship) as well as a clear understanding of the mutual benefits and financial payoffs to be gained by engaging in the process including the prospects for establishing viable positions of competitive advantage.

At the time of this writing, ISO 14000 is on the takeoff roll. The first two sets of standards have been approved and are now global standards. Four remaining groups of standards under ISO 14000 will likely be approved within two years. The major section, ISO 14001, establishes EMS certification procedures. Experts expect the growth trend of ISO 14000 certification to mirror what biologists call a dominant tendency or a cascade effect, one that is triggered at the customer-buyer interface. As Rothery (1995) explains,

> As sophisticated buyers demand the standards (ISO 14000) from their imme-diate suppliers, those suppliers in turn pass on the demand to their suppliers

so that it cascades through the supply chain. . . . A very good example is a large international user of print and packaging for products sold worldwide . . . which demands that its print and packaging suppliers supply materials with environmental probity. The suppliers pass the demand back to the paper and board mills, which in turn insist that the timber come from managed forests. The mechanism for monitoring this up the supply system is an ISO 9000/ISO 14000 system in each facility from print and packaging to forest. (p. 5)

From a marketing perspective, ISO 14000 has the potential to have a profound impact on the future of sustainable practice. This is because being ISO 14000 certified may well become a routine customer requirement when dealing with large industrial firms, one that derives from the customer's real-world need to comply with legislation (i.e., the political-legal environment), which in turn is a manifestation of environmental public policy. Thus, the linking of a voluntary EMS to market transactions will literally create a market-driven mandate for thousands of companies. Under this scenario, channel members without ISO 14000 credentials will be at a distinct competitive disadvantage in the global marketplace of the future.

Channel Management: Implementing Sustainable Channels

A major lesson from life-cycle analysis is that it is generally not feasible for one firm, unless it is totally vertically integrated, to take on the gargantuan task of cradle-to-grave waste management. Rather, the efforts of many organizations must be joined in a common assault on waste management challenges. Implementation, then, involves building appropriate strategic alliances as well as achieving higher levels of integration within already functioning channel networks. In addition, conducting a sustainable marketing audit to develop appropriate decision support information is another important factor.

Building Logistical Strategic Alliances

The term *strategic alliance* was described in Chapter 4 as an interorganizational liaison in which participants (partners) make substantial investments in time, money, and expertise for the purpose of obtaining mutual benefits or seeking mutual objectives (Badaracco 1991; Barnes and Stafford 1993).

Because the relationships between independent firms in channel networks generally fulfill this definition, most channel networks are rightfully viewed as de facto strategic alliances (partnerships).

The ecological challenge represents a unique setting in which strategic alliances can be used to accomplish the logistics functions necessary to implement sustainable marketing strategies (Fuller 1994a). Generally, waste impacts occur at widely disparate times and locations over the PSLC, thereby making it operationally difficult for a single firm to control all the geographic and temporal dimensions of manufacturing and move-store activities that relate to P2 and R2 strategies. For example, any manufacturer in national distribution is instantly separated from its products in terms of time, place, and ownership (title) once they leave production facilities; this also means that all real manufacturer control over ultimate product disposal is lost. Developing a high-control corporate integrated (fully owned) network for managing the cradle-to-grave functions of waste management (e.g., operating reverse channel networks, hauling hazardous wastes, performing deinstallation and related activities) generally is beyond both the functional and administrative competence and economic capability of the product-originating firm. This opens the door to strategic alliances as a particularly straightforward approach for spinning off, or outsourcing, the technological and logistics efforts needed to accomplish sustainable programs.

The services offered by North American High Value Products (Exhibit 5.1), Canon's Clean Earth Campaign (Exhibit 5.2), and Xerox Corporation's reverse distribution and remanufacturing system (described earlier in this chapter) reflect such outsourcing in practice. In short, each represents the formation of a mutual benefit strategic alliance. For example, Canon's strategic alliance with Canada Post makes it possible to ensure the accumulation of depleted toner cartridges from thousands of business locations and their subsequent shipment to designated locations. Canon benefits by creating an image of environmental responsibility while also securing a source of recyclable materials and reusable components that have potential for incorporation in primary or remanufactured products. Canada Post benefits because the firm is paid for its expertise and the economies of scale it brings to the process of retrieving relatively small quantities of spent cartridges from thousands of individual and widely dispersed business locations.

Retailers can similarly effect strategic alliances that pool the complementary local expertise and functional capabilities of the parties involved. The relationship between Minneapolis-area Target Stores and Valvoline Rapid Oil Change Service Centers to facilitate the collection of used oil and oil filters is an example ("Valvoline and Target" 1996). In this case, Target retail stores are high-volume sellers of new oil and oil filters to the do-it-yourself market. Because of the nature of the products involved, Target management desires to be environmentally responsible by facilitating take-back of the waste components. However, Target retail stores are not equipped to handle used oil or oil filters on-site (the used products are classified as hazardous wastes). Valvoline locations do specialize in this function, and Valvoline's management desires to increase its volume of used oil and filters, which are salable commodities. This is accomplished when Target customers are routinely referred to the nearest Valvoline location for disposal of their used oil and filters. Thus, a complementary/symbiotic relationship is achieved by these firms.

Strategic alliances between government agencies and private enterprise also are a factor. For example, local governments traditionally have been responsible for the collection and disposal of municipal solid waste (MSW) management and now control the major sources of many of the postconsumer materials sought for recycling. An effective method of accumulating these materials from household sources is curbside collection, a process that essentially parallels traditional MSW collection activities. Because of this, a common local logistical strategic alliance is created by extending the services covered in private waste-hauler contracts with municipalities to include the curbside collection process. For instance, Waste Management Inc. and the city of Winter Park, Florida, have created a public-private sector alliance that designates Waste Management as the operator of the city's curbside collection program. Under this arrangement, Waste Management contributes not only the functional transportation and hauling expertise (e.g., vehicles customized for recyclables pickup) necessary to accomplish accumulation but also expertise in the marketing of recovered materials to intermediaries and end users after collection (Fuller and Allen 1991).

Integrating Channel Networks

Vertically integrating channel systems to achieve better coordination and control of marketing functions and programs has long been a standard channel management approach. The resulting vertical marketing systems (VMSs) unify partners' efforts around common objectives, usually stated in terms of sales/profits and customer satisfaction. This occurs because each partner's involvement in the systemwide marketing management process leads to a thorough understanding of the partners' respective functional roles and responsibilities; that is, organizational buy-in occurs across the VMS. The process is completed when channel leader organizations apply economic, legal, referent, and/or expert power as a control mechanism. Economic power refers to ability of one organization to provide meaningful financial incentives/rewards, or in some cases disincentives, to others in exchange for their cooperation; legal power refers to contractual and corporate ownership arrangements; referent power involves the belief by one channel partner that "the other partner(s) has our best interests in mind"; expert power means that one channel member believes in the marketing competence of the other party (parties) in the business relationship. Under the VMS concept, these power bases translate into three types of channel control formats: (1) administered, (2) contractual, and (3) corporate.

Administered Networks

These systems rely on voluntary programs and mutual self-interest to achieve their goals. To gain the voluntary cooperation of others in the channel, manufacturers typically offer incentive packages called reseller support programs. These often take the form of promotional support such as advertising, sales training, and point-of-sale materials. Because of their voluntary nature, administered relationships are based on economic, expert, and referent power bases. In short, the various partners must believe that the manufacturer's support programs represent true value added or participation will be sparse. This is particularly important when environmental issues are the target of the support package because this subject involves new information and involvements for many firms in the distribution trades. The manufacturer's potential role as environmental educator is apparent.

In the case of convenience goods, a given manufacturer in an administered system often is in the position of being one of hundreds or thousands of suppliers that service an industrial, wholesale, or retail account. In addition, the intensity of retail distribution for convenience goods can run into thousands of retail store locations, which makes it difficult for a manufacturer to orchestrate specific environmental programs at the point of sale. But two cases demonstrate that administered approaches can succeed under certain circumstances. The first is the refillable milk jug system put in place by the Schroeder Milk Company (cited earlier in this chapter). In this situation, limited market coverage (i.e., small number of locations) and total logistical support by the manufacturer (e.g., back-hauling of empties, processing of containers for refilling) appear to be the keys to success. The second case involves the take-back programs put in place by makers of single-use cameras, such as Konica USA and Eastman Kodak, who pay retailers a take-back allowance (approximately 5 cents per unit) to accomplish the functions of in-store handling of camera bodies, consolidation into bulk quantities, and shipment to designated locations.

Opportunities for environmental services companies to support retailer environmental programs in administered channels is demonstrated by Safety-Kleen Corporation, a major recycler of automotive oils-fluids, solvents, and chemical wastes. It has developed the WE CARE program for use by its retail channel partners (i.e., automotive services, printing establishments, photo processing facilities, auto painting-refinishing shops, and dry cleaners), a systematic approach for recouping local eco-costs from their customers through a voluntary invoice surcharge. Through this program, retailers ask their customers to voluntarily pay an added "environmental" fee (say 1 to 2 percent) to cover the costs of responsible waste management. Safety-Kleen's reseller support package includes the WE CARE environmental symbol (logo) that is the centerpiece for in-store signage, countertoppers (i.e., displays and other promotional devices designed to sit on counters), and national advertising campaigns that educate customers about recycling-resource conservation issues and generate an image of environmental responsibility for participating retailers. Further retailer support is provided by a marketing manual, *Building Business with WE CARE®,* which contains marketing checklists; sample press releases; 60-second radio spot scripts; tombstone drop-in small space advertisements for magazines, newspapers, and telephone yellow pages; and video presentations. Safety-Kleen's experience with the program suggests that participating firms can pass along reasonable eco-costs to customers and that using the program can create a local competitive advantage for the retailer based on demonstrated environmental responsibility (D. Besterfeldt, Safety-Kleen Corp., personal communication, August 19, 1997).

Contractual Networks

These systems use the legal power embodied in an enforceable contract to detail the relationships that bind the partners together for the purpose of marketing a product. For example, fast-food franchise contracts contain detailed provisions defining the exact product lines to be sold, use of promotional materials, hours of operation, advertising fund participation requirements, materials specifications relating to products and packaging contents, management information reporting requirements, participation in corporate training programs, and the percentage franchise royalty that must be paid on sales.

In contractual systems, it is relatively easy to incorporate waste management rules, regulations, and policies into contracts as simply another aspect of defining operating standards. For example, the 1991 partnership between McDonald's and the Environmental Defense Fund uncovered a number of waste management issues involving supplier and franchise outlet operations. As a result, improved practices have been incorporated into the firm's world-wide network of fast-food locations (McDonald's Corporation 1991).

Corporate Networks

These systems use corporate ownership of one or more levels of the distribution chain to gain control over marketing activities. This legal power base is the most absolute form of control; it essentially results in an absolute hire-fire, command-and-control style relationship. Corporate systems also are generally high volume in character. The fully integrated corporate system formerly used by the Reynolds Aluminum Company to recover and process used beverage containers was mentioned earlier as one of the alternative reverse channel networks making up the materials recycling infrastructure.

Many corporate integrated systems are partially integrated in that owner-ship extends only one level above or below in the channel organizational structure. For example, to accomplish outbound distribution, many large manufacturers own distribution centers rather than use independent wholesal-ers; this is a form of partial forward integration. Similarly, many large retail chains own distribution centers that function as internal supply depots; this is a form of partial backward integration. The repetitive shipping cycles and two-way information exchange that exists between manufacturing facilities and distribution centers (manufacturing facilities ↔ distribution centers), and between distribution centers and retail stores (distribution centers ↔ retail stores), is an ideal setting for implementing reusable packaging systems. Because networks often are large and management's control is relatively absolute, corporate policy can be quite effective in making environmental improvement happen. For example, in 1995 the world's largest retailer, Wal-Mart, operated more than 2,000 Wal-Mart and 400 Sam's Club stores in the United States, with an annual sales volume of $93.6 billion (Hoover Online 1995). The opportunities for reaping environmental gains from such operating formats are significant.

Sustainable Marketing Audit: Channels Assessment

Obtaining information through a marketing audit is a prerequisite of implementation. To assist in the channels assessment process, a number of generalized questions and issues are provided in Exhibit 3.7. It remains important to recognize that the "position(s)" of a firm in the PSLC will determine the significance of various channels-related factors in the analysis.

Chapter Summary

The role of marketing channels is to make products accessible to customers. In so doing, the intermediary organizations and customers making up channel networks engage in move-store and consumption activities that generate process and product/packaging wastes. Channel decisions involve two components: (1) logistics and (2) channel management. In the area of logistics, channel DFE focuses on reducing the volume of waste flowing from these sources (P2 strategies) and the need to manage any remaining unavoidable waste streams (e.g., disposable packaging) through R2 strategies. Channel management involves examining the role of retailing, channel partner selection, and various implementation issues associated with sustainable channel decisions.

The usual notion of channels is one involving the forward movement of products from manufacturing sources to customer markets. P2 initiatives involve moderating waste streams from outbound activities such as transportation, inventory, and fugitive emissions. This may involve the minimization of product movement (transportation), more efficient inventory programming, and enhanced vigilance against accidental (fugitive) discharges. Such actions translate into using fewer resources to meet equivalent customer needs, or "getting more from less."

In contrast to forward channels, the term *reverse channel* is used to designate those cases in which the flows of products or materials occur in the opposite direction and has become the label for the Stage 5 channels in the PSLC that manage unavoidable wastes. Reverse channels are an essential element of all R2 strategies (i.e., product reuse, materials recycling, materials transformation) because they represent the infrastructure that performs the necessary recapture and processing functions.

For consumer products, retailer selection is an important traditional channel management decision. Retailers are closest to the customer and serve as major interpreters of market preferences. They also may play a major role in educating consumers about environmental matters. As channel members, retailers spin off the same general types of logistics and product (packaging) wastes as do other channel members; however, they also may be points of mandated or voluntary take-back for specialized products/materials such as used oil, lead-acid batteries, automobile tires, and consumer containers.

Two categories of specialty green retailers have evolved: (1) eco-retailers and (2) green catalog retailers. Although generally small in terms of sales volume, some larger retailers fall into these categories. Most can be described as cause driven, in this case the cause being environmental social responsibility. Mainstream retailers with traditional profit motives also have engaged in sustainable initiatives. Some focus on greening store operations through "reduce, reuse, recycle" programs. Others incorporate design improvements into new store development strategy by focusing on energy-efficient design and the use of recycled-contents materials in building construction. Still others have placed green products lines on shelves in the form of store brands or by encouraging suppliers to offer green product alternatives. As a specialized large-scale form of retailing facility, shopping malls have adopted many of the same practices as those of individual stores but have concentrated most on facilities design, reducing energy and water use, and minimizing the functional costs of local waste management through materials recycling programs.

One approach to enhancing overall sustainable practice is to use environmental performance as a channel member selection criterion. So far, applications of green selection criteria have been largely individualized and qualitative in nature. But two factors are changing this state of affairs. First, advances in environmental science have resulted in more standardized approaches and measurement formats. Second, the International Organization for Standards currently is implementing ISO 14000, the EMS to be applied worldwide. Some suggest that ISO 14000 will become a buyer requirement in the near future and that suppliers will have to be properly certified to make buyers' "to consider" lists. In short, ISO 14000 may become a powerful market-driven greening factor.

Overall, life-cycle analysis often leads to the conclusion that it is generally not feasible for one firm to accomplish the task of managing cradle-to-grave waste management. Rather, a joint effort by the many organizations and customers making up the PSLC is necessary to accomplish environmental progress. Developing logistical strategic alliances and working within channels to achieve higher levels of vertical integration and cooperation among channel partners are ways in which to implement sustainable channel solutions. Developing appropriate decision support information via the sustainable marketing audit process is another important factor.

cHAptER 6

Sustainable Marketing Communications

Marketing communications decisions are not linked to waste outcomes in the same way as are product and channel decisions. Even though communications processes do consume resources and spin off waste to an extent, these activities are waste-generating lightweights when compared to the business of designing and making products and then making them accessible to customers through channel networks. Rather, communications is a transaction facilitator, one that supports a basic assumption of the free market economy— the customer's ability (and right) to make an informed choice.

Role of Marketing Communications

As an element of the marketing mix, the role of the marketing communications is to positively influence stakeholder behavior now and in the future. This is accomplished by developing a communications (promotion) mix consisting of the following standard tools: (1) advertising, (2) personal selling, (3) sales promotion, and (4) publicity-public relations (PR). Although marketing communications often have been criticized as a source of cheap hype, puffery, and misinformation, the legitimate purpose of marketing communications is to blend these tools in such a manner as to provide customers value added through information.

In general, much of the information contents of sustainable communications is generated by the decisions a firm makes in those areas of the marketing mix that do have a direct impact on waste generation, that is, (1) product and (2) channel networks. In competitive markets, "value added through information" means providing complete and appropriate information about product alternatives to foster the customer's ability to make an informed choice. Obviously, the firm has the opportunity to use environmental issues and product information to redirect buying decisions toward its ecologically compatible products and away from the ecologically destructive products of competitors.

Communications Design-for-Environment

Because environmental issues are intangible, illusive, and often misunderstood by customers, communicating the true substance of sustainability is a challenging proposition. The "bad guys" in the scenario—waste/pollution generation and its ultimate negative consequences in terms of human health, welfare, and quality of life—are difficult to quantify and make tangible in the minds of customers, and hard data often are subject to the conflicting interpretations that make up the ongoing scientific debate. Attaining positive results in terms of environmental quality improvement is a slow, long-term proposition; the immediate benefits to customers from behaving in environmentally beneficial ways often are not readily apparent to those same customers.

A Two-Way, Multifaceted Challenge

But people also recognize that the environment "isn't what it used to be" and are beginning to question the fundamentals of company and product environmental performance, that is, what goes into products, the impact of product manufacturing on the natural world, and the ultimate consequences of waste generation and disposal. The challenge of sustainable marketing communications, which is to provide meaningful environmental information, can be likened to the familiar analogy of separating the wheat from the chaff. This challenge is multifaceted, not singular. As Peattie (1995) points out, "Communicating successfully is not simply a question of putting out positive messages regarding eco-performance. It involves becoming involved in a multiparty dialogue about business and the environment" (p. 211).

Harrison (1994) supports this view by describing the practice of sustainable communications as "a continuous, multilevel, and consistent exchange between the organization and its customer-publics. It draws upon and reinforces a cooperative 'green' mentality in the organization, and it attracts useful input and output" (p. 8). He continues by emphasizing the interactive, two-way nature of the sustainable communications process. In short, marketers do not simply create and deliver preprogrammed messages to designated targets. Rather, the nature of environmental performance requires a give-and-take to create "the right kind of customer-public relationships . . . and [to] constantly deal with the changing forces and channels involved in environmental performance and reputation" (p. 8).

Communications as Pollution Prevention/ Resource Recovery Strategy Support

Marketing communications serve as the information support troops for the various pollution prevention (P2) and resource recovery (R2) strategies that are primarily outgrowths of product and channel design-for-environment (DFE) decisions. Therefore, the information presented in this chapter may be creatively adapted to the circumstances or conditions surrounding any P2/R2 strategy for the purpose of positively influencing purchase decisions and other outcomes.

Sustainable Communications Objectives

At a general level, sustainable communications objectives concern fostering an image of environmental responsibility that will lead to product purchase (see Exhibit 3.3). For business firms, this means that two-way sustainable communications must constantly address two specific objectives: (1) educating a diverse set of stakeholders about environmental issues and (2) establishing and maintaining the environmental credibility of both the product and the firm behind it.

These objectives assume unique importance in sustainable communications for at least two reasons. First, the subject of "the environment" represents a new and complex issue. Many mature adults living in advanced economies have grown up believing that maximizing customer convenience through disposable products equates with progress, that unrestrained use of resources is a basic right that goes with wealth, and that waste management is nothing more than an "out of sight, out of mind" garbage dump problem. Most have not had access to the formal education and training in ecology/earth science that today's children routinely experience in primary and secondary schools. Second, most consumers in the affluent (developed) countries do not understand that the eco-costs associated with their high levels of consumption can, and do, have a negative impact on world ecosystems and developing nations. Nor do they understand the competing demands placed on resources (and ecosystems) by the population explosion in the developing countries. Thus, the objective of educating stakeholders about environmental issues, including the global ramifications of sustainability, must be constantly tempered by the objective of learning their current perceptions and misconceptions about those same environmental issues.

It follows that when opinions are being formed, the credibility of information sources becomes a key factor. This is particularly true in the case of environmental issues because there are no easy scientific answers to begin with and the public debate often is rancorous. In addition, the marketing community has been regularly accused of taking green issues out of context, putting a spin on them, and using them as a marketing ploy in an attempt to fatten short-term, bottom-line profits at the customer's expense. This practice, coined "green washing" by Landler (1991), has done little to enhance the believability of business information sources when it comes to green issues. A 1991 Gallup poll of 1,514 consumers reported in *Advertising Age* noted that only 8 percent of respondents said they were "very confident" that product advertising provides accurate information about impact on the environment (Chase 1991:10). Therefore, the challenges of educating stakeholders and building credibility/trust are obvious and profound.

The linking of very specific sustainable communications objectives to P2 and R2 strategies is accomplished by focusing the subject matter on appropriate issues and then designating the promotion mix elements to be employed. Several examples of sustainable communications objectives are given in the following:

Pollution prevention:
1. To increase the percentage awareness of target customers of our joint programs with the Nature Conservancy from 10 to 80 percent by January 1, 20__
2. To communicate the comprehensive nature of our production process P2 programs to 100 percent of shareholders by publishing a separate "environmental annual report" by January 1, 20__

Resource recovery:

1. To increase the percentage of target customers aware of the fact that our product's new package is made with at least 25 percent recycled materials from 0 to 80 percent by January 1, 20__

2. To communicate the ecological value and availability of local curbside recycling programs by distributing 1 million point-of-purchase brochures in our stores by January 1, 20__

In addition, traditional nonfinancial objectives of marketing communications in relation to primary product benefits (e.g., image development, persuasion, the transfer of specific product information about primary benefits, achieving repeat purchases, moving outdated inventories) must not be overlooked. After all, it is the actual purchase of sustainable products that brings the desired result—positive environmental effects and profits—and effective marketing communications will facilitate this desired outcome.

Sustainable Communications Targets

As with traditional communications efforts, stakeholder targets for sustainable communications are diverse. In addition to customers (target markets), relevant stakeholder groups include company employees, shareholders, channel partners, regulators (local, state, federal, and international), and environmental advocacy groups. In particular, partnering with environmental advocacy groups in the area of sustainable communications makes it possible for businesses to avoid adversarial relationships through improved communications while implementing believable communications that meet the objectives of all concerned. This unique opportunity to form communications alliances is discussed later in this chapter.

Controversy over Message

In the late 1980s, a wave of green-washing in the United States and elsewhere led to calls for the regulation of green claims in marketing communications programs. The broad public policy goal was to avoid deception and provide customers and other stakeholders with more reliable, accurate, and relevant information about the environmental impact of products and the companies that make and market them.

Green Report I

In November 1990, the attorneys general of 10 states issued *The Green Report I* (State Attorneys General 1990). The work was critical of so-called green marketing because its zealous pursuit by business to take advantage of consumer interest in environmental issues appeared to be creating a plethora of unfounded environmental claims. In short, green marketing was rapidly becoming equated with "green hype." The report recommended the following:

1. Environmental claims should be as specific as possible, not general, vague, incomplete, or overly broad.
2. Environmental claims relating to disposability (e.g., degradable or recyclable) should not be made unless the advertised disposal option *currently* is available to consumers in the area in which the product is sold and the product complies with the requirements of the relevant waste disposal programs.
3. Environmental claims should be substantive.
4. Environmental claims should, of course, be supported by competent and reliable scientific evidence. (p. 3)

FTC Regulation of Environmental Claims

In response, the U.S. Federal Trade Commission (FTC) moved to clear the air (no pun intended) by setting initial guidelines that would serve to "reduce consumer confusion and prevent the false or misleading use of environmental terms . . . in the advertising and labeling of products" ("FTC Chairman Steiger" 1992:1). Published in July 1992, *Guides for the Use of Environmental Marketing Claims* deal mainly with establishing norms for the use of environmental terminology and the manner in which the FTC will apply its existing deception policy and substantiation policy statements in the environmental context (FTC 1992). In short, terminology or statements are deemed deceptive if they cannot be reasonably substantiated by fact. The *Guides* establish a voluntary compliance/preventive approach on this issue, rather than a mandated/legalistic one, by setting forth certain general principles followed by guidance about the use of terms in making specific environmental marketing claims.

The general principles apply to all environmental marketing claims and cover four areas: (1) qualifications and disclosures, (2) the distinction between benefits of product versus package, (3) overstatement of environmental attributes, and (4) comparative claims. The first factor refers to the general language used stating qualifications and disclosures; that is, its sufficiency in terms of clarity, type size, and prominence in or on the communication vehicle. The product versus package principle points out that when a package is recyclable but the contents are not, labeling that refers to the whole product as "recyclable" may be deemed deceptive (e.g., an aluminum container is recycled, whereas its contents are not). The overstatement principle is an attempt to stop deception via the mention of "trivial but true" environmental benefits (e.g., "We increased recycled contents 100 percent—from 0.5 to 1.0 percent"). Finally, when making a comparison, care must be taken to clearly state the basis for the claim and to be able to provide substantiation if required (e.g., "Our product has 25 percent more recycled contents" provides no basis for the comparison).

Actual guidance on specific environmental claims is provided in the form of a listing of a number of common terms/phrases that have been subject to misrepresentation along with examples of what might be appropriate. A partial listing includes the following: compostable, degradable, recyclable, ozone safe/ozone friendly, recycled contents, source reduction, and refillable. In general, misrepresentation can occur through their unsubstantiated or unqualified use. Exhibit 6.1 summarizes the FTC's suggestions concerning the use of two prominent environmental terms, *recyclable* and *recycled contents,* and provides examples of appropriate and inappropriate uses of each. Quite obviously, the complexity of the language demonstrated in these examples has raised as many questions as it has provided answers. But it does represent a necessary first step in an attempt to bring order to a very complex subject.

Environmental Message Design

Kotler (1997) notes several key areas that must be addressed by message design: (1) determining what to say (message contents), (2) determining how to say it logically and symbolically (message structure and format), and (3) determining who should say it (message source) (p. 611). In the discussions that follow, it is suggested that even though the research on green promotion messages has focused almost exclusively on consumer advertising, many of the findings to date likely have relevance for personal selling, sales promotion, and publicity-PR as well.

ᴇxʜibiт **6.1**

Examples of Inappropriate and Appropriate Use of Two Environmental Terms

Term: *Recyclable*

A product or package should not be marketed as "recyclable" unless it can be collected, separated, or otherwise recovered from the solid waste stream for use in the form of raw materials in the manufacture or assembly of a new product or package. This also means that facilities must be present to accomplish these processes.

Inappropriate use: A package is labeled with the unqualified claim "recyclable." It is unclear from the type of product and other context whether the claim refers to the product or its package.

Appropriate use: A product is marketed as having a "recyclable" container. The product is distributed and advertised only in Missouri, where collection sites and facilities are available to a substantial majority of residents.

Term: *Recycled contents*

A recycled contents claim may be made only for materials that have been recovered or otherwise diverted from the solid waste stream, either during the manufacturing process (preconsumer) or after consumer use (postconsumer). Substantiation must exist to show that the preconsumer component would have entered the solid waste stream.

Inappropriate use: A manufacturer routinely collects spilled raw material and scraps from trimming finished products. After a minimal amount of reprocessing, the manufacturer combines the spills and scraps for use in further production of the same product. A claim that the product contains recycled material is deceptive because these materials would not normally have entered the solid waste stream.

Appropriate use: A greeting card is composed 30 percent by weight of paper collected from consumers after use of a paper product and 20 percent by weight of paper that was generated after completion of the paper-making process, diverted from the solid waste stream, and otherwise would not normally have been reused in the original manufacturing process. The marketer may claim that the product contains "50 percent recycled material."

SOURCE: Federal Trade Commission (1992), *Guides for the Use of Environmental Marketing Claims*, Washington, DC: FTC, pp. 16-22.

Themes-Appeals: General Types

What themes-appeals are showing up in contemporary sustainable communications? A study by Banerjee, Gulas, and Iyer (1995) found the following types of themes-appeals used in 173 contemporary green print and television advertisements:

- Zeitgeist: Reflects the mood of the times by implying a pro-environmental stance that attempts to blend with the prevailing green climate, either through bland statements (e.g., this product is environmentally safe) or by linking the product to the green movement (i.e., the bandwagon effect)
- Emotional: The use of fear, guilt, humor, self-esteem, and warmth
- Rational/financial: The use of lower price, or the seller making a "contribution per unit sold" to an environmental cause or organization, tied to the product's purchase
- Health: Highlighting the health aspects of environmentalism or emphasizing the goodness of "natural" ingredients [and the like]
- Corporate: Emphasizing the commitment of the organization to social welfare and the taking of green actions
- Testimonial: The use of a celebrity, [an] expert, or [an] ordinary person to endorse a product's environmental benefits
- Comparative benefit: The direct comparison of green and regular products on a specific benefit (p. 23)

Claims: General Types

Although themes-appeals set the general tone or direction of a sustainable communication, specific claims, or statements about environmental issues, set the details. A content analysis of 100 environmental advertisements by Carlson, Grove, and Kangun (1993) produced the following generalized list of claim types:

- Product orientation claims: Focus on the environmentally friendly attributes that a product possesses.

  Example: "This product is biodegradable."
- Process orientation claims: Deal with an organization's internal technology, production technique, and/or disposal method that yields environmental benefits.

  Example: "Twenty percent of the raw materials used in producing this good are [from] recycled [materials]."

    ▒ Image orientation-enhancing claims: Associate an organization with an environmental cause or activity for which there is broad-based public support.

    Example (a): "We are committed to preserving our forests."

    Example (b): "We urge that you support the movement to preserve our wetlands."

    ▒ Environmental fact claims: Invoke an independent statement that is ostensibly factual in nature from an organization about the environment at large or its condition.

    Example: "The world's rain forests are being destroyed at a rate of two acres per second." (p. 31)

Claims: Relationship to Product System Life-Cycle Stages

A differentiating feature of sustainable marketing is that the product system life cycle (PSLC) is seen as the relevant decision framework. Therefore, the various stages of the PSLC also represent a logical taxonomy for assessing the type of claim in terms of environmental subject matter or focus. Earlier work by Iyer and Banerjee (1993) sorts 173 green advertisements into "levels of the eco-chain" as follows: (1) production (28.3 percent), (2) consumption (3.5 percent), and (3) disposition (16.2 percent), but 52.0 percent of the advertisements proved to be "not applicable" under this classification approach (p. 499). Similarly, in their analysis of regulatory challenges to environmental claims, Scammon and Mayer (1995) sort environmental claims into the life-cycle categories of (1) production (e.g., recycled content, no bleach/chlorine, source reduction) (17.7 percent), (2) consumption (e.g., ozone/CFCs, fewer/no pollutants or pesticides, energy efficiency) (23.4 percent), and (3) disposal (degradability, recyclability, compostability, harmless incineration) (44.4 percent), and only 14.5 percent were classified "not applicable" (p. 37).

The noted advertising giant J. Walter Thompson USA (1991) emphasizes the relevance of the life-cycle concept in environmental message design. Specifically, its work links the source of authority in green advertisements—which the firm describes as the distinctive language of Mother Nature, science, or ordinary people—to successive life-cycle stages. For example, a Mother Nature metaphor portrays a dolphin family in a Starkist tuna advertisement to show the need to protect one natural resource while harvesting another at the extraction stage; the precise language of science (e.g., numbers, statistics) conveys improvements in products and processes and the lowering of pollution levels at the manufacturing stage; and the colloquial and familiar language of ordinary people ties in every consumer's personal experience with garbage with the suggestion that they recycle containers at the disposal stage.

Claims: Structure and Format

Designing messages that meet legal requirements while also communicating environmental information in a meaningful way has been a persistent challenge. Four issues stand out: (1) character-quality of claim, (2) claim specificity, (3) claim emphasis, and (4) customer orientation.

Character-Quality of Claim

Using the classification of claim types described earlier (i.e., product, process, image, fact), Carlson et al. (1993) further characterized 122 individual environmental claims found in 100 advertisements (some contained multiple claims). This was accomplished by having judges evaluate the character-quality of each claim, a process that produced the following qualitative categories:

- Vague/ambiguous: The claim is overly vague or ambiguous; it contains a phrase or statement that is too broad to have a clear meaning.

  Example: "This product is environmentally friendly."
- Omission: The claim omits important information necessary to evaluate its truthfulness or reasonableness.

  Example: "This product contains no CFCs" (when in fact it contains other environmentally harmful chemicals).
- False/outright lie: The claim is inaccurate or a fabrication.

  Example: "This product is made from recycled materials" (when in fact it is not).
- Acceptable: The claim made was judged to be truthful and accurate.

  Example: "This product's package contains at least 25 percent postconsumer recycled materials" (when in fact it does). (p. 31)

Because the sample was small ($n = 122$), Carlson et al. offer the following tentative (qualitative) findings:

- More claims were judged to contain misleading/deceptive aspects (60 percent) than those judged to be acceptable (40 percent).

▓ Misleading/deceptive claims were judged to occur more often in the product (88 percent) and image (65 percent) claim categories than in the process (36 percent) and environmental fact (33 percent) categories.

▓ Image-oriented claims were more often cited as being vague/ambiguous (52 percent) than as omitting information (11 percent) or containing falsehoods (2 percent).

▓ More claims were judged to be vague/ambiguous (42 percent) than as omitting information (10 percent) or containing falsehoods (8 percent). (p. 35)

The message, then, for designers of environmental communications is this: it is necessary to deal with the perception of lack of specifics and inaccuracies that permeate past efforts from both a legal and customer point of view. Beginning with the current legal debate over environmental claims, Davis (1993) notes,

> From a marketer's perspective, a focus on legal and regulatory issues is important. . . . However, we do not believe that the resolution of regulatory issues and the subsequent strict adherence to resulting regulations . . . will determine the ultimate success of environmental marketing efforts. We do believe that marketing success will be the result of understanding and satisfying consumer needs, needs which may be significantly more stringent than, or possibly even different from, regulatory requirements. (p. 20)

He goes on to identify three subissues associated with environmental message structure and format that must be addressed if marketers are to develop an appropriate consumer's perspective: (1) the specificity of the environmental claim, (2) the level of emphasis given the environmental claim, and (3) consumer orientation toward environmental appeals.

Claim Specificity

This first issue involves the degree to which a stated claim is either specific in contents or vague and/or ambiguous. It is axiomatic that Carlson et al.'s (1993) finding that a large percentage of environmental advertising claims are perceived by consumers as "misleading/deceptive" reflects a downright unhealthy situation. Davis (1993) confronts this issue directly by first defining a "specific environmental claim" as one that (1) provides useful, detailed information; (2) presents real, not implied, benefits; and (3) represents meaningful benefits in terms of contributing to environmental improvement (pp. 21-22). His thesis that environmental claims should be "specific, not vague and/or ambiguous" is supported by the following research findings:

■ Environmental claims perceived as specific foster a positive advertiser image. Claims perceived as vague foster negative perceptions of the advertiser (p. 23).

■ Environmental claims perceived as specific foster positive perceptions of the product. Claims perceived as vague result in highly unfavorable product perceptions (p. 25).

■ Environmental claims perceived as specific are significantly more likely versus claims perceived as vague to be persuasive and to lead to higher levels of product purchase intent (p. 25).

These findings lead to the six guidelines for presenting environmental claims that are presented in Exhibit 6.2.

It also must be noted in passing that the terms *specific* and *scientific* are not meant to be equated when describing environmental claims. As pointed out in Chapter 2, the use of quantitative life-cycle assessment (LCA) inventory results as a source of specifics for sustainable communications has yet to become an acceptable practice. What *specific* does mean in this context is that a careful review of a product or an organization will likely uncover unique environmental linkages that can be used to positively communicate and support various aspects of P2 or R2 strategies while not citing quantitative claims that go beyond the ability of current science to support. Developing collateral, and sometimes reasonably quantitative, associations between products/organizations and positive environmental values is both possible and plausible. In short, the new standards of behavior being fostered by broad-based environmental concerns can be translated into important environmental messages that support both products and firms at a fairly general level and yet are specific enough to have meaning.

Rehak (1993) demonstrates this potential to build positive environmental associations through communications that are more sensitive to environmental values. Building on his experience at Ogilvy & Mather, he has cataloged 64 strategies, selected examples of which are summarized in Exhibit 6.3. Notice the direct tie-ins to various aspects of P2 and R2 approaches. Using a more quantitative approach, Procter & Gamble demonstrates a similar tone in the segments of ad copy presented in Exhibit 6.4.

Claim Emphasis

How much emphasis should be placed on environmental claims versus the product's traditional core attributes? The dilemma is this: placing increased emphasis on environmental attributes leads to a decrease in emphasis on traditional benefit-creating attributes. An emphasis on environmental attri-

exhibit 6.2

Guidelines for Presenting Environmental
Claims: A Focus on Delivering Specifics

1. Ensure that the promoted benefit has a real impact.

   Comment: Benefits that are likely to be positively associated with environmental improvement from the consumer's perspective include (a) reduced packaging, (b) the use of recycled materials, (c) biodegradability, and (d) reduced harmful emissions.

2. Identify the product's specific benefit; identify the specific product attribute that underlies the product's environmental contribution.

   Comment: Specific source attributes include recycled materials contents, downsized package, and so on.

3. Provide specific data.

   Comment: The claim should be supported by specific detailed information. For example, "100 percent recycled paperboard, minimum 35 percent postconsumer" is specific, whereas "contains recycled paperboard" is not.

4. Provide a context.

   Comment: The claim should have a benchmark for comparison or frame of reference. The advertiser should be able to complete the following statement: "The product makes an environmental contribution compared to _____ because _____." Benchmarks/frames of reference can include a product's previous package, prior formulations of the product, a competitive product's formulation or

---

butes suggests that they are a more important driver of the purchase decision than are traditional attributes when they likely are not.

Davis (1993) and others (Carson 1991; Ottman 1993) suggest that for many consumers, environmental attributes play a secondary or supplemental role in the purchase decision. In other words, all other factors being equal, traditional product category attributes serve as the primary driver of purchase decisions; environmental attributes generally serve as a "tie-breaker." This is especially the case when the competing products in a category are perceived to be relatively equal on traditional benefit-creating attributes (e.g., all toilet bowl cleaners clean equally well).

EXHIBIT 6.2 Continued

package size, and so on. For example, "This strengthened 32-ounce plastic container represents 20 percent less packaging materials than our previous 40-ounce package."

5. Define technical terms.

Comment: Definitions should be provided for all technical terms. For example, the term "postconsumer recycled plastic" should carry the notation that this is material that is collected after consumer use as opposed to materials generated during production runs in manufacturing facilities.

6. Explain the benefit.

Comment: The reason the benefit is real or important might not be apparent to consumers. The phrase "this package made from chlorine-free paper" might fall on deaf ears unless consumers are advised as to the association between dioxin contamination and chlorine bleaching processes.

Overall: Marketing research can be employed to determine the meaning of environmental product attributes in the customer's mind, which are seen an having real impact.

SOURCE: Adapted from Davis, Joel J. (1993), "Strategies for Environmental Advertising," *Journal of Consumer Marketing,* Vol. 10, No. 2, pp. 19-36.

This consumer predisposition is reflected in Figure 6.1, where the grid dimension "product image" (i.e., how the product performs on traditional attributes relative to competitors) is classified as either "positive" (i.e., better than competitors) or "neutral/negative," and the dimension "source of product's environmental benefit" is described as either "physical" (e.g., reformulation) or "nonphysical" (e.g., packaging). This results in three distinct cells that are strategically interpreted as follows:

Cell 1: Product is positively perceived by consumers in terms of traditional benefit delivery; the environmental benefit is obtained through basic product changes (i.e., a reformulation, new functional approach, etc.)—this is essentially a "new" product. Therefore, because the traditional benefits drive the purchase, customers must *first* be reassured that the "new" product

ЕхнiвiT **6.3**

Advertising Support Strategies Based on Positive Environmental Value Themes

Description of Strategy	*Scenario/Logic*
Reinforce performance benefits with environmental benefits.	Consumers buy products for their basic benefits, not environmental benefits; however, "environment" can be a tie-breaker. ***Example:*** Exxon 93 Supreme gasoline couples expected high performance with low emissions.
Portray environmentally responsible behavior as cost-conscious—saving money and more.	Builds on the idea that waste represents inefficiency and that overcoming inefficiency reduces costs. ***Example:*** Downey, backed by Downey Refill, results in less packaging; it costs less to make and less "per use."
Emphasize quality, durability, and longevity.	This reduces materials and disposal volume, and it discourages the development of a "disposable" mentality. ***Example:*** Toyota advertisements feature owners whose vehicles have exceeded 100,000, 200,000, or 300,000 miles.
Help customers minimize waste.	Products that directly address the waste reduction issue fit this scenario. ***Example:*** Food container systems (e.g., Rubbermaid, Tupperware) minimize spoilage. Other applications include showing customers how to use products more efficiently (e.g., power company conservation programs, Shell showing drivers how to get more miles per gallon).
Provide customers with a way in which to repair and upgrade products.	This strategy extends the product service lives of ancillary components. ***Example:*** Personal computer upgrades through the installation of high-speed chips.
Develop reusable products.	This approach emphasizes the "throwaway" versus "reuse" contrast. ***Example:*** Millenium Rechargeable Power Cells are positioned as an alternative to a "lifetime supply of throwaway batteries."

SOURCE: Rehak, Robert (1993), *Greener Marketing and Advertising: Charting a Responsible Course*, Emmaus, PA: Rodale Press. Reprinted by permission.

---

exhibit 6.4

▨▨▨▨▨▨▨▨▨▨▨▨▨▨▨

Procter & Gamble Environmental Advertising Copy

Working together we can help efforts to reduce solid waste

Procter & Gamble is committed to minimizing the impact our products and packaging have on the environment. Our goal is to reduce the materials used in packaging our products, to use recycled materials in making our packages, and to explore ways in which our products and packages can be reused or recycled rather than simply thrown away. Here are some of the steps we are taking:

Source reduction

- *Downy® Refill* allows the reuse of the original 64 oz Downy bottle and uses 74% less packaging than the 64 oz bottle.
- *Ultra Tide®* and *Ultra Bold®* packages contain 10% less packaging per use than conventional size powder packaging.
- *Tide®* with *Bleach* and *Liquid Tide®* with *Bleach Alternative* reduce packaging by eliminating the need for separate detergent and bleach packages. *Bold®* reduces packaging waste by eliminating the need for separate detergent and softener packages.
- *Ivory® Bar Soap* is biodegradable. It reduces solid waste by using less packaging than many leading bar soaps.
- *Instant Folgers®* plastic jar uses 75% less packaging than glass jars.
- *Folgers®* Brick Bag reduces packaging by nearly 90% in weight.
- *Pampers®* and *Luvs®* have 50% less product material than previous diapers. The compact packaging uses 60% less material than previous packaging and the new paper shipping container reduces packaging material by 90%.

Using recycled materials

- *Tide® Bold®* and *Puffs®* boxes are made of 100% recycled paperboard (minimum 35 percent post-consumer).
- *Ultra Tide®* and *Ultra Bold®* package handles are made of 50% post-consumer recycled plastic and the scoops are made of 100% post-consumer recycled plastic.
- *Liquid Tide®* , *Liquid Bold®* , *ERA®* and *Downy® Liquid* (64 oz bottles and larger) are made with at least 25% post-consumer recycled plastic.
- *Pampers®* and *Luvs®* bags and *Bounty®* wrappers are made with 25% post-consumer recycled plastic (recycled from milk and water bottles).
- Learn responsible ways to handle your garbage and how recycling might help your community.

SOURCE: Davis, Joel J. (1993), "Strategies for Environmental Advertising," *Journal of Consumer Marketing*, Vol. 10, No. 2, p. 26. Reprinted by permisson.

---

will continue to deliver traditional benefits while environmental benefits should receive *secondary* emphasis.

Cell 2: Product is positively perceived by consumers in terms of traditional benefit delivery; the physical, functional product benefit remains essentially unchanged, and the environmental benefit is derived from nonphysical sources (e.g., a packaging change). The customer knows the product will "deliver" in terms of traditional benefits, and there are many equal,

	Product image versus competition in terms of traditionally important category benefits	
	Positive	Neutral/negative
Physical attribute (reformulation, etc.)	1	3
Non-physical attribute (packaging, etc.)	2	

Source of product's environmental benefit

Figure 6.1. Framework for Determining Environmental Advertising Claim Emphasis
SOURCE: Davis, Joel J. (1993), "Strategies for Environmental Advertising," *Journal of Consumer Marketing,* Vol. 10, No. 2, p. 30. Reprinted by permission.

look-alike competitors. Therefore, environmental benefits may function as a tie-breaker and consequently should be given *primary* emphasis.

Cell 3: Product is seen as having a disadvantage in the delivery of traditional benefits relative to competitors. Advertising must *first* develop positive associations with traditional benefits prior to any *secondary* emphasis on environmental claims. (Davis 1993:29-31)

Customer Orientation

Another factor affecting the efficacy of environmental claims is the target customer's motivation to respond (customer orientation). Research by Kinnear, Taylor, and Ahmed (1974), Davis (1993), and Ellen, Winer, and Cobb-Walgren (1991) suggests that consumers are more likely to positively respond to environmental claims if they believe that they are personally in control of the situation (i.e., their decisions-behaviors count, not luck, fate, or the controlling actions of others) and that their personal actions do make an environmental difference (i.e., the belief that buying a recycled contents product really does save resources). Davis (1993) sums up the need to understand consumer environmental orientation as follows:

> It is important for an environmental advertiser to stress the contribution and reward obtained from each individual's action of purchasing the advertised, environmentally sensitive product. Thus, the environmental advertising is likely to be more successful when the environmental problem addressed by the environmentally better product and the consumer contribution to environmental improvement are presented on a personal level, addressing these relevant attitudes in the advertising. (p. 31)

Exhibit 6.5

▨▨▨▨▨▨▨▨▨▨▨▨▨▨▨▨▨▨

Summary of Environmental Advertising Recommendations

1. Before advertising planning begins, consider concept testing the proposed environmental benefit to make certain that, *from the consumer's perspective*, the product:
   - is seen as providing a real and meaningful environmental benefit
   - benefit is seen as an improvement over competitive products

2. The environmental advertising claim should be written to provide specific and detailed information on the product's environmental benefit. Then, consider pretesting the claim to make certain that, *from the consumer's perspective* the claim:
   - states the specific aspect of the product in which the environmental benefit lies
   - provides specific data to permit the consumer to believe that the environmental product benefit is real
   - provides a context for evaluating the promoted environmental benefit
   - provides definitional support for all technical terminology
   - explains why the promoted environmental product attribute will result in an environmental benefit

3. When determining how much emphasis to give the environmental claim in the advertising examine the relationship between the source of environmental improvement and consumer attitudes toward the product:
   - first make certain that consumers' understand that the product delivers (or continues to deliver) expected levels of traditionally important category benefits
   - then promote the product's environmental benefit

4. When thinking about the context in which to place the product's environmental claim keep the advertising personal:
   - stress the contribution to the environment which *each individual* makes by purchasing environmentally-better alternatives
   - reinforce the target's environmentally conscious/responsible behaviors

---

SOURCE: Davis, Joel J. (1993), "Strategies for Environmental Advertising," *Journal of Consumer Marketing,* Vol. 10, No. 2, p. 32. Reprinted by permission.

A summary checklist of Davis's conclusions and recommendations concerning environmental advertising is provided in Exhibit 6.5.

Source Credibility

Kotler (1997) points out the importance of a message's source credibility in all marketing communications as follows:

Messages delivered by attractive or popular sources achieve higher attention and recall. . . . But what is equally important in the spokesperson is credibility. Messages delivered by highly credible sources are more persuasive. (pp. 615-16)

In research on spokesperson credibility, consumer stakeholders ranked their confidence in the various authority figures behind green product promises (claims) in advertisements in the following descending order: (1) approval by a well-known environmental group (39 percent), (2) approval by an independent laboratory (28 percent), (3) a scientist's testimonial (19 percent), and (4) a manufacturer's self-declared warranty/claim (9 percent) (J. Walter Thompson USA 1991:5). Clearly, there is a credibility gap when environmental messages are based only on the manufacturer's self-declared warranty/claim. This suggests that to establish consumer credibility, the firm must go outside and develop relationships with individuals and organizations that have inherently believable environmental credentials. The opportunity to form strategic alliances for this purpose is discussed later in this chapter.

By contrast, research by the Global Environmental Management Initiative (1996) among nonconsumer stakeholder groups on the credibility of voluntary corporate environmental reports (CERs) suggests that third-party attestation (e.g., supportive statements by accounting firms or environmental advocacy groups, certification by private sector agencies/companies) contributes little in the way of enhancing credibility. The stakeholder groups researched included investors, media reporters, regulators, environmental advocacy groups, and corporate environmental professionals. Those factors that tended to enhance credibility most included the following (rated 4 or higher on a 5-point scale):

- The presence of a balanced tone (both positive and negative aspects covered)
- Compliance trend information (including penalties paid)
- A description of environmental audit programs
- Quantitative information on environmental trends (other than Toxic Release Inventory emissions)
- Information on toxics use reductions
- Having a corporate environmental strategy
- The application of U.S. standards worldwide
- Oil and chemical spill trends
- Toxic Release Inventory emission reductions
- Occupational Safety and Health Administration (OSHA) information (p. 9)

Explicit versus Implicit Messages

The distinction between explicit and implicit messages in marketing communications is well stated by Bearden, Ingram, and Laforge (1995) as follows:

> Explicit communications convey a distinct, clearly stated message through personal selling, advertising, public relations, sales promotions, direct marketing, or some combination of these methods. Implicit communications are what the message connotes about the product itself, its price, or the place it is sold. (p. 430)

The limited ability of sustainable marketers to present incontrovertible facts about the environmental aspects of products and companies can lead to a natural focus on implicit message building. For example, despite the factual scenarios (explicit messages) presented in the advertisements by Glidden Company, Xerox Corporation, and Safety-Kleen Corporation shown in Exhibits 4.3, 6.6, and 6.7, respectively, probably the more valuable implicit message in each case is this: our organization has a serious and sincere commitment to environmental quality.

Environmental Labeling Programs

To encourage the use of environmentally compatible products by consumers, it would be extremely helpful to have available labels (symbols) that instantly differentiate the environmentally "good" products from the sea of offerings currently available in most product categories. In response to this need, a number of so-called third-party environmental labeling programs have evolved to provide this type of information. These programs typically use an independent governmental, quasi-governmental, or private entity as the source of an explicit environmental label or symbol, which is then applied to the product and/or package or used in marketing communications as evidence that the product meets certain standards or criteria. Exhibit 6.8 gives a worldwide sampling of what is now available or is in various stages of development.

Three outcomes are achieved by third-party programs: (1) an independent evaluation of the product takes place, (2) a consumer protection tool is created, and (3) environmental public policy goals are achieved. The U.S.

exHibit 6.6

A Positioning Statement Advertisement by Xerox Corporation

Sustainable Development
Corporate Citizens of the Earth

Sustainable development cannot occur without near universal participation. That means it is everyone's responsibility, including especially the business sector. Accepting that responsibility leads to a new agenda, not just of eco-efficiency or of stewardship, but a social agenda too – as citizens of the Earth.

Corporations are increasingly trans-national entities with operations in many countries and many communities. The same scales – global, national, and local – must characterize their citizenship responsibilities.

Just as the Earth Summit in Rio was the first United Nations conference at which non-governmental organizations played a major role, it was also the first time business organizations helped to shape the agenda and the output. The corporate activity organized by the Business Council for Sustainable Development, chaired by Swiss industrialist Stephan Schmidheiny, set an important precedent, but it is one that needs to be followed up.

Energy companies, for example, should be actively preparing to support the Climate Convention that will come into force later this year. They should also be preparing to participate in shaping the national plans aimed at stabilizing carbon dioxide emissions.

Pharmaceutical companies and bio-technology companies should be engaged in the North-South dialogue over biodiversity prospecting rights and responsibilities and intellectual property concerns that remain to be sorted out before the Biodiversity Convention can have full effect. Merck, for example, has initiated a pioneering agreement with Costa Rica that trades up front support for local biodiversity conservation efforts and possible future royalties for access to the country's biological and genetic riches.

Global citizenship also means, at the least, that corporations must themselves apply the same environmental and safety standards in poor countries with ineffective enforcement as they do in rich, well-regulated countries.

At a national level, citizenship in an era of sustainability means leadership and participation:

■ Leadership by public support of policies that move the country toward sustainable development and by private actions to make environmental citizenship a meaningful agenda at all levels of a corporation. DuPont, for example, was the first CFC manufacturer to commit to phasing out production; it also made progress in reducing toxic emissions a part of the salary review of every plant manager. Leadership also means taking initiative to set up needed industry-wide or nation-wide recycling systems, such as aluminum can and some plastics manufacturers have, or to establish eco-efficiency standards.

■ Participation in national groups and voluntary activities that can make a difference. The President's Council on Sustainable Development, established this summer, is co-chaired by David Buzzelli of The Dow Chemical Company and Jonathan Lash of the World Resources Institute and includes seven other corporate leaders as well as key Cabinet members and NGO leaders. It is charged with developing a national strategy that can be implemented by the public and private sectors.

Active participation is also the best way corporations can encourage and endorse voluntary government programs rather than regulatory regimes. The EPA Green Lights, Energy Star (for energy-saving computers and electronic equipment), and 33/50 (reduction of toxics emissions) programs deserve, and are getting, widespread corporate participation.

At a local level, citizenship means community involvement and public education – in the schools, in the home, in the workplace, and in the community. Sustainable development is not a familiar concept to many people, and not even experts can say all that it might mean. It will take time and deliberate efforts at communication to make it work. Environmental education has only a fragmentary toehold in primary school and secondary school curricula; corporations can support the creation and dissemination of better materials. Xerox has taken the initiative to help children become environmentally active by hosting local youngsters to an environmental seminar at Xerox's Stamford, Conn. headquarters, and through its "Kids on Earth" environmental education guide.

Many adults need better information too, to cope with local environmental challenges and to gain a perspective adequate to the challenge of sustainable development. Enlightened companies, aware that an informed citizen is ultimately their best neighbor, are not only seeking open dialogues with the communities in which they operate but also using their own employees to teach environmental concepts and improve public awareness.

No strategy for sustainability can, in the long run, succeed unless corporations accept their responsibilities as corporate citizens of an increasingly finite planet. ●

> *"Enlightened companies, aware that an informed citizen is ultimately their best neighbor, are using their own employees to teach environmental concepts and improve public awareness."*

Brought to you by Xerox: The Document Company

SOURCE: Reprinted from a series of special advertising sections in *Business Week*, November 3, 1993. Sponsored by Xerox. Copyright 1993 by McGraw-Hill Inc.

Exhibit 6.7

Safety-Kleen WE CARE Program Small Space
Advertisement for Automotive Services

While you're changing your oil... change the world.

Every year this country generates 1.4 billion gallons of used
oil that *could* be *re*-used. Recycled. Re-refined. If you get your oil
changed at a place like ours that shows the WE CARE® sticker —
you can be sure that your used oil is being recycled. So let *us*
change your oil — and help change the world, for the better.

BUSINESS NAME

SOURCE: Reprinted courtesy of Safety-Kleen Corporation, Elgin, IL.

Environmental Protection Agency (EPA 1993a) divides these labeling activities into two broad categories (Figure 6.2): (1) mandatory disclosure programs
and (2) voluntary environmental certification programs (ECPs).

Exhibit **6.8**

Examples of Worldwide Environmental Labels

SOURCE: U.S. Environmental Protection Agency (1993a), *Status Report on the Use of Environmental Labels Worldwide,* Washington, DC: EPA, Pollution Prevention Division, Office of Pollution Prevention and Toxics, EPA Contract No. 68-D0-0020.

NOTE: Row 1: Sweden, Singapore, U.S. Federal Trade Commission, U.S. State of Vermont; Row 2: Australia, U.S. Scientific Certification Systems, U.S. Green Seal, Japan; Row 3: New Zealand, Earthtrust Hawaii, the Netherlands, Canada; Row 4: Germany, European Community Ecolabel, U.S. Environmental Protection Agency, Nordic Council (Norway, Sweden, Iceland, Finland).

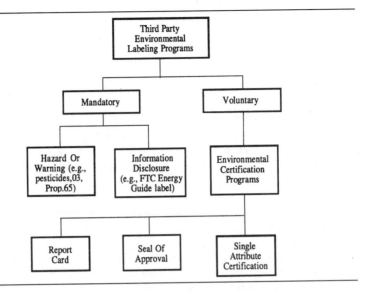

Figure 6.2.   Characterization of Third-Party Environmental Labeling Programs
SOURCE: Adapted from U.S. Environmental Protection Agency (1993a), *Status Report on the Use of Environmental Labels Worldwide,* Washington, DC: EPA, Pollution Prevention Division, Office of Pollution Prevention and Toxics, EPA Contract No. 68-D0-0020.

Mandatory Disclosure Programs

Mandatory programs are represented by federal, state, and local statutes that deal with issues such as "hazard warnings" and "required information disclosure" (Figure 6.2). Hazard warnings are negative by definition (see Vermont's household Hazardous Products label in Exhibit 6.8). Required information disclosure labels detail environmental facts that may or may not have been voluntarily offered by a manufacturer (see the EPA Energy Guide label in Exhibit 6.8). Depending on the situation, the impact can be either positive, negative, or neutral. However, from a marketing perspective, these are nondecisions in the sense that compliance with the given statute is necessary if the product is to be legally for sale.

Voluntary Environmental Certification Programs

The voluntary category consists of ECPs administered by government agencies and nonprofit organizations. The EPA (1993b) has identified three types of ECPs: (1) seal of approval, (2) single-attribute certification, and (3) report card.

Seal of Approval

A seal-of-approval program attempts to generally identify a product as being "less harmful to the environment than similar products/services with the same functions" (EPA 1993a:11). Products that meet given standards are licensed to use the prescribed logo. The process of arriving at this determination is as follows:

> Seal-of-approval programs award use of a logo to products judged to be less environmentally harmful than comparable products, based on a specified set of award criteria. First, product categories are defined based on similar use or other relevant characteristics. Award criteria are then developed for a product category. All products within a product category are compared against the same set of award criteria. How these product categories and award criteria are set defines the most important differences among seal-of-approval programs currently in existence. It is a complex task requiring the consideration of many factors including environmental policy goals, consumer awareness of environmental issues, and the economic effects on industry. (p. 12)

A sampling of seal-of-approval programs include Scientific Certification Systems (SCS) and Green Seal (both United States) and Environmental Choice (Canada) (Exhibit 6.8). In general, these programs have similar administrative setups. Typically, responsibility is vested in a central decision-making board composed of environmental groups, academics and scientists, business and trade representatives, consumer groups, and government/ regulatory agency representatives. Further technical advice is provided by the government, standards-setting organizations, consultants, and expert panels/ task forces set up to address specific issues. An example of the use of the SCS seal of approval by Glidden SPRED 2000 zero-VOC (volatile organic compound) paint is given in Exhibit 4.3.

Of course, a central issue associated with seal-of-approval programs is consistency in the award-granting process across venues. In an attempt to provide guidelines for standardization, the United Nations Environmental Programme sponsored the Global Environmental Labelling: Invitational Expert Seminar, which settled on the following basic features to be included in seal-of-approval programs:

- Determination of award criteria based on life-cycle review of a product category
- Voluntary participation of potential licensees
- Run by not-for-profit organization, including governments, without commercial interests
- Recommendations for product categories and environmental award criteria determined by an independent, broad-based board
- A legally protected symbol or logo
- Open access to potential licensees from all countries
- Endorsements from governments
- Award criteria levels established to encourage development of products and services that are significantly less damaging to the environment
- Periodic review and, if necessary, update of both environmental award criteria and categories, taking into account technological and marketplace developments (EPA 1993a:14)

Single-Attribute Certification

Single-attribute certification means that an independent firm has tested or otherwise examined a particular (single) product attribute (e.g., percentage recycled materials contents) and attests to its truthfulness/authenticity of a given claim. The concept is described by the EPA (1993a) as follows:

> Single-attribute certification programs certify that claims made for products meet a specified definition. Such programs define specific terms and accept applications from marketers for the use of those terms. If the programs verify that the product attributes meet their definitions, they award the use of a logo to the marketer. (p. 21)

Environmental Choice Australia and SCS's Single Claim Certification are the two single-attribute programs currently in operation. The former is sponsored by the Australia and New Zealand Environmental Conservation Council and includes a scientific committee that defines terms and verifies claims as well as a broad-based advisory committee that consults on major decisions. The program also features random testing of products to ensure compliance and the power to levy significant fines on those who misuse the Environmental Choice logo.

SCS is a private, nonprofit organization operating in the United States. Its Single Claim Certification serves as an independent audit to back up claim specifics. The EPA (1993a) reports that more than 500 individual products have been certified to date in subject areas such as recycled materials content, recycling rates, biodegradability, energy and water efficiency, VOC content, and the practice of sustainable forestry (p. 22). The process of certification includes gaining full access to company records and on-site visitations to verify information. After winning certification, the manufacturer is authorized to display an authorized certification emblem along with an exact description of verified claims.

Report Card

The report card category can be described as follows:

> The report card approach to (environmental) labeling involves categorizing and quantifying various impacts that a product has on the environment. Values for each impact category (e.g., kilograms of carbon dioxide released during manufacturing) are listed on the label and displayed in a bar graph. . . . Because report card labels provide the consumer with more information than standard seal-of-approval labels, the consumer has more specific information to consider when choosing a product. (EPA 1993a:23)

SCS is the only organization currently offering this system. Given reliable information, several advantages are apparent over single-attribute and seal-of-approval systems. The major advantage of the report card approach is that is provides a broader array of information. For example, whereas a seal of approval might label two recycled-contents products in exactly the same way (e.g., 25 percent postconsumer recycled contents), the additional variables shown on the report card bring to bear other areas, such as water and energy consumption during manufacture, in which the products might differ in important ways. The SCS Certified Eco-Profile (see Exhibit 2.2) shows this multiple variable comparison for the case of Fortrel EcoSpun 100 percent recycled polyester fiber versus virgin polyester fiber.

Green Gridlock over Environmental Certification Programs

The general thrust of all ECPs is to provide an indicator of what is good for the environment and what is not. Whether they are government, quasi-government, or privately sponsored, achieving certification costs money, so the motivation behind any marketing investment in environmental certification is to positively influence customer purchase behavior. This raises two questions. First, are ECPs an effective marketing tool; that is, do they have a positive impact on consumer purchases? Second, are ECPs a credible source of information?

In the report, *Determinants of Effectiveness for Environmental Certification and Labeling Programs,* the EPA (1994) does a good job of isolating determinants but fails to provide a real answer to the question of consumer purchase impact. For example, the report cites minimal survey evidence that consumer awareness of ECP labels is up in places such as Germany, where such labeling is old hat (80 percent of Germans are aware of the Blue Angle program that was initiated in 1977). The report continues by noting that "consumers are willing to accept a label if they can be convinced of its impartiality and credibility" (p. 21). Yet, isn't that the question—are they really convinced? Finally, the EPA admits that although some certifiers claim proof that ECPs improve market share, "most such evidence is anecdotal, does not control for other factors that may affect a product's marketplace performance (e.g., economic climate), or tracks changes only over a very short time" (p. 21). Clearly, the jury is still out on the effectiveness issue.

In regard to the second question, ECPs operate under the assumption that it is possible to measure/quantify the life-cycle impacts of products in a meaningful manner. In other words, they are an operationalized form of LCA inventory analysis, and many responsible analysts simply disagree with the use of LCA data in such applications (Fava, Consoli, and Denison 1991). Furthermore, some believe that the information provided or implied through ECPs might be misleading at best, and environmentalists have attacked the paid-for nature of ECPs (e.g., certification costs of $25,000 to $100,000 are not uncommon) as simply "science for sale" (Holmes 1991:45) (see also Chapter 2).

This is not just a troublesome state of affairs; it has created what might be called a state of green gridlock that awaits a scientific green light in terms of LCA methodologies. The harmonization issue also has arisen, referring to the need to standardize the methodologies and procedures that underlie the many programs now in place including the labeling schemes shown in Exhibit 6.8. Groups such as the International Organization of Standards, the Society of Environmental Toxicology and Chemistry, and the American Society for Testing and Materials are working toward developing international standards at this time.

In summary, it probably is fair to say that mainstream manufacturers remain noncommittal, and perhaps unconvinced, about the marketing value of the ECP concept; at least, they are not rushing to sign up when the program is truly voluntary. For example, the rivalry between ECP arch-competitors

Green Seal and SCS in the United States has been described by one industry spokesman as a "pissing match between two organizations that don't have much credibility" (Holmes 1991:48). The consensus among manufacturers about ECPs is well stated by a spokesperson for a prominent baking soda products company: "The risks of getting involved in green advertising until [the labeling controversy] is sorted out are too high" (Reitman 1992:B1).

Role of Promotion Mix Elements

The various elements of the promotion mix—(1) advertising, (2) personal selling, (3) sales promotion, and (4) publicity-PR—have unique roles and applications in sustainable marketing communications. Each is examined in the following subsections.

Advertising

Because it is a mass media, advertising represents an opportunity to contact and educate large numbers of customers and other stakeholders about environmental issues. One useful way in which to gain insights about its use as a sustainable communications tool is to look at some of the general types of advertising and how they may be strategically employed by sustainable marketers. The types included in this discussion are (1) product, (2) institutional, (3) trade association, and (4) public service.

Product Advertising

The major objective of environmental product advertising is to spell out the specific attributes and benefits of products so that customers will buy them. But as we have already noted, there are many issues associated with doing exactly that when "environment" is the subject. So, probably a good description of the present consensus about whether or not to use environmental themes in product advertising is "damned if you do, damned if you don't." To forgo product advertising means missing a major opportunity to inform the public of valuable product benefits. On the other hand, commercial advertising is viewed as a less than reliable source by many, so to engage in an aggressive green campaign invites customer backlash and cynicism.

A good trade-off suggested by Ottman (1995) is to advertise but to use environmental issues in a low-key (understated/implicit) manner in product advertisements until updated consumer research points to a different course. As she explains, "Don't wrap your company in a green flag. Understatement, such as ARCO's headline "Gasoline is part of the problem. It's also part of the solution," helped to build credibility for the introduction of EC1 [Emission Control 1, the first reformulated gasoline]" (p. 8). This means making collateral, but specific enough, environmental claims about product composition or use that leave a positive impression at the general level while not overshadowing the primary benefits that drive most products' sales. For example, Glidden advertises that its new SPRED 2000 "contains no volatile organic compounds, or VOCs, that can react with nitrogen oxides in the presence of sunlight to form ground-level ozone," a statement that leaves it up to the buyer to conclude (implicitly) whether this is a positive environmental attribute. The copy also reveals SCS certification, but with little fanfare, while also carefully reaffirming the product's basic benefits as follows: "Yet, in both lab and field testing, SPRED 2000 wall paint has been shown to sacrifice nothing in terms of coverage or durability. In fact, it meets the same standards established with Glidden's best-selling SPRED Satin wall paints" (see Exhibit 4.3). Another low-key example is a recent advertisement by Philips Lighting that ties together its product (fluorescent lighting tubes), the "mercury issue" (i.e., some brands contain significant amounts of hazardous mercury, but ours does not), and the authority of a regulatory agency (i.e., our brand meets the EPA's nonhazardous waste standard) to create both explicit and implicit messages in support of Philips's environmental image.

Institutional Advertising

The objective of institutional advertising in sustainable communications is to clearly position the firm or industry as ecologically sensitive, responsible, credible, and trustworthy. After all, it is not just the company's products but all aspects of its operations and business relationships over the PSLC that create waste or eliminate it. Corporate image advertising also is consistent with the low-key approach that appears to be winning favor. Ottman (1995) notes, "In these days of environmental and social responsibility, the support of all corporate stakeholders is critical to conduct business smoothly. A key first step in courting your stakeholders: project a green corporate image" (p. 8).

Using institutional advertisements, firms may extol their ecological concerns, present their environmental records, and even attempt to explain environmental accidents in the hope that this image will carry over to the products they offer for sale. For example, Mobil has run a continuing series of institutional advertisements/advertorials in the *Wall Street Journal* on subjects including (1) the EPA's proposal for changing air quality standards, (2) the issue of global warming/climate change, and (3) the firm's introduction of double-hulled tankers to enhance transportation safety (Mobil Corporation 1997a, 1997b, 1998). Similarly, as a response to the adversity surrounding the *Valdez* oil spill on March 24, 1989, Exxon placed advertorials in major U.S. daily newspapers on April 5, 1989 titled "An Open Letter to the Public." Signed by Chairman L. G. Rawl, the purpose was to show top management's concern, explain the circumstances surrounding the accident, and describe the actions the company was taking in the days following the incident.

Other corporations, such as Canon and Xerox, attempt to environmentally position themselves through advertorials that project basic environmental values. Canon has used this appeal in a continuing series of advertisements in *National Geographic* that reflect on the urgency surrounding the preservation of endangered species in Africa and elsewhere. Exhibit 6.6 shows a particularly comprehensive and philosophical "positioning statement" advertorial sponsored by Xerox in *Business Week* on the subject of sustainable development.

At the local level, the Safety-Kleen WE CARE program, discussed earlier in Chapter 5 as a reseller support program, provides a retailer institutional advertising campaign customized to the type of business. For example, a Safety-Kleen-supplied small space automotive services advertisement shown in Exhibit 6.7 uses appropriate copy and the WE CARE logo to educate customers about recycling/resource conservation issues related to used oil while building an image of environmental responsibility for the participating local firm.

Trade Association Advertising

Because much of the controversy over waste management is about how various generic types of materials (e.g., plastics, paper, glass, ferrous metals, nonferrous metals, chemicals) affect our lives and the environment, trade association-sponsored advertising is a natural sustainable marketing tool for certain industries. Such advertisements can help engender a positive image about a given material and the products made from it.

Two cases in point are the American Plastics Council (APC) and the Chemical Manufacturers Association (CMA). Responding to the popularly held belief among consumers that plastics are "bad for the environment," the APC mounted a multimedia campaign to communicate three things: (1) plastics have a positive impact on modern lifestyles, (2) plastics are recyclable, and (3) postconsumer plastics are being recycled. This last point is important because postconsumer plastics recycling rates were literally zero just five years ago. Available evidence indicates that the campaign currently is reaching more than 95 million people, has appreciably altered the public's perception of plastics, and has contributed greatly to the increased recycling rate for this generic material category (APC 1995:3).

Similarly, the CMA stresses waste reduction (i.e., the release of fewer chemicals by the chemical industry into the ecosystem) and product steward-ship as its dominant themes. Directed by Ogilvy & Mather, the multimedia campaign features print and television segments that deliver the "Responsible Care" theme through cleverly portrayed cartoon characters. The advertisements claim that the industry has diverted more than 640 million pounds of chemicals through recycling programs, chemicals that were formerly released into the environment (K. Hodges, CMA, personal communication, March 11, 1994).

Public Service Announcements

Because one general objective of sustainable communications is to educate and create awareness among business leaders and consumers, doing so through public service announcements (PSAs) also is a natural communications approach. Such endeavors represent partnerships among various organizations including government regulators, trade associations, businesses, and environmental advocacy organizations. The message usually is designed to create an awareness of, and provide information about, one environmental issue. Exhibit 6.9 provides three examples from one local radio station that demonstrate both sponsorship and message aspects of 30-second public service spots focusing on the issues of buy recycled, water quality, and environmental quality, respectively. Note that all include direct response provisions (toll-free phone numbers) that encourage listeners to obtain additional information.

Personal Selling

Sales personnel often are the only point of contact that channel organizations and final customers have when dealing with manufacturers. In this capacity, a well-informed sales force can do much to communicate a firm's environmental policies, profile, and commitment to its PSLC partners.

exhibit **6.9**

Examples of 30-Second Environmental
Radio Public Service Announcements

Date and Title	Sponsorship	Environmental Message/Theme
November 20, 1994: "Buy Recycled"	Ad Council, Environmental Protection Agency, Environmental Defense Fund	Need for consumers to buy products made from recycled materials; this "saves" resources. Direct response for additional information: 1-800-CALLEDF (for brochure).
December 3, 1994: "Water Quality"	Environmental Protection Agency, Natural Resources Defense Fund	Nature of the water problems in the United States; need for water conservation. Direct response for additional information: 1-800-504-8484 (for brochure).
March 5, 1995: "Keep Florida Beautiful"	Keep Florida Beautiful, Florida Association of Broadcasters	What every citizen can do to keep the environment clean; litter and related waste disposal issues. Direct response for additional information: 1-800-828-9338 (Enviroline).

SOURCE: WWNZ 740 AM radio, Orlando, FL. All examples are based on personal observations by the author on the dates cited.

Relationship to Sales Tasks

The purpose of selling activity is to provide information and assistance to customers while closing sales. In carrying out this function, three fundamental types of sales tasks can be identified: (1) order processing, (2) creative selling, and (3) missionary sales (Boone and Kurtz 1992). Order processing may be described as a routine activity in which both the needs of customers and the ability of the seller's product to satisfy those needs are well known. Creative selling often requires providing significant amounts of information in the form of in-depth proposals that represent solutions to customers' problems. Missionary sales may be viewed as an indirect support activity that sells "goodwill" and provides customers with ongoing information and technical assistance. Although a given salesperson may specialize in one task to a large degree, all tend to perform the other tasks to some degree.

The importance of sales personnel as an environmental information delivery system will vary in relation to the types of sales tasks that must be carried out at various levels of the channel network. Those undertaking the most basic forms of order processing (e.g., retail clerks who simply scan merchandise at checkout) might have little usefulness in this regard. However, as the creative selling and missionary sales tasks become more dominant in a transaction, the stage is set for using the sales force as a conduit for delivering important environmental messages.

Key Areas of Environmentally Relevant Selling Information

It is crucial that sales personnel be well educated about the environmental factors surrounding the products they represent. Three key areas of information are important: (1) product environmental benefits, (2) regulatory/environmental compliance issues, and (3) ISO 14000 certification.

Product environmental benefits. An understanding of general ecosystem concepts, such as PSLC, product versus process waste generation, and the baseline strategies (P2 and R2) as they apply to the firm's products is essential if sales personnel are to successfully communicate the desired environmental message. A thorough knowledge of the environmental reseller support programs also is necessary.

Regulatory/environmental compliance issues. When a product or product class is subject to a complex web of environmental statutes and regulations, having the product solution simultaneously address all regulatory/compliance requirements is one of the most important benefits sought by customers. Many industrial raw materials, chemicals, and similar products fall under multiple federal environmental statutes and also are subject to state and local regulations. Sales forces must be able to respond to the issues and customer questions raised by applicable statutes.

For example, the Toxic Substances Control Act establishes rules for the manufacture and distribution of a wide range of industrial chemicals and products made from chemicals. Sales representatives for these products must know the implications of use on the environment as well as the details of the federal-level record keeping and reporting requirements that are mandated under the act, OSHA, and the Department of Transportation. Similarly, sales forces selling pollution abatement and control equipment must be familiar with the details of the Clean Air Act, the Clean Water Act, and the Safe Drinking Water Act to recognize the legal and appropriate applications of the systems they offer. The provisions of the federal Insecticide, Fungicide, and Rodenticide Act are crucial knowledge for sellers of pesticides, fertilizers, and related products (Arbuckle et al. 1993).

State statues and local ordinances often preempt federal statutes and impose stricter, not more lenient, requirements on product use, handling, and storage. Thus, sellers of underground storage tank systems in Florida must be familiar with the Underground Storage Tank program, a provision of the Federal Resource Conservation and Recovery Act, as well as the stricter regulations imposed unilaterally by the Florida Department of Environmental Protection.

ISO 14000 certification. As noted in Chapter 5, the broad process of screening for green channel partners is moving forward due to the adoption of ISO 14001, the subsection that defines the international environmental management standard (EMS) and establishes certification procedures. This strongly suggests that ISO 14000 certification will become a buyer requirement in the foreseeable future and that to get on and stay on the "to consider" list the selling firm will have to routinely update and disseminate information about its ISO 14000-instigated environmental management system. The sales force can play a major role in accomplishing this objective.

Educating and Involving Sales Personnel

As an analogy to the case of a highly technical product or line, the "environment" is a complex and highly technical issue that demands schooling before the typical sales representative will be competent in the key areas of sales information described heretofore. This can occur in a number of ways including (1) formal sales training programs, (2) sales meeting presentations, and (3) through the salesperson's involvement on cross-functional teams.

In regard to formal sales training, Kotler (1997) notes that "the median training period is 28 weeks in industrial-products companies, 12 in service companies, and four in consumer-products companies" (p. 695). Obviously, as environmental factors become more important in relation to closing sales, more training dollars and time should be spent on this topic. Because the expertise required to cover subjects such as environmental law is not likely to be found in-house, educational specialists have evolved to fill the need. For example, Government Institutes of Rockville, Maryland, offers the "Environmental Laws and Regulations Compliance Course" several times a year for $949. Training sessions on ISO 14000 standards and certification also are available from Government Institutes and a number of other sources.

Of course, environmental education/training can be addressed more locally through sales meeting presentations and through the active representation of sales personnel on cross-functional product development teams within the organization. Drafting internal experts to brief sales personnel on the linkage between marketing and the environment and other topics also encourages cross-pollination between departments and functional areas of the firm. Sales force representation on cross-functional product development teams brings firsthand market/customer input to the table while exposing the sales force to the environmental issues, concerns, and technical needs of other functional areas.

Sales Promotion

Sales promotion might well be described as those communications efforts that do not neatly fit within one of the other promotion mix elements. As described by Boone and Kurtz (1992), the general purpose of sales promotion is to "enhance consumer purchasing and dealer effectiveness" (p. 579). The activities involved generally are short-term oriented and designed to induce some sort of desired customer action while also reinforcing the other elements of the promotion mix.

Sales promotions are commonly directed at a number of targets including (1) customers (i.e., consumers and organizations) and (2) internal and/or middleman marketing personnel. Some of the more common forms of sales promotion activities include coupons/rebates, point-of-purchase displays, frequency programs, allowances/trade-ins, trade shows, catalogs/brochures, sales contests/spiffs/bonuses, selling aids, and sales training. Just adding the adjective *environment* to this list often will result in an appropriate vehicle for communicating the notion of sustainability. In any event, one also must remember that the dual objectives of educating stakeholders and enhancing credibility must be a constant factor in these efforts.

Sales Promotion Aimed at Customers

Customers (end users) include both consumers and organizations; both are valid targets for sales promotion efforts. In regard to consumers, an article in *Advertising Age,* titled "Green Products Sprouting Again" (Lawrence 1993), suggests that sales promotions can be a viable element in low-key programs promoting green products. It reports that in the household cleaner category, Benckiser Consumer Products Inc.'s Earth Rite line has appeared in a special retail end-cap display in Wal-Mart Stores in an attempt to draw attention to the merchandise. In support of this in-store effort, Benckiser Corporation also has developed several full-color product line brochures that quietly feature the SCS Biodegradable Cleaning Product certification logo, a toll-free hotline to handle any customer inquiries, and a manufacturer's coupon for 30 cents off any product in the line. In another example of consumer-targeted sales promotion, Publix Super Markets has developed a set of consumer sales promotion brochures to further the environmental image of the chain. Titles include *Every Day Is Earth Day; Our Future Is in Your Cans; Reduce, Reuse, Recycle; Save Your Place;* and *Plato's Funbook on Nutrition and Recycling.* Prominently located in a rack at the front of each retail store, the contents are decidedly educational in nature while also subtly pointing out the firm's low-key strategic alliances with the following organizations: Food Marketing Institute, EPA, Environmental Defense Fund (EDF), Keep America Beautiful, and Florida Beverage Industry Recycling Program (Publix Super Markets 1996).

An application of sales promotion targeted at organizational users is demonstrated by Canon's Clean Earth Campaign (see Exhibit 5.2). This program arose because of two factors: (1) low-priced remanufactured toner cartridges began competing heavily against virgin (new-manufacture) replacement products (Pierson 1990) and (2) the negative environmental impacts of landfilling spent toner cartridges became a factor that manufacturers no longer could ignore. The solution was to design a product take-back system (a reverse channels decision) that uses sales promotion to stimulate customer awareness and to maximize the long-term take-back rate. In designing this program, the major functional challenge was getting customers to routinely initiate the return of spent cartridges from the point of use to manufacturer-designated facilities. The sales promotion elements consist of (1) the inclusion of a prepaid postage return label, (2) a dual role outbound/return package, and

(3) a detailed instructional brochure. This sales promotion brochure is a carefully worded, multilingual presentation (English, French, Spanish, German, and Italian versions are available) designed to communicate two things: (1) the ease of participation regardless of country of origin and (2) Canon's association with environmental causes. This last factor is communicated in the brochure by announcing a $1 donation for every cartridge returned, to be equally shared by the World Wildlife Fund and the Nature Conservancy.

Sales Promotion Aimed at Internal or Middleman Marketing Personnel

Sales training materials, videos, brochures, point-of-purchase materials, trade show participation, and various environmental reseller support programs can be classified as sales promotion devices aimed at the trade (middleman) and internal marketing (sales) personnel. The need for educating sales forces was mentioned earlier; the use of internally generated educational manuals is an obvious opportunity. For sellers of waste management products, participating in the trade show circuit is a major sales promotion endeavor. For example, the annual Waste Expo sponsored by the Environmental Industry Associations provides worldwide exposure to sellers of waste systems and services; it ranks as one of the top 100 trade shows in the United States ("Waste Expo '95" 1994:40). In addition, reseller support packages, such as the WE CARE program by Safety-Kleen described earlier in this chapter, can be used as a major sales promotion tool by a firm's sales representatives.

Publicity-Public Relations

Only in recent years has the marketing discipline begun to appreciate the power of publicity-PR as an element of the promotion mix. In the world of sustainable marketing, this power is exacerbated. This is because positive publicity-PR tends to be a believable/credible source. Because establishing credibility is a clear objective of all sustainable communications, the use of publicity-PR must be considered a priority within any low-key program.

Negative Inbound Publicity

The environmental image of the firm can be damaged through events that translate into negative publicity. For example, the words "Exxon *Valdez*" and "Bhopal" would likely score very high levels of recognition on surveys of adults in developed countries. This recognition also would likely be associated with very negative overtones because these words are now commonly associ-

ated with the idea of "environmental disaster." This state of affairs is a
testament to the need to quickly respond to image problems created by
inbound negative publicity stemming from corporation-induced environmental disasters. For example, Exxon Chairman Rawl's "Open Letter to the
Public" advertisement in U.S. daily newspapers was published 12 days after
the *Valdez* incident, thereby allowing perhaps too long a time for the media's
garish reporting to go unanswered.

The control of fugitive emissions is not something left to chance in the
United States. As noted in Chapter 5, procedures for handling environmental
crises are mandated by the Emergency Planning and Community Right-to-
Know Act, passed in 1986 as part of the Superfund Amendments and
Reauthorization Act (Arbuckle et al. 1993). This statute requires firms to
develop specific emergency response plans, one outgrowth of which has been
the recognition of the importance of properly communicating with the various
publics (e.g., the community, regulators, local governments, the media, shareholders) during any period of environmental crisis. Whereas this publicity-PR
activity serves the purpose of image damage control, it also should play a very
important role in reporting accurate and factual information about the situation, the actions being undertaken to remedy any problems, and any likely
ecological consequences.

Negative environmental publicity can have significant ramifications for
other elements of the promotion mix. For example, as the Exxon *Valdez* drama
was unfolding in 1989, the full-page newspaper "Open Letter to the Public"
advertisements described earlier served as a much-needed response to the
intensely negative inbound publicity that the company was receiving. In the
ensuing months, Exxon also used newspaper advertising to suggest that a
nationwide boycott of Exxon dealers (suggested by outraged environmentalists) would do little to harm the firm but would do much to harm
franchisees who were important members of local small business communities. The suggested boycott never materialized. The point: negative publicity
often triggers other marketing communications actions.

Positive Outbound Publicity-Public Relations

It is equally important to be proactive and to generate positive publicity-
PR in support of the firm's environmental image. This "aggressor" versus
"defender" role has several interesting applications in sustainable marketing.

One guideline suggested by Rehak (1993) as an advertising approach, but
which applies equally to publicity-PR endeavors, is to "tell customers [and

coincidentally the general public, stockholders, and other stakeholders] about your company's environmental record" (p. 18). This can be done through local news coverage of the firm itself or through the firm's participation in environmental events/activities. For example, when shopping malls participate in seasonal community-wide recycling programs involving items such as Christmas trees and telephone directories, the news coverage represents publicity that has the potential to enhance corporate environmental image (Fuller 1994b).

"Telling the firm's environmental story" also can be accomplished through a modified version of the traditional annual report called the voluntary CER. For example, the *Baxter Environmental Performance Report 1995* clearly positions the firm in regard to environmental issues with the following policy statement: "Baxter will be a global leader in respecting the environment. Environmental excellence is vital to Baxter's business interests and is consistent with our mission and shared values" (Baxter International Inc. 1995:4). Obviously, this type of print vehicle represents a specialized outlet through which firms can communicate their commitment to the environment, as well as the progress they are making in meeting environmental improvement objectives, to a variety of publics and constituencies. (Note: Some ways in which to enhance the credibility of corporate environment reports were given earlier in the "Source Credibility" subsection.)

Another specialized PR medium of more recent vintage, the Internet, also provides a platform for communicating the firm's environmental position to broad audiences. For example, Northern Telecom's (1996) World Wide Web site (http://www.nortel.com) provides a detailed and insightful statement about the company's commitment to "enhancing the environment . . . [by] managing its products from conception to final disposition." This Web site also provides a literal library of environmentally relevant information about the company and industry-trade activities that is regularly updated.

The recent history of McDonald's Corporation provides a second approach involving proactive publicity-PR—partnering with environmental activist organizations. After sparring in the media over the supposedly large quantities of waste generated by the fast-food restaurants, McDonald's and the EDF, a major advocacy organization, shelved their adversarial relationship in 1989 and formed an alliance to study the issues. The *Waste Reduction Task Force Final Report* (McDonald's Corporation 1991) outlined strategies for improved waste management as well as the discovery that "almost 80 [percent] of McDonald's on-premise waste, by weight, is generated 'behind the counter' " (p. ii). The positive publicity generated by this unheard-of private

enterprise-environmental activist partnership undoubtedly did much to solid-
ify the image of McDonald's as a firm genuinely committed to ecosystem
concerns. It also may have started a new trend toward more cooperative and
less adversarial relationships between the business and environmental communities.

Other forms of positive PR include the corporate media kit and the
corporate environmental video. Anheuser-Busch Companies has made extensive investments in both areas. Its media kit typically contains 35-millimeter
slides, a set of Environmental News Fact Sheets, and several other brochures
detailing environmental issues and the company's responses (R. Buckley,
Fleishman-Hillard Inc., personal communication, May 1, 1995). The firm also
has produced a 15-minute corporate video, titled *Pursuing Environmental
Excellence,* that portrays the company's wide-ranging environmental initiatives over several decades. This video is appropriately hosted and narrated by
August A. Busch, III, president and chairman of the board (Anheuser-Busch
Companies 1995).

Implementing Sustainable Communications

The mechanics of implementing sustainable promotion programs are no
different from those of the traditional kind; only the subject matter and PSLC
orientation differ. The idea is to implement an integrated marketing communications program that focuses on defined stakeholders (target markets),
includes realistic objectives, develops relevant themes and information, and
is cost-effective. Particularly relevant are decisions concerning (1) the use of
internal departments or external specialists and (2) the implementation of
communications strategic alliances. The development of appropriate decision
support information through the sustainable marketing audit process also is
an important factor.

Integrated Marketing Communications

The premise of integrated marketing communications is that the effectiveness of the communications process is increased when a unified approach
is taken. Unification can be achieved along a number of dimensions. First, it
manifests itself when the elements of the promotion mix are united through a
common, consistent message or theme, sometimes referred to as a common
positioning statement. Second, unification occurs when the promotion mix

elements themselves (i.e., advertising, personal selling, sales promotion, publicity-PR) are thoroughly coordinated. In this latter case, coordination must occur horizontally within the firm as well as vertically among the firms in the channel network.

What sets sustainable integrated marketing communications apart is that decision makers must acclimate to new subject matter and expand their vistas beyond traditional channel networks to include the realm of the PSLC. In real terms, more potential players are involved, which exacerbates the vertical coordination challenge. Within this context, it is necessary to identify the natural expertise and promotion role of each potential player as well as those players unique to the environmental arena such as advocacy groups and trade associations. For example, given the challenge to "turn around" the negative public image of plastics, trade groups such as the APC and the National Association for Plastic Container Recovery (NAPCOR) evolved as obvious choices through which unified, coordinated programs could be delivered using multiple elements of the promotion mix (see discussion in "Building Communications Strategic Alliances" subsection).

Internal versus External Function

The sustainable communications function can be accomplished by either an internal staff/department, an outside/external specialists, or a combination of the two. This decision likely will be based on the presence or lack of appropriate expertise within the organization. The use of outside specialists is a natural choice for many firms when it comes to advertising, sales promotion, and publicity-PR because of a lack of in-house expertise on sustainable (green) marketing issues. Cognizant of this fact, J. Walter Thompson USA is an example of an advertising agency that has developed and makes available highly specialized green marketing services that apply strategy to the specific challenge of marketing communications. In addition, publications such as *The Green Business Letter* (by Tilden Press), *Business and the Environment* (by Cutter Information Corporation), *JWT Greenwatch* (by J. Walter Thompson USA), and *Green Gauge Report* (by Roper Starch Worldwide) are available to provide continuing advice and counsel about sustainable communications and related issues to those firms supporting internal efforts. As noted earlier, when it comes to educating internal sales forces, numerous external specialist firms also are available to provide green training seminars on relevant subjects such as environmental law, waste management practices, and ISO 14000 certification.

Building Communications Strategic Alliances

It was noted earlier that when looking at the issue of spokesperson credibility, "approval by a well-known environmental group" received the highest credibility rating by consumers at 39 percent, compared to a 9 percent rating for "a manufacturer's self-declared warranty/claim" (J. Walter Thompson USA 1991:5). This suggests that communications strategic alliances are an appropriate vehicle for delivering environmental messages. In particular, such liaisons can serve to build positive associations between businesses and nontraditional partners, such as environmental advocacy groups, as well as foster mutual self-interest through the leveraging power of trade associations.

Aligning with Environmental Groups

Developing alliances with high-profile environmental advocacy groups helps businesses develop a "sustainable aura." This is a key benefit of both the McDonald's-EDF partnership (detailed earlier in this chapter) and Canon's financial support of the National Wildlife Federation and the Nature Conservancy through the Clean Earth Campaign (see Exhibit 5.2). In both cases, the commercial association remains decidedly low-key. For example, Canon uses only name and logo displays along with an explanation of the per-transaction model (i.e., 50 cents per unit) that determines the contribution to each organization (Shannon 1996). But the implicit message is very clear: the advocacy group vouches for the manufacturer's credibility and/or intentions. Douglas Hall, director of communications at the Nature Conservancy, sums it up as follows:

> [We] think strategically about the nature and duration of our corporate couplings. Call us old-fashioned, but we wisely favor long-term, multifaceted relationships. . . . Smart companies know that environmental concerns will continue to affect their work and customer base far into the future. Smart nonprofits need to put more trust in the longevity of their issues by demanding quality and diversity in their relationships with corporations. Going for the quick buck, media gimmicks, and one-shot associations yields few results for business or the environment. (Hall 1992:26)

Trade Association Alliances

Trade associations obviously exist to support the mutual self-interests of their members. As discussed earlier, they are well suited to be primary operatives in alliances that communicate the basic environmental benefits associated with certain generic materials and entire industries; they also are in a position to develop broad-based college, primary, and secondary school education programs for dissemination. For example, the APC, an alliance of plastics resin producers, fabricators, and recyclers, is uniquely positioned and funded to carry out a variety of integrated campaigns (e.g., multimedia advertising [print and television], PR) with the continuing objectives of (1) educating the public about the positive contribution of plastics to modern daily living and (2) increasing the plastics recycling rate (APC 1995). NAPCOR has developed an extensive educator's kit for primary and secondary schools, called PETE'S Pack, that details the feasibility of recycling a specific polymer, polyethylene terephthalate (PET). NAPCOR (1995) also makes available brochures, television and radio PSAs, editorial articles, and bus signs/mall posters/outdoor boards. Similarly, the Steel Recycling Institute, which is made up of steel makers, recyclers, and fabricators, has developed multimedia campaigns (e.g., billboards, television, primary school educational kits) and a newsletter, *The Recycling Magnet,* for the purpose of reinforcing the fact that steel is easily recycled and already is the most recycled material in the world ("The New Steel" 1997:5). In all of these cases, maintaining the public's awareness of the positive environmental attributes of a given generic material is a benefit sought not just by producers but also by multiple members of the PSLC functioning as an alliance.

Sustainable Marketing Audit: Communications Assessment

The sustainable marketing audit process introduced in Chapter 3 can serve to develop a fact base to support the implementation of sustainable communications. To assist in the communications assessment, a number of generalized questions and issues are provided in Exhibit 3.7. Again, it remains important to recognize that the "position(s)" of a firm in the PSLC will determine the significance of various communications factors in the analysis.

Chapter Summary

Marketing communications is not a decision area that generates waste in the direct way that product and channels decisions do. Rather, communications is a facilitating function that supports P2 and R2 strategies already based on product and channel DFE decisions.

Communications DFE is a multifaceted challenge involving the multiple tools of the promotion mix; numerous stakeholder publics; and interactive, two-way information exchanges that support P2 and R2 strategies. Two generalized objectives are paramount: (1) educating customers about environmental issues and (2) establishing and maintaining the environmental credibility of products and the firms that make them. The multiple targets of sustainable communications include customers, employees, shareholders, channel partners, regulators, and environmental advocacy groups.

The unscrupulous use of green claims in marketing promotion programs in the early 1980s led to charges of green-washing and has cast a pall on their continued use. It also led to a call for regulation. Although the FTC issued guidelines for green marketing claims in 1992 and solicited comments, little guidance has emerged beyond the listing of a number of common phrases and terms along with examples of appropriate usage. Therefore, green promotion claims remain a contentious issue.

Research into environmental message design has uncovered a set of general basic appeals as well as a set of specific claims. The appeals include (1) zeitgeist (i.e., reflection of the mood of the times), (2) emotional, (3) rational/financial, (4) health, (5) corporate (i.e., commitment by), (6) testimonials, and (7) comparative benefits. Specific claim categories include (1) product attributes oriented, (2) process attributes oriented, (3) image enhancement oriented, and (4) environmental statements of fact. It also is possible to relate many of these claim types to stage in the PSLC. Research also has uncovered that a majority of consumers believe environmental advertisements are vague/misleading, omit important information, and/or contain false information or outright lies. This leads to the suggestion that environmental claims should be presented in specific terms because this tends to foster positive advertiser image and positive product perceptions and also leads to higher levels of purchase intent. It also is important to adopt a customer orientation that emphasizes, on the personal level, the contribution that each individual makes when purchasing an environmentally compatible product. Furthermore, research into the issue of spokesperson credibility reveals high levels of consumer confidence in product environmental information that is associated with the approval of a well-known environmental group or an independent testing laboratory. Finally, the use of implicit messages is an important aspect of message design in an area where explicit facts might be hard to substantiate and even harder to communicate.

Another controversial aspect of sustainable communications is the area of environmental labeling programs. In particular, third-party programs are evolving through which an explicit label is applied to a product to denote positive ecological attributes. The label is earned by meeting certain standards, which results in the awarding of a user license for a fee. The central issue remains the consistency and science behind award-granting processes across various venues. Three labeling formats currently are used: (1) seal of approval (e.g., the product generally is identified as environmentally sound), (2) single-attribute certification (e.g., a certain percentage recycled materials is certified), and (3) report card (e.g., several attributes are quantified). But the lack of conclusive LCA technology and the potential for financial abuse (e.g., certification is bought for a fee) have caused many firms to shy away from adopting any form of third-party environmental labeling.

Each element of the promotion mix—(1) advertising, (2) personal selling, (3) sales promotion, and (4) publicity-PR—has a particular role to play in sustainable communications. Product advertising probably is best accomplished using low-key, implicit environmental appeals that do not overshadow the basic benefits associated with the product. Institutional advertising in either traditional or advertorial format may be used to deliver messages signifying ecological concern, sensitivity, and responsibility. Trade association advertising represents an obvious approach for marshaling the resources of many firms around a basic material, such as plastic or aluminum, for the purpose of emphasizing its pro-environmental attributes. PSAs cosponsored by coalitions of businesses, advocacy groups, and/or regulatory agencies represent another natural advertising opportunity in the environmental arena.

Personal selling can be used to deliver a variety of environmental messages/information to potential customers, especially when creative selling is the major task. Key areas of environmentally relevant sales information include product environmental benefits, regulatory/environmental compliance issues, and details of the firm's ISO 14000-inspired environmental management system. To ensure that sales forces have the necessary knowledge, appropriate sales training must be undertaken.

Sales promotion activities can focus on either (1) customers (i.e., consumers or organizations) or (2) internal or middleman marketing personnel. Consumer programs consist of brochures, end-cap displays, toll-free hotlines, and coupons. Sales promotions aimed at middleman or internal marketing personnel consist of videos, trade show participation, sales training, and other selling tools for field representatives. It is simply the environmental subject matter that differentiates these approaches from normal sales promotion activities.

Publicity-PR can play a key role in both enhancing and destroying the environmental image of a product or firm because it is the most credible/ believable source. It should be employed in the low-key manner generally recommended for environmental communications. Performing damage control in response to negative inbound publicity is one major application, one that is particularly relevant to products, industrial processes, or companies that may experience fugitive emissions. From the positive point of view, publicity-PR can serve as an outbound vehicle to "tell the firm's environmental story" through actions and formats such as press releases, participation in events, and CERs as well as by posting environmental information on a Web site. An application of publicity that is particularly useful is for a firm to partner with a well-known environmental advocacy organization for the purpose of addressing local environmental issues.

Implementing sustainable marketing communications generally parallels traditional practice. Integrated marketing communications is the standard framework for ensuring that the various elements of the promotion mix are designed to be supportive of one another and that message delivery is consistent. However, extending the challenge to include the broader set of organizations making up the PSLC is a differentiating feature. Because of inexperience with environmental subject matter, some organizations might tend to employ external organizations when designing sustainable marketing communications. Joining in strategic alliances with environmental groups and trade associations represents a major implementation opportunity. The development of decision support information through the sustainable marketing audit process is yet another vital consideration.

CHAPTER 7

Sustainable Pricing

In his landmark treatise on sustainability, *The Ecology of Commerce,* Hawken (1993) offers this observation:

> I believe customers and buyers are getting incomplete information because markets do not convey the true costs of purchases. When customers start receiving proper information—the whole story—things will change. (p. 81) . . . The economics of restoration rests on the premise that people, if given honest information, not only about price, but about cost, will make intelligent and appropriate decisions that will improve both their own lives and the life around them. (p. 155)

By "incomplete information," Hawken is referring to the continuing distortion of the market mechanism caused by the exclusion, or understatement, of eco-costs in the unit cost structures of products. This practice leads to the setting of unrealistic market prices and keeps us heading down the road to environmental degradation described in Hardin's (1968) "The Tragedy of the Commons." The need to change this practice represents a most compelling challenge.

Role of Pricing

As the fourth, and final, element of the marketing mix, the role of pricing is to provide an overall indicator of transaction value for consideration by the

271

customer. In this role, value can reflect two transaction formats: (1) traditional ownership value (i.e., a title transfer transaction) and (2) product as service equivalent value (i.e., a rent/lease transaction). In addition, price reflects terms of sale through quantity discounts, allowances, payment timing, and other special considerations accorded the customer by the seller. In any event, price is a tentative offer, made by the seller to the customer, that can be either accepted or refused. If the customer refuses, then the seller may counteroffer with lower and lower prices until agreement is reached. Because it is relatively easy to execute short-term price changes, price can be described as the quick-change artist of the marketing mix. It also follows that adjusting price and terms of sale is a major ways and means through which sellers respond to changing market conditions and customer preferences over time. In short, price is a major competitive weapon.

The monetary price of a product/resource has two components: (1) unit cost and (2) a profit component. Unit cost is derived by allocating to the product the cost of manufacturing processes, labor inputs, materials purchases, making products accessible through channel systems, and an assortment of other marketing and administrative expenses. The profit component represents "value added beyond costs," that is, "earned" by a business through its insightful and anticipatory performance of marketing functions/activities that deliver the following outcomes:

- The right product is developed; that is, the form and function attributes fit/meet the customer's need.
- The product is in the right place at the right time; that is, channel networks provide appropriate access.
- The customer has foreknowledge; that is, marketing communications provide appropriate transaction-supporting information.
- The product's price is in line with the customer's expectations given the circumstances surrounding the transaction.

Pricing Design-for-Environment

Pricing has a profound impact on the decisions customers make in the marketplace and, consequently, on the acceptance or rejection of sustainable product offerings. Economic theory teaches that the market mechanism, which consists of buyers and sellers making free and informed choices at prevailing market prices, is the best way in which to allocate resources. This model assumes that prevailing market prices reflect the true costs of resources and all other factors that make up the cost of doing business. But so-called "value-empty economics" (Olson 1991) often fails to make good on this assumption. And, as Schmidheiny (1992a) notes, "markets will not support sustainable development until they can be made to tell the environmental as well as [the] economic truth" (p. 20). Peattie (1995) sums up the situation:

> For those who believe that the path toward sustainability depends on the use of market mechanisms, the integration of environmental costs [eco-costs] into product costings and prices is a vital step. While consumption continues to expand, taking advantage of prices which do not reflect the environmental costs [eco-costs] of products, the environment will continue to be unsustainably consumed. (p. 278)

Product price is the universal indicator of value or, more correctly, the value of the product in the context of physical access (channels), available information (marketing communications), and competitive offerings. It should reflect positive and negative environmental attributes, all other costs of doing business, and the value of the ultimate benefits sought by customers.

Influences on Pricing Decisions

At the micro level, sustainable marketing managers are concerned with traditional decision areas including the determination of price level, terms of sale, channel price structure, and pricing strategies/objectives. Three major influences on pricing decisions are (1) unit cost structure, (2) customer perception, and (3) competitive products and prices. Known as the "three C's" of pricing, these "drivers" suggest that for a price to be profitable it must fall within a "floor-ceiling" range, where the floor is the unit cost and the ceiling is the maximum perceived value (demand) assigned by customers, and it must reflect adequate perceived value in relation to competitive offerings.

Unit Cost Structure

Unit cost structure plays a fundamental role in setting prices as follows: it quantifies the expected unit cost-volume relationship, sets the floor below which price may not go, and is one of two factors (price is the other) that determines a product's profit spread. Because profit is a major criterion for retention, inappropriate costing sends false signals about what is profitable and what is not.

The unique costing dilemma facing sustainable products is summarized by Peattie (1995):

> The idea that green products are in some way unusually expensive is perhaps something of an illusion. The reality is that grey [i.e., traditional, nonsustainable] products are unrealistically inexpensive. The costs associated with environmental degradation in grey products are largely not reflected in their prices, so the environment is effectively providing a subsidy. (p. 284)

The challenge, then, is to first identify the various sources of eco-costs and then develop procedures through which they are fairly allocated to the products responsible for them. In terms of business functional specialization, the task of developing full-costing approaches is being addressed by the emerging discipline of environmental accounting. In the foreword to *Green Ledgers: Case Studies in Corporate Environmental Accounting* (Ditz, Ranganathan, and Banks 1995), Jonathan Lash, president of the World Resources Institute, comments on the need to advance the practice of full-cost/environmental accounting:

> From the boardroom to the shop floor to the marketplace, business decisions are skewed when environmental costs (eco-costs) are hidden. Common accounting practices hide these costs in two ways: by burying them in "nonenvironmental" accounts and by failing to link costs to the activities that spawn them. As a result, managers are forced to make decisions—what products to manufacture, what technologies to employ, and what materials to use—without command of the relevant facts. Now, more than ever, these managers are on the line as regulation, public concern, and corporate commitments make it increasingly important to account for environmental costs (eco-costs). (p. v)

Customer Perception

As defined by Kotler (1997), perceived-value pricing is based on recognizing "the buyers' perceptions of value, not the seller's cost, as the key to pricing" (p. 505). As further explained by Monroe (1990),

> Perceived value is a trade-off between perceived quality and perceived benefits with the perceived monetary sacrifice. . . . Buyers do not determine a product's value solely on the basis of minimizing the price paid. Customers

must be educated about the use and value of products and services. Moreover, the price set must be consistent with customers' value perceptions. (p. 92)

Stated another way, customers pay for value added based on their perception of the primary and secondary benefits brought to the transaction by a product. This relationship is generalized as follows:

$$\text{Perceived Value} = \frac{\text{Perceived Primary and Secondary Benefits}}{\text{Price}}$$

By positively influencing customers' perception of a product's primary and secondary benefits, manipulating the monetary price up or down, or doing some combination of these things, perceived value in a given transaction will be directly affected.

As pointed out earlier in Chapter 4, ecological benefits usually take the form of intangible promises about future quality of life and assume a decidedly secondary role in many transactions compared to primary benefits. In addition, customers are not particularly knowledgeable about them. This is partially true because the downside threats associated with not engaging in sustainable behavior (e.g., pollution, health hazards) lack the exigency that often accompanies the satisfaction of other customer wants/needs. Therefore, a positive association between perceived ecological benefits and value added might not be present. This leads to the assumption that many customers tend to lump ecological benefits into the category of "okay—nice to have but not crucial" as a purchase decision factor.

This assumption appears supported by segmentation research conducted by Roper Starch Worldwide Inc. (1997). Its work identifies five consumer segments in the United States (subsequently dubbed "Shades of Green" segments) based on self-reported pro-environmental behaviors (see Chapter 8 for a full discussion). However, only one segment, the "Greenback-Greens," exhibits the propensity to pay a significant premium for products with identifiable ecological attributes. Because this segment accounted for only 6 percent of the total consumer market in 1997 ("Marketplace Getting Greener" 1998:3), this also means that the vast majority of consumers (94 percent) exhibit little or no interest in paying a "green premium" for ecological value added. So, although many studies report that customers would pay more for products that provide ecological benefits, the fact is that most customer behavior is just the opposite (Sims 1993; Wood 1990).

Recent experiences in the marketplace back up this contention. Seventh Generation, the largest catalog retailer of green goods in the United States, has undertaken a major downward restructuring of prices in an attempt to broaden its appeal and increase sales. The higher prices it was charging for deep green products simply did not generate the volume necessary for profitable operations. The firm's chief executive officer, Jeff Hollender, recently noted, "The research that says people will pay more for socially [ecologically] responsible goods simply isn't true" (quoted in Gupta 1994:B1). In another case, Fieldcrest Canon Inc. confirms that its attempt to sell ecologically correct organic cotton towels through high-volume Wal-Mart Stores was a dismal failure. In reporting on this situation, the *Wall Street Journal* concluded, "Even though consumers claim they want eco-sensitive goods, 'if the price tag's a dollar more, they won't buy it' " (Ortega 1994:B2). Attempts to market cleaner-burning automotive fuel in the United States evoked a similar response from consumers. Several smog-riddled cities have been required to sell this fuel to comply with air quality standards under the Clean Air Act of 1990; it cuts emissions by 15 to 20 percent and costs an additional 5 cents per gallon. Several other urban areas initially opted to do so voluntarily for the purpose of improving local environmental quality, but due to consumer grumbling over the higher price, many later withdrew from the program. As Makower (1995a) comments, "So much for the polls saying that consumers would gladly pick a green product over a less-green one, even if it cost a bit more, assuming it performed as well and didn't cause them any other inconvenience to buy or use" (p. 8).

However, a consensus is emerging that rising consumer awareness of environmental issues is gradually transforming ecological attributes into a purchase decision factor that comes into play only when perceived product price and quality are equal across a number of purchase alternatives. As Ottman (1992) notes,

> Consumers appear to be most receptive to products perceived as green when their primary needs for performance/quality, convenience, and affordability are met and when they understand how a new product or package can help solve an environmentally related problem. (p. 16)

Ottman (1993) adds,

> While environmentally sound product attributes may not always motivate consumers to pay a premium . . . research strongly suggests that environmental attributes can act as a powerful *tie-breaker* and, in general, provide a source of differentiation and value added. (p. 44)

Competitive Products and Prices

Available competitive offerings and their prices provide a comparative benchmark for establishing the perceived value of a given brand. Thus, the unwillingness to pay a premium for secondary ecological benefits might be understandable in the case of consumer products, where primary benefits are the dominant purchase driver and where many brands with well-known prices and acceptable features are available in the marketplace.

The translation to everyday marketing is this: sustainable products usually face stiff, entrenched competitors. But when price and quality are perceived as equal across products or brands, "tie-breaker" ecological attributes have a chance to come into play. Products possessing these attributes empower the ecologically savvy customer "to do the right thing and buy an environmental product" without spending more and giving up valued benefits (Quintana 1995:13). In this context, ecological attributes can become a viable source of competitive advantage for both new and existing products. For example, Loblaws International Merchants, Canada's largest supermarket chain, has a policy of setting prices for environmental products deliberately level with those of standard offerings. As anecdotal evidence that this strategy works, after adding "dolphin-free" albacore tuna to its product line at the same price as standard competitive offerings, sales of dolphin-free tuna increased 68 percent in one year (Walley 1991:12).

Pricing as Pollution Prevention/Resource Recovery Strategy Support

Along with marketing communications, pricing is an element of the marketing mix that serves in a facilitating capacity; that is, it does not have a direct linkage to waste generation or moderation (see Exhibit 3.1). Rather, pricing decisions reflect the outcomes of product and channel design-for-environment (DFE) decisions that underlie pollution prevention (P2) and resource recovery (R2) strategies.

Sustainable Pricing Objectives

At the general level, sustainable pricing objectives address the challenge of integrating eco-costs into unit cost structures so that the resulting prices better reflect the full costs associated with the resources being converted and offered for consumption (see Exhibit 3.3). The importance of this issue cannot be understated. As Hawken (1993) points out,

Markets are the place at which production becomes consumption, but at present they do not recognize the destruction and waste caused by that production. Because markets are a price-based system, they naturally favor traders who come to market with the lowest price, which often means the highest unrecognized costs. (p. 79)

Both Peattie (1995) and Hawken (1993) point out the biggest reason to insist on a full-cost objective: the potential threat of underpricing a product as opposed to overpricing it. Returning to the familiar floor-ceiling concept, not recognizing eco-costs allows a company to sell below the real floor because the real floor is misstated due to lost eco-costs, which are in reality being shifted to other products or to society at large. The full-cost objective eliminates this masking or subsidy effect. So, for those seeking to improve the ecological equity of market transactions, a bold sustainable pricing objective for a firm might be stated as follows:

▓ To set product prices that reflect the inclusion of full eco-costs in unit cost structures by January 1, 20__

Traditional financial and nonfinancial pricing objectives also will continue to play a major role in directing price setting and price variation strategy decisions. These objectives may involve (1) setting exact price levels in relation to competitors; (2) varying price through the use of price substitutes (e.g., discounts, allowances, special deals) to influence purchase timing, quantity, and other aspects of customer behavior; (3) attaining certain financial goals (e.g., market share, sales volume, profitability, return on sales or equity/investment); (4) enhancing competitive position and product image; and (5) neutralizing competitors' prices. Of course, any pricing strategy that results in the meeting of traditional objectives while also advancing the sale of products with positive ecological attributes represents a welcomed contribution toward achieving sustainability.

Sources of Eco-Costs

It was noted earlier that sustainable pricing faces the unique challenge of eliminating the ecological subsidies that now skew cost structures against environmentally sound product choices. In theory, manufacturers selling truly full-costed products, as well as customers willing to buy them, would be shouldering their fair share of the ecological load, so to speak. Products heavy with ecological burdens would tend to have higher cost structures and prices. In market transactions, they would tend to lose sales to products that deliver equivalent benefits but have lower eco-costs and prices. This scenario reflects the "polluter pays principle" (Cairncross 1992a).

Although straightforward in concept, identifying eco-costs for the purpose of operationalizing the polluter pays principle is not easy. Five eco-cost sources (drivers) that may alter unit cost structures are listed in Exhibit 7.1. As will be discussed later in this chapter, some are internal in character (i.e., under management's control), whereas others are external (i.e., costs controlled/imposed by other members of the product system life cycle [PSLC], regulators, legal action, or public policy mandates). The term *alter* is carefully chosen because the circumstances facing individual companies operating in different industries and in different stages of the PSLC will transform some drivers into cost increasers, whereas others will become cost reducers (Peattie 1992).

Product

These costs may result from changes in physical construction, product form, materials, and energy use or through the deliberate addition of green features. Examples include the following: deciding to use recycled contents paper may result in higher costs; product redesign minimizing the quantity of materials and energy required may reduce costs; packaging downsizing will reduce packaging materials procurement costs; and adding a separate per-transaction/unit "green premium" to a product (e.g., Canon donates 50 cents to both the Nature Conservancy and the World Wildlife Fund for every toner cartridge returned through its Clean Earth Campaign [see Exhibit 5.2]) adds to unit marketing costs, on the one hand, but serves as an "offset" marketing communications (sales promotion/publicity) expenditure, on the other.

Processes/Facilities/Management Personnel Overhead

Changing industrial and channel handling processes and facilities to take advantage of advances in P2 technologies results in capital expenditures that may be offset by savings from decreased energy consumption and reduced future waste processing costs. For example, environmental initiatives undertaken by 3M Corporation's Pollution Prevention Pays (3P) program are

Exhibit 7.1

Sources and Examples of Eco-Costs

1. Product
   - Increased costs from introducing environmentally friendly materials
   - Reduced costs (savings) from reducing product inputs of raw materials and energy
   - Reduced costs (savings) from reducing unnecessary packaging
   - The stipulation of a donation to an environmental group or cause that is directly tied to product sale but obviously separate from core product attributes

2. Process/facility/management
   - Capital expenditure on cleaner processes and technology
   - Green overheads associated with changing the management and marketing of the company
   - Reduced costs (savings) in company overheads in terms of reduced use of office supplies, heating, and lighting

3. Fugitive emissions cleanup
   - The physical costs of after-the-fact spill or accident site cleanup operations and administration
   - Costs of setting up and maintaining a contingency plan/equipment
   - Insurance costs associated with potential environmental liability

4. Environmental legal actions
   - Fines for illegal behavior and noncompliance with statutes
   - Jury awards for losses of natural resources/future compensation
   - Superfund cleanup: Actual costs for carrying out a Superfund operation under the U.S. Superfund Amendments and Reauthorization Act statute and the contingent liability costs (hedge against future U.S. Environmental Protection Agency actions)

5. Routine regulatory compliance
   - Complying with product construction/standardization mandates
   - Administrative overheads associated with monitoring, reporting, training, materials tracking, and inspections
   - Routine disposal of hazardous and nonhazardous waste
   - Paying and administering required taxes/deposits
   - Legal costs

SOURCES: Kreuze, Jerry G. and Gale E. Newell (1994), "ABC and Life-Cycle Costing for Environmental Expenditures," *Management Accounting,* Vol. 75, No. 8, pp. 38-42; Peattie, Ken (1992), *Green Marketing,* London: Pitman; Peattie, Ken (1995), *Environmental Marketing Management,* London: Pitman.

reported to have saved the firm more than $500 million during the 1975 to 1989 period (Ottman 1993:60).

Hiring personnel or retaining consultants to supervise and implement sustainable programs also can result in predictable increases in overhead expenditures in both general management and marketing functions. For example, Powdercraft Services Inc. of Anaheim, California, hired an environmental consultant to minimize the disruption caused by having to deal with 22 local, state, and federal environmental agencies. The cost: $40,000 per year ("Regulations Add to Company's Costs" 1994). Obviously, this cost must be spread over the firm's sales. By contrast, process/facility efficiency moves described as "environmental belt tightening," such as lighting and transportation conservation programs and office wastepaper recycling, may serve to cut waste while also reducing some overhead costs.

Fugitive Emissions Cleanup

The classic case of fugitive emissions cost is the 11-million-gallon Exxon *Valdez* oil spill that occurred in Prince William Sound, Alaska in 1989. As of May 25, 1995, the firm estimated it had spent $2.5 billion on remediation efforts alone (Sullivan 1995:B1).

Environmental Legal Actions

Lawsuits associated with unplanned environmental disasters and violations of current statutes also can lead to sizable, and unexpected, cash outlays in the form of fines, penalties, and jury awards for damages. Recently, Regency Cruise Lines was fined $250,000 in U.S. district court for dumping 40 plastic bags containing garbage into the ocean off St. Petersburg, Florida (Associated Press 1995); L.A. Gear was fined $70,000 by the state of Minnesota for including a prohibited mercury switch in a line of running shoes (mercury is a hazardous material banned from products in Minnesota) ("L.A. Gear to Pay" 1994); and a federal jury recently awarded Alaska fishermen $286.8 million in damages for lost fisheries stemming from the Exxon *Valdez* incident ("Alaska Fishermen" 1994). Exxon also paid $1.1 billion as a penalty to settle federal criminal charges related to the *Valdez* incident (Sullivan 1995:B1).

In the United States, cleanup costs associated with the Superfund Amendments and Reauthorization Act, a subsection of the federal Comprehensive

Environmental Response, Compensation, and Liability Act, have become a special challenge for U.S. companies. The statute deals with the cleanup of nonfugitive emissions that have occurred over time at industrial sites, waste processing facilities, and similar locations. It contains a "broadened liability" provision stating that any firm that generates hazardous waste, any transporter that hauls it, or any disposal facility that processes it remains liable for any future cleanup costs related to that material if the U.S. Environmental Protection Agency (EPA) deems such action necessary. This has been further interpreted by the courts to mean that a joint and several liability exists, meaning that the EPA can choose to pursue "deep-pockets" firms and ignore the others in the chain of liability if the agency cares to do so (Arbuckle et al. 1991:516).

The threat of a Superfund action represents an important and continuing exposure to financial risk for firms that have disposed of hazardous materials in the past or continue to do so in the present. To date, the historical average cost to clean up a Superfund site has been $30 million (Portney 1994:16). The overall known environmental liability of U.S. businesses has been estimated at between 2 and 5 percent of gross national product (Willits and Giuntini 1994:45). This translates into a potential remediation bill of between $500 million and $1 trillion over the next 50 years (Hirschhorn 1994:15).

As an example of the continuing long reach of the Superfund statute, the federal government has only recently finished collecting $5.7 million from a group of local governments and businesses in Central Florida that contracted with the City Chemical Company of Orlando, Florida, to dispose of its hazardous wastes during the 1972 to 1983 period (a rather modest Superfund site in view of the $30 million average). City Chemical's chief executive officer, Arthur Greer, was convicted in 1988 of illegal dumping at the site, thereby contaminating it with toxic metals, solvents, paints, inks, and other chemicals. Although he spent 13 months in federal prison for this crime, City Chemical has paid for none of the cleanup because the firm went bankrupt (Quintana 1994).

Routine Regulatory Compliance

The majority of the eco-costs paid by businesses in the United States are in response to mandates imposed by local, state, and federal authorities, which is essentially an exercise in the transfer of external/social costs to businesses. Two categories of costs may be distinguished. The first involves costs required to meet basic rules concerning specific product construction and operation.

For example, the EPA recently has proposed new rules that will curb air emissions from gasoline and diesel engines installed in boats and for small gasoline engines powering lawn mowers and similar home-use tools. The rules are estimated to increase the direct costs of marine engines by 10 to 15 percent per unit (Noah 1994a:B9) and the direct costs of lawn mowers and similar consumer yard equipment by $5 per unit (Associated Press 1994b:A1).

The second category consists of the continuing regulatory costs associated with complying with the broad and complex web of "command-and-control" regulations governing almost every facet of business operations. Called pollution abatement and control costs (PACO), their magnitude is shown in Table 7.1, which compares 1987 and 1992 in constant 1987 dollars. Thus, total PACO costs amounted to $87.6 billion in 1992; the share of PACO accounted for directly by U.S. business was $56.0 billion and represented nearly 64 percent of the total of all such expenditures (PACO also includes government and consumer spending on selected items). It is important to note that business PACO increased 23.1 percent between 1987 and 1992, a factor nearly double that of the total PACO increase of 12.7 percent and nearly triple the increase of gross domestic product, which was 7.9 percent. Within business PACO, the largest increases were in the categories of total water at 23.0 percent and total solid waste at 44.9 percent. These numbers simply reflect the continued addition of regulations during the late 1980s and early 1990s (Rutledge and Vogan 1994).

Of course, the real question is, "How much does PACO add to the cost of doing day-to-day business?" Although a global answer is not possible, a case study can show the possibilities. Returning to the Powdercraft Services example mentioned earlier, a sampling of the costs the firm faces that are directly attributable to environmental regulation include the following:

1.	Annual emissions fees	$10
2.	Annual equipment permit costs	$18,000
3.	Annual consultant's fees to interpret the environmental rules and regulations associated with dealing with 22 state, local, and federal agencies	$40,000
	Total	$58,010

In a recent letter to customers, the firm announced the addition of an across-the-board 3 percent fee to all invoices to cover exponentially increasing costs of environmental regulation ("Regulations Add to Company's Costs" 1994:D7).

TABLE 7.1

U.S. Pollution Abatement and Control Expenditures: 1987 versus 1992

	1987		1992		
	(billions of 1987 dollars)	Percentage Down	(billions of 1987 dollars)	Percentage Down	Percentage Change Across
Total PACO	77.7	100.0	87.6	100.0	12.7
Total business PACO	45.5	58.6	56.0	63.9	23.1
Within business					
Total air	16.0	35.2	16.7	29.8	4.4
Total water	18.3	40.3	22.5	40.2	23.0
Total solid waste	12.7	28.0	18.4	32.9	44.9
Other	−1.5	−3.3	−1.5	−2.7	0.0
U.S. gross domestic product	4,625.5		4,991.5		7.9
Percentage of U.S. gross domestic product					
Total PACO		1.7		1.7	—
Business PACO		1.0		1.1	—
Per capita, United States					
Total PACO	321		343		6.9
Business PACO	187		219		17.1
Per household, United States					
Total PACO	858		923		7.6
Business PACO	500		591		18.2

SOURCE: Rutledge, Gary L. and Christine R. Vogan (1994), "Pollution Abatement and Control Expenditures, 1972-1992," *Survey of Current Business,* Vol. 74, No. 5, pp. 36-49.

NOTE: PACO = pollution abatement and control expenditures.

Impact of Eco-Costs on Price

Many of the eco-cost sources shown in Exhibit 7.1 suggest that gains in environmental performance only lead to across-the-board cost increases, which suggests that price increases will follow. But as noted earlier, the potential also exists for some firms to achieve cost reductions as a result of eco-cost scrutiny and allocation procedures.

Cost-Push Relationship

Cost-push simply means that when an increase in unit cost is experienced by product, it is passed on to customers in the form of a higher price to maintain the profit spread. Because ecological burdens often were costed as "free" in the past, some addition to cost, and attendant pressures on prices, must be expected if products are now to be required to pay their ecological way. As was suggested earlier, it might not be so much a matter of having to pay more now than it is a matter of having unwittingly accepted eco-subsidies, and unrealistically low prices, in the past. But as Commoner's (1972) Fourth Law notes, "There is no such thing as a free lunch" (p. 41). In conjunction with Tenet 1 (see Chapter 1), this means that it is likely a case of paying fairly allocated eco-costs now or paying even more later.

The generalization that cost-push will increase prices across the board has particular relevance for those short-term waste management approaches that represent "end-of-pipe" solutions. In such cases, the solution to pollution may be viewed as an add-on to present system technology forced by command-and-control regulations. In other words, present system technology is tinkered with or adjusted without addressing its underlying propensity to make waste and pollute. As Peattie (1995) comments,

> A catalytic converter [and] a sulphur scrubbing system for a coal-fired power station are obvious examples of "end-of-pipe" technologies. Since these are added on to the existing products or production systems, they inevitably involve additional cost. (p. 281)

An exception will be when an add-on (1) creates a marketable by-product out of what formerly was considered a waste that was disposed of at a cost or (2) results in a direct savings of materials. For example, adding on Viatec Recovery Systems Inc.'s WADR (waste acid detoxification and reclamation) Spent Acid Recovery System (see Chapter 4) purportedly reduces both hazardous waste disposal costs and new materials purchases, thereby resulting in net savings over time.

Cleaner, Cheaper, and Smarter

The most desired impact is to achieve a designed-in cost savings. This is the "win-win-win" outcome in which an ecologically sound product delivers the required primary benefits and is delivered at lower cost (which implies enhanced profits). This result stems mainly from P2 initiatives consisting of "clean sheet of paper" system redesigns (reinventions) that factor DFE into every decision upfront. EPA Administrator Carol Browner has described these solutions as the "cleaner, cheaper, and smarter" approaches sought under the EPA's Common Sense Initiative (Browner 1994:3).

The use of soldering technologies in electronics manufacturing that feature "no-clean" fluxes is a case in point. No-clean is an approach that allows a formerly required solvent-based cleaning process to be eliminated with no change in product quality. This cuts upstream demand for solvents, which reduces eco-costs associated with solvent manufacturing and distribution. Because solvent-based cleaning generates hazardous wastes, its elimination reduces the firm's internal disposal costs as well as any external disposal costs borne by society. The Pacific Northwest Pollution Prevention Resource Center notes the following internal operational savings associated with no-clean systems (Leviten, Thorndike, and Omenn 1997):

- IBM Corporation reported saving 10 percent in assembly costs after changing to no-clean flux in a flip chip on ceramic carrier assembly plant.
- Researchers at Sandia National Laboratory reported that large-scale manufacturers can expect to pay about $25,000 to convert to a no-clean approach, with savings of $100,000 to $200,000 per year. (p. 53)

The preceding examples demonstrate a major ingredient associated with the long-term redesign challenge: the incorporation of advanced technology into production systems. This technological solution to pollution, also called the Porter hypothesis (see Chapter 3), is heralded by several authorities as one of the true benefits to be expected of properly managed economic growth (Cairncross 1992a; Porter 1991; Porter and van der Linde 1995). The point: innovative technologies will emerge that reduce the costs of environmental preservation and even create sources of long-term competitive advantage for individual firms.

Market Expansion

A factor that will serve to generally lower the unit cost structures of some sustainable products relates to economies of scale and learning curve efficiencies. As with any emerging market situation, small, specialized production runs and the inherent newness of products and processes breed inefficiencies. As products become accepted and markets expand, economies of scale are realized as fixed costs are written off over the larger volume. Simultaneously, accumulated experience and learning over time translate into fewer errors, which results in higher production and marketing productivity and contributes to lower unit costs. Biddle (1993) suggests that this trend already is in place by noting that in some instances "recycled products like paper and carpets are now cheaper than their virgin counterparts" (p. 150).

Full-Cost/Environmental Accounting

Full-cost/environmental accounting is an emerging discipline that deals with the process of internalizing eco-costs and allocating them to specific products so that prices based on full costs will influence customer behavior. The concept is straightforward: the full-cost price of a product includes "the cost of production plus the cost of any environmental damage associated with it" (Schmidheiny 1992b:17). As noted in Chapter 1 and earlier in this chapter, prices that do not account for eco-costs send false signals to markets. By contrast, prices based on full costs send proper signals, and markets will self-correct accordingly. Because the terms *life-cycle costing* and *full-cost pricing* are approximately synonymous, they are used interchangeably in the following discussions (Ditz et al. 1995; Keoleian 1996; Keoleian, Koch, and Menerey 1995; Schmidheiny 1992b).

Managerial Accounting Orientation

Accounting practice generally is divided into two areas: (1) financial accounting and (2) managerial accounting. Financial accounting focuses on the development of financial statements for tax authorities, investors, securities regulators, and other stakeholder groups desiring to measure financial performance. It is guided by an explicit set of standards known as generally accepted accounting principles.

By contrast, the practice of managerial accounting is dedicated to enhancing the productivity and profitability of the firm. Its goal is to creatively provide information for decision makers. As a subset of managerial accounting, the purpose of full-cost/environmental accounting is to provide relevant in-house information that will support the making of environmentally compatible decisions by management.

Life-Cycle Orientation

As noted by Kreuze and Newell (1994), the objective of environmental accounting is to apply the concepts of managerial cost accounting to the measurement of the eco-costs generated during a product's life cycle so that "a company can attempt to eliminate, or at least minimize, the costs related to those activities that do not add value to the product" (p. 38). In linking eco-costs to product design issues, Keoleian et al. (1995) similarly describe the mission of life-cycle costing as the determination of

> all costs associated with a product system throughout its life cycle, from materials acquisition to disposal. Where possible, social costs are quantified; if this is not possible, they are addressed qualitatively. Traditionally, [the term has been] applied in [the] military and engineering to mean estimating costs from acquisition of a system [product] to disposal. (p. 125)

The preceding suggests two degrees of application. The first is cradle-to-grave coverage consistent with PSLC decision framework and full-blown life-cycle assessment (LCA). This represents the ideal state of being able to accurately track all costs associated with a product system including societal burdens, beginning at the point of raw materials extraction and continuing through the point of final disposal after consumption. The second is a more limited scoping restricted to those costs that are within the control of the individual firm or customer.

Internal versus External Eco-Costs

These two degrees of application define two categories of costs that should be covered in a full-blown full-cost analysis: (1) internal and (2) external (White, Savage, and Shapiro 1996). These cost categories must be interpreted from the viewpoint of a given company; for discussion purposes, they are further subdivided in Figure 7.1.

Internal Costs

From the viewpoint of hypothetical Company A, internal costs are the total company costs over which it exercises some degree of control through the decisions it makes. Also called private costs, two types are present that make up a company's internal cost domain: (1) Type I (conventional internal

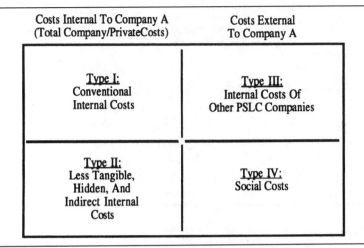

Costs Internal To Company A (Total Company/PrivateCosts)	Costs External To Company A
Type I: Conventional Internal Costs	**Type III:** Internal Costs Of Other PSLC Companies
Type II: Less Tangible, Hidden, And Indirect Internal Costs	**Type IV:** Social Costs

Figure 7.1.   Company A's Costs: Internal versus External Perspective

SOURCE: Adapted from Ditz, Daryl, Janet Ranganathan, and R. Darryl Banks (1995), "Environmental Accounting: An Overview," in *Green Ledgers: Case Studies in Corporate Environmental Accounting,* edited by Daryl Ditz, Janet Ranganathan, and R. Darryl Banks, Washington, DC: World Resources Institute; White, Allen L., Deborah Savage, and Karen Shapiro (1996), "Life-Cycle Costing: Concepts and Applications," in *Environmental Life-Cycle Assessment,* edited by Mary Ann Curran, New York: McGraw-Hill, pp. 7.1-7.19.

NOTE: Company A's Internal Costs = Type I + Type II. Company A's External Costs = Type III + Type IV. Life-Cycle Costs = Type I + Type II + Type III + Type IV.

costs) and (2) Type II (less tangible, hidden, and indirect internal costs) (Figure 7.1). The distinction between the two is as follows (White et al. 1996):

- *Type I—conventional costs:* [These] appear in typical company accounts for use in process control, product costing, investment analysis, capital budgeting, and performance evaluation. They include both annual operational costs, such as labor, materials, and product transportation, and one-time capital costs, such as new equipment and buildings [and] engineering and design for new installations.

- *Type II—less tangible, hidden, and indirect costs:* [These] tend to be less measurable and quantifiable, frequently are contingent or probabilistic in nature, and often are obscured by placement in an overhead account (instead of being allocated directly to a product or process). Examples . . . include environmental permitting and licensing, waste handling, storage, and disposal. . . . Also included are costs for waste cleanup, toxic tort actions, natural resource damages, and personal or property injury associated with the use and disposal of hazardous materials; worker productivity, employee health insurance, and worker compensation related to exposures to hazardous substances in the workplace; production losses due to hazardous materials incidents; and corporate image and market share effects of toxic use reduction or elimination. (p. 7.2)

In summary, Type I and II costs represent Company A's statutory responsibility, or its internal costs domain, at a given point in time under the rules of accepted business practice and the prevailing regulatory/legal framework. This same idea applies to the military/engineering use of the term *life-cycle costing,* in which case it refers to the total costs a customer must bear over time (Types I and II) associated with the purchase, operation, maintenance, and ultimate disposal of a product system.

External Costs

From the perspective of Company A, there is a second category of costs, called *external,* over which it has neither control nor statutory responsibility. Two types of costs make up a company's external cost domain (Figure 7.1): (1) Type III (the internal costs of other companies in the PSLC) and (2) Type IV (social costs) (Ditz et al. 1995; White et al. 1996).

From an LCA viewpoint, all companies making up a PSLC have their own sets of internal costs (Types I and II). But from Company A's perspective, the Type I and II costs of other companies clearly are external and beyond management's control, so they are defined as Type III in Figure 7.1. Although it would be most desirable to calculate a PSLC total cost, this is unlikely to happen for three reasons. First, it is unlikely that the firms included in the PSLC would willingly share this type of information with each other. Second, sharing of cost information might be construed to be an antitrust violation in the United States. Third, if cost information were legally shared, then there would remain the gargantuan and costly task of managing the information to serve some valid purpose.

Social costs, designated Type IV in Figure 7.1, reflect yet another dimension that is external to Company A as well as the other companies making up the PSLC. These costs include broader factors such as health care costs associated with polluted air, the unemployment impact of overharvesting fisheries, groundwater pollution from landfills, and the like. Although the commercial activities of companies and customers might be regarded as the ultimate cause of these costs, individual companies and customers are held responsible for them only to the extent that current public policy has formally transferred them to firms via current regulations, statutory requirements, and legal actions. Examples include increased landfill tipping fees and current compliance costs under the U.S. Clean Air Act.

The shifting of external social costs to the internal cost structures of companies (i.e., the process of internalization) is a hot political issue subject to rapid change. A contemporary example that parallels eco-costs is the host of class-action lawsuits filed in the United states against cigarette makers to get them to pay for health care and personal injuries associated with the diseases their products cause. A lower court judgment of $750,000 against Brown & Williamson demonstrates the potential for a rapid shift of external costs to the internal cost structure of a firm ("Jury's Tobacco Verdict" 1996:A1). In the environmental arena, the passage of Germany's Green Dot take-back legislation in 1991 made manufacturers instantly responsible for managing the packaging wastes their products create and the costs that go with it (see Chapter 8) (Fishbein 1994). The point: external social costs that once were part of an individual company's external cost domain can be dramatically shifted to the internal cost domain on very short notice via political/legal interventions.

Channel Network Accounting Integration

If each firm in the PSLC identified and properly allocated internal eco-costs when developing its cost structure and prices, and all external (social) eco-costs were factored in via public policy and voluntary initiatives, then full costs would be built in at each level. This would mean that the influence of eco-costs would trickle down the PSLC and find its way into the unit cost structures and prices of the manufacturers of appliances, automobiles, and other everyday consumer products. But the reality of contemporary full-cost/environmental accounting is that companies cannot be expected to venture much beyond their internal costs domain. In short, comprehensive full-cost models that include all internal and external costs remain an ideal state of affairs awaiting future development (Global Environmental Management Initiative 1994). Therefore, current full-cost applications must be considered as interim solutions that generally only examine a given firm's available internal costs.

The integration of distribution networks was described earlier in Chapter 5 as a channels decision that enhances the control and coordination of marketing programs in vertical marketing systems (VMSs). It follows that the degree of integration can affect the range of PSLC firms across which accounting system standardization could take place. The three integrative formats described in Chapter 5—(1) corporate, (2) contractual, and (3) administered—suggest some possibilities. Under the corporate model, ownership of the various levels of distribution (full or partial channel integration) defines the range over which a standardized marketing plan can be implemented with absolute authority. It follows that an environmental accounting system also could be applied over this same range. The trend toward corporate integration in large-volume channels suggests that applications of environmental accounting could have a significant effect within a relatively wide internal domain if corporate management has the will to implement the concept. Imagine the impact that fully implemented environmental accounting systems could have on the millions of decisions made by consumers "at the shelf" in the thousands of Kmart, Wal-Mart, and Sears Roebuck retail stores in the United States alone.

Under the contractual VMS approach, the main thrust of standardization creates a favorable setting for the effective implementation of environmental accounting systems. For example, franchise contracts usually contain clauses that mandate accounting reporting systems for the purpose of enhancing the franchisor's administrative control over large numbers of duplicated operations. Again, imagine the opportunity that exists to fully implement environmental accounting systems at the thousands of locations operated by McDonald's, Burger King, and KFC (Kentucky Fried Chicken) in the United States alone.

Administered channel networks are problematic because a lack of standardization defines the essence of the relationships between the partners making up such channels. One could say that a sort of automatic diversity exists and that getting deeply involved in the accounting systems of partner organizations will likely be seen as a meddlesome invasion of proprietary turf. But even in this case, two options are available for enhancing the prospects for achieving the practice of environmental accounting within the broader channel network. Under the first option, a strong channel leader (captain) provides reseller support in the form of formal training in environmental accounting methods (e.g., materials, funding, schooling) to be applied at the partner's discretion behind closed doors. Critical in the acceptance of this type of reseller support is the recipient organization's belief that it represents legitimate value added in the marketing relationship. The second option is for a channel leader to add the practice of environmental accounting to the list of channel partner selection criteria.

Allocating Internal Eco-Costs

The allocation of internal eco-costs to the products and processes responsible for them is where "the rubber meets the road" in contemporary ecological
accounting. This section first examines current accounting practice in this area
and then discusses activity-based costing (ABC) as a solution to the allocation
challenge.

Decision Support Potential

In a nutshell, current managerial accounting practice often lumps environmental charges into general overhead accounts, where they lose any
potential to influence individual product costs. This is a matter of minor
consequence when the share of nonallocated eco-costs remains small. But a
recent study suggests that the eco-costs sector may account for as much as 20
percent of total costs for some companies/industries, a share that cannot be
dismissed (Ditz et al. 1995:8). Obviously, the potential misallocation of costs
at this level opens the door to allowing products with lower eco-costs to
subsidize those with higher eco-costs—exactly the scenario that sustainable
marketing is attempting to eliminate.

Environmental (managerial) accounting's potential to meaningfully allocate costs brings to the table the ability to support decision making at two
levels. First, the allocation of already-discernible internal eco-costs on management's plate can help improve short-term decisions, and the use of such
environmental inputs also can become a routine aspect of the organization's
decision-making process.

A second, and perhaps more exciting, use of allocated eco-costs lies in
applications as a pro-forma decision-making tool. Given emerging indications
of customer preferences for cleaner products and the need to avoid future
environmental liabilities, better cost accounting information can serve as
economic signals that show managers which longer term alternatives to pursue
and which to avoid. Furthermore, not using eco-cost information likely will
lead to unfavorable consequences. As Ditz et al. (1995) note,

> Firms that fail to detect and respond to these signals will shoulder larger
> economic burdens that can only weaken their competitiveness. . . . The wiser
> course of action is to truly internalize environmental costs [eco-costs]—not
> merely to bear them, but to anticipate and manage them. Firms must be able
> to generate, evaluate, and implement alternatives to the status quo. They must

exhibit 7.2

Marketing/Managerial Uses of Environmental
Cost Accounting Information

Goal: Enhance productivity and profitability of the company.

1. Product mix decisions
   Product profitability is one key determinant of inclusion in a product mix.
   Total revenues minus total costs equals total profits ($TR - TC = TP$). Any
   misallocation of eco-costs influences the TP outcome. In particular, distortion
   occurs when firms undervalue the direct economic benefits of products with
   lower eco-costs, thereby subsidizing those with higher eco-costs.

2. Choosing manufacturing inputs
   The choice of materials and other production inputs is dependent on unit
   purchase costs and eco-costs as well as safety, reliability, performance, and
   other criteria. A "cheap" (i.e., unit purchase cost) material may "trigger" high
   compliance costs for permits (preparation and fees), monitoring, and disposal.
   An "expensive" material may lead to the avoidance of any/all of the above,
   thereby more than offsetting its higher initial unit cost. Therefore, understanding the correlation between eco-costs and input unit cost is important
   when assessing the cost-effectiveness of substitutes.

3. Assessing pollution prevention projects
   A switch is under way from controlling pollution (end-of-pipe solutions) to
   preventing it (P2 solutions). However, the typical managerial accounting
   systems now in place treat costs in such a manner as to not fully credit P2
   projects with the success they deserve. Thus, comparisons between current
   pollution control/waste disposal programs and P2 programs often are made
   on an unequal basis. Modifying accounting procedures can resolve this
   discrepancy.

4. Evaluating waste management options
   When end-of-pipe waste management programs are warranted, the evaluation
   of alternatives is a necessary step in the decision-making process. Properly
   allocated eco-costs and the careful scrutiny of both fixed and variable-cost
   components can be determining factors.

5. Comparing eco-costs across facilities
   Cross-facilities comparisons are a common aspect of assessing the operations
   of a given firm. Environmental accounting procedures can help identify those

---

exhibit 7.2 Continued

▬▬▬▬▬▬▬▬▬▬▬▬▬▬▬▬▬▬▬▬▬▬▬▬

"best-performing" facilities that can serve as stewardship models. Many fixed costs of shared environmental facilities (e.g., incinerators, wastewater treatment plants) continue on regardless of where a product is manufactured. Other eco-costs may shift, depending on point of manufacture and on local regulation and internal factors. Eco-cost information also may serve as a benchmark of comparative performance data.

6. Pricing products
Including true eco-costs in the unit cost structures (private internal costs) of firms is the fundamental notion driving the "polluters pay principle."

SOURCE: Ditz, Daryl, Janet Ranganathan, and R. Darryl Banks (1995), "Environmental Accounting: An Overview," in *Green Ledgers: Case Studies in Corporate Environmental Accounting,* edited by Daryl Ditz, Janet Ranganathan, and R. Darryl Banks, Washington, DC: World Resources Institute, pp. 21-28. Reprinted by permission.

NOTE: P2 = pollution prevention.

---

be able to motivate executives, managers, and employees toward this common goal. In this endeavor, more effective, accurate accounting is crucial. (pp. 11, 13)

Some of the areas in which environmental cost (eco-cost) accounting information can support sustainable marketing decisions are summarized in Exhibit 7.2.

Activity-Based Costing

Developing and applying overhead rates for all cost-bearing activities associated with a product is called *activity-based costing* (ABC) (Lere 1991). To accomplish this, one must first determine which costs are relevant and then eventually assign them to specific products based on important differences. In other words, if no differences are apparent, then equal allocation is the rule. The word *relevant* is extremely important in this context. To reiterate earlier discussions, it is realistic in the case of eco-costs to focus only on the allocation of internal (private) costs; that is, *relevant* life-cycle eco-costs are defined as those that will be experienced by the firm in question, now or in the future. Note that this perspective does not attempt to formally account for and allocate Type III and IV costs that fall outside a given company's internal costs domain. For example, the consumer's cost of monthly waste disposal payment to a municipality is not considered a relevant element of a given manufacturer's unit cost structure because this cost simply does not occur within the jurisdiction of the manufacturer.

Relevant costs do include future costs that must be discounted to the present to make valid comparisons. Using the example of hazardous waste, Kreuze and Newell (1994) note,

> Responsibility for hazardous waste, for example, lasts forever. Therefore, all costs are discounted to the present to facilitate comparisons with competing products. Life-cycle costing may reveal that a product with low acquisition costs but high operation, maintenance, environmental, or disposal costs may be a less desirable alternative than a competing product with a higher initial cost. (p. 38)

The basic premise of ABC is to "cost" activities, which then become the ways and means for assigning/allocating costs to products. Subsequently, relevant environmental costs are allocated on the basis of the individual product's demand for those activities. Allocation bases, called *cost drivers,* serve to operationalize the "quantification of the activities performed" (Kreuze and Newell 1994:39) and include measures such as machine hours, number of quality inspections, number of machine setups, and percentage value added. The allocation of activities occurs at four levels: (1) unit, (2) batch, (3) product sustaining, and (4) facility sustaining. Unit-level activities are those performed on the individual units of a given product (e.g., machine time, energy use, waste generated per unit). Batch-level activities are those supporting batch processing systems (e.g., an acid reclamation process necessary to clean units in a batch). Product-sustaining activities relate to the product as a general class (e.g., environmental reporting necessary because of hazardous materials used in product construction). Facility-sustaining activities are those necessary to support a manufacturing plant, processing facility, distribution center, retail/wholesale location, and the like (e.g., air and water pollution abatement devices, staff necessary to implement and monitor environmental regulatory standards).

An example of ABC allocation of eco-costs for hypothetical Products A and B is summarized in Tables 7.2 and 7.3 (this example has been adapted

TABLE 7.2

Activity-Based Costing: Example Levels/Activities, Cost Drivers, and Amounts

Level and Activity	Driver	Amount (dollars)
Unit level		
Machine costs	Machine hours used	2,400,000
Energy	Machine hours used	1,000,000
Disposal of hazardous waste	Product B exclusively	400,000
Batch level		
Inspection	Number of quality inspections	1,200,000
Material movements	Number of production orders	1,450,000
Support services	Number of machine setups	1,800,000
Disposal of hazardous waste	Product B exclusively	300,000
Environmental reporting		
requirements	Product B exclusively	200,000
Product level		
Research and development		
and parts maintenance	Number of subcomponents	2,110,000
Environmental reporting		
requirements	Product B exclusively	200,000
Environmental inspections	Product B exclusively	500,000
Waste treatment costs on site	Product B exclusively	1,000,000
Landfill disposal costs	Product B exclusively	800,000
Contingent liability costs[a]	Product B exclusively	250,000
Facility level		
Plant maintenance	Percentage value added	2,000,000
Buildings and grounds	Percentage value added	1,000,000
Heating and lighting	Percentage value added	600,000
Environmental standards	Percentage value added	290,000
Total overhead costs		17,500,000

SOURCE: Kreuze, Jerry G. and Gale E. Newell (1994), "ABC and Life-Cycle Costing for Environmental Expenditures," *Management Accounting,* Vol. 65, No. 8, pp. 38-42. Copyright by Institute of Management Accounting, Montvale, NJ.

a. Annual contingent liability costs related to waste treatment on site, transportation, and landfill disposal/SuperFund exposure, estimated at $250,000 per year, discounted at current cost of capital rate. This is a life-cycle cost.

from Kreuze and Newell 1994). Product A is described as a high-volume item (200,000 units annually) produced through a single process; it uses no hazardous materials, creates no hazardous waste, and subsequently has zero environmental compliance costs associated with it. Product B is low volume (50,000 units) and generates hazardous waste that is subject to a number of handling regulations and reporting requirements administered by the EPA, the Occupational Safety and Health Administration, and the Department of Trans-

TABLE 7.3

Total Manufacturing Costs per Unit: Activity-Based Costing versus Direct Labor Hour Allocation for Products A and B

	Product A		Product B	
Level and Activity	Event	Amount (dollars)	Event	Amount (dollars)
Panel I: Activity-based costing allocation				
Unit level				
Machine costs at $120 per hour	15,000	1,800,000	5,000	600,000
Energy at $50 per machine hour	15,000	750,000	5,000	250,000
Disposal of hazardous waste	—	—	All	400,000
Batch level				
Inspection at $480 per inspection	1,000	480,000	1,500	720,000
Material movements at $2,900 per order	300	870,000	200	580,000
Support services at $1,200 per setup	1,000	1,200,000	500	600,000
Disposal of hazardous waste	—	—	All	300,000
Environmental reporting requirements	—	—	All	200,000
Product level				
Research and development and parts				
maintenance at $211,000 per component	6	1,266,000	4	844,000
Environmental reporting requirements	—	—	All	200,000
Environmental inspections	—	—	All	500,000
Waste treatment costs on site	—	—	All	1,000,000
Landfill disposal costs	—	—	All	800,000
Subtotal value added (percentage across)	47.6	6,366,000	52.4	6,994,000
Contingent liability costs	—	—	All	250,000
Facility level				
Plant maintenance		952,000		1,048,000
Buildings and grounds		476,000		524,000
Heating and lighting		285,600		314,400
Environmental standards		138,040		151,960
Total overhead costs		8,217,640		9,282,360
Number of units produced	200,000		50,000	
Overhead per unit		41.09		185.65
Direct material cost per unit		100.00		80.00
Direct labor cost per unit		60.00		60.00
Total manufacturing cost per unit		201.09		325.65
Panel II: Direct labor hour allocation				
Overhead cost per unit: $17,250,000 / 750,000 hours =				
$23 / direct labor hour; (3 hours × $23)		69.00		69.00
Direct material cost per unit		100.00		80.00
Direct labor cost per unit		60.00		60.00
Total manufacturing cost per unit		229.00		209.00

SOURCE: Kreuze,, Jerry G. and Gale E. Newell (1994), "ABC and Life-Cycle Costing for Environmental Expenditures," *Management Accounting,* Vol. 75, No. 8, pp. 38-42. Copyright by Institute of Management Accounting, Montvale, NJ.

portation. Both require three direct labor hours (DLHs) for completion (3 × 250,000 = 750,000 per year), which translates into $60 per product at a labor rate of $20 per hour. Direct materials costs are $100 for Product A and $80 for Product B.

Table 7.2 shows activity levels, cost drivers, and dollar amounts. This information is allocated to Products A and B in Panel I on Table 7.3 using the ABC approach and includes a net present value discounted contingent liability cost of $250,000 as a life-cycle factor. A standard approach based on DLHs and no life-cycle considerations is shown in Panel II. The end result reveals startlingly different unit cost estimates when the methods are compared. Specifically, the comparison shows that Product B's ABC-generated and life-cycle-relevant unit cost is nearly 56 percent higher than when using the DLH approach ($325.65 / $209.00 = 1.558), whereas Product A's unit cost dropped approximately 12 percent ($201.09 / $229.00 = 0.8778).

The analysis is extended by comparing the total manufacturing contribution of the ABC and DLH allocation alternatives (Panels I and II in Table 7.4). In Panel I, the culprit behind the dramatic decline in profitability of Product B is the $3,650,000 in charges related to waste management, environmental reporting and inspections, and contingency liability that are not relevant to Product A. At the very least, this state of affairs suggests examining the feasibility of replacing the hazardous materials used in Product B with an alternative formulation, a review of P2 activities that might cut the waste stream, a review of hazardous waste handling procedures within the firm, and the need for repricing Product B. These decision possibilities are masked by the DLH allocation shown in Panel II of Table 7.4.

Design-for-Environment Pricing Strategies

Pricing strategies influence how a company attains its sales volume and profit goals in the context of its unique product-market circumstances. In this section, a number of distinctive pricing strategies are linked to sustainable marketing practice for discussion purposes.

Meet-the-Competition/Level Pricing

For many consumer products that fall in the "commodity convenience" category, the factor of sustainability is of secondary importance in the pur-

TABLE 7.4

Total Manufacturing Contributions: Activity-Based Costing versus Direct
Labor Hour Allocation for Products A and B

	Product A		Product B	
	Amount in Dollars	Percentage	Amount in Dollars	Percentage
Panel I: Activity-based costing allocation				
Total revenue (Products A				
and B at $400 per unit)	80,000,000	100.0	20,000,000	100.0
Less manufacturing costs	40,218,000	50.3	16,282,500	81.4
Manufacturing contribution	39,782,000	49.7	3,717,500	18.6
Percentage across	—	91.5	—	8.5
Panel II: Direct labor hour allocation				
Total revenue (Products A				
and B at $400 per unit)	80,000,000	100.0	20,000,000	100.0
Less manufacturing costs	45,800,000	57.2	10,450,000	52.2
Manufacturing contribution	34,200,000	42.8	9,550,000	47.8
Percentage across	—	78.2	—	21.8

SOURCE: Kreuze, Jerry G. and Gale E. Newell (1994), "ABC and Life-Cycle Costing for Environmental Expenditures," *Management Accounting,* Vol. 75, No. 8, pp. 38-42. Copyright by Institute of Management Accounting, Montvale, NJ.

chase decision. In other words, the product's pricing strategy must be developed around the customer's perception of traditional core (primary) benefits and quality delivered in comparison to competitive offerings. As mentioned earlier, this suggests a low-key tie-breaker role for ecological attributes in these highly routine transactions. This is especially true when the seller is faced with the need to maintain a relatively large market share in the face of heavy "look-alike" competition. Therefore, an appropriate response is a "meet-the-competition," or level, pricing strategy that matches a price line, or the customary price level, of competitive offerings. This essentially treats ecological attributes as added benefits that serve (hopefully) to break the tie.

This approach also reflects a product improvement strategy in which minor product changes (e.g., packaging downsizing, environmental labeling) are executed in the short run while essentially preserving the core benefits delivery system of the original product. This is demonstrated in Table 7.5, where two variants of Procter & Gamble's powdered Tide detergent are analyzed in terms of units cost per load by package type—regular (i.e., paperboard box) versus environmental (i.e., Enviro-Pac plastic bag). The

TABLE 7.5

Price Comparisons for Powdered Tide Laundry Detergent:
Regular versus Environmental Packages

Package Type	Product	Loads	Price (dollars)	Price per Load (dollars)
Regular	Tide with bleach, box	67 loads	14.99	0.2237
Environmental	Tide with bleach, Enviro-Pac bag	51 loads	11.59	0.2273
Regular	Tide regular, box	85 loads	14.99	0.1764
Environmental	Tide regular, Enviro-Pac bag	65 loads	11.59	0.1783

SOURCE: Personal observations by the author in a Publix supermarket in Orlando, FL, September 15, 1998.

nearly identical unit prices shown clearly give customers the option of selecting tie-breaker environmental benefits given identical product core benefits/quality. In fact, the miniscule price increases associated with the Enviro-Pac package very likely are attributable to the smaller quantities of product (loads) being offered in them.

Premium Green Pricing

As will be discussed in Chapter 8, research by Roper Starch Worldwide Inc. has uncovered a consistently small 5 to 6 percent segment of the consumer market, called the Greenback-Greens, that indicates a willingness to pay a significant green price premium to obtain environmental benefits. Members of this segment have above-average incomes, which suggests that they can afford to support the environment through everyday purchases. More important, the vast majority of consumers do not exhibit this expressed propensity to pay a green premium. In addition, because Roper's survey data are based on self-reports and not actual behavior, the Greenback-Greens might even be contaminated by the "fair-weather environmentalist" phenomenon. As described by Hemphill (1991), this refers to the tendency of survey respondents to give socially acceptable answers when asked environmental questions while failing to put their money where their mouths are when it comes to actually making greener purchases. Therefore, the presence of a substantive premium green segment remains shrouded in doubt.

Larger Quantity Pricing

From a materials intensiveness point of view, purchases of consumer and industrial products in larger package sizes usually are more environmentally efficient because they generally require significantly less packaging material per unit of product (see Table 4.1). Table 7.6 demonstrates how this phenomenon relates to quantity discounts offered on two larger sizes of laundry detergent (i.e., 42 and 85 loads) in standard paperboard packages. Although the correspondence between "package weight saving" and "quantity discount" percentages is not perfect, significant noncumulative quantity price discounts are evident as package size increases along with concurrent reductions in packaging materials. This situation could be promoted as a low-key environmental tie-breaker by informing customers that quantity discounts also invoke significant eco-cost savings in terms of reduced packaging waste per unit of product consumed.

Complementary Product Pricing

This may be considered a form of meet-the-competition pricing involving similar products, but it is further distinguished by the linkage of the product to be priced to another product that it supports or complements. A classic example of this approach is what has been occurring in the office copying machine market during the past decade. Basically, the traditional linkage of equipment sales to continuing complementary sales of proprietary new-manufacture toner cartridges could be described as the "protected turf" of original equipment manufacturers (OEMs). However, remanufacturers have challenged this position by developing remanufacturing/reconditioning/repairing channels to recapture spent cartridges, remanufacturing them to new product specifications, and selling them at deep discounts. (Note: This also doubles as an example of take-back pricing discussed later in this chapter.) In response, most major manufacturers have countered with prices on new-manufacture units that are more competitive along with the ecological benefit associated with easy, no-cost return of used cartridges to the manufacturer (i.e., recapture systems featuring prepaid postage and return shipping packages [see Chapter 5]). Of course, the driving force behind these changes has been the outcry to stop disposing of toner cartridges in landfills because of the long-term pollution consequences associated with this practice. But sales promotion/publicity tie-in benefits also are evident because the cartridge return process is linked to contributions to well-known environmental advocacy groups, thereby potentially enhancing corporate environmental image (see Exhibit 5.2).

TABLE 7.6

Quantity Discounts for Powdered Tide Laundry Detergent

Package Weight and Volume[a]	Package Weight per Load (grams)	Package Weight Saving[b] (percentage)	Price (dollars)	Price per Load (dollars)	Quantity Discount[c] (percentage)
105.58 grams, 18 loads	5.8656	—	4.39	0.2439	—
212.31 grams, 42 loads	5.0550	14	6.49	0.1545	37
386.36 grams, 85 loads	4.5454	23	14.99	0.1764	28

SOURCE: Personal observations by the author in a Publix supermarket in Orlando, FL, September 15, 1998.

a. All packages are standard paperboard construction.

b. Example calculation for 42 loads: $\text{Savings} = 1 - \frac{5.0550}{5.8656} = .138 = 14\%$

c. Example calculation for 42 loads: $\text{Discount} = 1 - \frac{0.1545}{0.2439} = .367 = 37\%$

Service-Life Pricing

Service-life pricing is the customer's side of life-cycle costing. Its general premise is that a stream of customer benefits over time is accompanied by a parallel stream of recurring costs. Therefore, factors such as operating costs, replacement costs, disposal costs, executive time, and disruption of business operations can be linked to price. Service-life pricing vividly demonstrates the potential of relationship marketing, which views a customer as a long-term, continuously unfolding stream of needs to be met over time. From the seller's perspective, the goal is to "lock in" customers by providing a corresponding stream of future benefits at a recognized lower total price over time and/or by providing other incentives linked to continuity. At least three types of service-life pricing are discernible: (1) straight service-life pricing, (2) disposables versus reusables system pricing, and (3) take-back pricing.

Straight Service-Life Pricing

This applies to products that experience continuing operating costs (e.g., insurance, maintenance components replacement, the use of fuel or energy) while in the possession of the customer. Reducing total costs over the long term (e.g., lowering average fuel/energy costs, extending the service life of an asset prior to replacement) reduces the quantity of resources necessary to deliver equivalent benefits, and lower eco-costs are experienced.

But the "entry price" required to gain access to the long-term savings made possible by incorporating ecological attributes might appear exorbitant compared to the usual short-term alternatives. In financial terms, *entry price* represents an advance payment to secure a stream of future benefits, the value of which must be discounted to the present. The compact fluorescent bulb (CFB) is a case in point. When compared to an ordinary incandescent bulb (IB) in Table 7.7, the initial price comparison of $17.75 for the CFB versus $0.75 for the IB is truly a shocking contrast. However, when the six-year product service life and the lower energy consumption rate of the CFB are factored in to determine "real costs" (price) over time, the CFB emerges with a positive service-life savings of $24.46 in unadjusted dollar outlays. When analyzed on a net present value basis at 4 percent, the savings is $19.22. When annualized, the savings are $4.08 and $3.20, respectively. With such small real savings per year and high entry price, it is easy to see why many customers would not be attracted to the environmentally correct CFB alternative. However, in an industrial application involving thousands of bulbs and a long-term decision orientation to begin with (e.g., a large manufacturing plant or office facility), the "sell" would be relatively straightforward.

However, one might hypothesize a situation in which durable products, such as home appliances and automobiles, could deliver enough real savings over time to attract a substantial number of customers if the savings were emphasized at the time of purchase. Suppose that a sustainable automobile was created using the latest DFE approaches and could be delivered at a cost/price comparable to that of a conventional automobile. In this case, if annual operating savings of as little as $1,000 ($2.74 per day) were deliverable over a six-year time span, then the net present value calculation at 4 percent would yield approximately $5,242 (see Table 7.7 for net present value factors), an amount that translates into an important selling point.

Disposables versus Reusables System Pricing

When both disposable and reusable product forms compete head-on as substitute products and a long-term, routine purchasing pattern is the norm, cost comparisons (the total price to the customer) can be presented in a life-cycle framework. Each alternative has a set of cost factors as follows:

- Disposables: the costs (including environmental) of periodically replacing the single-use product and the costs of recycling or other waste disposal

TABLE 7.7

Straight Service-Life Pricing: Compact Fluorescent versus Incandescent
Bulb—Cash Outlays over Time and Net Present Value

| | Cash Outlays | | | | | Net Present Value at 4 Percent | |
| | Compact Fluorescent Bulb | | Incandescent Bulb | | | | |
Year	Electricity (dollars)	Bulb (dollars)	Electricity (dollars)	Bulb (dollars)	Cash Difference (dollars)	Factor	Amount (dollars)
Start bulb	—	17.75	—	0.75	17.00	—	17.00
1	1.97	—	7.88 +	1.00	6.91	0.9615 =	6.64
2	1.97	—	7.88 +	1.00	6.91	0.9246 =	6.39
3	1.97	—	7.88 +	1.00	6.91	0.8890 =	6.14
4	1.97	—	7.88 +	1.00	6.91	0.8548 =	5.91
5	1.97	—	7.88 +	1.00	6.91	0.8219 =	5.68
6	1.97	—	7.88 +	1.00	6.91	0.7903 =	5.46
Totals	29.57		54.03		24.46		19.22
Per year	4.93		9.01		4.08		3.20

NOTE: Energy factor: compact fluorescent bulb = 15 watts; incandescent bulb = 60 watts. Six years = 9 incandescent bulbs at $0.75 replacement cost. Annual electricity costs-annual usage: 4 hours per day × 365 = 1,460 hours; compact fluorescent bulb = 1,460 hours × 15 watts = 21,900 watt hours, 21.9 kilowatt hours × $0.09 = $1.97; incandescent bulb: 1,460 hours × 60 watts = 87,600 watt hours, 87.6 kilowatt hours × $0.09 = $7.88. Break-even/payback on original $17.00 investment, cash basis: $17.00 / $6.91 per year = 2.46 years. Net present value calculations are courtesy of Stanley M. Atkinson, University of Central Florida.

⬚ Reusables: the costs (including environmental) of building a more durable product to begin with; the costs (including environmental) associated with recapture, refurbishing, and remarketing until the product reaches its trippage limit; and the costs of recycling or other waste disposal

Because comparisons between disposables and reusables are a variant LCA, the analysis requires proper scoping to include relevant activities/ processes associated with each alternative. In Chapter 2, a comparison between disposable and reusable diapers made this point, but without the addition of customer cost (price) information. Factoring costs into the picture is an attempt to further quantify the overall ramifications of using product systems over time.

But product usage rates, waste management infrastructure, and other local circumstances of individual customers (e.g., ordinances, geographic ecological sensitivities, customer with unused back-hauling capacity) play a major role in any given cost/price outcome. Specifically, "canned" or "pat" answers are to be avoided. For example, Pomper (1993) reports that a 10-trip refillable container with 90 percent recovery is equivalent to a 65 percent recycling rate for disposables (p. 3). What this says is this: when the two systems (reusable and disposable) are properly supported, they may exhibit fairly equivalent environmental efficiency. So, the answer to the question "Which is better?" is "It depends on local circumstances." This further suggests that selling personnel, especially those in the industrial markets, must be trained to conduct such analyses in the field given the specific conditions of specific customers rather than relying on a standard scenario that covers all cases.

When dealing with consumer products, it sometimes is possible to quantify disposable/reusable trade-offs in terms of a break-even point or payback period. Consider the example of a coffee maker that offers two purchase configurations: (1) a lifetime metal filter (the reusable ecological option) and (2) the standard disposable paper filter option. The upfront marginal cost of the metal filter is $17.95; disposable paper filters sell for $1.75 per 40 or $.04375 per unit. Considering only these rough costs and a use rate of one coffee-making cycle per day, it will take 410 days ($17.95 / $0.04375 per day = 410 days), or 1.12 years, for the customer to reach the break-even point on the purchase of the metal filter system.

Analyses of disposable versus reusable pricing options in industrial markets typically involve the use of detailed LCAs to establish comparative system costs. An industrial market example is the comparison between reusable and single-use/disposable surgical gowns in hospitals. The scenario presented in Exhibit 7.3 shows a comparison between Johnson & Johnson's single-use (disposable) brand, FABRIC 450, and two reusable alternatives, standard linen (a generic product) and ComPel (a reusable brand marketed by Standard Textile Company) (McDowell 1993). It is provided to demonstrate the variety of information and basic assumptions that are necessary to undertake an analysis of this type.

It must be reemphasized that a given customer's local circumstances play an extremely important role in these decision outcomes. For example, if a hospital already has invested in a laundry facility, then the use of disposables might well be uneconomical given this circumstance; however, a new facility under construction that already has made the decision not to have a laundry will experience lower costs using disposables. Other factors, such as community environmental sentiment and the medical efficacy, also will be factors that take the decision beyond costs. For example, community perceptions regarding the undesirable impacts disposables might have on the environment

---

εxhibiτ 7.3

Comparison of Disposable and Reusable Surgical Gowns: A Life-Cycle Cost Analysis

Comparison: FABRIC 450 (a Johnson & Johnson disposable brand) versus standard linen (a generic reusable) versus ComPel Fabric (a Standard Textile Company reusable brand)

Scoping: manufacturing of product through final disposal outlined by Arthur D. Little as follows:

| Manufacturing | → | Transportation | → | Laundering, Reprocessing, and Sterilization | → | Waste Management |

Data sources:

1. Data on hospital use patterns, laundering, reprocessing, and disposal patterns came from a survey of 30 hospitals across the United States.
2. Data on disposables manufacturing came from Johnson & Johnson operations.
3. Data on reusables manufacturing came from secondary sources.
4. Cost data came from a review of the literature, hospital surveys, telephone interviews, and cost data provided by Johnson & Johnson.
5. Health and clinical efficacy data came from a review of the literature, the U.S. Food and Drug Administration, commercial launderers, and a sterilizer manufacturer.

Assumptions:

1. The single-use product (FABRIC 450) is a 50% polyester and 50% wood-pulp blend.
2. The standard linen product is a woven 50/50 blend of cotton/polyester.
3. The ComPel product is a tightly woven 100% polyester.
4. All fabrics were fluorocarbon repellent treated.
5. The standard unit of comparison was the average abdominal operation.
6. All standard linen products were assumed to be laundered and reprocessed by the hospital.

(continued)

exhibit **7.3**   Continued

7. All ComPel products were assumed to be laundered and reprocessed by a contract service (RePak).

8. Reusable products were laundered each time they were reprocessed.

9. Fully 80% of the single-use products were disposed of as infectious waste, and all reusable products were disposed of as regular trash at the end of their useful lives.

10. An average of 3.7 surgical gowns were used per abdominal procedure.

11. Large-size gowns were used as a basis for comparison.

12. The maximum number of reuses for reusable surgical gowns was 85 for standard linen and 75 for ComPel.

13. The lower estimates of the number of reuses of surgical gowns was 10 or 30 for standard linen and 10 or 30 for ComPel.

14. Life-cycle assessment inventory findings were based on 100 average abdominal procedures.

15. Costs tracked: (a) direct cost, (b) setup and changing cost, (c) reuse cost (applies to reusables only), (d) storage cost, and (e) disposal cost.

16. All costs expressed in 1991 dollars.

Results: Standard linen gowns appear to be less expensive than either single-use or ComPel gowns as follows:

Product	Number of Reuses	Total Cost[a] (dollars)
FABRIC 450	0	11.11
Standard linen	10	10.78
	30	7.09
	85	5.90
ComPel	10	9.82
	30	9.82
	75	9.82

SOURCE: McDowell, John W, (1993), "An Environmental, Economic, and Health Comparison of Single-Use and Reusable Surgical Drapes and Gowns," a report on an independent study conducted by Arthur D. Little Inc. and prepared for Johnson & Johnson Medical Inc., Arlington, TX. Reprinted by permission.
a. Total cost per average abdominal operation.

can cause hospitals to switch to reusables even if it does cost more (Johnson 1993). In addition, some medical experts argue that in terms of medical efficacy (i.e., the maintenance of sterile conditions), "single-use drapes and gowns seem to offer better protection than standard linen reusables to patients, operating room personnel, and other hospital workers" (McDowell 1993:11). In other words, the products were not equivalent to begin with, which confounds making a direct price/cost comparison.

Take-Back Pricing

Take-back pricing involves pricing products in such a way as to recover the costs of future disposal. This may entail internalizing a front-end disposal charge in the product's initial price or simply charging an end-user fee for any future product recovery/processing services (Davis 1996). It usually is discussed in the context of durable products and represents an implementation strategy through which manufacturers take ultimate responsibility for end-of-life product handling/disposal. However, the implementation of the German Green Dot legislation clouds this distinction because it applies to a wide range of both durable and nondurable products (Fishbein 1994). The result is that products have to be priced to recover the mandated added costs of future waste management services that have been shifted from the public sector to the private/internal cost structures of companies.

Outside the German experiment, some in industry see the voluntary implementation of take-back pricing by durable products producers as a hedge against ill-advised future government mandates (for additional discussion, see the "Voluntary Action versus Mandated Take-Back" subsection in Chapter 5). For example, an appliance manufacturer might feel that implementing a voluntary take-back approach for a product with an assumed average six-year service life would forestall less desirable, and likely more costly, government mandates. Using the discount factor of 4 percent in Table 7.7 and an anticipated future handling fee of $50 (incurred in the sixth year), this would translate into an internalized upfront take-back fee of approximately $40 to be built into the price at the time of purchase.

Another take-back pricing approach is to share the cost of end-of-life handling/disposal with the customer. For example, Sony Corporation asks customers to fund the shipping of used electronic products back to a designated facility, at which point Sony supports the cost of recycling by a third-party supplier ("Sony Pilots Takeback Programs" 1996). Sony's support takes the form of the costs associated with setting up and operating the required reverse channel recapture network, which are now also factored into the costs of doing business.

Including take-back as part of the terms of sale on traditional ownership transactions (i.e., title transfers, outright purchases) involving consumer durables generally would facilitate the return of these items to the original manufacturer or to a designated agent/location. Take-back on the back end of a transaction can be facilitated by a trade-in discount, a practice that tends to occur when a product retains significant residual value, when it is formally titled, or when a secondary market exists for its resale. Automobile trans- actions traditionally have been handled in this manner, whereas transactions involving other consumer durables, such as appliances and furniture, have not.

The take-back pricing strategy of trade-in discounts also can be applied in other cases to support the R2 substrategies of reuse and even materials recycling. For example, machine components, such as timers for dishwashers and clothes dryers and toner cartridges for office copiers, are innocuous, standardized units (components) that sometimes can be routinely remanufac- tured (i.e., fitted with new parts as necessary and upgraded to new-manufac- ture specifications) and offered at much lower prices than new units bearing the same warranties. In such systems, the take-back is again facilitated by a trade-in discount through which defective/failed units, or "carcasses," are generated for routing through reverse channel networks to appropriate loca- tions. As a factor in pricing, the traded-in carcass is a value-added component for which the seller is given a standard credit/discount tied to the replacement purchase. In the Sony Electronics example cited earlier, the recaptured prod- ucts serve as inputs to materials recycling systems, which points out that take-back is not always for the express purpose of remanufacturing.

A university department's purchase of replacement laser printer toner cartridges demonstrates many of these points. A local remanufacturer offers a replacement Hewlett-Packard Laserjet 4L 92274A unit for $39.95. This price is subject to receiving an empty cartridge in exchange (take-back); a $10 core fee applies if an empty is not turned in, and a $10 drum fee is assessed if the unit's drum requires replacement. At the same time, the university computer store charges $69 for a virgin OEM unit. Given that an empty cartridge is exchanged, the worst-case scenario for a remanufactured unit (with drum replacement) is a 28 percent savings ($69.00 − $49.95 / $69.00 = 0.276), and the best-case scenario (no drum replacement) is a 42 percent savings ($69.00 − $39.95 / $69.00 = 0.421).

The point is that many consumer durable products could be redesigned to be efficiently remanufactured (see Chapter 4). This would represent a more efficient use of resources that could be accomplished through take-back strategy. The following additional side effect of take-back is suggested by Hawken (1993):

> By placing both the responsibility [for take-back] and the cost of mitigation with the originator of the problem, vast and compelling incentives are created for companies to redesign, even reimagine, their business and processes. (p. 71)

Rent/Lease Pricing

Under a rent/lease pricing strategy, the right to product use is transferred for a specified period of time, but no title transfer occurs; at the end of the period, the product reverts back to its owner. For customers, rent/lease strategies create an alternative to the traditional ownership of large permanent inventories of durable products, sometimes jokingly referred to as "the goods life." This raises three implications. First, in rent/lease transactions, managed take-back is built in from the beginning. For example, an automobile that is leased for a five-year period is automatically returned to the dealership at the end of the contract, and from there its disposal (e.g., repair for continuing use, recycling for raw materials, cannibalization for reusable parts) takes place in a business setting; nothing is left to chance. A shorter-term example is a video rented at a Blockbuster Video store that is returned within the designated 24- to 48-hour window of use. Thus, a rent/lease pricing strategy triggers automatic take-back.

Second, durable goods rent/lease contracts can be written so that product upgrades could be obtained over time. For example, new computer chips could be routinely installed to upgrade automobile engines to accommodate ethanol or other new fuels as technological advances make them available. Overall, rent/lease is a clear alternative to the linear "make → use → dispose → replace" cycle that now occurs in the case of most owned durable products such as appliances, electronics, and automobiles. This also would open up a more extensive "upgrade" market to manufacturers, suppliers, and retailers.

The third implication is more subtle. Many durable products experience low levels of use in relation to their intended design capacity. For example, a consumer rents a residence and buys a chainsaw. Whether rented or owned, the residence experiences 100 percent use because "occupancy" is a continuous phenomenon. On the other hand, for most people, the use of a chainsaw is an occasional undertaking. In a nutshell, the thousands of chainsaws in consumer garages remain idle 99.99 percent of the time because each individual customer has purchased much more sawing capacity than necessary in relationship to the need to be fulfilled. Normalizing the approach of paying the price of a short-term rental to accomplish occasional sawing work would make it possible to meet the combined needs of all "occasional users" with far fewer rented chainsaws, thereby incurring much lower manufacturing and marketing eco-costs.

A shift to rent/lease pricing on a large scale would result in mass dematerialization (see Chapter 3). From a resource use perspective, this simply means accomplishing the customer's objectives (meeting his or her needs) while using fewer material and energy resources in doing so. From a marketing perspective, this means that the customer focuses on buying benefits, not on material objects per se (i.e., the products as services concept is implemented); therefore, marketers must focus on developing appropriate new benefit delivery mechanisms in terms of the channels, communications, and pricing elements of the marketing mix. This is consistent with the old marketing maxim "It's not what the product is, but what it does, that customers buy." It also reminds traditional marketers that the myopic view "We make products" rather than "We sell benefits" remains totally out of touch with reality as we cross the bridge into the 21st century.

A particularly innovative application of lease pricing has been developed in the carpet market by Interface Inc. (1997) (see Exhibit 7.4). Called the Evergreen Program, product benefits (i.e., the ambiance of a high-quality carpeted surface) are delivered through a seven-year lease arrangement during which the carpeted surface is systematically maintained over time through a physical product design that allows the selective replacement of 18-inch carpet squares. Because carpet wear patterns follow a consistent 80/20 rule (i.e., 80 percent of the wear occurs on 20 percent of the surface), replacing only worn squares during the lease period maintains the surface at the 100 percent level while consuming far fewer resources in the process (i.e., dematerialization occurs). Because ownership is retained, replaced squares are routinely accounted for (recaptured) and returned to the manufacturer for recycling. In addition to the obvious environmental benefits, the continuing customer contact represents a relationship marketing tactic that has the potential to grow both brand loyalty and repeat purchase behavior.

exhibiт 7.4

Interface's Evergreen Program: Innovative Lease—
Pricing in the Carpet Market

EcoSense

Eco-Efficiency and the Evergreen[TM] Program

Interface, Inc.

The Evergreen[TM] Program is an embodiment of the "Product of Service" concept discussed in Paul Hawkins' book, in the form of flooring services. This concept was brought to the United States by McDonough Braungart Design Chemistry. Interface, Inc. manufactures carpet tile for commercial and institutional use. In the Evergreen Program, Interface not only makes the carpet but also assists with designing the floor aesthetics and takes responsibility for lifting existing furniture systems, installing the carpet and maintaining it to a predetermined appearance standard. Because of the attributes of free-lay carpet tiles (not glued to the floor), Interface selectively replaces worn and damaged areas, one 18" square at a time, implementing a sort of rolling, progressive, continuous facelift by periodically, over the years, replacing modules; and most importantly recycling the carpet tiles that come up. Interface continues to own the carpet. Title for the carpet tiles never passes to the user; it stays with the manufacturer, along with the ultimate liability for the used up, exhausted carpet tiles. The customer pays by the month for color, texture, warmth, beauty, acoustics, comfort under foot, cleanliness, safety and healthier indoor air. Interface delivers these benefits but continues to own the means of delivery - theoretically for as long as the building stands.

The Evergreen Program is designed to lower the long term cost of Interface carpet, a natural resource-based product, while utilizing the flexibility of modular carpet to extend the asset's life. The building block of the program is a 7 year lease which allows for a reduction in front end cost, plus a guarantee that, at the end of the carpet's useful life, Interface will take the carpet back and recycle it.

Selective replacement design techniques (20% of your carpet receives 80% of the wear) are outlined prior to the first lease term. Considerable savings are then achieved during the second lease term, when traffic aisles only are refurbished instead of complete replacement. A complete restoration is feasible, at the client's option, in the third lease term with a combination of new and refurbished products. New materials saved during the two lease terms can amount up to 20% of the original carpeted area. New materials saved during three lease terms can amount to more than 50% of the original carpeted area.

The most important benefit in the products of service concept is the opportunity to begin radically redesigning the form, materials and functions of products to drastically "de-materialize" industrial processes. Through the long term relationship inherent in the Evergreen Program, Interface is determined to not only extend the life of the majority of the material through selective replacement, but to develop methods of leaving un-exhausted materials of the carpet in place through multiple rejuvenations.

Four paradigms in the selection and installation of interior finishes must be overcome for the Evergreen Program to become common place.

1. Product ownership versus leasing - Even though leasing is becoming popular for automobiles and copiers, the leasing of building finishes has not been widely considered. Leasing relieves the customer from long term liability of the disposal of exhausted products.
2. Transaction product sale versus long term relationships - Many purchasing professionals are uncomfortable with contractual, long term relationships. The Evergreen Program works to minimize the total life cycle costs of all products and services while making Interface contractually accountable to deliver the predetermined performance and economics.

(continued)

exhibit 7.4   Continued

3. Product specifications versus total accountability - The building industry is comfortable and experienced with using a myriad of product specification information to predict future performance. In the Evergreen Program, Interface assumes direct and total accountability for the performance of the product. Product specifications become a minor issue relating only to safety and accessibility concerns.
4. Capital costs versus operating costs - Particularly in building renovations, the true cost of the money used for the purchase of interior finishes is rarely realized. The three available options for financing carpet are cash, existing bank or credit lines and third party funding (leasing). Cash and available credit lines are becoming highly valued corporate assets and managed very tightly. Though the easiest to use, cash is probably the most expensive option when you consider the true value of cash to a corporation. Additionally, in the purchase of a durable good with cash or credit, the business is paying today's dollars for a future value. In the Evergreen Program, the business is paying for the value as they use it. Thirdly, capital budget items (cash or credit) traditionally require elaborate authorizations. Payments for the Evergreen Program can be considered as operating expenses requiring lower levels of authorization.

The World Business Council for Sustainable Development considers the following categories as important in developing "Eco-Efficient" products and processes:
1. Make products with less material
2. Make products with less energy
3. Make products with less toxics
4. Enhance product recyclability
5. Maximize the sustainable use of renewable materials
6. Extend product durability
7. Increase service intensity

The Evergreen Program is focused on delivering value with significantly reduced material and energy, extending the life cycle of products through material selection and maintenance and increasing service intensity by bundling design, furniture lifting, carpet installation and maintenance services with its products. These improvements are being realized today at the Energy Resource Center of Southern California Gas Company and the City of San Diego. A number of major corporations, medical facilities and municipalities have expressed interest in the concept for their facilities or in adaptation of the concept for their products. In the future, the long term relationships that the Evergreen Program will provide will eliminate some barriers to innovations in product design using less materials and energy and with enhanced recyclability. Over the long term, the Evergreen Program will deliver more value and with less, sharing those savings with Interface customers and the environment.

SOURCE: Interface Inc. (1997), Interface homepage: http://www.ifsia.com, January 10. Reprinted by permission.

Implementing Sustainable Pricing

Pricing is an issue that hardly escapes the attention of top management. Making price changes is risky business, especially when a long and venerable status quo position has been the norm. Attempting to convince senior executives that products are underpriced or that they need to be repriced because of environmental factors might even be seen as treasonous. Cultivating an accounting connection and developing adequate decision support information through the sustainable marketing audit process are crucial to the implementation of sustainable pricing.

Cultivating an Accounting Connection

Marketers must first establish a relationship with the people in accounting and get the facts concerning the unit cost structures of present products. Most firms have a standardized managerial cost-accounting system. Getting a firm grip on how this system works and how it presently allocates eco-costs is a vital first step.

Given that the firm has not adopted an environmental accounting perspective, the next logical step is to sell this approach to top management. The point is to start a continuing dialogue with the function that controls "the numbers" that eventually will lead to accounting systems that routinely allocate environmental charges to the products that are responsible for them.

Sustainable Marketing Audit: Pricing Assessment

The sustainable marketing audit process introduced in Chapter 3 can serve to develop quantitative and qualitative information to support the implementation of sustainable pricing. To assist in the pricing assessment, a number of generalized questions and issues are provided in Exhibit 3.7. Again, it remains important to recognize that the "position(s)" of a firm in the PSLC will determine the significance of various pricing factors in the analysis.

Chapter Summary

The pricing element of the marketing mix provides the customer with an indicator of value. As such, it generally should reflect the true costs of resources and all other costs of doing business. Unfortunately, most prices do not reflect the relevant eco-costs of products. This sends the wrong signal to customers as they go through the process of making free and informed choices in the marketplace. Ideally, products with low eco-costs would have lower prices than similar products that have high eco-costs. Under such circumstances, customers would tend to buy the lower price alternative, which would serve environmental interests. Shielding conventional products from eco-costs has the effect of subsidizing their profit because eco-costs go unreported.

Pricing DFE decisions act as support for P2/R2 strategies already based on product and channel waste management decisions. The major influences on price are (1) unit cost structure, (2) customer perception, and (3) competitive prices. The unique cost dilemma facing sustainable products is incorporating eco-costs into their unit cost structure; this challenge involves the identification of relevant sources of eco-costs and the fair allocation of these costs to the product(s) responsible for them. Customer perception deals with the fact that ecological attributes usually are secondary considerations in marketing transactions for which customers will not pay a premium; however, positive ecological attributes may serve as a tie-breaker given that all else, including price, is equal. In addition, the prices of available competitors (substitutes) serve as a benchmark against which the value of sustainable products is constantly compared.

Sources of eco-costs include product, process/facilities/management personnel, fugitive emissions, environmental/legal actions, and routine regulatory compliance. Allocating eco-costs from these sources to products may alter their unit cost structure. However, because of differences across industries, both cost increases and cost savings may occur. The costs involved may induce a cost-push effect that puts upward pressure on prices. This is particularly true when the strategy involved is an R2 end-of-pipe solution. In such cases, the remedy usually is an add-on to an existing system that usually also adds to costs. However, clean-sheet-of-paper system redesigns (reinventions), which often represent P2 initiatives, can result in cost savings. Another factor having an impact on cost structures is market expansion. Emerging sustainable products may initially be characterized by small production runs, little product experience, and high unit costs. Market expansion implies larger production runs and the accumulation of more product experience, which generally leads to lower unit costs.

Full-cost/environmental accounting is an emerging discipline within managerial accounting that deals with the issues involved in allocating and internalizing both internal and external eco-costs. In the ideal case, this allocation and internalization process would occur over the product's total life cycle (i.e., all PSLC stages). However, practical constraints exist that effectively sidetrack the ideal in favor of more limited partial applications involving a firm's internal (controllable) cost structure. Even these limited applications run into monumental challenges because they must address the less tangible, hidden, and indirect costs associated with waste management issues. External costs, which include social costs over which the individual firm has no direct control, may be shifted (allocated) to firms through the political (public policy) process. This has occurred, and continues to occur, through the present environmental regulatory framework and via swift social change legislation and class action litigation.

The integration of marketing channel networks (i.e., VMSs) holds out promise for advancing environmental accounting practice in the future. This is particularly true in corporate-integrated systems that represent a single firm within which standardized environmental accounting procedures could be instituted by top management edict. Many contractual systems have a high degree of standardization that could be capitalized on to initiate environmental accounting procedures, at least within the domain of the traditional marketing channel. However, because of their lack of standardization, administered systems are problematic. However, a strong channel leader organization could institute voluntary educational/reseller support programs that would trigger in-house efforts to adopt standardized environmental accounting practices to a degree. Alternatively, channel partner selection criteria could be amended to include evidence of environmental accounting practice as a forward partner or supplier selection criterion in administered channels.

Allocating the internal costs of firms to products is accomplished through the process of ABC. When internal eco-costs are not allocated and end up as general overhead, they fail to provide vital information to management about current costs and profits that could lead to improved management decisions in relation to present products. Recent studies indicate that this can be a serious omission because the eco-costs sector may account for as much as 20 percent of total costs. In addition, the adoption of ABC techniques can improve pro-forma new product decision-making capabilities.

ABC is a complex process that establishes overhead rates for all cost-bearing activities associated with a product. It first determines relevant costs and eventually assigns them to various products based on important differences. The basic premise of ABC is to first cost activities; a given product's use of an activity determines the final allocation. Such procedures can generate major differences in allocations when compared to traditional DLH allocation methods.

DFE pricing strategies represent approaches unique to the issue of sustainability and can be used to support a variety of P2/R2 strategies. *Meet-the-competition pricing* reflects the presence of many look-alike competitors and emphasizes the tie-breaker role of ecological attributes. *Premium green pricing* raises the issue as to whether customers will pay more to get ecological attributes; the general conclusion is that only a small segment will do so. *Larger quantity pricing* focuses on the materials intensiveness issue by pointing out that larger quantity packages consume fewer materials and, therefore, feature reduced eco-costs. *Complementary product pricing* relates to that fact that one product often creates a need for another, for example, a continuing stream of replacement cartridges for copiers. Therefore, a low-price (deep-discount) pricing challenge by remanufactured replacement cartridges affects the pricing of traditional virgin replacement cartridges. *Service-life pricing* develops a long-term cost/price approach for three types of situations: (1) durable products that have significant ongoing operating costs over time, (2) products with purchase cycles over which disposable and durable versions can be compared over time, and (3) durable products subject to take-back at the ends of their useful lives. In each case, the idea is to compare total costs (price) over the life cycle, with lower total costs translating into lower eco-costs and (hopefully) lower prices. *Rent/lease pricing* addresses the issue of shifting transactions from traditional product ownership to the use of a product for a specific period of time on a rent/lease basis, at the end of which the product reverts to the owner. Rent/lease transactions are seen as a way in which to dematerialize consumption to a significant degree.

Implementing sustainable pricing centers on selling top management on the need for full-cost accounting. Its adoption is crucial for establishing cost structures and prices that reflect the true costs of consumption. Cultivating a liaison with the firm's accounting function and developing adequate decision support information through the sustainable marketing audit process are critical implementation factors.

cHApTeR 8

Markets and Market Development

$\mathbf{S}$ince the earliest days of commerce, the term *market* has come to signify the coming together of sellers of products and potential customers for the ultimate purpose of satisfying the wants and needs of both. In this exchange process, sellers strive to make a profit, whereas customers seek benefits through the products obtained. In the Western world, once simple products have blossomed into the unprecedented arrays of goods and services now available through supermarkets, convenience stores, department and specialty stores, banks, shopping malls, mail-order catalogs, automobile dealerships, health care institutions, and even universities—just to name a few. Under the free enterprise system, almost any imaginable variant is available somewhere. For example, the Disney Institute, a division of Walt Disney World, offers alternative upscale vacation packages that promise customers intellectual fulfillment through participation in experiential activities involving the culinary arts, photography, animation, gardening, canoeing, and rock climbing.

Role of Markets

Modern marketing has likewise evolved to become the omnipresent manager of the exchange process. The traditional, and quite logical, view of this process is that marketers assess customers' wants and needs, devise appropriate "form and function" product solutions to meet those needs, and then deliver these product solutions to the marketplace via channels, promotion, and pricing decisions. The point is that identified target markets (i.e., potential consumers and/or industrial customers) serve as a sounding board for the various marketing mix decisions. Again, as Drucker (1973) notes, "There is only one valid definition of business purpose: to create a customer" (p. 61). Thus, the marketing strategist's job is to optimize the marketing mix around the wants and needs of specified target markets.

Consumer Markets: Decision Process Factors

The nature of the consumer markets challenge, given the new sustainable marketing criteria that product systems must be "compatible with ecosystems," is well stated by Polonsky and Mintu-Wimsatt (1995): "Customers must learn to base their purchase decisions not only on how well products satisfy individual needs but also on how these products affect the natural environment" (p. xix). Obviously, understanding the consumer purchase decision process will provide insights for improving the efficacy of marketing mix decisions designed to achieve the goal of sustainability.

The Decision Process Model

Consumers seek out products to satisfy their own personal needs and sometimes the needs of those around them such as family members, friends, and colleagues. This involves both mental and physical effort. Loudon and Della Bitta (1988) define consumer behavior as "the decision process and physical activity individuals engage in when evaluating, acquiring, using, or disposing of goods and services" (p. 8). Note that the definition includes product disposition as the logical and final element in the consumer behavior sequence. It also translates neatly into the traditional four-stage decision process model (Figure 8.1) that depicts potential customers as engaged in a problem-solving activity that may be either (1) aborted/postponed at any point or (2) carried through to eventual closure (a purchase outcome occurs). The stages are viewed as interactive and simultaneous in character rather than as occurring in strict linear sequence.

The level of involvement in the decision process is an important aspect of this approach. At least three types of consumer problem-solving processes based on involvement level have been identified: (1) routinized response behavior (low involvement), (2) limited problem solving (moderate involve-

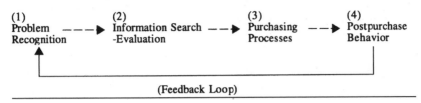

Figure 8.1. The Consumer Decision Process Model

ment), and (3) extended problem solving (high involvement) (Boone and Kurtz 1992:217). These levels of involvement also reflect how fast the typical decision maker goes through the process. A "knee-jerk" convenience product decision can be characterized as a low-risk/low-price, routinized transaction; buying a $100 blouse likely will require more personal involvement, information, and time because financial and fashion risks are present, and building a $1 million retirement home certainly would be an intensely time-involving, high-risk, extended problem-solving exercise for most people. Of course, the overall idea is that understanding the customer's buying process (what the typical customer goes through) will inspire marketing mix decisions by sellers that will facilitate the movement of the customer through the process to a favorable conclusion—completion of a transaction rather than abortion or postponement.

In the past, marketers have concentrated their analysis efforts more on the acquisition aspects of the decision process (Stages 1, 2, and 3) than on postpurchase behavior (Stage 4). But it is important to note that in addition to actually realizing the benefits of consumption, the postpurchase stage of consumer behavior includes both the waste-generating aspects associated with consumers' product use over time and the act of disposition at the end of product useful life. These aspects of consumer behavior are of major concern to sustainable marketers.

Problem Recognition

The consumer decision process model begins by raising the dual issues of (1) what needs are to be met and (2) what triggers the need satisfaction process. Loudon and Della Bitta (1988) state,

> Problem recognition results when a consumer recognizes a difference of sufficient magnitude between what is perceived as the desired state of affairs and what is the actual state of affairs, enough to arouse and activate the

decision process. The "actual state" refers to the way in which the need is already being met, and the "desired state" is the way a person would like for the need to be satisfied. (p. 590)

In the usual marketing setting, customers can be described as having either expressed or latent needs. In the case of expressed needs, customers seek benefits through products to meet needs they are generally aware of, or become aware of, during the buying process. For example, they want/need an automobile to transport them to work, housing to provide shelter from the elements, food to provide nourishment and enjoyment, life insurance to provide future cash for loved ones, copies of tax returns from Kinko's to document important correspondences, and so on.

A clean, habitable ecosystem also is a legitimate need, without which the customer literally cannot survive. But in the case of most consumers, this need for sustainability is hardly expressed; rather, it is latent, and in most cases it is not recognized as all. Even if it were, meeting an ecological need is not particularly associated with any one product or transaction. Unlike an automobile purchase, which directly addresses the expressed need to be moved daily over land from Point A (home) to Point B (work), the customer is not able to satisfy his or her need for a safe, clean world through the purchase of given Product X such as "green" toilet bowl cleaner or 50 percent postconsumer recycled-contents toilet paper. Rather, the benefits of sustainability remain an underlying factor linked to the elimination of the hidden wastes generated to some degree by all products. Because of this, ecological needs are unlikely to serve as the primary trigger of the purchase decision process.

Search-Evaluation

Once the existence of a problem is recognized, the potential customer moves on to search out and evaluate appropriate information. Levels of consumer awareness and the importance consumers attach to given issues are important drivers of the search process.

Consumer Awareness: Salience of the Issue

When it comes to the environment as an issue driving buying behavior, the crux of information search-evaluation is that customers must be aware of, understand, and value the subtle, and sometimes not so subtle, relationships among consumption decisions, waste/pollution, and environmental quality. If this is not the case, and it is not for most customers at this time, then ecological attributes will play a diminished role in the search-evaluation stage.

There is ample evidence that the general public tends to relegate pollution and other environmental risks to the back burner. Focusing on the U.S. market, large-sample public opinion surveys by Roper Starch Worldwide Inc. over the past three decades show that concern about "pollution of air and water" ranked consistently low in comparison to issues such as "crime and lawlessness," "drug abuse," and "the way the courts are run." In fact, on the 1994 survey, "pollution of air and water" ranked 17th out of 20 items tested, with only 12 percent indicating it was a personal concern (Ladd and Bowman 1995:19). More recent work by Ladd and Bowman (1996) confirms this continuing state of affairs.

Two things about this situation must be noted. First, as has been stressed throughout this book, reforming consumption practices and meeting "sustainability needs" is not a choice; it is a mandate, whether the customer likes it or not. So, even if the market is less than interested, marketers have a professional obligation to advance the issue and find the least offensive solutions to pollution.

Second, just because "the environment" is rated lower in importance than other issues having more immediate impact on the public does not mean that it is grossly unimportant and forgotten. In fact, quite the opposite may be the case. Roper Starch Worldwide Vice President Peter Stisser puts forth an interesting hypothesis that covers this eventuality, which he labels the "social issue life cycle." It involves three stages (Frankel 1994):

▓ Phase 1: Anxiety is high, and activities about the issue are relatively low.
▓ Phase 2: People become more informed about the issue, and activity overtakes anxiety.
▓ Phase 3: These activities become "embedded"—integrated into people's lifestyles. (p. 2)

Under Stisser's model, one might argue that well-known ecological disasters, such as the Exxon *Valdez* oil spill in Alaska and the Bhopal chemical plant poisonings in India, have had two effects. One is to increase anxiety simply by their occurrence (i.e,. Phase 1 is instigated); surely this was the result of the media's graphic portrayal of both events through images of environmental devastation and death for weeks. But a second effect could have been that, after a while, the detailed media coverage was tantamount to a large dose of awareness-increasing educational information that would tend to provoke a transition to Stisser's Phase 2. Later still, environmental disasters become part of the American scene that are "expected" on the nightly news; Stisser's Phase 3 has arrived.

All of this suggests that higher levels of awareness probably will have a generally positive impact on integrating "ecological thinking and action" into lifestyles and perhaps enhance the "tie-breaker" role of ecological attributes in product purchases. But there are other reasons beyond media exposure that support the belief that environmental awareness levels will continue to in-crease and continue the process of "embedding" ecological considerations into customer behavior. First, as Cairncross (1992b) notes,

> Not a schoolchild in the industrial world can have failed, in the past two years, to do a project on some aspect of the environment. Teachers have found it a wonderful way to combine the aspects of natural science, public policy, and a smidgeon of economics in a package that a 10-year-old can enjoy. (pp. 13-14)

Therefore, a whole generation of ecologically educated young people gradu-ally will be entering the consumption mainstream, where they eventually will establish ecological values as a norm influence on personal buying behaviors.

In addition, personal contact with waste management activities has been forced on consumers in the United States through the widespread implemen-tation of local curbside collection programs. These programs divert large quantities of municipal solid waste from landfills to recycling systems; they require observance of a daily ritual—the personal hand sorting of materials for separate pickup (e.g., paper, glass, plastics, metals, compostables, yard waste) prior to household garbage collection. State-level legislative mandates are the primary instigators, but coverage is nationwide in scope. As of early 1998, approximately 136 million Americans were served by curbside recy-cling programs, up from 108 million in 1995 (Glenn 1998:41; Steuteville 1996:54), and these programs have achieved very high levels of voluntary participation. Could it be that daily contact with garbage fosters respect for the environment and the further embedding of ecological values in daily life?

Finally, as the distribution of so-called "sustainable/green products" begins to go mainstream on a volume basis (see Chapter 5), customer aware-ness also is heightened by retail shelf exposure. For example, it is logical to conclude that people involved in curbside collection programs will be more aware of recyclable and recycled-contents products (RCPs) and packaging on supermarket shelves, the net effect of which is to translate this everyday ecological experience into a pro-environmental influence on personal decision making and lifestyle, as described in Stisser's Phase 3.

Maslow's Hierarchy of Needs

Maslow's hierarchy of needs model (i.e., physiological needs, safety needs, social needs, esteem needs, self-actualization needs) provides an interesting psychological characterization of factors that trigger customer behavior while providing insights about how to communicate environmental appeals/information in terms potential customers might understand. For example, the ecosystem support services listed in Exhibit 1.2 can be used to demonstrate how ecosystems health is necessary to support basic physiological needs; any perceived health advantage of a sustainable product (e.g., organically grown cotton uses no harmful pesticides, low-emission pollution automobiles release fewer pollutants into the atmosphere, zero-VOC [volatile organic compound] paints contribute to higher in-door air quality) can be translated into basic safety needs; concerns over future environmental quality in regard to loved ones can be translated as social needs; the purchase and use of green products may be seen as a "personal statement" that fulfills esteem needs; and customers may experience self-actualization through the belief that their local pro-environmental actions have a global impact.

Other Needs

Whereas the needs characterized by Maslow's hierarchy are important, other obvious economic and convenience factors are drivers of customer behavior. For example, when it comes to purchasing a specific brand, Russell and Lane (1996) assert,

> Despite all the press about quality, past experiences followed by price, quality, and recommendations from other people lead the reasons why people buy a brand. These factors haven't significantly changed over the past two decades; however, price has become more important. (p. 86)

Thus, many customers are creatures of habit and must observe the general economic constraint imposed by price. They lapse into routine and convenient patterns of purchase behavior. In short, they tend to buy the same brands over and over so long as the brands are affordable and convenient to purchase and customers' needs continue to be satisfied. This creates the barrier to market entry described in the next subsection.

Barrier to Market Entry: Tie-Breaker Role

The lack of salience of environmental issues, while disappointing to environmentalists and sustainable marketers, probably is something to be expected; it certainly is something to be dealt with strategically. In addition, customer experience with green product alternatives is bound to be somewhat limited, and the price-quality image of so-called green products certainly is not notably positive. Overall, these circumstances represent a barrier to market entry for new green products. They also suggest that placing heavy emphasis on green claims, at the expense of traditional benefits, might be misguided in the case of either new or established brands (see Chapter 6). One strategic solution that applies to both cases is to use ecological attributes as a tie-breaker (see Chapter 7) that "kicks in" when product quality, price, and convenience are equivalent. Noted British environmental marketing expert Ken Peattie spells it out nicely: "The vast majority of people, if offered credible green products with similar prices and technical performance to conventional products, would discriminate in favor of the green product" (Peattie 1995:155). The lesson at this time is as follows: let primary benefits win an Oscar as best actor, and let ecological attributes serve in the important capacity of supporting actor.

Purchasing Processes

This stage of the decision process defines the point at which the customer selects and carries out a course of action based on the preceding stages. Marketing analysis focuses on two aspects: (1) purchasing patterns, which include where to buy (location), quantity to buy, and when to buy (timing); and (2) purchasing outcomes, which represent the customer's final behavioral action(s).

Purchasing Patterns

In terms of where to buy, retailer environmental image and product availability are important considerations. A limited set of consumers might prefer specialty green retailers (both eco-retailer stores and non-store specialty green catalogs) as sources for green products, whereas the majority are likely to rely on the availability of "green lines" at the traditional mainstream retailers they already patronize (see Chapter 5).

The "where to buy" factor for many products already is influenced by the efficiency of the shopping experience. For example, supermarkets and shopping centers facilitate one-stop shopping. This has a positive environmental side effect: fewer trips, each of which results in the purchase of more goods and services, is more energy efficient than multiple trips that produce a lower average purchase quantity, assuming the automobile is the mode of transportation and exhaust emissions are the measure of impact. But these retailing strategies already are in place; what remains to be done is for retailers to recognize and promote the positive environmental attributes of those strategies.

Purchase "quantity" decisions are a pattern that can reflect resource conservation through (1) the downsizing of purchases of complementary/supporting products, (2) the purchase of products in larger package sizes, and (3) the downsizing of purchases to lead a simpler lifestyle that requires fewer material resources to support. These customer behaviors are demonstrated in sequence through the following examples:

- A high-mileage car is purchased, requiring 25 percent less fuel to be purchased over its service life.
- Milk is purchased in a 1-gallon (124-ounce) high-density polyethylene (HDPE) container rather than in two ½-gallon (64-ounce) HDPE containers, thereby resulting in a 22 percent saving in packaging materials (see Table 4.1).
- A professor purchases five pairs of Levi's Dockers pants and five mix-and-match shirts rather than five suit ensembles (suit, shirt, tie, matching shoes, etc.), with the motive of leading a simpler existence.

The "when to buy" (timing) factor may be reflected by the postponement of purchase by those waiting for a viable sustainable/environmental alternative to appear. For example, General Motors' EV1 electric cars were made available on a lease basis in late 1996 (Blumenstein 1996; "GM Electric Cars" 1996). Among the first buyers likely will be those who have postponed earlier purchases until the introduction of this technology by a major, and more reliable, manufacturer such as General Motors.

Purchasing Outcomes

The product acquisition sequence (Stages 1, 2, and 3) ends in a purchase outcome that defines the action (purchase or not) finally taken. There are a number outcomes possible, each reflecting active or passive behaviors by customers (Peattie 1995):

▓ Nonpurchase: repair old product, do without, simplify one's lifestyle to require fewer products to begin with (e.g., perform do-it-yourself auto repairs, become a vegetarian)

▓ Borrowing, hiring, and leasing/renting: to match a low-volume or intermittent real need or to reduce customer risk on the introduction of new sustainable technology (e.g., rent a chainsaw for occasional use, lease the General Motors EV1 electric car, borrow a book or video from the library)

▓ Buying secondhand: to make use of a product's remaining useful life and embedded investment in energy and resources (e.g., buy a used car, purchase a remanufactured copier toner cartridge)

▓ Alternative product purchase: shift to a radically different approach to attaining the desired benefits (e.g., substitute a bicycle for automobile transportation, buy a book in CD-ROM format)

▓ Alternative brand purchase: switch to an alternative green brand from a green supplier or a green brand marketed by a conventional supplier (ecological attributes may play a tie-breaker role) (e.g., switch to a "dolphin-free" brand of tuna)

▓ Life-span-based purchasing: purchase premium-priced, high-quality durable products that feature lifetime warranties or switch to reusables from disposables (e.g., buy 100,000-mile radial tires, use returnable beverage containers, purchase a permanent/reusable coffee filter)

▓ Continue existing brand purchase: shift to or simply accept the existing brand's green variant (feature) when it is introduced (e.g., buy Tide in the Enviro-Pac plastic bag, buy Tide in the largest paperboard package size) (pp. 88-90)

Product Ownership: The Norm

It is instructive to note that all of the preceding purchasing outcomes except "nonpurchase" and "borrowing, hiring, leasing/renting" are forms of traditional outright product ownership (i.e., title transfer). This certainly is consistent with the notion of "possession-defined success" (i.e., he who dies with the most toys wins) that is prevalent in Western culture (Richins and Dawson 1992). By contrast, it is important to reemphasize the need to consider the role of "products as services" in the dematerialization of resource-intensive durable goods use, a goal that is achievable through lease/rent transactions (see chainsaw dematerialization example in Chapter 3).

Postpurchase Behavior

The waste management orientation of sustainable marketing makes the study of consumers' postpurchase behavior an area of particular interest. Two aspects are of worthy of investigation: (1) the avoidance of postpurchase dissonance and (2) understanding the nature of product disposition patterns that represent the finale of consumption.

Avoiding Dissonance

For a customer to want to repeat a purchase or recommend one to someone else, he or she has to have a positive experience the first time around. In the decision process model, the positive/negative influence of customer satisfaction is shown as a feedback loop that fuels or aborts repeat purchase behaviors. When a purchase is less than satisfactory for whatever reason(s), it creates a state of tension called *postpurchase dissonance.* Loudon and Della Bitta (1988) describe this as a form of behavior that occurs because of a discrepancy between benefits expected and benefits actually delivered by a product.

It is axiomatic that products with sustainable benefits will gain higher levels of acceptance and respect faster if postpurchase dissonance is absent. Whereas this is important in convenience purchases, it is doubly so in the case of higher risk limited and extensive problem-solving scenarios. Take the case of the purchase of a first-generation General Motors EV1 electric car, a product lease-priced in the $30,000 to $40,000 range. Its electrical propulsion system requires different driving techniques (the way in which the car is operated by the customer) when compared to the conventional gasoline engine vehicle. Battery recharging procedures and timing also represent a total change from the norm of a service station gasoline fill-up. In addition, electric car technology has not seen widespread applications on conventional highways in the United States, so technology- and maintenance-related problems are anticipated to arise. Therefore, the first customers of this product face unusually high levels of risk. To moderate potential dissonance, General Motors has chosen to make the car available initially only on a lease basis, with maintenance risks borne 100 percent by the manufacturer, until the bugs are wrung out of the product's technology and support systems (Blumenstein 1996).

Product Disposition Patterns

A 1977 *Journal of Marketing* article by Jacoby, Berning, and Dietvorst (1977) titled "What about Disposition?" demonstrates the potential for research about what customers do with products at the end of service life. This work produced a "disposition decision taxonomy" (Figure 8.2) that remains a useful framework for research in the 1990s.

The idea behind disposition patterns research is to understand exactly what actions are required of customers to foster sustainability as well as the nature of product and other marketing enhancements necessary to facilitate those actions. With this knowledge in hand, the design of sustainable marketing mixes that make it easy for both customers and channel members to participate can proceed. For example, the shift to refillable beverage containers in markets where disposable systems have reigned for decades would require basic changes in both manufacturer and customer behavior. Bottlers and distributors would have to develop appropriate packages, as well as reverse channel networks, to perform recapture logistics and processing functions (see Chapter 5); customers would have to be informed about take-back/redemption procedures, as well as the reasons it is important to participate, to maximize the trippage rate. Similarly, if a manufacturer planned to continue the use of disposable packaging, then this process could be facilitated by incorporating design-for-recyclability considerations into packaging design and by engaging in marketing communications programs that promote the importance of high levels of consumer participation in local public sector curbside collection programs.

Consumer Markets: Green Segmentation Analysis

As noted earlier, the marketing strategist is charged with optimizing the marketing mix in relation to the wants and needs of the target market. Doing so requires the possession of detailed market-based data to serve as inputs to the decision-making process.

Market Segmentation: The Conventional Wisdom

Where do these data come from? The conventional wisdom is to conduct research that divides markets into subgroups, or segments, for detailed analysis. The point is this: "one size fits all" thinking, or mass-undifferentiated marketing, often will miss the mark when it comes to the realization of customer satisfaction and profits. By contrast, the segmentation/target marketing approach, sometimes described as "different strokes for different folks," provides a more diverse and honest interpretation of reality that

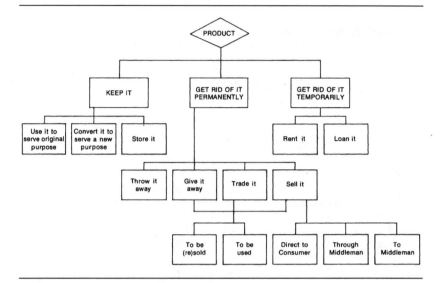

Figure 8.2. Disposition Decision Taxonomy
SOURCE: Jacoby, Jacob, Carol K. Berning, and Thomas F. Dietvorst (1977), "What about Disposition?" *Journal of Marketing,* Vol. 41, No. 2, pp. 22-28. Reprinted with permission of *Journal of Marketing,* published by the American Marketing Association.

marketers can respond to with differentiated marketing mixes. The details concerning survey techniques and general classes of market segmentation variable/base approaches (i.e., demographic, geographic, psychographic, behavioral, product usage, benefit segmentation) are well covered in most basic marketing texts and are not discussed here.

Roper's Shades of Green Segments

But what variable(s) should be used as the basis of the segmentation approach? A natural inclination among sustainable marketers has been to use variables that measure an individual's green proclivities to identify green segments (Coddington 1993; Peattie 1995). In 1990, the respected Roper Organization (1990) conducted a landmark study titled *The Environment: Public Attitudes and Individual Behavior* for S. C. Johnson & Son of Racine, Wisconsin. Later dubbed "Shades of Green Segments" by the marketing community, it identified five U.S. consumer segments (Table 8.1) defined by a set of self-reported environmental behaviors (Table 8.2). The study has since been converted into Roper Starch Worldwide's *Green Gauge Report,* an

TABLE 8.1

Shades of Green Segments: Demographic Profile (percentages)

Characteristic	Total Public	True-Blue Greens	Greenback-Greens	Sprouts	Grousers	Basic Browns
Sex						
Male	48	43	63	44	46	52
Female	52	57	37	56	54	48
Median age (years)	42	42	37	43	42	42
Median income (thousands of dollars)	28	33	33	33	28	22
Education						
Less than high school	18	10	10	13	18	27
High school graduate	36	30	21	32	41	40
Some college	23	29	26	28	22	17
College graduate	22	29	44	26	19	15
Occupation						
Executive/professional	19	29	31	24	12	14
White collar	18	20	25	18	21	16
Blue collar	25	19	30	24	26	27
Marital status						
Married	58	66	67	62	58	52
Single	42	34	33	37	42	48
Political/social ideology						
Conservative	39	31	24	39	42	40
Middle of the road	37	36	44	36	34	39
Liberal	20	29	28	20	21	16
Region						
Northeast	20	22	19	21	23	18
Midwest	23	29	35	23	24	20
South	35	27	22	30	40	43
West	21	22	24	26	13	19
Race						
White	84	91	92	90	78	79
Black	12	4	5	6	20	17
Asian	2	1	2	2	1	2
Other	2	2	1	3	1	2
Other characteristics						
Employed full-time	51	54	72	53	46	48
Employed part-time	11	16	14	11	14	9
Children under 13 years of age	36	45	40	33	41	33
(n)	(1,991)	(205)	(91)	(655)	(297)	(729)

SOURCE: Roper Starch Worldwide Inc. (1996), *Green Gauge Report.* Reprinted by permission.

TABLE 8.2

Shades of Green Segments: Pro-Environmental Activities Done on a
Regular Basis (percentages)

Pro-Environmental Activities/Behaviors	Total Public	True-Blue Greens	Greenback-Greens	Sprouts	Grousers	Basic Browns
At purchase						
Read labels	19	63	28	25	14	1
Use biodegradable soaps/ detergents	22	60	27	36	13	2
Avoid buying aerosols	20	50	30	31	15	1
Avoid products from specific companies	11	48	22	9	8	1
Buy products made from/ packaged in recycled materials	18	55	32	23	16	3
Buy products in refillable packaging	16	40	32	18	18	3
Avoid restaurants using styrofoam containers	8	44	15	4	4	1
After purchase						
Return bottles/cans	51	78	65	74	45	22
Recycle newspapers	46	77	52	70	39	16
Other						
Contribute money to environmental groups	5	31	9	2	3	1
Cut down on car use	6	24	8	5	4	1
Write to politicians	3	26	2	(a)	(a)	(a)
Bought a product because ad/label said it was environmentally safe (in past month or two)	26	60	45	33	21	7
Ever bought a product because ad/label said it was environmentally safe	45	80	69	59	37	20
Average price increase willing to pay for nine green products	4.5	6.6	20.1	3.8	3.2	1.6
(n)	(1,991)	(205)	(91)	(655)	(297)	(729)

SOURCE: Roper Starch Worldwide Inc. (1996), *Green Gauge Report*. Reprinted by permission.
a. Less than 0.5 percent.

annual proprietary marketing information service starting at approximately
$10,000 (M. T. Brouder, Roper Starch Worldwide Inc., personal communica-

tion, March 16, 1994). It has been selected as a benchmark for review here because contemporary studies by J. Walter Thompson USA, Angus Reid, and others tend to confirm the general patterns found in this continuing primary research effort (Coddington 1993).

Methodology and Segmentation Variables

The annual *Green Gauge Report* is the result of approximately 2,000 in-home interviews of individuals age 18 years or over conducted annually in the continental United States. A *k*-means clustering procedure is employed to determine membership in the five major segments that are tracked by the study.

The segmentation variables consist of self-reported pro-environmental activities such as returning bottles/cans for recycling and contributing money to environmental groups (Table 8.2). Whereas the exact items used and statistical criteria are proprietary, the clustering technique examines each respondent's pattern to see whether it is similar to that of any existing group and simultaneously different from the those of respondents making up other groups and then classifies accordingly. Occasionally, a small number of respondents turn out to be unclassifiable and are removed from the analysis. (Note: Most of the data cited in the following subsections come from Roper Starch Worldwide Inc.'s [1996] *Green Gauge Report* [Tables 8.1, 8.2, and 8.3]. Table 8.4 is from the 1997 *Green Gauge Report* [Roper Starch Worldwide Inc. 1997].)

Differences between Segments

The percentage shares of the five segments for the 1990 to 1997 period are shown in Table 8.4. For the latest available year, 1997, the segment shares are (1) True-Blue Greens, 12 percent; (2) Greenback-Greens, 6 percent; (3) Sprouts, 37 percent; (4) Grousers, 13 percent; and (5) Basic Browns, 29 percent. Each segment reflects a position on a continuum of environmental intensity/involvement, where True-Blue Greens represent the highest position and Basic Browns the lowest.

Detailed segment profiles in terms of demographics, pro-environmental activities, and reasons for not doing more about the environment are provided in Tables 8.1, 8.2, and 8.3, respectively. The reader is reminded that segment profiles provide measures of "tendencies" as opposed to being absolute

TABLE 8.3

Shades of Green Segments: Reasons for Not Doing More about the
Environment (percentages)

Stated Reason	Total Public	True-Blue Greens	Greenback-Greens	Sprouts	Grousers	Basic Browns
Companies, not people like me, should solve the problems	40	43	36	29	78	33
Alternatives (products) are too hard to find and no time to shop around	45	53	48	42	86	30
Too busy to get around to make changes	47	42	49	47	88	34
Alternatives (products) are too expensive	46	58	56	37	93	33
Alternatives (products) don't work well	41	52	48	32	97	22
Other people aren't making sacrifices	26	29	23	13	67	18
Family won't accept alternatives (products)	25	33	24	13	66	18
(n)	(1,991)	(205)	(91)	(655)	(297)	(729)

SOURCE: Roper Starch Worldwide Inc. (1996), *Green Gauge Report.* Reprinted by permission.
NOTE: Table shows percentages reporting "major reason" or "something of a reason."

indicators of correlation. A thumbnail sketch of each segment is provided in
the following:

■ True-Blue Greens (12 percent)
  – represent the most involved in a wide range of pro-environmental activities
    and behaviors and may be described as activists and leaders.
  – have high socioeconomic status (SES) (i.e., education, income, and occu-
    pational level).
  – consistently score nearly double the national rate or higher on the vast
    majority of pro-environmental behaviors tested.
  – are connected to environmental issues through money contributions to
    advocacy groups and interaction with politicians.
  – are best summed up as committed, hard-core environmentalists.

■ Greenback-Greens (6 percent)
  – are distinguished by their expressed willingness to pay a premium for
    environmentally sound products (average increase of 20.1 percent reported).

TABLE 8.4

Shades of Green Segments: Trends in Share, 1990 to 1997
(percentage shares)

Segment	1990		1991		1992		1993		1994		1995		1996		1997	
True-Blue Greens	11		19		14		14		11		11		10		12	
Greenback-Greens	11	48	6	57	5	55	6	55	4	48	7	49	5	48	6	55
Sprouts	26		32		36		35		33		31		33		37	
Grousers	24		17		11		13		13		14		15		13	
Basic Browns	28	52	26	43	33	44	32	45	37	50	35	49	37	52	29	42
(n)	(1,413)		(1,995)		(1,987)		(2,020)		(1,993)		(1,998)		(1,991)		(2,016)	

SOURCE: Roper Starch Worldwide Inc. (1997), *Green Gauge Report.* Reprinted by permission.

- have high SES (i.e., education, income, and occupational level) but are generally younger.
- rank well below the True-Blue Greens on all pro-environmental activities but generally are much higher than the other segments on these same factors.

▓ Sprouts (37 percent)
- represent a large/key swing group that can serve as "feeder" to the Greenback and True-Blue segments.
- have high SES (education, income, and occupational level).
- rank well above the total public on nearly all pro-environmental behaviors.
- are best described as "middle of the road" in terms of political/social ideology.

▓ Grousers (13 percent)
- mark the entry into segments defined as relatively uninvolved in pro-environmental behaviors and the issue in general.
- have a consistently lower SES (education, income, and occupational level).
- rank well below the total public on all pro-environmental behaviors that reflect a general lack of involvement.
- are distinguished by scoring highest on all "reasons for not doing more about the environment" (Table 8.3).

▓ Basic Browns (29 percent)
- this segment represents the basement in terms of environmental concern and involvement.

- exhibit a low, almost disadvantaged, SES (education, income, and occupational level).
- do not blame others for environmental problems or lack of action; simply have much more pressing, immediate, day-to-day priorities with which to contend.

Correlates of Green Behavior

The 1996 *Green Gauge Report* shows that two obviously linked demographic variables, income and education, are important correlates of green (sustainable) behavior (Table 8.1). This is particularly apparent when the segments with the highest levels of involvement (i.e., True-Blue Greens, Greenback-Greens, and Sprouts) and compared to the two exhibiting the lowest involvement (i.e., Grousers and Basic Browns). For openers, acting on environmental concerns might be considered a matter of affordability. If so, then making a financial contribution to improve the environment (e.g., paying a higher price for a green product, contributing to an environmental cause) would come only after covering the basics and, therefore, would be much less likely to occur at all under a low-income constraint.

Likewise, higher educational levels also tend to parallel pro-environmental behaviors. The higher levels of college exposure among the top three segments suggests that a better understanding of environmental problems and issues in general might lead to the conclusion that action is necessary, worth it, and appropriate at this time.

Segment Trends and Summary

Table 8.4 reveals trends in the Shades of Green Segment shares for the 1990 to 1997 period. As the U.S. economy passed through recessionary times in the early 1990s, the Greenback-Greens segment immediately diminished to 6 percent in 1991 (a 46 percent decline from 11 percent in 1990) and since then has held steady in the 4 to 7 percent range. Overall, the top three segments as a group vacillate from a position of just under half of the market (e.g., 48 percent in 1990, 1994, and 1996; 49 percent in 1995) to slightly over half (e.g., 57 percent in 1991; 55 percent in 1992, 1993, and 1997).

What does all of this mean? In many respects, the jury is still out. But, a few things are apparent. First, the Sprouts continue to occupy one-third of the market, and when combined with the True-Blue Greens and Greenback-Greens, the share rose to majority status (55 percent) in 1997. On the other hand, the combined Grousers and Basic Browns remain simultaneously steady at majorities or near majorities of the market. Because the True-Blue Greens, Greenback-Greens, and Sprouts generally share higher SES (i.e., income, education, and occupational level), some experts suggest that these segments should be combined and interpreted as a generalized pro-environment group made up of both confirmed greens, defined as the True-Blue Greens and Greenback-Greens, and emerging greens, defined as the Sprouts (Frankel 1994; " 'Green Gauge' " 1996; "Marketplace Getting Greener" 1998; Stisser 1994). To them, this clearly is a "cup half-full" scenario. To others, this is a "salt-and-pepper" scenario in which roughly every other American consumer is either "with us" or "against us" on the environmental issue.

The consistently low share of the Greenback-Greens (5 to 6 percent in the 1996 to 1997 period) appears to confirm that few customers are willing to pay above market (premium) prices for products with ecological attributes. This finding is supported by several North American and European sources including Wasik (1996), who reports "a gap between those who want to shop green but do not want to pay premium prices for green products" (pp. 10-11). As discussed earlier (see discussions in Chapters 6 and 7), this suggests that environmental attributes should be delegated the role of tie-breaker that comes into play after the customer's primary needs have been met; they are not something for which customers will pay extra. This means that businesses likely will have to design-in environmental attributes without the perk of being able to recover a premium price for their efforts.

Positioning on Sustainability

Loudon and Della Bitta (1988) point out that one of the major uses of segmentation information (segment profiles) is to position or reposition products in the minds of target customers. As defined by Kotler (1997), "Positioning is the act of designing the company's offerings and image so that they occupy a meaningful and distinct competitive position in the target customers' minds" (p. 295). In short, differences between segments can provide a basis for customizing (positioning) the marketing mix so that a company may distinguish itself from competitors.

But Kotler (1997) cautions that "not all brand differences are meaningful or worthwhile. Not every difference is a differentiator. Each difference has the potential to create company costs as well as customer benefits" (p. 294). He suggests the following criteria for assessing the "worth" of differences as positioning dimensions:

- ▓ Important: The difference delivers a highly valued benefit to a sufficient number of buyers.
- ▓ Distinctive: The difference either is not offered by others or is offered in a more distinctive way by the company.
- ▓ Superior: The difference is superior to other ways of obtaining the same benefit.
- ▓ Communicable: The difference is communicable and visible to buyers.
- ▓ Preemptive: The difference cannot be easily copied.
- ▓ Affordable: The buyer can afford to pay for the difference.
- ▓ Profitable: The company will find it profitable to introduce the difference. (pp. 294-95)

How do product ecological attributes stack up as potential positioning dimensions on these criteria? Given their generally low perceived *importance* in the minds of customers, the lack of a way in which to operationalize their *distinctiveness,* the lack of a way in which to demonstrate their clear *supe- riority,* the ongoing difficulties of *communicating* environmental claims, and the obvious predisposition of most customers not to pay more for ecological benefits (*affordability*), it appears that positioning on sustainability will fall short at this time.

However, as sustainable practice and thinking by customers and companies advances and evolves, the salience of "the environment" likely will increase as a product purchase factor. At noted in earlier chapters, economy and ecology still are viewed as separate and opposing forces by many in today's world, resulting in a separation of the concepts of market position and eco-position (Peattie 1995). But as ecology and economy become reinvented as "one and the same" through consumer education and changing values, sustainability may emerge in the future as a viable positioning dimension in terms of Kotler's criteria. Peattie (1995) offers this prospect:

> The concept of eco-position [i.e., using the sustainability dimension] for a product is a relatively new idea. . . . As the importance of the relationship [among] the environment, society, and the economy becomes increasingly clear, . . . the market positions and eco-positions of products and companies will begin to merge in consumers' minds. An excellent market position may not be compromised by a poor eco-position today, but this may not hold true tomorrow. (p. 165)

Deconsumers: A Lifestyle Segment?

In the master equation for environmental impact (see Chapter 1), affluence (*A*) reflects consumption or the level of living. Logically speaking, reducing consumption is a straightforward option for reducing the consumption burdens (eco-costs) being placed on the earth's ecosystems. However, as an overall government or corporate policy, reducing consumption is not a popular idea; it flies in the face of Western society's values, where "more" generally is equated with "better." In other words, "the good life" is the same as "the goods life."

Several authors have advocated "the simple life," or deconsumption, as a solution to environmental ills (Durning 1992; Shi 1985). People embracing this philosophy opt for a lifestyle that requires fewer material resources to support and, therefore, reduces their individual impact on ecosystems. This lifestyle is a "statement of personal responsibility" that rejects the notion that high levels of consumption lead to personal fulfillment. The personal desire to a live a simpler life must be respected; the potential for this sort of "less is more" thinking to emerge as a viable future consumption trend must not be trivialized. Calling such individuals "environmentalist wackos" is an act of ignorance.

Consumers opting for deconsumption (i.e., deconsumers) could properly be regarded as a market segment with specific needs to be addressed. For instance, DeGrandpre and Buskist (1991) segment consumers into two broad classes based on conservationist behaviors. They define primary conservationists as those implementing "major changes in lifestyle aimed at reducing the consumption of all goods" (p. 519), a clear fit with the notion of deconsumers. Secondary conservationists, by contrast, exhibit behavior that "involves no changes in consumption patterns but does entail actions aimed at reusing or recycling what is consumed or developing technologies that offset consumption" (p. 519). Presently, they believe that secondary conservationists represent what most people call green consumers, that is, those willing to make minor environmental adjustments in purchasing behaviors while essentially supporting a status quo consumption level.

A more operational surrogate for the deconsumers segment might be Roper Starch Worldwide's True-Blue Greens, which held a modest 12 percent share in the United States in 1997 (Table 8.4). As shown in Table 8.2, this segment is distinguished by high levels of pro-environmental activities. Marketers choosing to target this segment probably can expect its size to remain small. However, their differential response might be significant to marketing appeals that stress environmental and life simplification themes (e.g., less is better; slow your life down and smell the roses; enjoy people more and material goods less; you don't have to consume, consume, consume to get respect).

A recent article in the *Wall Street Journal* (Graham 1996) may confirm that at least a variant deconsumption segment might be in the initial stages of emergence. The article, "How to Sell More to Those Who Think It's Cool to Be Frugal," notes the following:

> The engines of postwar prosperity have been oiled by Madison Avenue's relentless message that more is better than less and that dreams can be fulfilled with a flash of plastic. . . . These marketers have [now] concluded that shoppers who already own everything now hanker for simple, practical, environmentally friendly gear, that is, all the trappings of the simple life. (p. B1)

In the same article, a spokesperson for one well-known seller of environmental sportswear products, Patagonia Inc., adds this twist: "The idea is to buy less, but buy our stuff" (p. B1). To support this pitch, Patagonia has simplified product lines, has put a new emphasis on product longevity by touting the rugged characteristics of its products, and offers a repair service for used goods damaged by wear-and-tear. Its premium prices reflect a variant of the service-life pricing strategies discussed in Chapter 7.

Green Segments or Traditional Segments with Green Implications?

The lack of salience exhibited by the environmental factor seems to suggest another course for bringing sustainability into target market analysis. Why not continue to segment using the traditional variables that meet the (1) measurable, (2) meaningful, and (3) marketable criteria suggested by many authorities (Peter and Donnelly 1995:91) but extend the marketing research analysis within segments to include their environmental predilections? I would summarize this perspective as follows:

> Let's not offend our customers in their rightful, and logical, search for primary benefits; rather, let's concentrate on how to attach an "ecological rider" to our basic selling proposition *without offending them*. We know that ecological attributes are secondary; we also have the opportunity and an obligation to continually remind our customers that their unexpressed and latent need for sustainability must be concurrently addressed at every point along the path to and from consumption. Our constant quest must be to deliver ecological benefits without detracting from the primary benefits sought by our customers.

Superimposing "the environment" on every transaction would have the effect of bringing the tie-breaker to the attention of those who would be responsive to this information while also exposing the nonresponsive to the issue through a sort of continuing educational experience. This perspective reinforces the need to actively research and analyze markets through market segmentation studies; the "target market as sounding board" approach remains totally relevant in marketing mix design decisions. In addition, it points out that in the case of most customers, the real question is, "How do we deliver ecological benefits most palatably without detracting from primary benefits?"

Sustainable Marketing Audit: Target Market(s) Assessment

Because target markets serve as a sounding board for all marketing mix decisions, it follows that the implementation of sustainable marketing programs might be seriously impeded by a lack of timely consumer research relating to environmental matters. An active primary and secondary marketing research program can eliminate this gap between what needs to be known and what is known, and it would represent valuable support for the sustainable marketing audit process. Exhibit 3.7 provides some general questions that might be applicable to a variety of primary consumer research scenarios. The availability of environmentally focused secondary research information sources, such as *JWT Greenwatch* (J. Walter Thompson USA), *Green Gauge Report* (Roper Starch Worldwide), *The Green Business Letter* (Tilden Press), and *Business and the Environment* (Cutter Information Corporation), has been noted throughout this book.

Industrial Markets: Environmental Products

As one moves through the value chain represented by marketing channel networks, the presence of industrial markets linked to the day-to-day challenges of sustainability becomes apparent. The purchases of products (i.e., both goods and services) to meet compliance standards, to staff in-house waste management functions, to modify/upgrade manufacturing technology to attain cleaner levels of practice, and to design sustainable marketing strategies all are examples of direct environmental needs that must be addressed. Such needs define the broad industrial-environmental products sector of the economy.

Jobs Substantiate the Market

Some in the business community believe that maintaining a clean and healthy ecosystem is a luxury, the cost of which reduces profits and acts as a drag on competitiveness and business expansion in general. They argue that unproductive environmental "command-and-control" programs sponsored by governments result in lost jobs and decreased productivity—a double jeopardy situation that is devastating to industry (Easterly 1993). Others see the sustainable paradigm as a positive influence for gaining and maintaining competitive advantage in the global marketplace. Accepting the fact that ecosystem quality is a real problem requiring real solutions, Porter (1991)— the originator of the Porter hypothesis (see Chapter 3)—believes that regulations that encourage eco-cost integration do not have to be counterproductive forces stifling competitiveness; instead, flexible regulations can be devised that provide incentives for companies that cover ecological costs while also expanding business opportunities. The point is to stimulate the development of cost-effective innovation that will propel those firms to an enviable position of long-term competitive advantage. This scenario suggests the creation of jobs.

On another dimension, one aspect of recycling and remanufacturing strategies is that they employ large numbers of workers as opposed to being highly automated. A recent analysis of recycling by the Environmental Defense Fund reports,

> Recycling creates jobs and makes manufacturing industries more competitive. . . . The industrial development effects of recycling are significant. For example, one recent study found that in ten northeastern states alone, recycling adds $7.2 billion in value to recovered materials through processing and manufacturing activities. Approximately 103,000 people were employed in recycling processing and manufacturing jobs in this region in 1991, 2.7 percent of the region's employment. (cited in Ruston and Denison 1996:2)

Other sources estimate that the environmental sector of the economy employed more than 1 million people in 45,000 organizations in the United States in 1994 (Hoerner, Miller, and Muller 1995:13; National Science and Technology Council 1994:42).

In regard to remanufacturing, McConocha and Speh (1991) confirm employment opportunities as one of the major benefits of this strategy. Specifically, they note,

Remanufacturing is labor intensive, but most of the required labor is unskilled
or semiskilled. Thus, remanufacturing may create new job opportunities for
unskilled domestic workers or lead to ventures with less developed countries
with whom America seeks political alliance. (p. 28)

Interestingly, advances in remanufacturing applications even mesh nicely with
recent changes in U.S. welfare system laws that are forcing large numbers of
unskilled and semiskilled workers off welfare rolls and into the job market.

Environmental Services Industry Segments

Whether driven by creative innovation or regulatory compliance, the
process of achieving sustainability creates a need for environmental services
and the jobs that go with them. This fact—that the environment is a real issue
that must be continuously dealt with from now on—translates into the multi-
billion-dollar market served by what has been labeled the "environmental
services industry" (ESI) (Wilson 1994). The pollution abatement and control
expenditures discussed in Chapter 7 represent a rough measure of the sales of
firms competing in ESI markets. The $87.6 billion reported in 1992 (stated in
1987 dollars) (Rutledge and Vogan 1994:46-47) clearly demonstrates that
meeting the needs of environmental protection has created a "sales-generat-
ing, profit-making, job-creating industry" (Bezdek and Wendling 1992:197).

The ESI has numerous segments defined largely by functional needs, and
21 segments are listed in Exhibit 8.1. They reflect adjustments in business
activities and processes necessary to support sustainability and to meet regulatory compliance standards. The following selected scenarios give some
indications of the depth and nature of various ESI submarkets:

- Asbestos abatement market: More than 50 asbestos makers have reached a $200
  million settlement with more than 30,000 U.S. school districts to accomplish
  abatement programs to rid classrooms of this known carcinogen ("Asbestos
  Makers" 1994:B4; Associated Press 1994a:A10).

- Underground storage tank removal market: The University of Tennessee's
  Waste Management Research and Education Institute estimates the cost of
  cleaning up between 350,000 and 400,000 leaking underground storage tanks
  at between $32 billion and $67 billion. A typical site costs $100,000 to clean
  up ("Mega-Billion-Dollar Outlays" 1992:2).

- Trade associations and organizations: Declining fisheries and concern over
  ocean quality have spawned environmental organizations such as the Harbor
  Branch Oceanographic Institution in Fort Pierce, Florida. This organization
  offers services in areas such as aquaculture, underwater engineering, and

biomedical research in support of ocean sustainability. It employs more than 200 research scientists and operates at an annual funding level of nearly $18 million (Harbor Branch Oceanographic Institution 1993).

▓ Environmental products manufacturing: Church & Dwight, maker of Arm & Hammer Baking Soda, has an established market as an ingredient in a wide variety of consumer food products and as a cleaning/deodorizing agent in personal care items (e.g., toothpaste, detergents, deodorants). But nearly 25 percent of its baking soda revenues now come from industrial applications that are environmental in character (e.g., smokestack scrubbers, solutions that replace chlorofluorocarbons in circuit board manufacturing) (Makower 1995c). As a general indicator of environmental product activity, a recent issue of *Pollution Equipment News* (October 1996) lists 395 suppliers of waste management-related products on its reader service card.

▓ Solid and hazardous waste management market: As discussed in Chapter 7, the total costs for site cleanups under Superfund legislation are estimated at between $500 million and $1 trillion over the next 50 years (Hirschhorn 1994:15), thus creating what was described earlier as a recession-proof market for several ESI segments well into the next century (Easterly 1994). BioSafe International Inc. has developed a landfill remodeling concept that increases the physical capacity of a given location by as much as 70 percent. The process involves excavating and compacting the waste from an old section of an existing landfill, installing an approved liner system in that section, and then reburying the waste. A 23-acre site currently under development is expected to reap $55 million in revenue over a 10-year period (Williams 1996:B11B).

Environmental Technology Segments

Another overlapping view is that industrial-organizational markets for sustainable products reflect the general need for environmental technology applications. As noted in the master equation in Chapter 1, technological innovation is a major variable driving ecosystem impact—both positively and negatively. As Vice President Gore notes,

> The scientific and technological revolution has almost completely changed the physical realities of our relationship to the earth. With a dizzying array of new tools, technologies, and processes, we have extended our senses and magnified our ability to work our will on the world around us. (quoted in National Science and Technology Council 1994:6)

Gore's view, which is simply a restatement of the pollution prevention (P2)-oriented Porter hypothesis, suggests that the future potential of ESI markets is directly linked to the development, transfer, and implementation of environmental technology that will serve as a solution to pollution. An

exhibit 8.1

Environmental Services Industry:
Functional Market Segments

1. Asbestos abatement
2. Remediation
3. Solid and hazardous waste management
4. Environmental engineering/consulting
5. Site assessment
6. Emergency response
7. Laboratory services
8. Air and water treatment
9. Environmental data and information
10. Transportation
11. Sustainable marketing/management consulting
12. Architectural/building design
13. Pollution prevention
14. Environmental products manufacturing
15. Software development
16. Trade associations and organizations
17. Trade and regulatory services
18. Recycling
19. Publishing
20. Underground storage tank removal
21. Education and training

SOURCE: Adapted from Wilson, David N. (1994), *Marketing Environmental Services,* Rockville, MD: Government Institutes Inc., p. 2.

environmental technology is one that "reduces human and ecological risk, enhances cost effectiveness, improves process efficiency, and creates products and processes that are environmentally beneficial or benign" (National Science and Technology Council 1995:3). Various aspects of environmental technology include hardware, software, systems, and services. The global market for environmental technology was estimated at more than $200 billion in 1990 and is projected to exceed $300 billion by 2000 (Hoerner et al. 1995:8).

The National Council of Science and Technology (1994) further delineates the environmental technology market into four segments for the purpose of focusing the development of appropriate policy scenarios. The segments are (1) avoidance, (2) monitoring and assessment, (3) control, and (4) remediation and restoration. They provide yet another means of visualizing and defining the emerging opportunities that accompany the gradual shift to the sustainable paradigm.

Avoidance Segment

The avoidance segment represents the current trend toward solving ecosystem problems through upfront P2 approaches rather than relying on "end-of-pipe" resource recovery (R2) solutions. The objective is to prevent or minimize the generation of pollutants, hazardous substances, or other damaging materials that eventually would be released into ecosystems. Specific technologies include (1) equipment, processes, and process sensors and controls; (2) product/materials substitutions; and (3) the in-house reclamation of useful raw materials, products, and energy from residual materials streams. Avoidance involves changes in both business procedure and practice, everything from total production system redesign, to the routine recycling of all materials that spin off from production processes, to the use of life-cycle assessment and full-cost accounting to provide decision support information. Design-for-environment (DFE) is the general label often given to these applications.

Monitoring and Assessment Segment

The objective of monitoring and assessment technologies is to provide an ongoing stream of information concerning the physical condition of ecosystems. Included in this segment are technologies involved in the design, development, and operation of the instrumentation associated with quality assurance and the risk assessment aspects of regulatory compliance. Specific areas include microsensors, chemical sensors, biosensors, sampling services, and systems used to identify and track pollutants over time.

Control Segment

Control technologies serve the purpose of rendering hazardous materials harmless prior to their planned release into ecosystems. Included in this segment are technologies that eliminate or reduce environmental or human risks via treatment protocols as well as those that reduce the initial volume of such materials/residuals so that natural recycling systems can safely dispose of them. The use of catalytic converters on automobiles is a classic example. Other examples include various forms of incineration, oxidation, reduction, bioprocessing, filtration, and substance neutralization.

Remediation and Restoration Segment

Remediation and restoration technologies are "after-the-fact" applications that render harmless hazardous or harmful substances that previously have been released into ecosystems. They include the various cleanup technologies necessary to either remove or contain the risks posed by past waste dumping practices. Similarly, restoration technologies seek to improve ecosystems that have declined through either human negligence or natural circumstances. Reforestation, the building of artificial reefs, aquaculture, and the stabilization/containment of old landfills sites are examples.

Industrial Markets: Recycled-Source Materials

Another unique industrial market associated with sustainability deals with substituting recycled-source materials for virgin materials in product making and other applications. Recycled-source materials, although originally derived from virgin sources, bear the characteristic of having been "already made" at least once. They represent a potentially valuable source of resources for redeployment in future product systems; doing so results in the further write-off of the eco-costs that were incurred during the first conversion process. Redeployment is accomplished through the strategy of materials recycling.

Markets Complete the Materials Recycling Process

As noted in both Chapters 3 and 5, materials recycling is a normative marketing process, the success of which is dependent on the development of markets for recycled-source materials. Simply put, market transactions are the linchpin, or point of closure, in the circular materials use life cycle. Consequently, maintaining and expanding end-user product and materials/ commodities markets remains an ongoing challenge for marketers of recyclables.

As emphasized in earlier chapters, providing large quantities of specific quality feedstocks is a prerequisite for competing against virgin-source materials in industrial markets. Highest and best-use markets are defined by both closed-loop and open-loop applications that require feedstock materials to meet high-quality specifications, but these markets also command the highest resource prices. Closed-loop applications are defined as use in the original application (i.e., postconsumer glass is used to make new glass containers), whereas open-loop applications use high-quality materials in an alternative but similar quality application (Hunt, Sellers, and Franklin 1992). For example, Seattle-based TriVitro Corporation is using the open-loop strategy to establish a market for recycled-source glass by processing it into an "industrial mineral" form for use in abrasive blasting, art glass, tile, and water filtration media applications. This requires a specific processing capability that meets the contaminant removal and crushing size specifications required for different industrial applications (White 1996). By contrast, downcycling markets employ recycled-source materials in low-quality applications, which in turn command low resource prices. Mixed plastic lumber is an example product application.

Many observers believe that a fundamental transition is under way, one eventually leading to economic systems that routinely use recycled-source materials of all types as a first priority, not merely as "sometimes" substitutes or replacements (Cairncross 1992a; Kovacs 1988; Schmidheiny 1992b). This would represent realization of the Type III "zero-waste, zero-discharge" systems envisioned by Richards, Allenby, and Frosch (1994), which are characterized by very high levels of materials conservation and reuse (see Chapter 2). But *transition* is the key word. Progress toward "recyclables first" will come slowly because extensive capital investment is required to (1) upgrade industrial technology, (2) develop new technologies that can more efficiently use recycled inputs, (3) build recycling infrastructure near recycled materials sources, and (4) build industrial-user facilities near recycled materials sources.

The last two factors just mentioned, building recycling infrastructure and industrial-user facilities near recycled materials sources, relate to the peculiar geographic challenge that recycled-source commodities must contend with to be competitive. Densely populated urban areas are the major high-volume source of postconsumer recyclables. Production facilities, however, traditionally have been located near sources of virgin materials in rural/remote areas. Given that most recyclables are low-value commodities, transporting them over long distances might result in delivered cost structures that are not competitive with virgin alternatives, thus impeding the growth of markets. Because moving the source is not feasible, phasing in new recycling infra-structure and industrial-user facilities in urban areas is one long-term solution that might be called a "market relocation" strategy (Alexander 1993).

"Buy-Recycled" Programs

The purchase of products totally or partially made with recycled materi-als, known as recycled contents products (RCPs), generates derived demand for recycled-source commodities. The development of such demand tends to be material (commodity) specific. For example, postconsumer aluminum containers (used beverage containers) always have been a high-value recycla-ble because of the massive energy savings (95 percent) associated with their reuse in the production of new containers. As a result, aluminum containers claim the title of "highest postconsumer recycled contents rate" at 66.5 percent (Ridgley 1998a:1), and used beverage containers have experienced few prob-lems in being rapidly absorbed by markets during past decades. By compari-son, postconsumer newspapers, glass, steel, and plastic packaging are inher-ently low-value materials that often face off against low-cost, tax-subsidized, virgin-source competitors. As a result, they have been recycled less system-atically and often subjected to downcycling.

One key approach for creating demand for recycled-source materials has been the development of organizational "buy-recycled" initiatives that focus on establishing a clear preference for the purchase of RCPs as opposed to virgin products. These initiatives apply equally to private sector (i.e., busi-ness/corporate) and government (i.e., local, state, federal) procurement pro-grams.

Private Sector "Buy-Recycled" Initiatives

Integrating RCPs into the mainstream corporate purchasing routine re-quires several adjustments. First, purchasing specifications/rules that dis-criminate against (prohibit) nonvirgin products must be reviewed and replaced if no functional reason can be found for their existence. Second, RCPs of equal performance must be given at least equal, and in some cases preferential, treatment in terms of pricing. Cases of preferential treatment for RCPs may be economically justified by management because as they enhance the firm's environmental performance, they also tend to create value added in terms of heightened corporate environmental image. In other situations, organizational buyers are beginning to impress green standards on their suppliers in an attempt to "green the supply train" (see Chapter 5); accepting only products with specified recycled materials content levels is among the approaches used. In these cases, RCPs have literally attained the status of a direct customer requirement that must be met by the supplier or else the account relationship will be terminated.

Private sector "buy-recycled" involvements evolve from a number of circumstances. For example, companies subscribing to the International Chamber of Commerce Business Charter for Sustainable Development agree to generally work toward promoting sound environmental practices among suppliers, which may logically include the offering of RCPs (Willums and Goluke 1992:357). Similarly, McDonald's Corporation adopted RCPs as an important supplier purchasing guideline after a joint McDonald's-Environmental Defense Fund study of the fast-food giant's waste impacts identified its potential as a waste moderating strategy (McDonald's Corporation 1991).

At a broader level, the Buy Recycled Business Alliance is a voluntary project of the National Recycling Coalition. It was formed in 1992 by two dozen large U.S. corporations (Allen 1992) whose purpose is to promote the growth and development of markets for RCPs by "integrating recycled-content purchases into a company's daily operations" (K. Griswold, Buy Recycled Business Alliance, personal communication, April 19, 1993). This is accomplished by disseminating general information, conducting workshops, and developing "how to" manuals to increase understanding of the value, reliability, and performance of RCPs. The alliance reports that in 1993, its 950 members spent $8.1 billion on purchases of RCPs (Rabasca 1995:1). A sampling of leading companies' expenditures in this area includes Anheuser-Busch, $2.1 billion in 1993; McDonald's, more than $900 million over four years; and DuPont, $75 million annually ("Closed Loop Policies" 1995:1).

Public Sector "Buy-Recycled" Initiatives

Making public sector purchases subject to RCP preferences is another obvious way in which to build end-product market demand. As in private sector programs, the issues of arbitrary discrimination in specifications (prohibitions against recycled-contents and preferential pricing for virgin materials and products) must be addressed. At the state level, one notable program is set forth in the Northeast Maryland Waste Disposal Authority's (1993) *Buy Recycled Training Manual,* which details everything from product checklists to the names and addresses of vendors offering RCPs in the state. A similar program is outlined in *Source Reduction Now,* a public service monograph offered by the Minnesota Office of Waste Management (Brown 1993).

At the federal level, President Clinton signed the Buy-Recycled Executive Order on October 20, 1993 as a means of integrating RCP preferences into federal-level purchasing policies. This order "directs every agency of the federal government to purchase printing and writing paper containing 20 percent postconsumer material by the end of 1994 and 30 percent postconsumer content by the end of 1998" (Rabasca 1993:1). Although the order applies only to federal agencies, the extremely large volume of business associated with this model program obviously will have "spillover" effects that influence both state and private industry purchasing practices, resulting in a derived demand ripple effect on the purchase of recycled-source commodities that are RCP inputs.

Recycled-Source Commodities Markets

Moving away from finished products to the materials/commodities level, markets for recyclables are in rapid transition. Although short-term market volatility still is a key issue, other factors appear to support the contention that markets for recyclables are beginning to "jell" as never before. These factors include (1) advances in technology and product design, (2) impact of state and local legislation, (3) impact of federal legislation, and (4) the gradual growth in industrial capacity.

Market Volatility

Until recently, recycled-source materials generally suffered from the syndrome of being absolute stepchildren in economic systems that assumed virgin resources were infinite in supply and better in terms of quality and quantity; these same economic systems typically subsidize low-cost waste disposal (e.g., landfilling, dumping). But in mid- to late 1994, the U.S. demand for postconsumer recyclables such as paper, steel, and plastics appeared to turn the corner and began to catch up with the supplies being made available by reverse channel networks (McCreery 1994a, 1994b; Norton 1994; Rabasca 1994b; White 1994b); demand stability appeared in sight.

But demand volatility continues. The scenario of U.S. prices for old newspaper (ONP) demonstrates this point. On November 2, 1993, *Recycling Times* reported the price paid by mills/end users in the Northeast for ONP at $0 to $20 per ton ("The Markets Page" 1993:5); the paper market outlook was pictured as bleak for the foreseeable future. Approximately one year later, ONP was quoted at $65 to $110 per ton ("The Markets Page" 1994:5), and an analysis in the *Wall Street Journal* concluded, "The reality is we're seeing the sharpest increases in paper prices in the last 50 years" (Levingston and Chipello 1994:C1). Although a combination of many factors was commonly cited as explaining this overnight surge in demand, industry observers generally credited the incremental development of additional de-inking capacity for ONP and the coming on-line of new advanced technology recycling mills and upgraded older facilities that handled larger quantities of recycled materials inputs as the major causes (National Solid Wastes Management Association 1990; Woods 1994).

But what goes up is bound to come down. From January through June 1995, ONP prices rose dramatically to peak at a little more than $200 per ton; but by December 1995, the price had fallen to approximately $50 per ton (Petrush 1996:14). This decline continued throughout 1996. The September 3, 1996 issue of *Recycling Times* ("The Markets Page" 1996) reported that the mills/end users price in the Northeast for ONP had dropped to $10 to $30 per ton (p. 15). Although there is no consensus about what caused the decline, two factors appear to be leading contenders: (1) a slowdown in the economy caused the demand for finished paper products to fall in the face of high supplies of input recyclables and (2) the new paper-making capacity specifically designed to handle recycled-source inputs was not yet up and running at full speed (Egan 1996c).

A different yet equally unstable scenario has unfolded in the recycled plastics markets for the commodity polyethylene terephthalate (PET), the clear plastic out of which soda bottles, other food packages, and polyester fibers are made. Since early 1996, the market price for PET has fallen drastically from 3.5 to 1.3 cents per pound in August, a 60 percent decline (Egan 1996a:1). The reason? An oversupply of virgin PET resin caused by industry overcapacity, which is dumped on the market at prices lower than some recycled-source materials. The point: virgin-source competitors are highly entrenched and will defend to the death their traditional markets.

The lesson in all this might be that commodities markets for recyclables always will be uncommonly unstable so long as industries maintain "virgin materials first" policies. But as if they see the handwriting on the wall, some virgin suppliers concurrently are pursuing major recycling ventures. For example, E. I. DuPont de Nemours and Company, a major supplier of virgin PET, has developed DuPont Petretec, a polyester regeneration technology described in the next subsection. Because the process uses recycled-source PET as its major input, the company is working hard to develop large-volume reverse channel networks to collect and deliver this material to DuPont facilities ("It Starts with a Little Imagination" 1996). Clearly, DuPont now has dual interests that encompass both virgin-source and recycled-source materials. This sort of commitment may dampen market swings as disparate interests (recycled-source vs. virgin-source materials) merge into one.

Technology and Product Design Advances

Technology has not ignored the need to enhance the efficiency of handling and processing recyclable materials to make them more consistent in quality and price competitive. For example, DuPont's Petretec polyester regeneration technology is a cost-effective process that reduces recycled-source PET to dimethyl terephthalate and ethyl glycol. These monomers are the building-block ingredients of new polyester, so new-manufacture products made from them are comparable to virgin-source polyester in every way ("It Starts with a Little Imagination" 1996). Among other things, this means that recycled-source polyester films can be safely used in food contact applications, a factor that opens up previously restricted markets (National Food Processors Association 1993). In addition to food contact applications, recycled-source PET is finding use in products such as fiberfill, packaging strapping, and polyester fiber clothing. In short, advances in recycling technology have the potential to make virgin-source and recycled-source commodities one and the same.

The industrial design community also is continuing to affect future demand for recyclables through an emphasis on design-for-environment (DFE) applications that make products more ecologically compatible (Allenby 1991; Office of Technology Assessment 1992). As mentioned in earlier chapters, DFE is creating products "born" to be recycled, meaning that they are easier to disassemble, have simpler and more standardized mixes of materials, and avoid the use of hazardous/toxic materials (Abler 1990; Burnette 1990). The result is a more cost-effective and higher quality output of materials from downstream recycling processes.

Impact of State and Local Government Initiatives

Because waste management is an inherently local issue, state legislatures and municipal governments have taken the lead in passing recycling mandates that stimulate supply, market development, and infrastructure development (i.e., the basic enabling conditions described in Chapter 5). History has shown that mandates to create supplies of recyclables and infrastructure take effect quickly. By contrast, it takes much longer for demand-creating/market-developing public policy to "take hold" and produce tangible results.

Table 8.5 shows a sampling of state-level program elements used to develop markets for recyclables in the United States ("State Recycling Market" 1993). Because much of the legislation backing these alternatives was passed in the mid- to late 1980s, it is reasonable to suggest that its true impact is beginning to be felt nearly a decade later. This is especially true because market development is by nature a high-risk, long-term enterprise that requires substantial investment in processes and physical facilities as well as a major shift in corporate and consumer buying practices.

Impact of Federal Government Initiatives

At the federal level in the United States, there is no standardizing legislation that governs national recycling policy. But lobbying efforts are again underway in support of the passage of a national recycling bill and to remove the legislated advantages of primary materials, both of which would make recycled-source materials more competitive in terms of costs. The National Recycling Coalition has long favored such legislation, which it believes will "ensure the development of nationally uniform standards, definitions, and public policies . . . and expand the recycling infrastructure" (Goff 1994b:92). Admittedly, the issues of health care, crime and drugs, income tax relief, and balancing the budget have totally eclipsed any possibilities of action during recent congressional sessions.

But the U.S. Environmental Protection Agency (EPA) has exhibited interest in experimenting with innovative approaches for expanding recycling activity. In a novel federal partnership initiative, the EPA has agreed to fund an ambitiou attempt to develop/expand markets using market information created by trading recyclables (as commodities) on the Chicago Board of Trade (Goff 1994a). This move represents an alliance with industry trade associations and also involves setting up a network of commodities inspectors to verify product quality. Initial recyclable commodities to be traded included plastics (PET and high-density polyethylene) and glass (Rabasca 1994a).

TABLE 8.5

Sampling of U.S. State Recycling Market Development Program Elements

Program Element	Number of States Participating
Grants for:	
Recycling equipment	31
Recycled product procurement	5
Market development	23
Landfill reduction and alternative waste reduction	18
Demonstration projects	22
Promotion programs/education	25
Research and feasibility studies	20
Program planning and implementation	20
Low-interest loans and loan guarantees	23
Tax incentives	
Sales tax	10
Property tax credits	7
Recycling equipment income tax credits	21
Material/product purchase tax credits	1
Franchise tax exemption	1
Disposal fee waiver	2
Technical assistance	
Voluntary recycled contents newsprint program	20
Product vendor and processor information	32
Recycling market development zones	2
Market reports/information	37
Business/government recycling councils	27
Local market development planning requirements	8
Materials exchange programs	26
Technical assistance programs	34
Job training and development	5
Buy-recycled conferences/campaigns	26
Market development workshops	22

SOURCE: Compiled from "State Recycling Market Development Programs" (1993), *Green MarketAlert,* Vol. 4, No. 11, pp. 6-7.

At the federal level in Germany, the Ordinance for the Avoidance of Packaging Waste (nicknamed "Green Dot") sets an intricate system that shifts the social costs of waste management directly to manufacturers (Exhibit 8.2). This radical departure from "business as usual" relies on two assumptions: (1) industry is the key to efficient waste and materials use policy because it determines the final designs of products and (2) incentives are a more effective public policy tool for modifying industry practice and consumer behavior than either taxes or the implementation of extensive government regulations (i.e., punitive command and control). The philosophy behind it can be stated in one sentence: "Those who produce waste are responsible for recycling and dis-

exhibit 8.2

German "Green Dot": Packaging Take-Back by Manufacturers

In an attempt to legislate the handling of packaging in an ecologically responsible manner, Germany passed the Ordinance on the Avoidance of Packaging Waste of 1991, nicknamed "Green Dot." The legislation has four objectives: (1) to ensure that packaging is made from materials that are compatible with recycling processes, (2) to minimize the weight and volume of packaging materials, (3) to encourage the use of refillable packages when feasible, and (4) to ensure that packages not refilled are recycled.

Packaging is defined as one of three types: (1) transport, (2) secondary, or (3) primary. These definitions basically define when a package loses its primary function and becomes subject to manufacturer take-back, that is, becomes the responsibility of manufacturers once again. Green Dot mandates that primary (consumer) packaging be returned to retailers; a mandatory advance deposit ($0.30 to $1.20 per unit) is to be collected on all nonrefillable beverage, cleaning agent, and paint containers. The regulation of transport and secondary packages began immediately. Manufacturers and distributors must physically accept (take-back) transport packaging; retailers must install bins in stores to handle secondary packages left at points of purchase by consumers.

Recognizing the diversity and large quantities of materials associated with primary packages presented potential control problems, the legislation allowed German industry to come up with a plan to accomplish the mandate satisfactory to the government. "Satisfactory" means that it would meet collection and sorting quotas of 80 percent by 1995 and also maintain the present refill rates of 17 percent for milk containers and 72 percent for beverage containers. Industry proposed the "dual system" for primary packaging to be run by the firm Duales System Deutschland GmbH—and the government accepted—therefore allowing industry to design and test its own system, which is independent of the public waste processing system. DSD uses a combination of dropoff and curbside collection approaches to enhance "collection convenience" for consumers. In addition, DSD licenses a trademarked "Green Dot," which serves as a symbol on packages to signify that they will be recycled. To obtain the license, a firm must (1) provide a guarantee from a designated recycler stating that the material in question will be recycled and (2) have a contract with DSD showing that the license fee has been paid.

(continued)

ɛxhibiт 8.2   Continued

▓▓▓▓▓▓▓▓▓▓▓▓▓▓▓▓▓▓▓▓▓▓▓▓▓▓▓▓▓▓

In theory, German manufacturers will now "internalize" waste management costs through design-for-environment initiatives. Shifting the managerial and financial responsibility for waste management to industry also assumes that industry can carry out this function more cost-effectively than a government bureaucracy.

SOURCE: Fishbein, Bette K. (1994), *Germany, Garbage, and the Green Dot: Challenging the Throwaway Society,* New York: INFORM Inc.

---

posing of it" (Fishbein 1994:7). The recycling of industrial and consumer packaging materials is one of the key outcomes desired.

Will Green Dot succeed? Because the program has been in place a few years, the jury is still out—but the experiment is still on. However, at least one unanticipated short-term result has been glutted markets for recyclables. This has caused Green Dot to be accused of greatly distorting European markets because supplies of recyclable materials far exceed what German and European industry presently can accommodate. This has led to further charges that recovered materials are being quietly exported and landfilled in Third World countries (Goff, Rabasca, and White 1994) along with continuing exports of toxic and hazardous waste (Stein 1993). So, it remains unclear whether setting up mandated sources of recycled-materials supply is an effective way in which to stimulate the concurrent development of markets to absorb those materials.

Growth in Industrial Capacity

The gradual coming on-line of industrial capacity that uses recycled feedstocks is progressively affecting U.S. markets, but the impact is materials specific. In the paper industry, past market demand for recycled feedstocks had been hampered by lack of the specialized processes required to handle recycled-source materials. However, available supplies of low-cost recycled newspaper and office paper led manufacturers in 1992 to commit to nearly 100 new projects designed to use wastepaper. Representing a $3 billion investment in future markets (Glenn 1992:40), manufacturers began ramping up this additional capacity late in 1994, the result being skyrocketing wastepaper prices. As noted by Alexander (1995),

> While a notable portion of the paper industry's recycling investment was motivated by cost savings associated with manufacturing with recovered fiber, most has been made in response to government prodding and consumer demand for recycled content in paper products. (p. 50)

Another promising area of demand growth is in steelmaking. The initial jump of 12 percent in scrap steel prices experienced in August 1994 was at least partially due to a surge in demand by integrated steel mills, a form of steelmaking that uses a "charge" containing approximately 25 percent recycled scrap (Norton 1994:A2). The development of new electric-arc steel mini-mill capacity in Arizona and Pennsylvania, a process that uses 100 percent recycled steel inputs, provides further confidence in the emerging market for recyclables (White 1994b).

Finally, DuPont's Petretec polyester regeneration technology (described earlier) clearly recognizes the critical market-building linkage between expanding industry's capacity to use recyclables via technology advances and the development of supporting recycling infrastructure. As DuPont Vice President Mike Hartnagel notes,

> As an industry, we've set goals to avoid landfilling polyester waste, increase public awareness about the greenness of polyester, reduce our consumption of oil derivatives, and retain the chemical value of polyester. This is a tall order, and even a company with the resources and experience of DuPont cannot handle it alone. That's why we want to leverage our leadership with our customers, their industrial associations, and other polyester producers to establish reverse channel networks to collect scrap polyester that can be used in the Petretec process. (quoted in "It Starts with a Little Imagination" 1996:16)

Chapter Summary

The general role of markets is to provide a sounding board for marketing mix decisions. Such decisions generally are driven by "what the customer wants." But customers do not see their dependency of the earth's ecosystems as a "need" in the traditional sense. Therefore, customers eventually must learn to at least partially base their buying decisions on how products affect the natural environment.

Although the general public tends to relegate "the environmental issue" to the back burner on opinion polls, two things must be noted. First, sustainability is not a choice; rather, it is mandate. Whether customers like it or not, marketers must have the moral fortitude to advance the issue. Second, there is evidence that "environment" is becoming embedded in everyday life through formal education, media reporting of environmental catastrophes, and involvement in household recycling programs. As a purchase decision criterion, "environment" (or greenness) probably has assumed the role of tie-breaker for many customers. This means that if product benefits and price are equal, then the product perceived as better for the environment likely will be chosen.

Traditional segmentation analysis has been applied to identify so-called green market segments based on pro-environmental behaviors. A relatively small segment of the market (approximately 12 percent) is strongly motivated by environmental considerations. Combining this segment with two others results in approximately half the consumer market having at least some pro-environmental tendencies; however, this leaves half that do not. This suggests that using the sustainability dimension to position products will not be effective because of the lack of importance of the issue. Another way in which to interpret the small pro-environmental segment is to assume that it consists of deconsumers, that is, those who seek a simpler lifestyle requiring fewer material resources.

Because "environment" is not a dominant issue in the minds of most customers, one suggestion is to simply continue traditional segmentation approaches while investigating any green implications of those segments through market research. The point would be to determine how to best attach an "ecological rider" to the selling proposition without detracting from the primary benefits sought by customers.

The presence of environmental challenges has created industrial markets for the myriad of environmental products (i.e., goods and services) necessary to meet compliance standards, to modify/upgrade manufacturing technology in the move to attain cleaner levels of practice, and to engage in recycling and a host of other remedial activities. Segmentation of what is called the ESI is largely based on functional need (e.g., asbestos abatement, environmental product manufacturing, emergency response, education/training).

Because technology applications are expected to play such a prominent role in future environmental advances, this area has come under particular scrutiny as a potential market. Technology segments include (1) avoidance, (2) monitoring and assessment, (3) control, and (4) remediation and restoration. Avoidance focuses on developing P2 solutions; monitoring and assessment deals with the need to provide ongoing information concerning the physical condition of ecosystems; control deals with the challenges of making hazardous materials harmless prior to release into ecosystems; and remediation and restoration refers to the need to render harmless substances that previously have been released into ecosystems.

Another special case of markets involves recycled materials. As a form of R2, materials recycling is a normative marketing process that is dependent on the presence of markets for both end-user products and commodities. At the end-user level, market development has been fostered by both public and private sector buy-recycled programs, where the purchasing function gives preference to end products made with recycled materials. The federal government is playing an important role through directives that mandate such purchases by federal agencies.

At the commodities level, recycled-source materials compete directly with virgin-source materials. Although virgin-source materials have dominated in the past, the presence of large quantities of recycled-source materials generated by curbside recycling programs appears to be fostering a transition to the use of recycled-source materials as the norm practice. But markets for these materials traditionally have been volatile, and this trend continues. However, several factors have emerged that may serve as stabilizing influences. These include (1) advances in technology and product design, (2) the impact of state and local government initiatives, (3) the impact of federal government initiatives, and (4) the gradual growth in industrial capacity that can use recycled-source materials.

References

"A Perspective on the EDF-McDonald's Partnership." 1992. *Business and the Environment,* December, p. 3.

"An Ecostyle Listing." 1993. *In Business,* November-December, pp. 28-29.

Abler, Robert A. 1990. "Design with the Waste Stream in Mind." *Innovation,* Summer, pp. 20-22.

Adolph Coors Company. 1992. *Environmental Progress Report.* Golden, CO: Adolph Coors Company.

"Alaska Fishermen Awarded $286 Million in *Valdez* Spill." 1994. *Orlando Sentinel,* August 12, p. A4.

Alberini, Anna, David Edelstein, Winston Harrington, and Virginia McConnell. 1994. *Reducing Emissions from Old Cars: The Economics of the Delaware Vehicle Retirement Program.* Discussion Paper 94-27. Washington, DC: Resources for the Future.

Alderson, Wroe. 1957. *Marketing Behavior and Executive Action: A Functionalist Approach to Marketing Theory.* Homewood, IL: Irwin.

Alexander, Judd H. 1993. *In Defense of Garbage.* Westport, CT: Praeger.

Alexander, Michael. 1995. "The Restructuring of the Waste Paper Market." *Waste Age,* May, pp. 49-56.

Allen, Frank E. 1992. "U.S. Companies Plan Alliance on Recycling." *Wall Street Journal,* September 14, p. A1.

Allenby, Braden R. 1991. "Design for Environment: A Tool Whose Time Has Come." *SSA Journal* 5(3): 5-9.

American Plastics Council. 1995. *Progress Report,* January, p. 3.

Anderson, Ray C. 1996. "The E-Factor: Confessions of an Eco-Savvy CEO." *The Green Business Letter,* July, p. 8.

Anheuser-Busch Companies. 1995. *Pursuing Environmental Excellence* [video]. St. Louis, MO: Anheuser-Busch Companies, Corporate Environmental Affairs.

Ansoff, H. I. 1957. "Strategies for Diversification." *Harvard Business Review* 35(5): 113-24.

Arbuckle, J. Gordon, Mary Elizabeth Bosco, David R. Case, Elliott P. Laws, John C. Martin, Marshall Lee Miller, Robert D. Moran, Russell V. Randale, Daniel M. Steinway, Richard G. Stoll, Thomas F. P. Sullivan, Timothy A. Vanderver, Jr., and Paul A. J. Wilson. 1991. *Environmental Law Handbook.* Eleventh ed. Rockville, MD: Government Institutes Inc.

Arbuckle, J. Gordon, F. William Brownell, David R. Case, Wayne T. Halbleib, Lawrence J. Jensen, Stanley W. Landfair, Robert T. Lee, Marshall Lee Miller, Karen J. Nardi, Austin P. Olney, David G. Sarvadi, James W. Spensley, Daniel M. Steinway, and Thomas F. P. Sullivan. 1993. *Environmental Law Handbook.* Twelfth ed. Rockville, MD: Government Institutes Inc.

"Asbestos Makers Including W. R. Grace, USG Agree to Settle Class-Action Suit." 1994. *Wall Street Journal,* November 2, p. B4.

Associated Press. 1994a. "Asbestos Makers Reach Settlement with Schools." *Orlando Sentinel,* November 2, p. A10.

_____. 1994b. "Emission Standards Set for Gas-Driven Mowers." *Orlando Sentinel,* May 5, p. A1.

_____. 1994c. "Here's the Dirt on Higher Cost of Dry Cleaning." *Orlando Sentinel,* October 4, p. C3.

_____. 1994d. "Study Shows Conchs Aren't Recovering." *Orlando Sentinel,* June 1, p. C6.

_____. 1995. "Cruise Line Fine: $250,000 Dumping." *Orlando Sentinel,* March 5, p. D3.

_____. 1996. "New Mill Cleans Up Paper Trail." *Orlando Sentinel,* September 9, pp. B1, B6.

_____. 1997. "Cleaners' Pollution Has High Price Tag." *Orlando Sentinel,* July 29, p. C3.

Ayres, Robert U. 1994. "Industrial Metabolism: Theory and Policy." Pp. 23-37 in *The Greening of Industrial Ecosystems,* edited by Braden R. Allenby and Deanna J. Richards. Washington, DC: National Academy Press.

Badaracco, Joseph L., Jr. 1991. *The Knowledge Link: How Firms Compete through Strategic Alliances.* Boston: Harvard Business School Press.

Bailey, Ronald. 1993. *Eco-Scam: The False Prophets of Ecological Apocalypse.* New York: St. Martin's.

Ballou, Ronald H. 1985. *Business Logistics Management, Planning, and Control.* Englewood Cliffs, NJ: Prentice Hall.

Banerjee, Subhabrata, Charles S. Gulas, and Easwar Iyer. 1995. "Shades of Green: A Multidimensional Analysis of Environmental Advertising." *Journal of Advertising* 24(2): 21-31.

Barnes, John W. and Edwin R. Stafford. 1993. "Strategic Alliance Partner Selection: When Organizational Cultures Clash." Pp. 424-33 in *Enhancing Your Knowledge Development in Marketing,* edited by David W. Cravens. Chicago: American Marketing Association.

Baxter International Inc. 1995. *Baxter Environmental Performance Report 1995.* Deerfield, IL: Baxter International Inc.

Bearden, William O., Thomas N. Ingram, and Raymond W. Laforge. 1995. *Marketing: Principles and Perspectives.* Homewood, IL: Irwin.

Bechtel, Stefan. 1990. *Keeping Your Company Green.* Emmaus, PA: Rodale.

Bell, Maya. 1998. "Swordfish Are Sliced Off Menus." *Orlando Sentinel,* April 25, p. C1.

Berkowitz, Marvin. 1987. "Product Shape as an Innovation Strategy." *Journal of Product Innovation Management* 4:274-83.

Berube, Mario and Sylvie Bisson. 1991. *Life Cycle Studies: A Literature Review and Critical Analysis.* Saint-Foy, Quebec: Gouvernement du Québec, Ministère de l'Environnement, Direction de la récuperation et du recyclage.

Betts, Kellyn S. 1994. "The Coming Green Computers." *E Magazine,* March-April, pp. 28-35.

Bezdek, Roger H. and Robert M. Wendling. 1992. "Environmental Market Opportunities." Pp. 196-224 in *The Greening of American Business,* edited by Thomas F. P. Sullivan. Rockville, MD: Government Institutes Inc.

Biddle, David. 1993. "Recycling for Profit: The New Green Frontier." *Harvard Business Review* 71(6): 145-56.

"Big Three Automakers Will Open Recycling Research Center." 1993. *Business and the Environment,* September, p. 8.

Binkley, Christina. 1995. "Imperiled Mangrove Preserve Gets Support from an Unlikely Source." *Wall Street Journal,* December 27, p. F3.

Blaich, Robert. 1988. "From Experience: Global Design." *Journal of Product Innovation Management* 5:296-303.

Bleakley, Fred R. 1994. "How an Outdated Plant Was Made New." *Wall Street Journal,* October 21, p. B1.

Blumenstein, Rebecca. 1996. "GM to Lease, Rather Than Sell, Electric Cars." *Wall Street Journal,* February 15, p. B6.

_____. 1998. "Auto Industry Reaches Surprising Consensus: It Needs New Engines." *Wall Street Journal,* January 5, p. A3.

Boone, Louis E. and David L. Kurtz. 1992. *Contemporary Marketing.* Seventh ed. New York: Dryden.

Boulton, William R., Daniel D. Butler, Shigeko N. Fukai, and Roger Wolters. 1991. *The Pulp and Paper Industry: A Global Assessment.* Auburn, AL: Auburn University, College of Business, Center for International Business.

Bouma, Katherine. 1998a. "Is 'Cell from Hell' Invading Florida?" *Orlando Sentinel,* July 16, p. A1.

_____. 1998b. "Smog Alert—Stay Inside." *Orlando Sentinel,* May 20, p. A1.

Bounds, Wendy. 1996. "Card Makers Try New Ways to Greet a Paperless World." *Wall Street Journal,* March 19, p. B1.

Bowersox, Donald J. and David J. Closs. 1996. *Logistical Management: The Integrated Supply Chain Process.* New York: McGraw-Hill.

Breen, Bill. 1990. "Selling It: The Making of Markets for Recyclables." *Garbage,* November-December, pp. 42-49.

Brown, Kendra. 1995-96. "First Step to Corporate Environmental Stewardship: Put It in Writing." *Keep Florida Beautiful Magazine,* Fall-Winter, pp. 9-17.

Brown, Kenneth. 1993. *Source Reduction Now.* St. Paul: Minnesota Office of Waste Management.

Brown, Linda. 1995. "Life-Cycle Assessment In Practice." *P2 Pollution Prevention Review* 5(4): 41-47.

Browner, Carol M. 1994. *The Common Sense Initiative: A New Generation of Environmental Protection.* Washington, DC: U.S. Environmental Protection Agency, Office of Communications and Public Affairs.

Bruno, Kenny. 1992. *The Greenpeace Book of Greenwash.* Washington, DC: Greenpeace HEIP Campaign.

Buchholz, Rogene A. 1993. *Principles of Environmental Management: The Greening of Business.* Englewood Cliffs, NJ: Prentice Hall.

Burnette, Charles. 1990. "Principles of Ecological Design." *Innovation,* Summer, p. 4.

Cairncross, Frances. 1992a. *Costing the Earth.* Boston: Harvard Business School Press.

_____. 1992b. "UNCED, Environmentalism and Beyond." *Columbia Journal of World Business* 27(3/4): 12-17.

Callenbach, Ernest, Fritjof Capra, Lenore Goldman, Rudiger Lutz, and Sandra Marburg. 1993. *EcoManagement.* San Francisco: Berrett-Koehler.

"Canon Canada Taps Canada Post as Partner for Toner Cartridge." 1993. *Business and the Environment,* November, p. 7.

Carlson, Les, Stephen J. Grove, and Norman Kangun. 1993. "A Content Analysis of Environmental Advertising Claims: A Matrix Method Approach." *Journal of Advertising* 22(3): 27-39.

Carson, P. 1991. *Green Is Gold: Talking to Business about the Environmental Revolution.* New York: Harper Business.

Carson, Rachel. 1962. *Silent Spring.* Greenwich, CT: Fawcett.

Catron, Derek. 1996. "Water Customers Fight Planned Rate Increases." *Orlando Sentinel,* January 31, p. D3.

Chase, Dennis. 1991. "P & G Gets Top Marks in AA Survey." *Advertising Age,* January 29 (special issue), pp. 8-10.

Chem Systems Inc. 1992. *A Life-Cycle Assessment of Vinyl Packaging Material.* Wayne, NJ: Vinyl Institute.

Chrysler Corporation. 1995. "If We're Going to Save the Planet, We All Need to Lend a . . . Hand, Paw, Fin, Hoof, and Wing." Advertisement in *Smithsonian,* September.

Clark, John. 1993. "Green Regulation as a Source of Competitive Advantage." *Greener Management International,* January, pp. 51-58.

"Closed-Loop Policies." 1995. *The Green Business Letter,* January, pp. 1, 6.

Coalition for Environmentally Responsible Economies. 1993. *CERES: Guide to the CERES Principles.* Third ed. Boston: CERES.

Coddington, Walter. 1993. *Environmental Marketing.* New York: McGraw-Hill.

"Coke Crushes Experiment to Sell Soda in Shaped Can." 1998. *Wall Street Journal,* April 15, p. B10.

Colburn, Theo, Dianne Dumanoski, and John P. Myers. 1996. *Our Stolen Future.* New York: NAL/Dutton.

Coleman, Calmetta Y. 1996. "Spiegel Catalog to Publish CD-ROM Version . . . Again." *Wall Street Journal,* February 15, p. B4.

Commoner, Barry. 1972. *The Closing Circle.* New York: Bantam Books.

Corcoran, Elizabeth. 1992. "Green Machine: Volkswagen Gears Up to Recycle Autos." *Scientific American,* January, pp. 140-41.

Council of Logistics Management. 1993. *Reuse and Recycling: Reverse Logistics Opportunities.* Oak Brook, IL: CLM.

Coyle, John J., Edward J. Bardi, and C. John Langley, Jr. 1996. *The Management of Business Logistics.* Sixth ed. St. Paul, MN: West.

Cracco, Etienne and Jaques Rostenne. 1971. "The Socio-Ecological Product." *MSU Business Topics,* Summer, pp. 27-34.

Cronkite, Walter. 1995. *Environment Beware?* Video presentation on *The Cronkite Report,* September 14. The Discovery Channel.

Crosby, Lawrence A., James D. Gill, and James R. Taylor. 1981. "Consumer-Voter Behavior in the Passage of the Michigan Container Law." *Journal of Marketing* 45 (Spring): 19-32.

Crosby, Lawrence A. and James R. Taylor. 1982. "Consumers' Satisfaction with Michigan's Container Deposit Law." *Journal of Marketing* 46 (Winter): 47-59.

"Czech Republic's Air Pollution Sickens and Enrages Citizens." 1993. *Orlando Sentinel,* February 15, p. A9.

Davis, Joel J. 1993. "Strategies for Environmental Advertising." *Journal of Consumer Marketing* 10 (2): 19-36.

Davis, John Bremer. 1996. *Product Stewardship and the Coming Age of Takeback.* Arlington, MA: Cutter Information Corporation.

DeGrandpre, R. J. and William Buskist. 1991. "Culture, Contingencies, and Conservation." *The Psychological Record,* 41:507-22.

"Details." 1996. *Wall Street Journal,* May 17, p. B10.

Devalle, Bill and George Sessions. 1985. *Deep Ecology: Living as if Nature Mattered.* Salt Lake City, UT: Peregrine Books.

Discovery Communications Inc. 1995. *Finite Oceans.* Video presentation produced by Tim Cowling. Bethesda, MD: Discovery Communications Inc.

Ditz, Daryl, Janet Ranganathan, and R. Darryl Banks. 1995. "Environmental Accounting: An Overview." Pp. 1-46 in *Green Ledgers: Case Studies in Corporate Environmental Accounting,* edited by Daryl Ditz, Janet Ranganathan, and R. Darryl Banks. Baltimore, MD: World Resources Institute.

Drucker, Peter F. 1973. *Management: Tasks, Responsibilities, Practices.* New York: Harper & Row.

Durning, Alan. 1992. *How Much Is Enough?* New York: Norton.

Easterly, James H. 1993. "Business Opportunities during the 1990s Created by Solid and Hazardous Waste Control Programs in the U.S. and International Markets." *American Chemical Society Buyers Guide,* April, pp. 1-9.

_____. 1994. "Environmental Protection: A Recession-Proof Industry?" *Virginia's Environment,* February, pp. 9-10, 16.

Edwards, Mike. 1994. "The U.S.S.R.'s Lethal Legacy." *National Geographic,* August, pp. 70-99.

Egan, Katherine. 1996a. "Market for Recovered PET Is Expected to Stay Depressed." *Recycling Times,* September 17, pp. 1, 4.

_____. 1996b. "New Plastic Resin Receives Approval for Food Packaging." *Recycling Times,* July 23, p. 1.

_____. 1996c. "What Goes Up Must Come (Way) Down." *Waste Age,* September, pp. 111-18.

Egan, Katherine. 1997. "Reynolds Sells Operations." *Recycling Times,* November 10, p. 5.

Ehrlich, Paul. 1986. *The Machinery of Nature.* New York: Simon & Schuster.

_____. 1988. "The Loss of Biodiversity: Causes and Consequences." Pp. 21-27 in *Biodiversity,* edited by E. O. Wilson. Washington, DC: National Academy Press.

Ehrlich, P. R. and A. H. Ehrlich. 1990. *The Population Explosion.* New York: Simon & Schuster.

El-Ansary, Adel and Louis W. Stern. 1988. *Marketing Channels.* Third ed. Englewood Cliffs, NJ: Prentice Hall.

Ellen, P. S., J. L. Winer, and C. Cobb-Walgren. 1991. "The Role of Perceived Consumer Effectiveness in Motivating Environmentally Conscious Behaviors." *Journal of Public Policy and Marketing,* 10(Fall): 102-17.

Ember, Lois R. 1991. "Strategies for Reducing Pollution at the Source Are Gaining Ground." *Chemical and Engineering News* 69(27): 7-16.

"Every Day Is Earth Day at Publix." 1992. *Florida Retailer,* August, p. 7.

Fava, James A., Frank Consoli, and Richard A. Denison. 1991. "Analysis of Product Life-Cycle Assessment Applications." Paper prepared for the SETAC-Europe Workshop on Life-Cycle Analysis, Leiden, Netherlands, December 2-3, 1991.

Federal Trade Commission. 1992. *Guides for the Use of Environmental Marketing Claims.* Washington, DC: FTC.

Fishbein, Bette K. 1994. *Germany, Garbage and the Green Dot: Challenging the Throwaway Society.* New York: INFORM Inc.

Fisk, George. 1974. *Marketing and the Ecological Crisis.* New York: Harper & Row.

Fitzgerald, Kate. 1993. "It's Green, It's Friendly, It's Wal-Mart 'Eco-Store'." *Advertising Age,* June 7, p. 14.

Flemming, Richard A. 1992. "Designing for Recycling: A Plastic Bottler's Perspective." Paper presented at the meeting of the Society for the Plastics Industry Inc. and the Partnership for Plastics Progress, Washington, DC, February.

Frankel, Carl. 1994. "The Return of Roper's True-Blue Greens: Less Is More!" *Green MarketAlert,* February, pp. 1-2.

Franklin Associates Ltd. 1990a. *Resource and Environmental Profile Analysis of Foam Polystyrene and Bleached Paperboard Containers.* Prairie Village, KS: Franklin Associates Ltd.

_____. 1990b. *Resource and Environmental Profile Analysis of Polyethylene and Unbleached Paper Grocery Sacks.* Prairie Village, KS: Franklin Associates Ltd.

_____. 1992. *Energy and Environmental Profile Analysis of Children's Single-Use and Cloth Diapers.* Prairie Village, KS: Franklin Associates Ltd.

Freeman, Harry, Teresa Harten, Johnny Springer, Paul Randall, Mary Ann Curran, and Kenneth Stone. 1992. "Industrial Pollution Prevention: A Critical Review." *Journal of the Air & Waste Management Association* 45:616-56.

Freeman, Laurie. 1991. "The Green Revolution: Procter & Gamble." *Advertising Age,* January 29 (special issue), pp. 16, 34.

Friedland, Jonathan. 1997. "Chilean Salmon Farmers Test Free Trade." *Wall Street Journal,* October 13, p. A18.

"FTC Chairman Steiger Announces National Guidelines to Prevent Misleading Environmental Claims." 1992. *FTC News,* July 28, p. 1.

Fuller, Donald A. 1977. "Aluminum Beverage Container Recycling in Florida: A Commentary." *Atlanta Economic Review,* January, pp. 41-43.

_____. 1979. "Materials Recycling from Post-Consumer Sources: Concept and Case Studies." Pp. 567-71 in *1979 Educators' Proceedings: American Marketing Association.* Chicago: AMA.

_____. 1990. "Recycling Post-Consumer Plastic Containers: A Marketing Overview." Pp. 177-81 in *Progress in Marketing Thought,* edited by Louis Capella. Proceedings of the Southern Marketing Association.

_____. 1991. "Recycling Post-Consumer Aluminum Containers: A Marketing Commentary." Pp. 101-5 in *Developments in Marketing Science,* Vol. 14, edited by Robert L. King. Proceedings of the Academy of Marketing Science.

_____. 1993. "Strategic Green Marketing: Background-Need, Definition, and Call for Inquiry." Pp. 282-84 in *Marketing: Satisfying a Diverse Customerplace,* edited by Tom K. Massey. Proceedings of the Southern Marketing Association.

_____. 1994a. "Exploring the Role of Strategic Alliances in Sustainable Marketing." Pp. 315-19 in *Marketing: Advances in Theory and Thought,* edited by Brian T. Engelland and Alan J. Bush. Proceedings of the Southern Marketing Association.

_____. 1994b. "Shopping Centers and the Environment: Recycling Strategies for the 1990's: An Exploratory Investigation." *Journal of Shopping Center Research* 1(1): 7-37.

Fuller, Donald A. and Jeff Allen. 1991. "Consumer Recycling: A Review of Reverse Channels." Pp. 302-95 in *Marketing: Toward the Twenty-First Century,* edited by Robert L. King. Proceedings of the Southern Marketing Association.

_____. 1995. "A Typology of Reverse Channels for Post-Consumer Recyclables." Pp. 241-66 in *Advances In Environmental Marketing,* edited by Michael J. Polonsky and Alma T. Mintu-Wimsatt. New York: Haworth.

Fuller, Donald A., Jeff Allen, and Mark Glaser. 1996. "Materials Recycling and Reverse Channel Networks: The Public Policy Challenge." *Journal of Macromarketing* 16(1): 52-72.

Fuller, Donald A. and Daniel D. Butler. 1994. "Eco-Marketing: A Waste Management Perspective." P. 331 in *Developments in Marketing Science,* Vol. 17, edited by Elizabeth J. Wilson and William C. Black. Proceedings of the Academy of Marketing Science.

Fuller, Donald A. and Peter L. Gillett. 1990. *A Profile and Directory of the Recycling Industry in Florida.* Grant research project prepared for the Florida Department of Environmental Regulation, Tallahassee.

Garland, George A., Terry A. Grist, and Rosalie E. Green. 1995. "The Compost Story: From Soil Enrichment to Pollution Remediation." *BioCycle,* October, pp. 53-56.

Gatenby, David A. and George Foo. 1990. "Design for X (DFX): Key to Competitive, Profitable Products." *AT&T Technical Journal,* May-June, pp. 2-13.

Gies, Glenda. 1996. "Modular Management of Residential Organics." *BioCycle,* February, pp. 80-82.

Gilder, George. 1990. *Life after Television: The Coming Transformation of Media and American Life.* Knoxville, TN: Whittle Direct Books.

Ginter, Peter M. and James M. Starling. 1978. "Reverse Distribution Channels for Recycling." *California Management Review,* Spring, pp. 72-81.

Gladwin, Thomas N. 1995. "Sustainable Development and Sustainable Enterprise." Paper presented at the Bell Conference, a program of the Management Institute for Environment and Business, University of Texas at Austin, July 20.

Glenn, Jim. 1992. "Recycling Revolution in the Paper Industry." *In Business,* December, pp. 40-43.

_____. 1998. "The State of Garbage in America, Part 1." *BioCycle,* April, pp. 32-43.

Glidden Company. 1993. "Concern for the Environment Is Changing the Way We Live . . ." Advertisement in *National Geographic,* April, p. 141.

Global Environmental Management Initiative. 1992. *Total Quality Environmental Management: The Primer.* Washington, DC: GEMI.

_____. 1994. *Finding Cost-Effective Pollution Prevention Initiatives: Incorporating Environmental Costs into Business Decision Making.* Washington, DC: GEMI.

_____. 1996. *Environmental Reporting and Third-Party Statements.* Washington, DC: Environmental Information Service, Investor Responsibility Research Center.

"GM Electric Cars to Go on Sale in California, Arizona This Fall." 1996. *Atlanta Journal/ Constitution,* January 5, p. E9.

Goff, Jennifer. 1994a. "EPA and APC Fund CBOT Project." *Recycling Times,* August 5, p. 1.

_____. 1994b. "Is a National Recycling Bill Possible?" *Waste Age,* September, pp. 91-94.

Goff, Jennifer, Lisa Rabasca, and Kathleen M. White. 1994. "German Green Dot: The Debate Goes On." *Waste Age,* June, pp. 87-92.

Goldstein, Jerome. 1995. "Recycling Food Scraps into High End Markets." *BioCycle,* August, pp. 40-42.

Goldstein, Norma. 1997. "The State of Garbage in America, Part 1." *BioCycle,* April, pp. 60-67.

"Good Impressions." 1995. *The Green Business Letter,* August, p. 1.

Gore, Al. 1992. *Earth in the Balance.* Boston: Houghton Mifflin.

Gore, Rich. 1989. "Extinctions." *National Geographic,* June, pp. 662-99.

Government Institutes Inc. 1994. *Environmental Statutes.* Rockville, MD: Government Institutes Inc.

_____. 1995. *The Environmental Laws and Regulations Compliance Course.* Rockville, MD: Government Institutes Inc.

Graedel, T. E. and B. R. Allenby. 1995. *Industrial Ecology.* Englewood Cliffs, NJ: Prentice Hall.

Graham, Ellen. 1996. "How to Sell More to Those Who Think It's Cool to Be Frugal." *Wall Street Journal,* September 9, p. B1.

" 'Green Gauge' Tracks Public's Ups, Downs on the Environment." 1996. *The Green Business Letter,* December, pp. 4-5.

"Green Product Introductions 1997." 1998. *The Green Business Letter,* February, p. 3.

"Greening the Supply Chain: Programs Grow More Comprehensive." 1995. *Business and the Environment,* October, pp. 2-5.

"Greening the Supply Chain: What's Working." 1993. *Business and the Environment,* February, pp. 2-4.

Gruley, Bryan and Joe Davidson. 1995. "GM to Settle Case on Toxic Car Emissions." *Wall Street Journal,* December 1, p. A3.

Guiltinan, Joseph P. and Nonyelu Nwokoye. 1974. "Reverse Channels for Recycling: An Analysis of Alternatives and Public Policy Implications." Pp. 341-46 in *American Marketing Association Proceedings.* Chicago: AMA.

Guiltinan, Joseph P. and Gordon W. Paul. 1991. *Marketing Management: Strategies and Programs.* Fourth ed. New York: McGraw-Hill.

Gupta, Udayan. 1994. "Cause-Driven Companies' New Cause: Profits." *Wall Street Journal,* November 8, p. B1.

Hall, Douglas. 1992. "Building Green Corporate Partnerships." *IABC Communications World,* April, pp. 25-26.

Harbor Branch Oceanographic Institution. 1993. *Annual Report 1993.* Fort Pierce, FL: HBOI.

Hardin, Garrett. 1968. "The Tragedy of the Commons." *Science* 162:1243-48.

Harrison, E. Bruce. 1992. *Environmental Communications and Public Relations Handbook.* Rockville, MD: Government Institutes Inc.

_____. 1994. "The E-Factor: Going Green, Sustainably." *The Green Business Letter,* September, p. 8.

Hart, Stuart L. 1997. "Beyond Greening: Strategies for a Sustainable World." *Harvard Business Review* 75(1): 66-76.

"Hauling Food Residuals." 1995. *BioCycle,* August, p. 40.

Hawken, Paul. 1993. *The Ecology of Commerce: A Declaration of Sustainability.* New York: HarperCollins.

_____. 1996. "Introducing . . . The Natural Step." *The Natural Step News,* Winter, p. 1.

Hemphill, Thomas A. 1991. "Marketers' New Motto: It's Keen to Be Green." *Business and Society Review,* Summer, pp. 39-44.

Henion, Karl E. 1976. *Ecological Marketing.* Columbus, OH: Grid.

Herman, Robert, Siamak A. Ardekani, and Jesse H. Ausubel. 1989. "Dematerialization." Pp. 50-59 in *Technology and Environment,* edited by Jesse H. Ausubel and Hedy E. Sladovich. Washington, DC: National Academy Press.

Hirschhorn, Joel S. 1994. "What Will It Cost?" *Institutional Investor* 24(9): 15-16.

Hirschhorn, Joel S. and Kristen U. Oldenburg. 1991. *Prosperity without Pollution: The Prevention Strategy for Industry and Consumers.* New York: Van Nostrand Reinhold.

"Hoechst Announces Cleanup Plan after Recent Accidents." 1996. *Wall Street Journal,* February 1, p. A12.

Hoerner, J. Andrew, Alan S. Miller, and Frank Muller. 1995. *Promoting Growth and Job Creation through Emerging Environmental Technologies.* Washington, DC: National Commission for Employment Policy.

Holmes, Hannah. 1991. "The Green Police." *Garbage,* September-October, pp. 44-51.

Hoover Online. 1995. World Wide Web: http://www.marketguide.com, Wal-Mart Stores, accessed July 29, 1995.

Hopkins, Lynne and David T. Allen. 1994. *Study of the Energy Burdens/Environmental Tradeoffs Attributable to Transportation during Production and Distribution of a Patagonia Garment.* Los Angeles: University of California, Los Angeles, Graduate School of Architecture and Urban Planning and the Department of Chemical Engineering.

Houghton Mifflin. 1992. *American Heritage Dictionary of the English Language.* Third ed. New York: Houghton Mifflin.

Hunt, Robert G., Jere D. Sellers, and William E. Franklin. 1992. "Resource and Environmental Profile Analysis: A Life-Cycle Environmental Assessment of Products and Processes." *Environmental Impact Assessment Review,* December, pp. 245-69.

"Hydrogen Peroxide Supplies Stay Tight as Cyclical Demand Rises." 1995. *Wall Street Journal,* November 11, p. A1.

Integrated Waste Services Association. 1994. "High Court Rules Ash Not Exempt from Subtitle C Regulation." *Update,* Summer, p. 1.

Interface Inc. 1997. Interface homepage: http://www.ifsia.com, January 10.

"It Starts with a Little Imagination." 1996. *DuPont Magazine,* November-December, pp. 15-17.

Iyer, E. and B. Banerjee. 1993. "Anatomy of Green Advertising." Pp. 494-501 in *Advances in Consumer Research,* Vol. 20, edited by Leigh McAlister and Michael Rothschild. Provo, UT: Association for Consumer Research.

J. Walter Thompson USA. 1990. *JWT Greenwatch,* Autumn.

———. 1991. "The Meaning of Green: How Environmental Advertising Works." *JWT Greenwatch,* Spring-Summer, pp. 1-20.

Jacoby, Jacob, Carol K. Berning, and Thomas F. Dietvorst. 1977. "What about Disposition?" *Journal of Marketing* 41 (2): 22-28.

Johnson, Elaine. 1993. "Hospitals Return to Reusable Products." *Safety & Health,* January, pp. 48-52.

"Jury's Tobacco Verdict Suggests Tough Times Ahead for the Industry." 1996. *Wall Street Journal,* August 12, p. A1.

Kahl, Jonathan D., Donna J. Charlevoix, Nina A. Zaitseva, Russell C. Schnell, and Mark C. Serreze. 1993. "Absence of Evidence for Greenhouse Warming over the Arctic Ocean in the Past 40 Years." *Nature,* January 28, pp. 335-37.

Kaldjian, Paul. 1990. "Environmental Results through Industrial Design." *Innovation,* Summer, pp. 15-19.

Katzenbach, Jon R. and Douglas K. Smith. 1993. *The Wisdom of Teams.* Boston: Harvard Business School Press.

Kaufman, Donald G. and Cecilia M. Franz. 1993. *Biosphere 2000: Protecting Our Global Environment.* New York: HarperCollins.

Keep Florida Beautiful. 1996. "Publix Awarded for Environmentalism." *StateWatch,* March-April, p. 6.

Keoleian, Gregory A. 1996. "Life-Cycle Design." Pp. 6.1-6.34 in *Environmental Life-Cycle Assessment,* edited by Mary Ann Curran. New York: McGraw-Hill.

Keoleian, Gregory A., Jonathan E. Koch, and Dan Menerey. 1995. *Life-Cycle Design Framework and Demonstration Projects.* Washington, DC: U.S. Environmental Protection Agency, Office of Research and Development.

Keoleian, Gregory A. and Dan Menerey. 1993. *Life Cycle Design Guidance Manual.* Washington, DC: U.S. Environmental Protection Agency, Office of Research and Development.

Kinnear, T., J. R. Taylor, and S. Ahmed. 1974. "Ecologically Concerned Consumers: Who Are They?" *Journal of Marketing* 38(2): 20-24.

Kmart Corporation. 1993. *Kmart Cares Product News,* June.

Kotler, Philip. 1997. *Marketing Management: Analysis, Planning, Implementation, and Control.* Ninth ed. Upper Saddle River, NJ: Prentice Hall.

Kotler, Philip and Gary Armstrong. 1991. *Principles of Marketing.* Fifth ed. Englewood Cliffs, NJ: Prentice Hall.

Kotler, Philip and G. Alexander Rath. 1984. "Design: A Powerful But Neglected Strategic Tool." *Journal of Business Strategy* 5(2): 16-21.

Kovacs, William L. 1988. "The Coming Era of Conservation and Industrial Utilization of Recyclable Materials." *Ecology Law Quarterly* 15:537-625.

KPMG Peat Marwick. 1993. *Environmental Practice.* Internal company document. Dallas, TX: KPMG Peat Marwick.

Kreuze, Jerry G. and Gale E. Newell. 1994. "ABC and Life-Cycle Costing for Environmental Expenditures." *Management Accounting* 75(8): 38-42.

Kusz, John Paul. 1990. "Environmental Integrity and Economic Viability." *Innovation,* Summer, pp. 25-27.

"L.A. Gear to Pay for Mercury Shoes." 1994. *Recycling Times,* August 9, p. 4.

Ladd, Everett Carll and Karlyn H. Bowman. 1995. *Attitudes towards the Environment.* Washington, DC: AEI Press.

_____. 1996. "Public Opinion on the Environment." *Resources,* Summer, pp. 5-7.

Laitner, Skip, Marshall Goldberg, and Michael Skeeham. 1995. *Environment and Jobs: The Employment Impacts of Federal Environmental Investments.* Research Report No. 95-02. Washington, DC: National Commission for Employment Policy.

Landler, Mark. 1991. "Suddenly, Green Marketers Are Seeing Red Flags." *Business Week,* February 25, pp. 74-76.

Langreth, Robert. 1995a. "Commercial Fish Stocks Could Rebound with Oversight of Industry, Study Says." *Wall Street Journal,* August 25, p. B3.

_____. 1995b. "New Technique for Discovering Medicines Takes Hold." *Wall Street Journal,* September 11, p. B3.

Lawrence, Jennifer. 1993. "Green Products Sprouting Again." *Advertising Age,* May, p. 12.

Lehrburger, C., J. Mullen, and C. Jones. 1991. *Diapers: Environmental Impacts and Lifecycle Analysis.* Report to the National Association of Diaper Services.

LeMaire, William H. 1997. "Trendwatch: Coke's Contour Can Set for U.S. Debut and Battle of the Bulge." *Packaging Strategies Inc.,* February 28, p. 1.

Lemonick, Michael D. 1994. "Too Few Fish in the Sea." *Time,* April 4, pp. 70-71.

Lentz, R. and I. Franke. 1989. *Comparison of Environmental Balances for Products Taking as an Example Disposable and Cloth Diapers: Does the Use of Cloth Diapers Instead of Disposable Diapers Cause Less Environmental Impact?* Berlin: International Recycling Congress.

Lere, John C. 1991. *Managerial Accounting: A Planning-Operating-Control Framework.* New York: John Wiley.

Levingston, Steven E. and Christopher J. Chipello. 1994. "Paper Prices Seem Set for Extended Rally." *Wall Street Journal,* November 11, p. C1.

Leviten, David, Kristi Thorndike, and Jason Omenn. 1997. "P2 Technology Review: No-Clean Fluxes." *P2 Pollution Prevention Review,*.Winter, pp. 47-54.

Libreria Editrice Vaticana. 1994. *Catechism of the Catholic Church.* Liguori, MO: Liguori Publications.

"Life Cycle Analysis: An Emerging Market." 1993. *Environmental Business Journal,* August, p. 11.

"Life Ever After." 1993. *The Economist,* October 9, p. 77.

Limbaugh, Rush. 1992. *The Way Things Ought to Be.* New York: Pocket Books.

Long, Frederick J. and Matthew B. Arnold. 1995. *The Power of Environmental Partnerships.* New York: Dryden.

Lorenz, Christopher. 1986. *The Design Dimension, Product Strategy, and the Challenge of Global Markets.* London: Basil Blackwell.

Loudon, David L. and Albert J. Della Bitta. 1988. *Consumer Behavior: Concepts and Applications.* New York: McGraw-Hill.

Lovelock, James. 1979. *Gaia.* Oxford, UK: Oxford University Press.

Machalaba, Daniel. 1998. "As Old Pallets Pile Up, Critics Hammer Them as a New Eco-Menace." *Wall Street Journal,* April 1, p. A1.

Makower, Joel. 1995a. "Mixed Messages." *The Green Business Letter,* January, p. 8.

_____. 1995b. "The PCSD's Counsel." *The Green Business Letter,* July, p. 8.

_____. 1995c. "The Writing on the Wall." *The Green Business Letter,* April, p. 8.

"Mall Will Boast Its Own Recycling Center." 1992. *Chain Store Age Executive,* April, p. 62.

"Malls and Energy Management." 1990. *Stores,* October, p. 29.

Mare Holstrum Productions Inc. (1995). *The Last Hunters.* Video presentation on The Discovery Channel, April 15, produced by Tim Clark.

"Marketplace Getting Greener, Says New 'Green Gauge'." 1998. *The Green Business Letter,* January, p. 3.

McCarthy, E. Jerome and William D. Perreault, Jr. 1993. *Basic Marketing: A Managerial Approach.* Tenth ed. Homewood, IL: Irwin.

McConocha, Diane M. and Thomas W. Speh. 1991. "Remarketing: Commercialization of Remanufacturing Technology." *Journal of Business and Industrial Marketing* 6(1-2): 23-37.

McCreery, Patrick. 1994a. "In 1994, Recycling Was about Prices, Prices, Prices." *Recycling Times,* December 27, p. 1.

_____. 1994b. "New Mills Open, But Feedstocks Could Be a Problem." *Recycling Times,* September 6, p. 3.

McDaniel, Stephen W. and David H. Rylander. 1993. "Strategic Green Marketing." *Journal of Consumer Marketing* 10(3): 4-10.

McDonald's Corporation. 1991. *Waste Reduction Task Force: Final Report.* Report coauthored by the Environmental Defense Fund. Oak Brook, IL: McDonald's Corporation.

McDowell, John W. 1993. *An Environmental, Economic, and Health Comparison of Single-Use and Reusable Surgical Drapes and Gowns.* Report on an independent study conducted by Arthur D. Little Inc. and prepared for Johnson & Johnson Medical Inc., Arlington, TX.

"Mega-Billion Dollar Outlays Foreseen for UST Cleanups." 1992. *National Petroleum News,* March, p. 18.

"Minding the Store: How Gap Inc. Is Making Green Retailing in Style." 1996. *The Green Business Letter,* February, pp. 1, 6-7.

Mobil Corporation. 1997a. "Science Far from Certain." Advertisement in the *Wall Street Journal,* February 12, p. A11.

_____. 1997b. "Stop, Look, and Listen before We Leap." Advertisement in the *Wall Street Journal,* March 3, p. A8.

_____. 1998. "It's Two of the Safest Ships Ever Built." Advertisement in the *Wall Street Journal,* June 2, p. A19.

Monroe, Kent B. 1990. *Pricing: Making Profitable Decisions.* Second ed. New York: McGraw-Hill.

Moore, Stephen D. 1995. "Danish Firm Has an Epilepsy Drug That's Linked to Rain Forest's Betel Nut." *Wall Street Journal,* September 8, p. B12D.

Moyers, Bill, producer. 1990. *Global Dumping Ground* [video]. Washington, DC: Center for Investigative Reporting.

Murphy, Patrick E. and Ben M. Enis. 1986. "Classifying Products Strategically." *Journal of Marketing* 50(3): 24-42.

NaQuin, Dee. 1997. "New Machine Recycles Disposable Diapers into Reusable Paper and Plastic Pellets." *Recycling Times,* June 9, p. 6.

National Association for Plastic Container Recovery. 1995. *PET Projects,* November (special issue).

National Food Processors Association. 1993. *Interim Guidelines for the Safe Use of Plastics for Food Packaging Applications.* Washington, DC: NFPA.

National Science And Technology Council. 1994. *Technology for a Sustainable Future.* Washington, DC: Government Printing Office.

_____. 1995. *Bridge to a Sustainable Future.* Washington, DC: Government Printing Office.

National Solid Wastes Management Association. 1990. *The Future of Newspaper Recycling.* Washington, DC: NSWMA.

_____. 1991. *Special Report: Recycling in the States—1990 Review.* Washington, DC: NSWMA.

Neace, M. B. 1995. "Marketing's Linear-Hierarchial Underpinning and a Proposal for a Paradigm Shift in Values to Include the Environment." Pp. 55-73 in *Environmental Marketing: Strategies, Practice, Theory, and Research,* edited by Michael J. Polonsky and Alma T. Mintu-Wimsatt. New York: Haworth.

Noah, Timothy. 1994a. "EPA Proposes to Curb Air Emissions from Boats' Gasoline, Diesel Engines." *Wall Street Journal,* October 10, p. B9.

_____. 1994b. "U.S. Is Acting in New England to Curb Fishing." *Wall Street Journal,* December 8, p. A20.

Noah, Timothy and Phil Kuntz. 1995. "Gingrich Blasts Environmental Policies of Past 20 years as 'Absurdly Expensive'." *Wall Street Journal,* February 17, p. B2.

Northeast Maryland Waste Disposal Authority. 1993. *Buy Recycled Training Manual: A Guidebook for Government Buyers and Using Agencies.* Baltimore, MD: NMWDA.

Northern Telecom. 1996. World Wide Web: http://www.nortel.com, accessed November 12.

Norton, Erle. 1994. "Scrap Steel Prices Have Been Soaring Following a Slump." *Wall Street Journal,* August 8, p. A2.

_____. 1995. "Steel Firms to Show a Lighter Design for Auto Bodies." *Wall Street Journal,* September 6, p. A4.

Oates, Wallace E., Karen Palmer, and Paul R. Portney. 1993. *Environmental Regulation and International Competitiveness: Thinking about the Porter Hypothesis.* Discussion Paper No. 94-02. Washington, DC: Resources for the Future.

Odum, Eugene P. 1971. *Fundamentals of Ecology.* Third Ed. New York: Saunders.

"Of Consuming Interest: Will 'Sustainable Consumption' Become a New Corporate Strategy?" 1998. *The Green Business Letter,* August, pp. 1, 6-7.

Office of Technology Assessment. 1992. *Green Products by Design: Choices for a Cleaner Environment.* Washington, DC: Government Printing Office.

Olson, Robert L. 1991. "The Greening of High Tech." *The Futurist,* May-June, pp. 28-34.

Orloske, Del and Joan A. Davis. 1994. "John Shaeffer: Making Real Goods for Real People." *E Magazine,* May-June, pp. 14-16.

Ortega, Bob. 1994. "Organic Cotton May Feel Soft to Touch, But It's Hard to Sell." *Wall Street Journal,* November 8, pp. B1-B2.

Ottman, Jacquelyn A. 1992. "Sometimes, Consumers Will Pay More to Go Green." *Marketing News,* July 6, p. 16.

_____. 1993. *Green Marketing: Challenges and Opportunities for the New Marketing Age.* Lincolnwood, IL: NTC Business Press.

_____. 1995. "Mandate for the '90s: Green Corporate Image." *Marketing News,* September 11, p. 8.

"Paint Busters." 1993. *Orlando Sentinel,* June 9, p. C5.

Parfit, Michael. 1995. "Exploiting the Ocean's Bounty: Diminishing Returns." *National Geographic,* November, pp. 2-55.

Parker-Pope, Tara. 1995. "Body Shop Shares Jump on Reports It Will Go Private." *Wall Street Journal,* November 1, p. B11.

Parkin, Sara. 1991. "Power and Green Politics." *Resurgence,* May-June, pp. 4-7.

Parsons, Leonard J. 1989. "Product Design." Pp. 51-75 in *New Product Development and Testing,* edited by Walter Henry, Michael Menasco, and Hirokazu Takada. Lexington, MA: Lexington Books.

Peattie, Ken. 1992. *Green Marketing.* London: Pitman.

_____. 1995. *Environmental Marketing Management.* London: Pitman.

Peske, William. 1997. "Inventory Management Cuts Volatility in Economy, Helps Firms Avoid Errors." *Wall Street Journal,* August 8, p. B8B.

Peter, J. Paul and James H. Donnelly. 1995. *Marketing Management Knowledge and Skills.* Fourth ed. Homewood, IL: Irwin.

Petrush, Liza. 1996. "All Fiber Prices Fluctuated Dramatically during 1995." *Recycling Times,* January 9, pp. 1, 14.

Pierson, John. 1990. "Form + Function: Canon Has Had Its Fill of Reused Cartridges." *Wall Street Journal,* June 6, p. B1.

Polonsky, Michael J. and Alma T. Mintu-Wimsatt. 1995. "Preface." Pp. xix-xxii in *Environmental Marketing: Strategies, Practice, Theory, and Research,* edited by Michael J. Polonsky and Alma T. Mintu-Wimsatt. New York: Haworth.

Pomper, Steven D. 1993. "Winning the War on Packaging Waste." Paper presented at the Life-Cycle Assessment Training Course, Society for Environmental Toxicology and Chemistry, Washington, DC, September 23-24.

Poore, Patricia. 1993. "Is Garbage an Environmental Problem?" *Garbage,* November-December, pp. 40-45.

Porter, J. Winston and Jonathan Z. Cannon. 1992. "Waste Minimization: Challenge for American Industry." *Business Horizons,* March-April, pp. 46-49.

Porter, Michael E. 1986. *Competitive Advantage: Creating and Sustaining Superior Performance.* New York: Free Press.

_____. 1991. "America's Green Strategy." *Scientific American,* April, p. 168.

Porter, Michael E. and Claas van der Linde. 1995. "Green and Competitive: Ending the Stalemate." *Harvard Business Review* 73(5): 120-34.

Portney, Paul R. 1994a. "The Price Is Right: Making Use of Life-Cycle Analyses." *Issues in Science and Technology,* Winter, pp. 69-75.

_____. 1994b. "What Will It Cost?" *Institutional Investor* 24(9): 16.

Postel, Sandra. 1992. "Denial in the Decisive Decade." Pp. 3-8 in *State of the World 1992,* edited by Lester R. Brown. New York: Norton.

Publix Super Markets Inc. 1996. Brochures collected by the author in stores in Orlando and Fort Pierce, Florida. Lakeland, FL: Publix Super Markets Inc., Customer Relations.

"Pump Makers Plan Phaseout of Brass Parts Due to Lead Concern." 1994. *Wall Street Journal,* October 6, p. A13.

Purcell, Arthur H. 1980. *The Waste Watchers.* Garden City, NY: Anchor Books.

"Quietly, Kmart Makes Environmental Push." 1993. *Discount Store News,* November 1, p. 16.

Quintana, Craig. 1994. "Liabilities Nearly Settled in City Chemical Pollution Case." *Orlando Sentinel,* September 10, p. D3.

_____. 1995. "Big Retailers Cash in on the Green Movement." *Orlando Sentinel* (Central Florida Business Supplement), February 6-12, pp. 12-13.

Rabasca, Lisa. 1993. "Clinton Signs Buy-Recycled Executive Order." *Recycling Times,* November 2, pp. 1, 8.

_____. 1994a. "CBOT to Trade PET, HDPE, and Glass First." *Recycling Times,* April 5, p. 7.

_____. 1994b. "Will OWP Follow OCC's Rapid Rise?" *Waste Age,* September, pp. 63-72.

_____. "BRBA Spending Slows in 1993, Reveals $2-Billion Error in 1992." *Recycling Times,* April 4, pp. 1-2.

Random House. 1958. *American College Dictionary.* New York: Random House.

Ray, Dixy Lee. 1990. *Trashing the Planet.* New York: Harper Perennial.

Regan, Mary Beth. 1993a. "Lakes in Central Florida Added to Mercury Warning." *Orlando Sentinel,* January 7, p. B3.

_____. 1993b. "Shetlands May Benefit from Lessons of Valdez Cleanup." *Orlando Sentinel,* January 6, p. A9.

"Regulations Add to Company's Costs." 1994. *Orange County Register,* September 18, p. D7.

Rehak, Robert. 1993. *Greener Marketing and Advertising: Charting a Responsible Course.* Emmaus, PA: Rodale.

Reilly, William K. 1991. *The Next Environmental Policy: Preventing Pollution.* Washington, DC: U.S. Environmental Protection Agency, Office of Communications and Public Affairs.

Reinhart, Debra R. 1994. "Future Concepts in Landfill Operation: Active Landfill Management-Optimizing Landfill Disposal Operations." Pp. 1-20 in *Proceedings of the Modern Double-Lined Landfill Management Seminar.* Saratoga Springs: New York Department of Environmental Conservation.

Reitman, Valerie. 1992. " 'Green' Product Sales Seem to Be Wilting." *Wall Street Journal,* May 18, p. B1.

Reuters. 1996. "Lawsuit Says Wal-Mart Sold Bad Blinds." *Orlando Sentinel,* July 7, p. B5.

Richards, Deanna J., Braden R. Allenby, and Robert A. Frosch. 1994. "The Greening of Industrial Ecosystems: Overview and Perspective." Pp. 1-19 in *The Greening of Industrial Ecosystems,* edited by Braden R. Allenby and Deanna J. Richards. Washington, DC: National Academy Press.

Richins, Marsha L. and Scott Dawson. 1992. "Consumer Values Orientation for Materialism and Its Measurement: Scale Development and Validation." *Journal of Consumer Research* 19 (December): 303-16.

Ridgley, Heidi. 1997. "City/Industry Plastic Bottle Redesign Project Heats Up." *Recycling Times,* September 29, p. 1.

———. 1998a. "Aluminum Container Recycling Hits Record." *Recycling Times,* April 1, pp. 1, 4.

———. 1998b. "New Pepsi Labels May Be Contaminant: However, Company Committed to Bottle." *Recycling Times,* March 16, p. 13.

Robert, Karl-Henrik, Herman Daly, Paul Hawken, and John Holmberg. 1996. "A Compass for Sustainable Development." *The Natural Step News,* Winter, pp. 3-5.

Robinson, Warren C. 1998. "Global Population Trends: The Prospects for Stabilization." *Resources,* Spring, pp. 6-9.

Roper Organization. 1990. *The Environment: Public Attitudes and Individual Behavior.* Report commissioned by S. C. Johnson & Sons, Racine, WI.

Roper Starch Worldwide Inc. 1996. *Green Gauge Report.* New York: Roper Starch Worldwide Inc.

———. 1997. *Green Gauge Report.* New York: Roper Starch Worldwide Inc.

Rose, Matthew. 1996. "Body Shop Gets Taken to Task in 'Social Audit'." *Wall Street Journal,* April 19, p. A7B.

Rosenbloom, Bert. 1991. *Marketing Channels: A Management View.* Fourth ed. New York: Dryden.

Ross, David Frederick. 1996. *Distribution Planning and Control.* New York: Chapman & Hall.

Rothery, Brian. 1995. *ISO 14000 and ISO 9000.* Brookfield, VT: Gower.

Ruckelshaus, William D. 1989. "Toward a Sustainable World." *Scientific American,* March, pp. 166-74.

Russell, J. Thomas and W. Ronald Lane. 1996. *Kleppner's Advertising Procedure.* Thirteenth ed. Englewood Cliffs, NJ: Prentice Hall.

Ruston, John R. and Richard A. Denison. 1996. *Advantage Recycle: Assessing the Full Costs and Benefits of Recycling.* Environmental Defense Fund World Wide Web site: http:/f.pubs/reports/advrec.html, accessed September 9.

Rutledge, Gary L. and Christine R. Vogan. 1994. "Pollution Abatement and Control Expenditures, 1972-1992." *Survey of Current Business,* May, pp. 36-49.

Sagoff, Mark. 1997. "Do We Consume Too Much?" *Atlantic Monthly,* June, pp. 80-96.

Sandborg, Verie. 1995. "Corporate Presentation: Baxter International." Paper presented at the Bell Conference, a program of the Management Institute for Environment and Business, University of Texas at Austin, July 19.

Saphire, David. 1994. *Delivering the Goods: Benefits of Reusable Shipping Containers.* New York: INFORM Inc.

———. 1995. *Case Reopened: Reassessing Refillable Bottles.* New York: INFORM Inc.

"Saturn Reuses Polymer Panels in New Automobiles." 1995. *Business and the Environment,* July, p. 9.

Sauer, Beverly J., Carol C. Hildebrant, William E. Franklin, and Robert C. Hunt. 1994. "Life Cycle Assessment: Resource and Environmental Profile Analysis of Children's Diaper Systems." *Environmental Toxicology and Chemistry* 13:1003-9.

Scammon, Deborah L. and Robert N. Mayer. 1995. "Agency Review of Environmental Marketing Claims: Case-by-Case Disposition of the Issues." *Journal of Advertising* 24(3): 33-43.

Schatz, Amy. 1996. " 'Good Wood' Winning the Green Crowd." *Wall Street Journal,* May 17, p. B10.

Schmidheiny, Stephan. 1992a. "The Business Logic of Sustainable Development." *Columbia Journal of World Business* 27(3-4): 18-24.

_____. 1992b. *Changing Course: A Global Perspective on Development and the Environment.* Cambridge: MIT Press.

Schoonover, Jennifer. 1993. "The Garment Industry Gets a New Foundation." *In Business,* November-December, pp. 25-28.

"Science Newsfront: Coke Is Out." 1991. *Popular Science,* December, p. 24.

Scrap Tire Management Council. 1997. *A Statistical Review of International Trade in Tire and Tire-Related Rubber Waste for the Period 1990-94.* Washington, DC: STMC.

"Seventh Generation Repositions Catalog in Lighter Shades of Green for Wider Market Appeal." 1994. *Business and the Environment,* June, p. 9.

Shannon, Daniel. 1996. "Doing Well by Doing Good." *PROMO: The Magazine of Promotion Marketing,* February, pp. 29-33.

Sheth, Jagdish and Atul Parvatiyar. 1995. "Ecological Imperatives and the Role of Marketing." Pp. 3-20 in *Environmental Marketing: Strategies, Practice, Theory, and Research,* edited by Michael J. Polonsky and Alma T. Mintu-Wumsall. New York: Haworth.

Shi, David E. 1985. *The Simple Life: Plain Living and High Thinking in American Culture.* New York: Oxford University Press.

"Shoe Company Sees the Light." 1994. *In Business,* July-August, p. 10.

Silver, Cheryl Simon and Dale S. Rothman. 1995. *Toxics and Health: The Potential Long-Term Effects of Industrial Activity.* Washington, DC: World Resources Institute.

Simison, Robert. 1995. "Detroit Is Retooling Its Economic Models." *Wall Street Journal,* August 7, p. A2.

Simon, Julian L. 1981. *The Ultimate Resource.* Princeton, NJ: Princeton University Press.

Sims, Rodman. 1993. "Positive Attitudes Won't Make the Cash Register Ring." *Marketing News,* June 7, p. 4.

Singer, S. Fred. 1992. "Sustainable Development vs. Global Environment." *Columbia Journal of World Business* 27(3-4): 155-62.

Smith, Therese K. 1993. "Catalogers Bask in Newfound Attention." *Advertising Age,* June 28, p. 5.

Smithers, Richard. 1993. "A Clean 135 mpg." *In Business,* May-June, pp. 332-33.

Society of Environmental Toxicology and Chemistry. 1991. *A Technical Framework for Life-Cycle Assessment.* Washington, DC: SETAC.

_____. 1993a. *A Conceptual Framework for Life-Cycle Impact Assessment.* Pensacola, FL: SETAC.

_____. 1993b. *Guidelines for Life-Cycle Assessment: A "Code of Practice."* Pensacola, FL: SETAC.

"Sony Pilots Takeback Programs for Mass-Market Consumer Electronics." 1996. *Business and the Environment,* June, pp. 4-7.

"Source Reduction." 1990. *Modern Plastics,* April, pp. 21-25.

Stanton, William J., Michael J. Etzel, and Bruce J. Walker. 1994. *Fundamentals of Marketing.* Tenth ed. New York: McGraw-Hill.

State Attorneys General. 1990. *The Green Report I: Findings and Preliminary Recommendations for Responsible Environmental Marketing.* St. Paul: State of Minnesota, Office of the Attorney General.

"State Recycling Market Development Programs." 1993. *Green MarketAlert,* November, pp. 6-7.

Stein, George. 1993. "Toxic Waste Exports Are Black Mark on Green Reputation of Germany." *Journal of Commerce,* May 28, p. 7A.

Stern, Louis W., Adel I. El-Ansary, and Anne T. Coughlin. 1996. *Marketing Channels.* Fifth ed. Upper Saddle River, NJ: Prentice Hall.

Steuteville, Robert. 1994. "The State of Garbage in America, Part I." *BioCycle,* April, pp. 46-52.

_____. 1996. "The State of Garbage in America, Part I." *BioCycle,* April, pp. 54-61.

Stipp, David. 1991. "Life-Cycle Analysis Measures Greenness, But Results May Not Be Black and White." *Wall Street Journal,* February 28, p. B1.

Stisser, Peter. 1994. "A Deeper Shade of Green." *American Demographics,* March, pp. 24-29.

Stock, James R. 1992. *Reverse Logistics.* Oakbrook, IL: Council of Logistics Management.

Stutzman, Rene. 1993. "Milk Jugs: Color Them Yellow." *Orlando Sentinel,* September 3, p. C1.

Sullivan, Allanna. 1995. "Exxon Begins Final Defense in *Valdez* Spill." *Wall Street Journal,* May 5, p. B1.

Suris, Oscar and Gabriella Stern. 1995. "Auto Industry Finds Even a Soft Landing Isn't Very Comfortable." *Wall Street Journal,* September 19, p. A1.

SustainAbility Ltd. 1993. *The LCA Sourcebook: A European Guide to Life-Cycle Assessment.* London: SustainAbility Ltd.

Tchobanoglous, George, Hilary Theisen, and Samuel A. Vigil. 1993. *Integrated Solid Waste Management: Engineering Principles and Management Issues.* New York: McGraw-Hill.

"Technology Watch: Mutant Frogs Divide Experts." 1998. *Popular Mechanics,* July, p. 22.

"Tending Wal-Mart's Green Policy." 1991. *Advertising Age,* January 29, pp. 20-22.

The Body Shop International PLC. 1996. *The Body Shop Environmental Statement 95.* West Sussex, UK: The Body Shop International PLC.

"The Design Principles of Environmental Stewardship." 1992. *Innovation,* Fall, p. 3.

"The EMS Mess: The Promise and Pitfalls of the ISO 14000 Environmental Management System Standard." 1996. *The Green Business Letter,* January, pp. 1, 6-7.

"The Greening of the Mall." 1996. *The Green Business Letter,* February, p. 6.

"The Hauler Perspective." 1995. *BioCycle,* July, p. 70.

"The Markets Page." 1993. *Recycling Times,* November 2, p. 5.

"The Markets Page." 1994. *Recycling Times,* November 15, p. 5.

"The Markets Page." 1996. *Recycling Times,* September 3, p. 15.

"The New Steel: Feel the Strength." 1997. *The Recycling Magnet,* Fall, pp. 1, 4-5.

"The Product Is the Problem." 1990. *The Economist,* September 8, pp. 12-18.

"The Status of Eco-Retailing." 1993. *In Business,* January-February, pp. 32-37.

Thierry, Martin, Marc Salomon, Jo Van Nunen, and Luk Van Wassenhove. 1995. "Strategic Issues in Product Recovery Management." *California Management Review,* Winter, pp. 114-35.

3M Corporation. 1990. *Pollution Prevention Pays* [video]. St. Paul, MN: 3M Corporation, Environmental Engineering and Pollution Control.

Tomsho, Robert. 1996. "More Hospitals Turn to Used Equipment." *Wall Street Journal,* April 4, p. B1.

Tracey, Dan. 1993. "OUC Sees Pollution Rights as Gold Mine." *Orlando Sentinel,* April 7, pp. A1, A8.

Ulrich, Karl T. and Steven D. Eppinger. 1995. *Product Design and Development.* New York: McGraw-Hill.

U.S. Bureau of the Census. 1997. *Current Population Reports.* Nos. P25-1045, P25-1103, and P25-1126. Washington, DC: Government Printing Office. (World Wide Web: http://www.census.gov/prod/3/97pubs/97statab/pop.pdf)

U.S. Congress. 1992. Public Law 102-486, Energy Policy Act, October 24.

U.S. Environmental Protection Agency. 1990. *Characterization of Municipal Solid Waste in the United States: 1990 Update, Executive Summary.* Washington, DC: EPA.

_____. 1993a. *Status Report on the Use of Environmental Labels Worldwide.* Washington, DC: EPA, Pollution Prevention Division, Office of Pollution Prevention and Toxics.

_____. 1993b. *The Use of Life Cycle Assessment in Environmental Labeling Programs.* Washington, DC: EPA, Pollution Prevention Division, Office of Pollution Prevention and Toxics.

_____. 1994. *Determinants of Effectiveness for Environmental Certification and Labeling Programs.* Washington, DC: EPA, Pollution Prevention Division, Office of Pollution Prevention and Toxics.

"Valvoline and Target Promote Used Oil." 1996. *Recycling Times,* October 1, p. 12.

Viederman, Stephen. 1992. "Sustainable Development: What Is It and How Do We Get There?" *Current History,* April, pp. 180-85.

Vigon, Bruce W., D. A. Toll, B. W. Cornaby, H. C. Latham, C. L. Harrison, T. L. Boguski, R. G. Hunt, and J. D. Sellers. 1992. *Life-Cycle Assessment: Inventory Guidelines and Principles.* Cincinnati, OH: Office of Research and Development, Risk Reduction Engineering Laboratory.

"Vinyl Miniblinds Pose Lead-Poisoning Risk." 1996. *Wall Street Journal,* June 26, p. B7.

Walley, Wayne. 1991. "Pricing Is the Key to Products' Success." *Advertising Age,* February 4, p. 12.

"Wal-Mart Explores Environmental Store." 1992. *In Business,* July-August, p. 20.

"Wal-Mart to Operate Microsoft Programs for On-Line Sales." 1996. *Wall Street Journal,* February 13, p. B5.

Walpert, Frank. 1994. "Involvement or . . . More Regulation." *Florida Retailer,* June-July, p. 49.

Walsh, John E. 1993. "The Elusive Arctic Warming." *Nature,* January 28, pp. 300-1.

Wasik, John F. 1996. *Green Marketing and Management: A Global Perspective.* Cambridge, MA: Blackwell.

"Waste Expo '95." 1994. *Waste Age,* July, p. 40.

"Waste Not." 1995. *The Green Business Letter,* June, pp. 1, 6.

"Waste Reduction Works Like Magic." 1993. *In Business,* May-June, p. 1.

Westerman, M. 1983. "A New Way to Make Friends and Money." *Progressive Grocer,* December, pp. 71-84.

Westerman, R. R. 1978. *Tires: Decreasing Solid Wastes and Manufacturing Throughput.* Washington, DC: U.S. Environmental Protection Agency.

Wheelwright, Steven C. and Kim B. Clark. 1992. *Revolutionizing Product Development.* New York: Free Press.

White, Allen L., Deborah Savage, and Karen Shapiro. 1996. "Life-Cycle Costing: Concepts and Applications." Pp. 7.1-7.19 in *Environmental Life-Cycle Assessment,* edited by Mary Ann Curran. New York: McGraw-Hill.

White, Kathleen M. 1994a. "JCI's Orlando, Fla., Plant Shifts Production to Favor Recycling." *Recycling Times,* March 22, p. 3.

_____. 1994b. "Two Major Steel Recycling Mini-Mills Planned for Ariz. and Pa." *Recycling Times,* September 6, p. 7.

_____. 1995. " 'Footware with a Past' Now a Thing of the Past." *Recycling Times,* June 27, p. 3.

_____. 1996. "New Glass Processor in Washington State Pursues Fresh Market Niche." *Recycling Times,* October 15, p. 5.

Wiekierak, Gaye. 1996. "Iowa Targets Organics to Meet Recycling Goal." *BioCycle,* July, pp. 33-37.

Williams, Christopher. 1996. " 'What a Dump' May Be a Compliment after BioSafe's Landfill Remodeling." *Wall Street Journal,* September 9, p. B11B.

Willits, Stephen D. and Ron Giuntini. 1994. "Helping Your Company 'Go Green'." *Management Accounting,* February, pp. 43-47.

Willums, Jan-Olaf and Ulrich Goluke. 1992. *From Ideas to Action: Business and Sustainable Development.* Oslo, Norway: Ad Notam Gyldendal.

Wilson, David N. 1994. *Marketing Environmental Services.* Rockville, MD: Government Institutes Inc.

Wilson, E. O. 1988. "The Current State of Biological Diversity." Pp. 3-18 in *Biodiversity,* edited by E. O. Wilson. Washington, DC: National Academy Press.

Winter, Georg. 1988. *Business and the Environment.* Hamburg, Germany: McGraw-Hill.

Witcher, S. Karen. 1995. "Australian Farmers Hoping to Find a Market for Naturally Colored Cotton." *Wall Street Journal,* January 9, p. B7C.

Wood, Leonard A. 1990. "U.S. Consumers More Concerned with Economy Than Ecology." *Marketing News,* March 19, p. 20.

Woods, Randy. 1994. "Progress Made on Several Recycled Paper Mills across North America." *Recycling Times,* November 15, p. 4.

World Commission on Environment and Development. 1987. *Our Common Future.* New York: Oxford University Press.

Young, John E. 1992. "Mining the Earth." Pp. 100-18 in *State of the World 1992,* edited by Lester R. Brown. New York: Norton.

Zaccai, Gianfranco. 1994. "The New DFM: Design for Marketability." *World Class Design to Manufacture* 1 (6): 5-11.

Zikmund, William G. and Michael d'Amico. 1993. *Marketing.* Fourth ed. St. Paul, MN: West.

Zikmund, William G. and William J. Stanton. 1971. "Recycling Solid Wastes: A Channels-of-Distribution Problem." *Journal of Marketing* 35(3): 34-39.

Index